LOVE AND REMEMBRANCE

A NOVEL BY

D. JOVANOVIC

ISBN: 1-4033-2100-0 (e-book)
ISBN: 1-4033-2101-9 (Paperback)
ISBN: 1-4033-2102-7 (Dustjacket)

Library of Congress Control Number: 2002091406

This book is printed on acid free paper.

Printed in the United States of America
Bloomington, IN

1st Books - rev. 10/16/02

Dedication

For MM
Then, Now, and Always...

Acknowledgments

I wish to convey my deepest feelings of gratitude to the following individuals, who gave to me their time, patience, concern, and in some cases, even understanding:

Sandra Warnken, Madge Kalish, Gayle Herschcopf, Paul Doganges, Yaffa Doganges, Ralph Mercer, Aurette Murante, Robin Moore, Susan Cairns, Marina Schwed, Ellen Weaver, and the late Dr. Sylvia Ardyn Boone.

I also wish to express my appreciation to the following persons, who rendered valuable assistance to my efforts:

Margel de Lauer, Brian O'Neill, Carol Mercer, Rhea White, Sherry Shaffer, Naomi Halvorsen, Kurt Kievel.

CONTENTS

LOVE AND REMEMBRANCE

(A Case Study in Paranormal Phenomena

from the files of Dr. E. Levy)

Compiled and Edited by

Dr. Shoshannah Levy-Goldstein

FOREWORD

The pages of this *Foreword* serve as an introduction to the work that follows, the compilation of transcribed taped therapy sessions and notes written at the conclusion of these sessions by Dr. Eliahu Levy. In the event this book is read by generations unfamiliar with the name of the Therapist, Dr. Eliahu Levy was a well-respected Psychiatrist, trained by both Freud and Jung.[1] Dr. Levy had a lengthy and distinguished career both in Europe and the United States, where he emigrated from Germany shortly before the outbreak of the Second World War.

After his arrival in this country, Dr. Levy opened a practise in New York City, and almost immediately developed a clientele which consisted mainly of the most wealthy and celebrated members of American intelligentsia. This troubled Dr. Levy, who held the firm belief that his services should be provided to the widest range of persons possible, not limited solely to the rich and famous.

It was not until the mid-1970s that Dr. Levy saw the realization of his views, and was able to reach a larger segment of the population of New York City and surrounding communities. His therapeutic sessions with the rich and famous continued; moreover, because of these connections, Dr. Levy was able to secure a half-hour time period on one of the smaller New York City radio stations, in the late night hours. The program became so successful that it was expanded to an hour, and continued on the air, with an enormous following, for more than 6 years, until Dr. Levy abruptly

---

[1] Dr. Eliahu Levy was also my Grandfather.

caused the show to be canceled, to the consternation of the public and the owners of Station WMMD.

The program was entitled, "Ask Dr. Eli."[2] Dr. Levy received telephone calls from listeners with problems, and dispensed therapeutic advice. Dr. Levy responded to his callers with tact, patience, and courtesy. He always reacted as if their problems were genuine and real, no matter how bizarre either the caller or his situation would appear to so-called "normal" listeners. He talked to each caller as would a friendly, concerned Grandfather.[3]

The popularity of Dr. Levy's program was not limited to those who needed help with mental problems. Insomniacs, those whose work schedules necessitated them being awake during late hours, and those who were curious to hear what the program was about, started tuning in and listening. Not only did the callers experience help with their problems, but those who shared similar problems but were afraid to call, or those who were just interested in the human condition, benefited from Dr. Levy's sage suggestions. His methods were never didactic, but always avuncular.

Much to his personal dismay, "Dr. Eli" became a cult figure with a cult following. This situation only heightened after a particular call Dr. Levy received in the final year of the program. A young man telephoned and told the Doctor (and the listening

---

[2] The management of Station WMMD was of the opinion that the name "Eliahu" would sound "too foreign" and be too difficult for Dr. Levy's audience to pronounce. "Eli," however, was a somewhat familiar name, particularly with the success of the actor, Eli Wallach.

[3] This fact has a certain irony. Both his son, my Father, Dr. Nehemiah Levy, and I, his only grandchild, found no such compassion forthcoming in his relationship with us. It appears as if his sympathy and empathy were reserved solely for his patients.

audience, as well, of course) that he (the young man, not the Doctor) had been abducted by aliens. While the snickering of station staff could be heard in the background,[4] Dr. Levy reacted to the question with great seriousness, and proceeded to ask the caller for detailed information about the "alleged" abduction.[5] When it was time for Dr. Levy to dispense his advice, he treated the subject with obvious sincerity, and delivered a scientific mini-lecture on the possibility of the existence of living creatures on worlds other than our own.

From that point, Dr. Levy became a media sensation, not just to his loyal late-night followers, but to the general public at large. The number of calls concerning alien abductions and paranormal phenomena increased until they dominated the content of the programs. Dr. Levy continued to respond to these callers with scientific objectivity; which gained him increased respect with some members of his profession, but general disdain from the majority.

Then, as stated above, Dr. Levy abruptly gave Notice that he was severing his ties with Station WMMD. No amount of pleading or threats from management, nor entreaties from the general public had any effect upon his decision, which was firm and unalterable. Most members of the scientific community believed Dr. Levy took this course of action in order to avoid further ridicule from fellow Psychiatrists, and to retreat to the safety of his exclusive, traditional practise. Most

---

[4] I obtained this information from his associates, as I was a very young child at the time and never heard Dr. Levy's program.
[5] The choice of the word "alleged," is mine; as Dr. Levy treated the subject as if the event had actually occurred.

members of the public believed it was the management of Station WMMD who discharged Dr. Levy because he was becoming too controversial. Nothing could have been further from the truth. Management wanted Dr. Levy to remain <u>because</u> of his controversy, which generated additional listeners and revenue from advertisers.

Dr. Levy never spoke of his abrupt decision; nor did he reveal the reason behind it during his lifetime.[6] It was not until recently, when I discovered the tapes and notations which make up the contents of this book, that the truth behind his decision was revealed.

Dr. Eliahu Levy died from the effects of Lung Cancer on September 21, 1984.[7] The residue of material utilized in the course of his profession had been sealed in boxes, and packed away in closets in his office, which was taken over by Dr. Nehemiah Levy[8] for use in his own practise. After the death of Dr. Nehemiah Levy, I took over these same offices for use in my practise of natural, non-toxic therapies concentrating upon whole-patient wellness. Wishing to cleanse the rooms of the negative vibrations accumulated through the years, I consulted a specialist in the utilization of *feng shui*, who made specific recommendations. Accordingly, I inspected the contents of the sealed boxes remaining from the practise of Dr. Eliahu Levy.

---

[6] He never told his colleagues, nor the few close friends he had. He certainly never told members of his family, in whom he confided nothing.
[7] He was a prodigious smoker, despite, as a Medical Doctor, his full awareness of the logical and scientific reasons against the use of tobacco.
[8] My father, Nehemiah Levy, Ph.D., was a Psychologist and <u>not</u> a Psychiatrist; a source of constant irritation between Eliahu Levy, M.D., and his son.

All but one of these boxes contained texts and Notes pertaining to the practise of medicine in general and psychiatry in particular. As a careful, conscientious, and compulsive individual, Dr. Eliahu Levy, shortly before his death, scrupulously erased or destroyed all tapes and notes which remained in his possession concerning the therapeutic sessions of his patients. I was, therefore, astonished to learn that the material which had been packed in this one box related to the therapy of a specific person, Ms. Sophie Jacobs, the subject of this book. In anticipation of the eventual discovery of these records, the final document prepared by Dr. Levy indicates his inability to destroy the tapes and notes of his sessions with Ms. Jacobs, because of the potential scientific value of their discussion of paranormal phenomena.

After listening to the tapes and reviewing Dr. Levy's notes, I was compelled to reach the same conclusion: i.e., that the information contained therein is of great significance to both the Scientific Community and the general public.

As we approach the end of the 20th century, there has been increased interest in metaphysical, spiritual, and paranormal subject matter. The rise in attendance, among intellectuals, at such Centers as Unity, The Science of Mind; among creative individuals in Scientology; and the formation of the so-called "thinktank" - The Institute of Noetic Sciences; serves as proof of the growing interest in metaphysics and spirituality. Information relating to the scientific experimentation and analytical findings of Parapsychological Studies conducted by

Professor J. B. Rhine and Dr. Ramakrishna Rao at Duke University has been widely disseminated among the general public. Unlikely sources such as police, forensic, and even military agencies have revealed the use of psychics to assist with their investigations. Therefore, the timing for the presentation of the material found in these tapes and Notes could not be more relevant.

The decision was reached to contact Sophie Jacobs and show her the material relating to her treatment.[9] As Ms. Jacobs is still a practising Certified Public Accountant, it was relatively simple to locate her. After discussing what I had found and providing the material for her review, Ms. Jacobs agreed to make the record of her sessions public for the further education of humanity. Her only condition was that her actual name and those of the individuals mentioned in her therapeutic sessions be changed, for the protection of their privacy. I agreed to her terms, and thus this book was submitted for publication.[10]

It is my opinion that there is much to be learned from its contents. Of course, each individual will have to decide, for her or himself, whether or not the experiences documented have personal truth and relevance.

Shoshannah Levy-Goldstein, NMD.[11]

---

[9] I am aware that it is not the usual ethical practise to permit a patient to see the Notes of her treating physician; however, because of the important service which could be rendered from revelation of the subject matter, I decided to approach Ms. Jacobs to obtain her permission to review the material and release it for publication.

[10] The title, *Love and Remembrance*, was taken from one of the sessions in which Ms. Jacobs described what she felt to be the essence of her experiences. It is also appropriate considering the contents of the Notes written by Dr. Levy immediately prior to the termination of Ms. Jacobs' treatment.

[11] Naturopathic Medical Doctor.

TAPE 1

March 18,1981
2:37 am [1]

"Hello?"

"Is this Dr. Levy? Have I reached Dr. Levy? Dr. Eliahu Levy?"

"Yes, this is Dr. Eliahu Levy. Who is calling, please?"[2]

"Dr. Levy, please forgive me for calling at this terrible hour, but --"

"Do you realize what time it is?"[3]

"I'm sorry. Please forgive me, I know it is after 2 o'clock in the morning, but I had to call you.

"Dr. Levy, my name is Sophie Jacobs. I'm a CPA and I'm usually a responsible person, but lately I've —"

"How did you get my private number, please?"

---

[1] Dr. Levy took calls from his clients at all hours. As the majority of his patients were involved in the arts (e.g.: writers, musicians, artists, etc.), he frequently received late night and early morning calls from individuals in the midst of creative as well as emotional crises. If he were in bed, Dr. Levy answered the call via speakerphone, and had the conversation recorded [with the consent of his patients, of course] so that he would have its contents available for study before the patient's next session. Because of this practise, his wife, Dr. Esther Oppenheim, had her own separate bedroom in their spacious apartment.

[2] I have literally transcribed every discernible word (some were inaudible) of each of the recorded sessions and telephone calls between Dr. Levy and Sophie Jacobs. The reader should imagine hearing the Doctor's voice as that of an almost stereotypical German-accented professor, and Ms. Jacobs having a New York accent, recognizable to those familiar with such dialects as emanating from Brooklyn. Any activity other than speech, such as crying, pausing, sighing, etc. has been duly noted in editorial parentheses. Lapses in the flow of dialogue between patient and therapist are indicated as follows: "Pause" refers to a fairly brief gap; "Silence" refers to a rather extended period without spoken language.

[3] Dr. Levy always asked patients who called at unusual times if they were aware of the hour, as a tool in assisting the recognition of their behavior.

1

Tape 1

"From my closest friend, Seymour Cohen, who
--"

"Ah, Seymour, yes. Continue."[4]

"I've been having some unusual experiences
lately which have been very disturbing. I've
been struggling to cope with them, and I've
talked to Seymour about them a lot, because
we've known each other since we were children
and he's one of the very few people I can
confide in. But it's only getting worse and
after what happened tonight -- it was <u>so</u>
bizarre[5] — I don't think I can take it any
more. I called Seymour and he told me to call
you. I told him it was so late, or early,
whatever, but Seymour insisted I call you.
[Pause.] Actually, he wanted me to call you a
long time ago."

"What is disturbing you so much, Miss
Jacobs? Can it wait for later today? Can you
come to my office during regular hours?"

[The sound of crying can be heard in the
background.]

"What is the problem, Miss Jacobs?"

"I don't even know how to tell you about it.
I don't know what to do anymore. It's
beginning to effect my work. I really think
I'm going crazy."

"Can you give me some idea of what the
problem is and then call my office when it
opens at nine and have my secretary arrange
for an appointment during regular hours. I
<u>promise</u> I will make time to see you, even if
it means rearranging other patients' times."

---

[4] As indicated in the *Foreword*, the names of all individuals, with the
exception of Dr. Levy, have been altered to protect their privacy. The
person referred to as "Seymour Cohen" (now deceased) was a renowned
'cellist, and a patient of Dr. Levy for many years.

[5] I have added varying levels of emphasis to the words spoken by Dr.
Levy and Ms. Jacobs which are stressed vocally.

2

"Forgive me. I know it sounds crazy, but I think I'm being courted by the Ghost of a man I used to know."

[Silence.]

"Do you want to tell me now about the specific experience that so upset you, or will you be able to wait and call for an appointment during regular hours."

[Silence; then sniffling.]

"I think I can wait. It's only a little longer anyway, and talking to you makes me feel better. I appreciate that you're listening to me, really. I'm sorry I called at this hour, but I just felt so desperate."

"Were you desperate enough to want to harm yourself?"

"No, not that desperate now, but there have been times since this began when I have felt that I didn't care whether I lived or died. Tonight, or this morning, whatever, when this experience occurred, I just felt so crazy that I knew I needed help, but I don't think I felt like harming myself in any way."

"Good. Now you will call and make an appointment for later today?"

"Yes, thank you Dr. Levy. I will call your office when it opens and come at whatever time is best for you. Thank you so much. I'm sorry for disturbing your sleep, but —"

"I understand, Miss Jacobs, and I will see you later in the day. Try to get some sleep. Goodnight."

"Goodnight, and thank you again, Dr. Levy."

March 18, 1981
10:00 am[6]

"Dr. Levy, I'm Sophie Jacobs. I'm so grateful to you for letting me have this early appointment."

"I must be honest with you that the fact that you stated you are such good friends with Seymour Cohen influenced my decision to rearrange my schedule today. I have high regard for Seymour."

"So do I. And again, I appreciate what you are doing for me."

"Please sit down, Miss Jacobs."

"Thank you, doctor."

•"I know you want to tell me about this specific disturbing incident, but first I feel I must ask if you think you need to come to me on a regular basis. Do you want to have continuing therapy?"

"I guess I've reached the point where I feel it is necessary. I have to get to the bottom of this and learn why this is happening to me. It may just be some sort of deep-seated neurosis that you can help me unravel."

"Good. When you leave you can have my secretary arrange a regular appointment schedule for you. But for now, do you feel calm enough to give me some background information, or would you rather talk about the troubling experience first?"

"I'm feeling much less upset now, but I think I'd better talk about what happened. For one thing, it's still fairly fresh in my memory, and I'm afraid that if I waited to

---

[6] The time of day of the start of recording is dutifully noted on the cover of each tape; however, there is no indication of the time of conclusion of the therapeutic session.

tell you I might not remember it all, and also I'd lose my nerve about wanting to tell anybody.

"I suppose I can give you a little general background. I'm a CPA now, but years ago, I was studying to be a concert musician. Seymour and I went to the same High School, where we majored in music. It was when I was in High School that I met this man, who meant a great deal to me."

"Did he attend your school, also?"

"No. He was an adult when I was in my teens, and I met him at a baseball game. It's a long story, and I know I have to tell you if I continue with therapy, but for now, all I can say is that I learned of his death, which disturbed me greatly, and shortly after, I began to - I know this sounds crazy, but I began to receive communications from him, even though he was dead."

"What kind of communications? Were they meant to frighten you, or to convey information?"

"Oh no, no. They were never meant to frighten me. It was nothing like that. You could say it was to convey information. He wanted me to know how much I loved him and that he had loved me, too."

"If that is the situation, then why were you so distraught that you had to call me so early this morning? Why do you feel as if you are 'going crazy', as you have put it?"

"Dr. Levy, I'm trained as an accountant. I work with numbers and logical analysis of facts and figures. In my world, there is no place for people to be talking with ghosts. And it's the way these contacts have occurred. There have been so many, and they have been varied and unpredictable. I've done a lot of

Tape 1

reading on paranormal phenomena and metaphysical subjects since this all started and it's as if Harry - that's his name,[7] the man who's dead and has been, you could say, hanging around me — I prefer to call it that rather than haunting, which sounds even more over the edge — anyway, it's as if Harry were giving me a crash course in psychic phenomena. I've had almost every type of experience recorded in the literature, except for what happened last night. I never read or heard of anything like that before and it was more than I could cope with."

"You will tell me about it now, please."[8]

"Yes, I know. I want to, but it's so difficult, because I <u>know</u> how crazy it will sound."

[Pause. Sigh.]

"Anyway, it was late, it's left over from my time as a musician I guess - I just naturally stay up late. I can't go to sleep early. I was in bed, sitting up, reading some book about paranormal experiences - I can't even remember now, but I read the book until my eyes started to feel tired and I knew it was time for me to turn off the light and get some sleep. That's when it happened."

"<u>What</u> happened, Miss Jacobs, please."

[Silence.]

"Miss Jacobs?"

"Yes. I'm sorry. It's just that now, in the light of day, I feel so foolish to talk about it."

---

[7] Although deceased, the name of the man referred to as "Harry" has been altered also, to protect his reputation and the privacy of his surviving family members.

[8] The word "please," when used by Dr. Levy at the close of a sentence, was spoken more as a command than a request.

"Yet you called me after 2am in the morning, and believe me, Miss Jacobs, you sounded quite agitated over the telephone."

"You're right. I apologize. I'm sorry. I called you and I came to your office, so I <u>know</u> I need to talk about it."

[Pause.]

"Anyway, I was ME - you'll understand in a minute why I say it like that - and I was ready to turn off the light to go to sleep. But then I felt a consciousness, and it was not my own. I was awake, Dr. Levy, believe me. I was <u>not</u> in a hypnagogic state[9], either. I've read about that, and I can assure you - you'll just <u>have</u> to believe me.

"The room I was in was no longer my own bedroom. I hadn't traveled via astral-projection or anything like that. One minute I was Sophie Jacobs, in my bedroom reading a book, getting ready to turn off the light, then the next minute I was someone else, another **I**, in another bedroom, reaching to turn off a different bedroom light."

"Explain please. I am not sure I understand what you are trying to tell me."

"I'm not surprised, as it's all so insane. And if it feels that way to me, how must it sound to someone else?"

"Don't worry about how it sounds, Miss Jacobs, just continue to explain what happened with as much detail as possible, please."

"Yes. Thank you, Dr. Levy."

[Sigh.]

"I felt a sense of consciousness, but <u>not</u> as Sophie Jacobs. For one thing, the bedroom was no longer my own. I could see everything around me. I was in a bed, but it was a

---

[9] A "hypnagogic state" is a condition between waking and sleep in which hallucinatory images often appear.

different bed. The walls that I could see were <u>very</u> different from my own, with different pictures - the entire room was different. The furniture was not the same, nothing in that room was the same."

[Pause.]

"You know, now that I think of it, as I tell you about what happened, I realize that part of my own consciousness <u>must</u> have been intact, in order for me to realize that what I was seeing was <u>not</u> my own bedroom."

[Pause.]

"Very good, Miss Jacobs. Now continue, please."

"The thing that made it <u>really</u> obvious that it was not me, I mean Sophie, who was turning out the light - well, first, before I forget, I need to tell you that the furniture was from the 1940s. It wasn't the furniture that is in style today. It was typical 1940s, maybe even 1930s style furniture, the kind I remember seeing when I was a kid.

"Anyway, the clincher was that when I went to turn off the light, which was to my right, I was reaching over the body of a woman, sleeping peacefully in the same bed, next to me."

"Was this woman someone you knew - and was the room one you had been in before? Was this a familiar scene to you, from your childhood, for instance?"

"No to everything you just asked. I had never seen that bedroom before in my life, nor did I recognize the woman who was in the bed next to the me who was reaching over to turn off the light. She was a woman in her late 20s or early 30s, I would imagine, from her appearance. And I could tell, from the way she was sleeping so peacefully, that this was her bed also, and that she was used to sleeping in it."

"Go on, please."

"So then I moved across her body to turn off the light, and I was actually pulling the - I don't exactly know how to describe them — you don't see them very much on lamps these days, but it was a brass chain or links or something like that — and when you pull on it, the light goes off. And it was when I started tugging on the chain to pull it and turn off the light, that I came to myself and was back in my own bedroom again."

[Momentary silence, then agitated speech.]

"The moment I started pulling on that chain, I snapped out of it and went back to being Sophie Jacobs in her own bedroom. I was in my bed, surrounded by my walls, with my paintings, decorations, etc., my furniture - everything was back to normal, except for my mind, you can believe that!"

"What do you mean by that, Miss Jacobs, please."

"Just that I knew that for the briefest time, I'm not sure at all how long this lasted, but I was NOT me. I was someone else, most likely Harry."

"What makes you think that, Miss Jacobs?"

"Because <u>who</u> else, <u>what</u> else could it have been? I mean, Harry's the <u>only</u> one, thank God, who's been hanging around me, and somehow, I can't explain it, but somehow, I knew that was Harry's bedroom and that was his wife who was —"

"Excuse me, Miss Jacobs, but you were never in this man Harry's bedroom?"

[Indignant tone, with clearly enunciated speech.]

"<u>Certainly not</u>, Dr. Levy."

"Forgive me, Miss Jacobs, but I had to be sure of your knowledge of that room."

"No. I <u>never</u> was in Harry's bedroom, yet somehow I knew that was the room, and I guess for that brief moment, I must have been Harry in that room, getting ready to go to sleep, and reaching over his wife as she slept, in order to turn out the light. This was so frightening to me. I thought I had completely lost my mind, and I called Seymour right away to tell him about it and he <u>insisted</u> I call you immediately. The entire experience completely unnerved me, although now that I talk about it, it doesn't carry the same terrifying emotion that it held for me then."

"Tell me, Miss Jacobs, now that you can describe the event objectively, how does it feel to you? Do you still think you are completely mad, or do you think there might be some other explanation for what happened?"

"What other explanation can there be, except that —. But I suppose that's why I've come to you. I need your help to sort this out. Believe me, Dr. Levy, this is only one of so many strange events, but none have had this powerful effect upon me, nor have they been this bizarre. Do you think it could be some deep-seated neurosis that has finally worked its way through when I learned of the death of this man? Many of my friends think that's the case. I was orphaned at an early age, and they think I have reacted this way to Harry's death in some kind of delayed response to the loss of my parents."

"Good, Miss Jacobs. That gives us someplace to begin our next session. You can tell me about your childhood and about your relationship with this man, Harry.

"I see our time is up. Please make an appointment with my secretary. How many times do you think you want to come each week?"

"Is that what you think I need, Dr. Levy? To see you more than once a week? [Pause.] Well, how often do you think?"

"Given the level of your anxiety about this particular experience and the number of others you say you have had, plus your fears for your sanity, I would think a minimum of twice a week would be necessary."

"All right. I'll make arrangements for appointments beginning with next week, if that's possible. And thank you again, very much, for seeing me on such short notice and for listening to me rant and rave at two o'clock in the morning."

"It was after two; and you are welcome."

End of Tape 1.

Notes Accompanying Tape 1. [10]

Miss Jacobs came to the 10am session precisely on time. She is an attractive woman whose age I would estimate, particularly since she stated she was a contemporary of Seymour's, to be in her mid to late 40s. Her appearance was business-like and well-groomed. She certainly did not look as if, nor did she convey the impression of someone facing an imminent breakdown. At times her speech rambled and she became somewhat hyper-active, however she did not exhibit obvious signs of psychosis or severe neurosis. There was some indication of obsessive-compulsive behavior, but nothing rising to the level of disorder. Her description of the episode which initiated her frantic phone call after 2am, was related in a very straight-forward, detached manner — even analytical, as if she were narrating a case history of someone other than herself.

The incident itself is fascinating. It seems likely that she was probably dreaming, or even fantasizing. Yet, what are these other occurrences to which she refers? She definitely will be an intriguing patient to work with. At this point I am not certain whether her rationality is a protective device that must be shattered in order to work on deep-seated problems of the subconscious. Perhaps it should not be ruled out that she actually _is_[11] a completely rational person to

---

[10] As indicated in the _Foreword_, after reviewing the audiotape of each session, Dr. Levy wrote his thoughts and impressions concerning the session on his Notepad.

[11] The underlining, markings, errors of grammar and punctuation, half-finished entries, etc., have been retained from the original Notes of Dr. Levy, written by hand in English.

whom events have occurred which are beyond our current knowledge of reality.

* * *

TAPE 2

March 25, 1981

4:30 pm

"Miss Jacobs."

"Good afternoon, Dr. Levy. Thank you for allowing me to have this as my regular appointment time. It's so much more convenient for me to come to your office after work. I really do appreciate the accommodations you've made for my convenience."

"It's not a problem. I try to arrange my appointments to fit the needs of my clients. I don't believe in adding more stress by making them worry about their work schedules.

"By the way, I have been meaning to ask, it is <u>Miss</u> Jacobs, is it not?"

"That's correct, Dr. Levy. I am not married."

"Please sit.

"Were you ever married?"

"Once, but only briefly. It became obvious in a very short time that we were not suited for each other. Our divorce was amicable, and we have not seen each other since. I have retained the use of my maiden name."

"Do you have children?"

"No, thank God."

"Tell me, Miss Jacobs, have you had any experiences similar to the one you described last week?"

"Nothing like that one, no. But I still am being contacted by Harry, the man I told you about."

"What do you mean - 'contacted?'"

"Just the usual stuff. What I've been used to having from him, like messages in songs,

14

messages through other people, for instance, in words they might say or gifts they might give me. Things like that. I can tell you specific details, if you'd like."

"What I would really like to know right now, Miss Jacobs, is how you are feeling about what you perceived as happening to you last week."

[Pause.]

"I'm much more calm about it, but you and Seymour are the only people I feel I could ever tell about it. It is too strange to tell anyone else, especially since most of my friends are accountants and attorneys. This sort of thing would be too way out for them, and they would <u>surely</u> think I had gone nuts."

"Good. Miss Jacobs, now that you are feeling somewhat calmer and seem to have your life under control, perhaps this would be an appropriate time for you to give me some background information about yourself, in particular, the events surrounding your meeting and relationship with this man Harry."

"Sure.

[Pause.]

"How far back do you want me to go?"

"You can start with something about your childhood, and go forward from there. Of course, we will come back to that as needed."

[Pause.]

"OK. I was born in Brooklyn and orphaned at an early age. My family was very poor and very sickly with no money to get proper medical treatment. My mother died within hours after my birth, and my father - well, it was the Depression and he didn't have the money to pay someone to take care of me, so he took off to look for work and nobody knew what became of him. I was sent to live with a series of aunts, but they died too, for the same reasons

15

as my mother did, poor health and no money to get medical attention.

"By the time I reached my teens, at age 13, I was living with an aunt who was also in frail health. I think she was alive mainly by sheer strength of will, because she had so many people to look after. The War had ended, and in my aunt's household there was my aunt and her husband, let me think now. [Momentary pause] Oh yes. Her husband's mother was there; my aunt's two sons who had just returned from fighting in the War; my aunt's two daughters, who were working adults at the time; and her two youngest sons; one a year older than I, and the other, a year younger.

"My uncle, you know, my aunt's husband, worked in the Post Office and his salary had to go to support all these people. The two veterans were going to school on the G.I. Bill, and the two daughters contributed something, I think, but I know times were tough. At least there wasn't any money to get anything for me.

"There was something else, too. I was kinda like Cinderella in some ways. I always got what was left over, if anything. I can remember especially that for dinner, we would have tea to drink. My aunt used one teabag, and it went for everybody at the table. You can imagine what kind of tea I had by the time the bag reached me. Let me see. [Sounds can be heard in the background of names of people being recited. Indistinguishable.] I was the tenth person to use the bag. Wow! I never counted it before. Tenth! [Pause.] That's truly pathetic!

"It was the same way with clothing. I never had any new clothes. I wore hand-me-downs from my aunt or her daughters. Here's the problem.

16

All the people in my aunt's family were stunning to look at. My aunt and her two daughters were beautiful. The older sons were handsome. I can't say much about the teen-age boys, as we were always fighting about something, so I didn't pay too much attention to how they looked, but I guess you could say they were good-looking also.

"But they were all thin. My aunt wore housedresses most of the time, but her daughters, going to work as they did, were always well-dressed and stunning to look at. And I was exactly the opposite. An ugly duckling in a family of beauties."

"Tell me about your appearance and why you think you were, as you say, 'an ugly duckling.'"

"Well, for one thing I was <u>very</u> fat. I'm not kidding. I was <u>really</u> ugly. I had very bad buckteeth – worse than Bugs Bunny. None of the clothes they gave me to wear fit properly, including the shoes, because they were bought for dainty people. My aunt and her daughters were short and slender, but I was tall and fat. My hair was bright red, coarse and thick, and very kinky.[1] The only thing that could be done with it was to braid it. So my hair was always in two long thick braids."

"Go on."

"About the only thing that my aunt and her family and I had in common was love for music and baseball. All of us felt passionately about those two things. We might not have liked the same kind of music, or the same

---

[1] The word "kinky," as used at the time these discussions were recorded, did not have the same connotation as it does today. It was used then to describe specifically the hair of Caucasian individuals with the same tight curls which occur naturally in most African-Americans.

17

teams, but we shared a love for those two things - music and baseball.

"I had developed a talent in playing piano, and a friend of my mother's, who had taken an interest in me, gave me piano lessons for free. I remember that in Junior High, I somehow got the nerve to take the extensive examination and testing to get into the special High School of Music and Art, and nobody was more surprised than I when I was accepted. I mean, only rich kids went to that school. Some of them had already been in movies and on Broadway, even had their own radio programs. But there I was, Sophie Jacobs, and I got accepted into Music and Art."

"You must have been very proud. How did your aunt and her family react?"

"It didn't mean much to them except more trouble for my aunt. The school was two hours one-way from where we lived, so she had to give me bus and subway fare to get there and back. She was not happy about that, you can believe me. And then there were lunches to make. In a way, I think she would have been happier if I had just gone to a local school where I could walk and come home for lunch, like her two boys did."

"How did you feel about attending this High School with all these special children?"

"It really frightened me, let me tell you. I really felt like a fish out of water. Here I was, fat, ugly, poor - everything the other kids in the school were not. The work schedule was grueling. We had a full college academic program, in addition to our specialized training in the Arts. And I had the four-hour round trip to the school, which was in Harlem by the way, then back home to Brooklyn.

"I felt so out-of-place to be there. Everything was <u>way</u> over my head. For the first time in my life, I did not get good grades. I was terrified of everything and everybody. I had no friends, except for a few odd-ball characters; boys who, like me, were baseball fans and who, for whatever reason, did not fit in with the mainstream."

[Long Silence.]

"Then everything changed when I met Harry."

"Ah. Yes. So now we get to Harry. Tell me about Harry, please. How did you meet him? In the last session you said he was not a student at your school; that he was an adult you met at a baseball game. Tell me about this, please."

"Looking back at it from an adult perspective, I can see that I needed to do something to call some attention to myself in my aunt's family. They were all fans of the Brooklyn Dodgers baseball team. To be different, I chose to be a fan of one of the arch-rivals of the Dodgers, the St. Louis Cardinals. That was even worse than being a Giants fan, because at least they were a New York team. Actually, one of the reasons I liked the Cardinals was because they had a really great looking young pitcher, Howie Pollette, a Cajun from Louisiana. I think he was only 19 or something. Anyway, he looked young enough to be a teenager, and I developed this big crush on him."

"His name was Howie? Did I not hear you correctly? Did I misunderstand you?"

"Oh no, Dr. Levy. I'm sorry. Howie Pollette is somebody completely different. I'm just leading up to how I became a St. Louis Cardinal fan and how I got to meet Harry. No. The man who is dead and does what I call "hang around" me - his name *is* Harry. You did not hear wrong."

"Thank you. Continue, please."

"Anyway, the Polo Grounds, the stadium where the Giants played their home games, was in Harlem. They tore it down in 1964, you know. What a pity. Just like Ebbett's Field. Even though I never was a Dodger fan, still it was a shame to see those two ballparks go and to have those teams leave New York.

"Anyway, to get back to how I met Harry. Because the Polo Grounds was a little over a mile from Music and Art, I used to walk there after school whenever the Cardinals were in town. I would get there after the game had already started, and because it would always be a weekday, not too many people were in attendance. For that reason, and because, to take one look at me, it was pretty obvious that I didn't have much money, the Gatekeepers used to let me in for nothing. But they would make me sit in what to them were the worst seats possible - the bleachers out in the sun, right next to the visiting team's clubhouse. Of course they didn't know that for me, those were the ideal seats, because I got to see the Cardinal players whenever they were going in or out or just hanging around the clubhouse. Naturally, I was hoping to see Howie Pollette up close."

"Did you?"

"To be honest, I really don't remember, because once I got to know Harry, nothing else and no one else mattered."

"Miss Jacobs, I see our time is up for now. When you come next week, we will begin with how you met this man Harry and what the nature of your relationship was with him."

[Silence.]

"Miss Jacobs, are you all right?"

"Yes, Dr. Levy, thank you. I'm all right. I'm sorry. It's just that when I talk or think about Harry, I become - it's hard to explain - it's just that I become overwhelmed by intense emotions, even just thinking about him."

"You will explain that to me next week, please."

"Yes. Thank you. Goodbye, Dr. Levy."

"Goodbye, Miss Jacobs."

End of Tape 2.

Notes Accompanying Tape 2.

Miss Jacobs always speaks in a self-deprecating manner. She is always saying "thank you" or apologizing for things she has not done. It would be obvious even to a layperson that her traumatic childhood experiences helped form an insecure personality. Still, there is no evidence of psychosis or hysteria. She is, however, a bit hyperactive, but that may simply be a manifestation of typical New York City behavior.

Once again, her narrative was straightforward and dispassionate. This does not seem to me to be a masking of hysterical behavior. It does not seem to indicate the flat-affect of Schizophrenia. It appears more to be the result of her training in analysis of facts and figures, relative to her profession as an accountant.

It was <u>very interesting</u> to listen to Miss Jacobs' description of herself as a child. This reinforces my theory that she has a very low opinion of herself. Of course, that may be fostered by the standards of beauty imposed upon the public by those in the entertainment and fashion industries. It is, in theory, quite similar to the NAZI emphasis on Aryan purity. The United States shows beauty in women as blond and blue-eyed, with slender bodies that are almost impossible for normal women to maintain. It is a standard suitable for women of White Anglo-Saxon origin, but excludes women with darker Mediterranean skin color, women of Semitic origin, and especially those who are non-Caucasian. For that reason, Miss Jacobs considers herself as a very ugly teenager. It would be interesting to know how she would describe herself today. I MUST remember to ask her that in one of our next sessions. (She is now scheduled to come twice per week.)

As noted before, Miss Jacobs was well-groomed and clothed in keeping with her profession. She wore a business-like jacket and skirt of solid dark color, with a pale turtleneck blouse. She wore no jewelry except for an unusual silver ring on the third finger of her left hand. She wore very little make-up, which was tastefully applied. She is well-proportioned, certainly not fat, and has an attractive figure, *etwas zaftig*.[2] Her hair is still vibrant red, long and thick, no longer in braids, but tied back in a "bun".

Her skin coloring is in America, strangely referred to as "olive," perhaps because it is used to describe peoples of the Mediterranean area. She has a rather large prominent nose — definitely a typical Semitic feature. Her most striking feature are her eyes, which, when she removes her glasses, are extraordinarily dark — the best characterization is the Russian phrase: "Ochi Chorneuyeh".[3]

Rather than being "ugly," Miss Jacobs has an intriguingly unconventional face and an attractive figure. Her facial appearance, and the unusual combination of her darker skin coloring with her bright red hair, makes discerning her ethnic origin difficult, as it defies stereotyping. I would imagine Miss

---

[2] German words, used to describe women who, in the United States, might be characterized as "somewhat chubby," or, "pleasingly plump."

[3] The phrase "Ochi Chorneuyeh" was written by Dr. Levy in the Russian Cyrillic script. As I am not familiar with this language, I consulted a translator, who approximated the sounds of the words into phonetic English, and translated them literally as "black eyes." This phrase does not carry the same connotation as it does in English, but, as she explained, simply means that the individual's eyes are so dark that they appear to be black in color.

Jacobs is asked often about her origins, as she could be imagined as Jewish, Italian, Arab, Puerto Rican — even a light-skinned Negro.[4] One would think these characteristics would make her attractive as a woman of mystery and intelligence, and that she would have no shortage of men interested in knowing more about her. Perhaps these <u>very</u> characteristics, including what she described as a certain determined rebellious nature, are what led to her relationship with this man Harry - a relationship which obviously had a profound effect upon her life at a time when, by her own narration, she had little opportunity to experience happiness.

My initial impression that this will be a most interesting case to analyze has been reinforced by today's session.

* * *

---

[4] Persons of African-American descent should not be offended by Dr. Levy's use of the term "Negro," which was considered in his time, to be the polite word to use in describing persons of African ancestry and Race.

TAPE 3

March 27, 1981

4:30 pm

"Good afternoon, Miss Jacobs."

"Dr. Levy. I feel so relieved to be able to come for these sessions. Seymour was right."

"Seymour was right?"

"Oh, yes. I've known Seymour for so long. He's like my closest friend. There never was any romance between us, or anything like that. I guess we've been friends for too long. But I can tell him anything. And in this situation, in particular, he has been the absolute <u>best</u> person for me to talk to - other than a professional such as yourself, I mean."

"Please sit down, Miss Jacobs, and tell me why you believe, rather strongly I can tell, that Seymour Cohen was the best person for you to talk to about these events in your life."

"Well, first of all, Seymour and I have always had intellectual discussions, even when we were kids. Our families were friends before the two of us were born. They were all members of the Socialist Workers Party."

"Oh. I see."

"And Seymour and I would be at meetings with the adults. But that's another story. You asked why Seymour was the absolute best person for me to talk to about these weird events in my life. Well, for one thing our close relationship enables me to tell him about these things knowing he will pay attention and not make fun of me, or reach a quick conclusion that I'm nuts. Also, Seymour and I were close friends during the time I knew Harry, so he knew about my relationship with

Harry. But <u>most of all</u>, Seymour was with me when we were teenagers <u>at the time when a VERY BIZARRE incident occurred</u> involving me and Harry."

[The emphasized words were spoken slowly and very deliberately.]

"Yes?"

"Yes. In fact, what's even <u>more</u> amazing is that every time since that particular incident, whenever Seymour would see me in-between concert tours, he would bring that incident up practically before he would say 'hello.' It used to annoy me terribly, because I didn't want to remember that incident at all, and I disliked his throwing it in my face every chance he got. I even asked him to stop talking about it, but that seemed to goad him into doing it even more.

"But now I'm glad Seymour talked about it so much, because he is someone, definitely not crazy, who can attest to the occurrence of at least one of these abnormal events that have always been a part of my knowing Harry."

"Harry was alive at the time of this incident when Seymour was present?"

"Oh yes. We were just teenagers at the time, and Harry was <u>very much</u> alive. It was a <u>terrible</u> thing, and I wish it had never happened. But at least it shows the nature of the deep connection between Harry and me."

"Do you want to tell me about this incident?"

"Of course. But maybe first I should continue telling you about how I met Harry so that you see how that event followed in the sequence of things."

"If that is what you wish. Continue with how you met this man Harry, please."

"I think I told you, in the last session, about how I would go to the Polo Grounds after school every time the Cardinals were in town playing the Giants. I would be let in free, but I would have to sit in the bleachers next to the clubhouse used for the visiting team. I preferred this arrangement - actually for me it was the best possible seat — because I got to see the Cardinal players come and go. Sometimes I could see them sitting around inside, or standing and looking out the window."

[Silence.]

"Yes. Continue, please."

[Sounds of crying.]

"Here, Miss Jacobs, take some tissues from this box, please."

[More sounds of crying, nose blowing, and eventual silence.]

"What made you cry, Miss Jacobs?"

"It's just remembering that day, the day I met Harry. He was so young, so full of life and the joy of living."

[Silence.]

"I'm sorry."

[Sniffling.]

"I'll go on."

[Pause.]

"Anyway, this one day, when I got to the bleachers, the game was already in progress, as usual. When I asked, the way I always did, someone in the stands what had happened before I got there, I was told that it was the bottom of the third inning, the Giants had scored four runs with nobody out and two men on base, the score was something like Giants - 6, Cardinals - 0, and the Cardinal manager had just sent his pitcher out of the game.

"Do you know anything about baseball, Dr. Levy?"

"Not a thing. Continue with how you met Harry, please."

"Anyway, the Cardinal pitcher had been sent out of the game, which meant he had to go to the clubhouse, take a shower, and be finished for the day. It's generally a disgrace for a pitcher, because it means he's doing a bad job. I'm oversimplifying things, but that's so you'll know the significance of what I'm going to tell next."

"Thank you. Continue please."

"Anyway, it's always been my belief that the Polo Grounds had the longest infield ever, and it was <u>really</u> a great humiliation for a pitcher to have to walk that long distance back to the clubhouse, with the crowd usually booing and shouting obscenities as the poor guy walked all the way. He'd been disgraced enough already, and this just rubbed salt in the wound."

"Yes. I understand. Continue please."

"Anyway, on this one day, I saw this pitcher coming toward the Cardinal clubhouse and right away, I could tell there was something different about him. He had a very special way of walking – it wasn't really walking, like people regularly do. Every step was a long stride, with a bounce, a spring to every step – almost jaunty, yes, jaunty, that's the word I'd use. Even in defeat, he had the nerve to have this bouncy spring to his steps, almost as if his spirit was so strong it was unconfined to this earth. [Almost a whisper.] Even then, when he was alive, nothing could contain his spirit, so why should it be confined in death?"

"Miss Jacobs, I'm sorry. What did you say? Your last words, could you repeat them please."

"I don't know if I remember. I guess I was just talking to myself out loud. I've been doing that a lot lately. I'm sorry. I'll get back to the story.

"Anyway, here comes the Cardinal pitcher, and the crowd is booing and yelling insults *et cetera* at him. As he came closer, I could see what looked like a scowl on his face, but that began to lighten and change into a grin. Then, as he heard the noise of the crowd yelling at him, he stopped dead in his tracks - that's funny to say that now - but he stopped right there on the outfield, he was near the clubhouse but still on the playing field, and his grin broke into a big smile and he started to laugh, probably at the absurdity of it all. Then he kept walking to the clubhouse, but that very act, that act of stopping, smiling, and laughing good-naturedly, won over the crowd, including me, and people in the bleachers ran down to the railing to see if they could get him to autograph their scorecards.

"I was one of those who ran down. I had never gotten a player's autograph before, but I certainly wanted this guy's. For one thing, I wanted to know who he was. So I went to where the crowd was standing and he did sign the scorecards, including mine. Only I had to be cute. Ball-point pens had only just come out and I had him sign with a red one - you know - red, for Cardinals - [Pause] - and sadly, over time, his signature faded, like he did, [Voice diminishing.] I guess, out of existence."

"What did he write, this fellow."

"He wrote his name. Just his name. Harry Gault."

"Ah. So <u>he</u> is the Harry you have been talking about."

"Yes. And after signing the autographs, he ran up the clubhouse stairs, two-at-a-time, and went inside."

"Then what happened? How did you get to know him?"

"The game went on, and I watched it and completely forgot about the Cardinal pitcher. The Giants kept getting runs, even with a new pitcher in the game, and by the time the seventh inning came, the Giants were way ahead. I don't remember the score now, but they were <u>way</u> ahead.

"Then came the seventh inning, when fans stand up to show support for their team. It's a baseball tradition, at least it was then, I don't know about now, because I haven't been to a ballgame since 1949."

"That's interesting. But tell me, Miss Jacobs, what year was this when you met Harry, and how old were you please."

"It was 1947 and I was 13 years old."

"Thank you. Continue please, except later you must tell me about why you have not been to a ballgame since 1949. Continue."

"Anyway, I stood up in the top of the seventh to show my support for the Cardinals. Naturally, I was the only person standing, since this was New York City and the St. Louis team wasn't particularly popular, <u>especially</u> because of their treatment of Jackie Robinson."

"Oh yes. Him I have heard of. A very courageous man with enormous strength of character and integrity. But continue, please."

"Anyway, I heard this voice yelling: 'Hey, kid!' I turned and saw that the Cardinal pitcher who had signed my autograph-"

"Harry."

"Yes. Harry. Anyway, he was yelling, leaning out the clubhouse window, yelling: 'Hey, kid!' I looked around to see what kid he could be calling to, and he yelled the same thing again: 'Hey, kid!' I couldn't possibly think he could mean me, so I kept looking around. This time he pointed and said, 'Yeah, you.' I was in shock. Why would he want to talk to me?

"Then he asked, 'Why are you standing?' And I answered, like he was some kind of dummy or something, 'It's the seventh inning stretch, and I'm standing for the Cardinals.' And he asked, like he couldn't believe what he had just heard: 'You're a Cardinal fan?' And when I told him I was, he asked if I was from Missouri. Well, he REALLY was surprised when I told him I was from Brooklyn. It was as if you could have knocked him over with a feather. So then he asked why, if I was from Brooklyn, I was a St. Louis Cardinal fan. And, naïve and young as I was, I responded simply with the truth. I told him, 'Because the Cardinals have such handsome pitchers.'

"That really caused him to laugh. What a beautiful laugh he had, and such a wonderful warm smile. He had such a big bright smile, so bright that it could light up a room. [Pause.] Anyway, he said, and I'll never forget his warm wonderful slow mid-western drawl, 'Well, I'm a Cardinal pitcher. I guess that means I'm handsome, right?' But the funny thing was I didn't know how to respond. He wasn't what you would call conventionally handsome, so I had to think about it for awhile before I could answer. This made him laugh even more. Then he

31

said, 'I guess since it's taking you so long, I'm getting worried about what your answer will be.' This time I laughed."

"Was he handsome, Miss Jacobs? Describe him for me please, as you remember him that first day you met."

[Pause.]

"You have to realize that at that time I was only 13, and I really wasn't sure if he was handsome or not. To me, Howie Pollette, who, as I said before, was probably still a teenager, maybe 19 or at most 20, was "cute." But Harry? At that time, handsome meant movie-star types, and I wasn't sure whether Harry fit that bill."

"Describe him please."

"After he asked that question, I looked at him intently. He was standing in the clubhouse, leaning out the window, and was naked except for a towel around his waist. I had never before in my life seen a man in such a state of undress.

"He was tall and had a beautiful muscular body, thin and wiry. He was dark-skinned, and also very tan, because of being in the sun so much. I found out later he was part Cherokee. He had thick jet-black hair, beautifully wavy. He had lots of hair, not only on his head, but all over his body, at least the parts I could see, and that was pretty much everything since he had only that towel wrapped around his waist. He was absolutely the hairiest man I have ever seen in my life.

"And what was fascinating — his eyes appeared to be dark from where I stood, because he had thick dark eyebrows and long thick dark lashes, but later, when I saw him up close, I realized his eyes were actually a brilliant sparkling blue - a deep blue hue —

bright and lively. He had a marvelous way of smiling, and a beautiful grin. I guess now I would say he was handsome, but then I didn't know what really constitutes being handsome. I think I would have called him 'good-looking.'"

"Thank you. Go on with what happened next, please."

"Well, we talked about the game, and he teased about how I could root for a team that was losing so badly. I remember the way it was between us even on that first day. There was such an ease of conversation between us, a teasing banter, a joking way of talking as if we had been friends for life already. Here I was, just a fat ugly kid, and here he was, a Major League pitcher with a champion ball team, and I could talk to him easier than I could talk to any of my classmates. In fact, the only person I could talk to with such ease at that time was Seymour. But Harry had a way of making me feel completely at ease, and safe to talk to, as if we were old friends teasing each other the way we had been for years.

"Then the real surprise came. The game was almost over, and he yelled to me that he would get dressed and he wanted me to meet him outside the ballpark by the clubhouse exit. He asked if I knew where it was. Of course I did. I waited there after every game to see the Cardinals leave, in hopes of seeing Howie Pollette. Funny how I can't remember if I ever did get to see him or not. I know I never got his autograph."

"I assume you agreed to meet Harry."

"Yes. I had to think about it for awhile, though. I knew I was only 13. He seemed so much older to me. Actually, he was almost 29 at the time, but I didn't know that then. And I knew I had homework to do, and practising.

And I knew somehow that it wasn't right for a girl my age to be meeting a man his age alone. Also, ballplayers didn't have too good a reputation in those days. I don't know whether that's changed since then, but back in the 40s, they weren't viewed with much respect. Certainly not the kind of people a 'good' girl would associate with.

"So I thought of all those things, but you're right. Of course I said 'yes.' And I met him outside the clubhouse.

"And that's how it began."

"Miss Jacobs, this will be a good place to close. I see we have gone over time, so we will have to continue this at our next session. You will tell me what happened at your first meeting, when you met Harry outside the stadium."

"Yes. Thank you, Dr. Levy. I'm sorry to have gone over time. I guess that was because I was crying so much. I'm sorry. I didn't mean to do that."

"There is no reason to apologize, Miss Jacobs. That is what this box of tissues is for. Goodbye now, and I will see you next week, correct?"

"Yes, Dr. Levy. Goodbye, and thank you."

"Yes. Goodbye, Miss Jacobs."

End of Tape 3.

Notes Accompanying Tape 3.

This is the first time since her distraught early morning telephone call, that this patient has expressed any emotion about her situation. Usually her manner, as detailed in previous Notes, has been dispassionate - as if she were relating an objective narrative about something quite distant and unconnected to her life. However, as she herself noted, Miss Jacobs becomes intensely emotional whenever she talks, or apparently even thinks, about this man Harry.

She continues to demonstrate a need to maintain order, such as when she refused to interrupt her background information to talk about this "terrible thing," whatever it was, and insisted on continuing her narrative in sequence. Could her insistent need for control betray a deeper underlying obsessive-compulsive disorder? This will bear watching for future indications.

At last we know something about this man Harry. He was a good-looking, possibly handsome, baseball player. He had a well-built muscular body, which is not surprising for a professional athlete. Apparently he was also what is known as a "smooth" talker, as he so easily captivated the emotions of this very young girl, barely in her teens.

However, at that time she was also a much-neglected orphan. She had no caring family members, and no father-figure to admire. Could this possibly be some kind of Elektra/Oedipus fixation? She was obviously starved for love and could easily have fallen prey to a good-looking adult male who would want to use her for his own purposes.

And what was the strange incident involving Miss Jacobs and this man Harry that so unsettled Seymour Cohen that he felt compelled to talk to her about it each time he saw her years later, despite her wishes to the contrary. This is something I must ask Miss Jacobs in our next session, but first I must also see if I can convince her to interrupt her material in its sequential order so she can tell me about it.

It is interesting that Seymour has never mentioned this incident in his own therapy sessions, despite its obvious strong impact upon him. But then, he has never talked about Miss Jacobs, either.

Also, I need to remember to ask Miss Jacobs why she has not been to a ballgame since 1949 - a strange fact, considering her obsession with the game until then.

***

TAPE 4

April 1, 1981

4:30 pm

"Good afternoon, Miss Jacobs."

"Good afternoon, Dr. Levy."

"Be seated, please."

"Thank you."

"Miss Jacobs, in reviewing the tape of our last session, I noted that you were quite upset about an incident involving you and this man Harry, at which Seymour Cohen was also present. Am I correct in saying that you were upset by this incident?"

"Yes. I was upset. That's correct."

"And from your words in discussing this incident, I received the distinct impression that this was not a normal occurrence - that it was unusual in some way, perhaps even a psychic phenomenon. Was my impression correct, please."

"Yes. It's correct."

"And I have also received the impression that in your mind this incident is just one of a number of paranormal events involving you and this man Harry, continuing even after his death. Is that not correct?"

"Yes. That is correct, Dr. Levy."

"Tell me, how did this man Harry die? What was the cause of his death? Was it an accident, or something unusual? Or do you know."

"Oh, I know, Dr. Levy. He died as a result of some sort of lung disease. He was a heavy smoker, and also a carpenter. It's possible that some of the materials he worked with could have gotten into his lungs."

"I thought you told me he was a baseball player."

"Yes. But in those days, ballplayers didn't make that much money, and unless you were really one of the true superstars, like DiMaggio or Williams or Feller - someone like that - you didn't make enough money to live on for the whole year. Most of the guys were country boys and returned to their farms during the off-season. Harry happened to be a carpenter, and worked at that during the off-season, and after he retired from the game."

"Did you continue to see him after he retired from baseball?"

"No. But I knew that was what he did. He had talked about it when I was seeing him, and I learned it after he passed away."

"What year was that, please."

"1979."

"When was - what year was it that you last saw Harry."

"I never saw him after the Spring of 1949."

"Does that have some connection with your never seeing a baseball game after that year?"

"Yes, it does."

"Miss Jacobs, will you talk about the incident that was so disturbing to you and Seymour, please."

"Really, Dr. Levy, I'd much rather do that later. I don't wish to be negative or difficult, it's just that I think it will make so much more sense if I can continue with the background material that shows the nature of my relationship with Harry. And I'm not trying to avoid the incident - it just will be more understandable to you, you'll know better why it was so upsetting."

"Very well, Miss Jacobs. Continue as you wish."

"I think our last session ended with my going to meet Harry outside the Clubhouse before the game ended. I did. When I saw him, I was somewhat taken aback. I had seen him in his uniform, and then with just that towel around his waist. But there he was, dressed in street clothes, and he, well — he was dressed really weird."

"Weird? In what respect, please, Miss Jacobs."

"Well, he was tall and thin, with a wiry, muscular build. He was well tanned with a dark complexion and thick black hair. But his choice of clothing was <u>unbelievable</u>! Nothing matched. Nothing matched his physique or his coloring, and nothing matched any other piece of clothing. After a few times of being with Harry, I used to scribble on whatever I could write on, what he was wearing, it was so unbelievable."

"An example, please."

"Well, he would - let me give you a typical type of outfit for him: maroon shirt, green pants, checkered jacket, plaid tie, and usually the same pair of tan shoes. Loafers, I think. Later, after he was dead, I wondered about his choice in clothes. Was it that he was too preoccupied with his inner thought processes to be concerned about his clothing? Or was it that he dressed that way deliberately, so people would notice him, look at him, then come under his spell."

"Miss Jacobs - what do you mean 'come under his spell.' Do you mean that literally?"

"Yes, I do, Dr. Levy. Harry was heavily into magic and the occult. But I'm way ahead of my story."

"All right. Continue, please."

"So the first thing I noticed about him was his weird choice of clothing. But I also saw how really good-looking he was. He smiled broadly, walked briskly over to where I was standing, actually took my hand and said something like, 'C'mon kid, let's run up the stairs and beat the crowd. There's something I want to show you.'"

"What stairs was he referring to."

"Since you don't know baseball, you probably are not familiar with the Polo Grounds. Well that was torn down in 1964. But the Yankee Stadium. I <u>know</u> you must have heard of that, or seen it. It is in the Bronx.

"Anyway, there was this elevated train. It came from somewhere, I don't really know where. But it stopped at the Polo Grounds, and from there went to its last stop, the Yankee Stadium. So Harry and I ran up the stairs to the train platform. He paid my fare - it was only a nickel then, anyway - and when the train came, we took it to the Yankee Stadium.

"I'll always remember that first time together. There we were, he was holding my hand, not like a sweetheart, but like a grownup holding a kid's hand, and we were standing like two pilgrims in front of a shrine.

"The stadium was closed, of course. Well, I forget you don't know baseball, but whenever the Giants were in town, the Yankees were away, and vice versa; because the parks were so close the management didn't want to divide the gate proceeds. And the sky was gray. I can see it so clearly, as if it were only yesterday.

"Dr. Levy? Have you ever had a day when something happened a long time ago but you can remember it as if it had only just happened?"

[Pause.]

"Yes."

[Pause.]

"I think we all have. Now continue Miss Jacobs, please."

"Anyway, we stood there staring at the empty closed Stadium. It looked so gray and large and mysterious. It was what you would call a magnificent edifice.

"Then Harry shared a secret of his with me. It was something very personal to him, but he wanted to tell me about it. It was his dream to pitch in a World Series against the New York Yankees. The Yankees were the hotshot team then. Well, I guess they always have been.

"And after that, after standing on this deserted street corner staring at the empty gray Yankee Stadium, he told me he knew where there was a little soda joint, and asked if I wanted to go have a soda with him. Well, you can imagine how I felt, so of course I said yes and went with him. I had never gone anywhere with any male other than my Uncle or cousins or Seymour."

"What happened next, please."

"Harry took me to this little candy store that he called a "soda joint," and he had black coffee, he always had black coffee and I had an egg cream. We sat there and talked and he told me about his family back in Missouri, his wife and baby girl.

"He said the sweetest thing to me."

"What was that, please."

"He told me that what made him notice me was that I had hair the same color as his little girl and that his wife would braid it and put it in two little pigtails. My color hair and

41

the two braids reminded him of his little girl.

"He hated being on the road so much. He missed his wife and baby. He had lost so much time during the War. His little girl was born while he was in the Service, and when he came back from the War, he was surprised to see her as a toddler, walking and talking. He was so very proud of her. He was barely home from the War when he had to report for Spring Training with the Cardinals. They made the Veterans have extra training to make up for the time they were away from the game. So he had to pack up and leave again and barely had time to spend with them. It was the same from then on, and he missed his wife and baby very much."

"He told you all that?"

"Yes. As we were sitting in the candy store."

[Silence.]

"Then what happened."

"He looked at his watch, and said he had better get me back to the subway so I could go home. Then, it was as if he had made a sudden realization, he said he hadn't asked me my name or how old I was. So I told him my name was Sophie, but I lied and told him I was 18."

"Why did you do that, Miss Jacobs?"

"Well, I didn't want him to think he had been having this serious talk with someone who was just a kid, and I figured he wouldn't want to have anything to do with me, and would feel like an idiot to be with a 13-year old. Also, I was very tall and so fat that I was always being taken for older than I was, so I figured I could get away with it. As I think of it now, he must have known I was not 18, although he might not have thought I was only 13."

"What happened next?"

42

"He stood up, went to the counter and paid the bill, and when he returned, I had gotten up also, and he did something that became a familiar gesture of teasing, and I guess now, affection, too, although I never realized it as such at the time."

"What was that, please."

"He pulled on my braids."

[Voice indicating difficulty in restraining tears.]

"He tugged on my braids, playfully, and said something like, let's go. He walked that wonderful, beautiful, bouncy quick walk of his, and I took off after him. It was quite a job to keep up with him when he walked like that, which was about 98 percent of the time, and as a result, I've developed this life long habit of walking faster than anyone else I know.

"We went back past the Stadium and took the el. to the Polo Grounds, which was now also deserted. We took the subway from there. He went to his hotel in midtown Manhattan where the Cardinals stayed when they had games in New York and Brooklyn. He asked if I was going that way, too, and I told him I was. But that was a lie also. I was living in Brooklyn and took a different subway line from the one that went to his hotel.

"When we came to his stop, he said something like: 'You know, Sophie is too fancy. I think I'll call you 'Sandy' instead. It goes with the color of your hair.' Then he asked if I would meet him tomorrow after the game, and I said 'Sure,' and then he got off.

"By the time I got home it was much later than usual, and my Aunt was getting ready to call the police. I was so excited about my meeting with Harry, that I actually told her everything, in the presence of her husband and children. That was a <u>big</u> mistake! From then on, I was subjected to either the teasing of the kids, or the anger of my Aunt. She was so worried about my associating with a married older ballplayer. I was so innocent then, and I couldn't understand why she felt that way. I thought she should be happy, as I was, that I had met someone important who had been nice to me. Of course, now as an adult, I can certainly appreciate why she would be upset. It got worse the more I saw Harry."

"Did you meet him that next afternoon."

"Yes. And what's more, I even got to talk to him again during the game. Even though he had started the game the day before, he loved to pitch so much, that he often volunteered to act as a relief pitcher, and the bleachers where I was sitting was also near where the Visiting Team relief pitchers stayed in what was called the "Bullpen."

"When I arrived, late as usual, I saw him sitting there on the bench, and I called to him. I was really being a show-off, letting the others know that I was friends with one of the Cardinal pitchers. Actually, I was a little nervous that he wouldn't want to remember me because he figured out my age, or I was so fat and ugly, whatever.

"But he beamed that wonderful warm smile of his, and actually got up and walked over to where I was in the stands. I walked down to the edge of the wall, and as I leaned over to say 'Hi,' my long braids fell over the railing. Of course, that gave him a good excuse to pull on them again, and he made some kind of joke about 'Rapunzel,' and how he liked to read that story to his little girl. There wasn't much going on during the game, and he never even got to warm up, so we just spent the time talking. Then we did the exact same thing as the day before. We took the el. to the Stadium, stood in awe, walked to the candy store, had coffee and egg cream, then went back on the subway, where he got off at the stop for his hotel.

"He had a break after that before one last game with the Giants, and then another break before going to Ebbett's Field to play the Dodgers in Brooklyn. I didn't get to see him then, because my school was in Manhattan. But I read the paper religiously to see how the Cardinals were doing.

"I didn't get to see him again until the next time the Cardinals were at the Polo Grounds. About a month, I think. Meanwhile, though, I told all the kids I knew in school - not too many, because I didn't have that many friends, and only a few who were interested in baseball - all about how I met this great ballplayer, who was so good-looking and so friendly. I must say that my stock went up with the kids I told, and then even some I didn't know, but were interested in baseball, came to find out about my experiences with Harry."

"What were your feelings for Harry at that time; do you remember?"

"I thought I had what could be referred to as a school-girl 'crush.' It wasn't until after he died, and I began receiving these communications from Harry, that I realized I was deeply in love with him."

"And how do you think Harry felt about you?"

"I never had any illusions then. I simply thought that he felt I was — well, that he felt sorry for me because I was so fat and ugly, and wanted to be kind to a poor slob.

45

Again, it wasn't until after he was dead and I began receiving these communications from him, that I realized he had deep feelings for me also.

"In the beginning, it was quite innocent for both of us, I believe. But I'm not sure of anything anymore. I've even gone to a Psychic, and she told me that Harry and I have always been together, in past lives, and will be together in the future as well."

"Do you believe that?"

"So many things have happened after Harry died and these psychic phenomena have occurred, that I don't know what I believe anymore. Except I <u>do</u> believe that Harry and I shared some form of love during the time we were together then."

"Can you tell me about that incident at which Seymour Cohen was present, please."

"Believe me, Dr. Levy, I'm not trying to be coy, or to deliberately keep you in suspense, but there is something else I need to tell you first before I can go into that incident. It involves what happened after Harry and I met the next month when the Cardinals came to play at the Polo Grounds. I promise that after I tell you about that, the incident will make much more sense to you and you'll be able to understand better why it was so devastating to me and so unnerving to Seymour."

"Am I right to assume that you told Seymour about your meetings with this ballplayer, Harry."

"Of course. I told Seymour more details than anyone. I had learned the hard way to be guarded about what I said at home, because my Aunt was very concerned about my behavior with this older married man. But it really was impossible for me to hide my feelings and I'm afraid I not only gave my aunt aggravation, but also allowed myself to become the brunt of all kinds of jokes from my male cousins who were near my age and followed baseball. They were Dodger fans because of Jackie Robinson, and so they really got on my case for being a Cardinal fan as well as my interest in Harry."

"Well, Miss Jacobs, I see our time is nearly up. Perhaps you will be able to tell me about this incident next time."

"Honestly, Dr. Levy, I'm not being coy or trying to hide anything. It's just that it makes more sense this way."

"I said nothing about your motivation, Miss Jacobs."

"I know. I guess I was just reading your mind."

"Good afternoon, Miss Jacobs."

"Good afternoon, Dr. Levy."

End of Tape 4.

Notes Accompanying Tape 4.

There seems to be a very interesting interplay between this patient and myself concerning this "incident" which was so disturbing to her and to Seymour Cohen. She was the one who brought it up during the previous session, yet she still refuses to talk about it. She keeps postponing her discussion of it.

Is she being "coy," as she suggested, or is this incident so disturbing that she is attempting to avoid any discussion and possible analysis of it on my part. But part of her must want to talk about it, otherwise she would not have mentioned it in her prior session. Perhaps she is being coy, however, and this was one of the things that the ballplayer found attractive in her.

It still remains obvious that Miss Jacobs has no self-assurance. She definitely suffers from a neurotic sense of inferiority, which is totally unjustified. She describes a childhood of poverty and neglect, yet she has achieved the profession of a CPA, which requires considerable education and a lengthy and complex examination. (I have not verified that this is her actual employment, but this can be done easily. At this time, I have no reason to doubt her veracity, at least as to her profession, and also to her relationship with Seymour Cohen, which Seymour himself referred to when he inquired as to whether she had actually sought my assistance.)

She gives herself no credit for her achievement in a difficult profession, and still seems to think of herself as the little girl she describes as being so fat and ugly. Yet, even if such description of herself as a child is accurate, she still attracted the attention of this good-looking athlete, who confided details to her of his personal life, which in itself says something about her character. She definitely has no concept of her own worthiness.

But I also need to search my inner self to find why exactly I am so curious as to this incident. Her case is certainly like no other I have at this time, or ever had.

Once again, except for a brief moment of tears and a choked-up voice, Miss Jacobs presented her life as if she were reciting a narrative from a play – with total objectivity and distancing – as if it were a tale of another human being, not herself. It begins to appear that she may have chosen the profession of accounting in order to place emphasis on logic and analysis of facts, thereby avoiding any need for emotions. Could she have done this in reaction to the powerful emotions of whatever happened between her and this man Harry when she was a child?

There are so many unanswered questions already in this case, where I have seen the patient only 4 times! What happened that ended her relationship with this man in 1949? Whatever it was, it must have been very traumatic, because she never attended a baseball game after that.

I wonder why she asked me about a day I would always remember for the rest of my life. Of course, all human beings have such days, but did she realize what an emotional question that would be for me? Nonsense. How could she! But what a strange thing for her to say about "reading my mind!" How did she know the word "coy" was exactly in my thoughts at that very moment.

Is this woman psychotic, or merely psychic?
It will be interesting to see whether she actually reveals this "incident" during her next session.

* * *

TAPE 5

April 3, 1981
4:30 pm

"Miss Jacobs."

"Dr. Levy."

"Sit down, please."

"Thank you."

"Miss Jacobs, I am curious if you are ready to discuss the incident that occurred during the lifetime of this man Harry, while you and Seymour Cohen were young teenagers – this incident which you described as 'bizarre,' if I remember correctly."

"Why is it so important to you that I discuss this incident, Dr. Levy?"

"Why is it so important to you that you <u>not</u> discuss it, after you have indicated that it was something neither you nor Seymour could forget, Miss Jacobs."

"Touché, Dr. Levy. Please understand though, I <u>really do</u> want to discuss it, and I'm not being evasive. I just feel it will make more sense to you after I've finished telling you about specific background information."

"Having things arranged in logical sequence is very important to you, is it not, Miss Jacobs?"

"Yes, it is, now that you mention it. It just seems more efficient to me."

"Did you always have this need for logic and order?"

[Long silence.]

[Voice, upon resumption, almost on the verge of crying.]

"No."

[Silence; not as long this time.]

"Until these events started to happen – these communications from Harry after his death – I viewed myself as a person who had <u>always</u> been logical. Then when I began reading about metaphysical theories and psychic phenomena, I started remembering my relationship with Harry – he certainly helped in that regard – and I realized that I had been a very emotional teenager, very volatile – with an extreme over-active imagination; and that I had repressed all this by assuming an ultra-logical persona. In fact, there was a time when I didn't even remember that I knew Harry, if you can imagine that."

[Pause.]

"Are you familiar with Science Fiction, Dr. Levy?"

"I know what it is, of course, but I do not read it."

"Do you watch television?"

"No. Quite frankly, I prefer to listen to symphonic and chamber music."

"Well, there was a program called 'Star Trek' on TV. It takes place in the distant future, and one of the main characters was from another planet in another Star system. His name is Spock, and he considered logic and reason far superior to emotions. On his planet, the inhabitants consciously inhibit the expression of emotion to the point where, as adults, they no longer experience it, but view every occurrence from the point of logic. This character Spock, however, is part human, and sometimes had to actively repress emotions which attempted to surface. Anyway, I'm telling you all this because I think of myself as Spock. I'm all logic on the surface, but with these events after Harry's death, I've come to realize that what I've done is repress emotion that I couldn't handle."

"You said in one of your earlier sessions that, like Seymour, you had prepared for a career as a concert musician - is that correct?"

"Yes."

"Tell me then, what made you become an accountant, please."

"Actually, there were many reasons. But I guess we have choices, and I know where you're leading. Yes, I suppose I did choose accounting because it involved straight facts and figures, all logic and no emotion."

"And why did you wish to rid yourself of all emotion, Miss Jacobs."

"I can see now that it was because of the overwhelming emotions I experienced associated with Harry. They were so intense as to be frightening, particularly after this one incident."

"Ah. I see once again we are back to that same incident, correct?"

"Yes. But please, Dr. Levy, let me tell it my way, because I don't think you will appreciate why it was so frightening without the background information."

"All right, Miss Jacobs. I agree that your approach is reasonable, if that is the <u>real</u> reason you are refusing to discuss this incident."

"I'm <u>NOT</u> refusing to discuss it, Dr. Levy. Let me go on, please."

"Yes. I believe you were going to tell me about what happened when you were with Harry the next time the Cardinals came to New York."

"That's right. Anyway, I was so excited to be able to see him again, but I was also afraid that he would not remember me, or that he would not want to be bothered by a pesky fat ugly kid.

"I went to the Polo Grounds the first chance I could when the Cardinals returned, but I didn't see Harry. He was not in the bullpen, and I didn't see him in the Clubhouse either.

"After the game ended, I rushed outside to wait for the players to leave, and there he was, dressed the same peculiar way as the last time — weird combinations of colors and styles, with those same tan shoes, but this time he was surrounded by other ballplayers. The famous ones were there: Musial, Brecheen, Marion, and one or two others, and they were all surrounding Harry, listening intently to whatever he was telling them. He was definitely center-stage. He saw me, winked and smiled a little crooked type grin, but kept on going."

"How did you react to this?"

"Well, at first I was sad to see that I could not get to talk to him, but then I felt so thrilled when he winked and smiled at me. And I also felt excited to see all these other famous players, much more famous than Harry, all wrapped up in whatever he was saying."

"What did you do next?"

"For some reason, I followed them. I walked behind them and got on the same subway train as they did. I sat where I could see Harry, and just kept staring at him. I guess I must have looked like some kind of love-sick teenager, which in fact I was, I guess, now that I think of it.

"But then, a strange thing happened."

"What was that, Miss Jacobs. And were you alone at the time."

"Oh yes. After school, I always went to the Polo Grounds by myself, except for one other

time I can remember. The incident where
Seymour was present was a totally different
set of circumstances; not my usual way of
seeing Harry.

"Anyway, while I was sitting on the subway
train, and Harry was still talking to the
others, who were still listening intently, I
actually heard Harry's voice in my head,
telling me, 'I'll see you after tomorrow's
game.' It was so real, but so strange. Nothing
like that had ever happened to me before. He
was there, across from me, actively engaged in
telling something to the others, but I
distinctly heard his voice in my head telling
me to meet him after the game the next day. It
was so bizarre."

"What did you do next, please."

"I didn't hear anything else, and I just
stayed on the train until they all got off at
their hotel stop, and I went to my connection
so I could get home to Brooklyn."

"What happened the next day, Miss Jacobs,
please."

"The next day, I was late getting to the
ballpark because of school work, and the game
was almost over when I arrived. But when I got
there Harry was in the bullpen. He was warming
up. It was such a thrill to see him pitch. He
had a unique style that I don't think anyone
ever had before or since, although of course,
I have to admit I haven't seen a ballgame
since 1949. Still, it's difficult to imagine
anyone having a style like Harry's, and in
fact, when I started reading all this stuff
about baseball after these weird events, I
found frequent statements both by ballplayers
and sportswriters, about the uniqueness of
Harry's style.

"Anyway, of course he was so preoccupied with warming up, that he did not acknowledge my presence. But again, I heard his voice in my mind. 'Meet me after the game,' he told me.

"He was called in as a relief pitcher, and I watched as he walked that wonderful, beautiful walk of his: long strides, with that special bounce -- it was like joy at being alive, so special.

"Anyway, he took over for someone else who had to make that long tortured walk back to the Clubhouse. Harry, who was a fabulous relief pitcher, got the Giants out and later hit a double that sent in the winning run for the Cardinals. He was also a very good hitter and infielder, as well. That was because he was a shortstop before he was a pitcher."

"I'm sorry, Miss Jacobs, but I do not know anything at all about baseball. But it appears that what you are telling me is that this Harry was an exceptional ballplayer."

"Yes. I thought so, and at the time, so did everyone else, I believe. He just never became famous, for a variety of reasons, I suppose."

"And you met him after the game, is that correct?"

"Yes. And here's where I want to tell you what is so important and necessary for you to understand about the nature of my relationship with Harry, in order for you to have a full appreciation of the event that occurred when Seymour was present.

"This time, when the game was over and I waited outside the Clubhouse, Harry was one of the last to come out. He was alone. He had his hands thrust deep into the pockets of his pants, and was walking that same beautiful brisk bounce. I waited to see what he would do next, and I heard his voice again, inside my

56

head, telling me to go up the stairs. It was so strange, but I did. I literally ran up the stairs to the elevated station, and when I reached the platform, he was right there, behind me.

"He didn't say a word as we waited for the train to arrive. He just stood there. It was so strange. I will <u>always, always</u> remember the image of how he looked that day. It comes to me often. I think of it so often. I see him standing there: hands thrust deep into his pants pockets, chewing gum as he rocked back and forth on the heels of his tan shoes. His head was down, but everytime he knew I was sneaking a look at him, he winked and smiled this delightful crooked grin of his, where his lips went up on the left side, almost as if in derision, at something, some hidden secret he knew that no one else did."

"But he said nothing."

"Not a word."

"And what were you doing at this time, please."

"I was just standing and watching him, and feeling an overpowering sense of emotion for this man. I can remember that now, but I had forgotten it for so many years.

"Anyway, we got off at the stop for the Stadium and rushed down the stairs. We still had not said a word to each other, at least not orally. We walked to the Stadium, and Harry found a groundskeeper, told him who he was, and we went inside and actually stood on the infield of the deserted Yankee Stadium. It was such a powerful feeling. The sky was cloudy and gray, and it felt damp and looked as if it might drizzle at any moment, which made the empty Stadium seem even more majestic and mysterious. We stood there in silence, again like two Pilgrims at a shrine, and then he took my hand, and we left. We went to our same candy store, and when we sat in our same booth, he started to talk to me, out loud this time."

"What did he say, please."

"He winked, and asked how I liked the 'game' we had been playing. I told him I wasn't sure what he meant, and he asked if I had gotten his 'messages.' At that point, I must admit to being somewhat scared, and I repeated that I didn't know what he meant. He asked again if I had gotten his 'messages.' I said that I thought I had heard inside my head that he wanted me to meet him outside after the game today. I felt crazy saying that, but he smiled a huge grin this time, and replied excitedly that it had worked. He said he somehow <u>knew</u> we could do it, that he could send messages to me and that I would know what he was thinking and what he wanted me to know. It wasn't until after his death that I learned he had a deep interest in psychic phenomena and the occult, and that he actually made use of this interest in his playing. I did know at the time that he was always doing magic tricks for his teammates, especially to amuse them when they were traveling on the road for long distances. There was no airplane travel then; the teams went from city to city by train mostly, sometimes by bus. The trips were long and that was one way he would help pass the time with his friends. He was actually referred to by some of the sportswriters as "The Merry Magician of the Mound," a title I used to tease him about, but which I really liked, because I thought it fit him so well, especially with his unique style. He was also a marvelous storyteller. He could capture the attention of whoever was listening to him spin a yarn. He really was quite a spellbinder.

"Harry was very popular, and gave the impression of a hale-fellow, well-met; but as I got to know him better, I came to realize that he actually was an introspective loner. After his death, when, as an adult I learned more about him, I understood that he held very profound and complex thoughts, and that he was particularly troubled by the experiences he suffered in the Second World War.

[Pause.]

"I'm sorry, I've gotten rather far afield."

"That is all right, Miss Jacobs. Continue, please."

"Anyway, after he told me that he had deliberately been sending these messages I had received, I asked if it worked both ways. Could I, as part of this game, send messages to him? Well then, he really smiled and became quite excited. He told me I could, and that if we wanted, we didn't have to speak at all. We could just try and see how much we could communicate to each other by just using our minds. As we had our coffee and soda, he talked, aloud, about how, if it worked, we could even influence the outcome of games with our communications. At that point, he was <u>way</u> ahead of me, and he sensed that and backed off. But the seed had been planted, much deeper than I ever realized at that moment.

"After we finished our drinks, we sat in silence for awhile; I mean, <u>real</u> silence, no talking, either external or internal. Then he looked at me with a very serious expression, and said aloud that I must <u>never</u> tell <u>anyone</u> about this 'game' we were playing, because very few people would understand what we were doing and would think we were both nuts. I had no trouble agreeing to that arrangement."

"Tell me how you felt about this 'game', Miss Jacobs, please."

"I had never experienced anything like it before, and it fascinated me. It was so incredible to be able to receive another person's thoughts in the form of a directed message. But then, you see, I had no idea of the future manifestations that would develop from this rather innocuous beginning. So, I guess to answer your question, I was thrilled by what I believed to be this special attention from Harry and delighted at the opportunity to continue the experience."

"Go on, please."

"When we finished our drinks and left the store, it had begun to drizzle. We walked as fast as some people run. I had trouble keeping up with that marvelous fast pace of his, but each time I was with him it became easier. When we reached the station and were waiting for the train to take us back to the Polo Grounds and the subway, he suggested that we practise. At that point, I really <u>was</u> beginning to think of it as some sort of game, so I went along with the idea, and it worked. We had an <u>entire</u> conversation without saying even one word aloud. It was <u>incredible</u>. I have <u>never</u> had such an experience with any human being in my life – before or since.

"But there were lots of down sides to it which I didn't realize then. For one thing, as time went on, and my feelings for Harry deepened, I began to feel his emotions as well as know his thoughts. When he was happy, I was happy. When he was sad, so was I.

"Dr. Levy, are you familiar with the story, I think by one of the Dumas, 'The Corsican Brothers'?"

"Yes. I am."

"Well, that's how it became for me. Every thought, every emotion of Harry's - it became mine as well."

"It must have been very difficult for you as such a young girl."

"I didn't realize just <u>how</u> difficult until this terrible thing happened that I've been postponing telling you about. But I wanted - I felt it was <u>absolutely necessary</u> [These words were spoken very slowly and very deliberately] that you understand all of this other stuff before I told you about the incident. It wouldn't have the same impact otherwise. I mean, you wouldn't understand why I was so effected by this incident and why I was so distressed whenever Seymour made reference to it."

"Did Seymour know about this 'game', as you call it, between you and Harry?"

[Again spoken slowly and deliberately.]

"<u>Absolutely</u> not. NEVER.

[Normal voice resumed.]

"Until now, I <u>never</u> spoke about this to anyone. For one thing, I had promised Harry never to tell. Also, as Harry anticipated. it would seem so insane. I guess that is another reason why I found such a haven in logic, facts and straight figures.

"Well, I suppose I can tell you about the incident now, if you are ready for it."

"Ah, but Miss Jacobs, we are not only out of time, but way over it. We will continue with it at your next session, please."

"Oh my God! I didn't realize how late it was. I'm so sorry, Dr. Levy. I really – I'm so sorry."

"Please. Miss Jacobs, it is not a mortal sin. I will see you next week."

"You will put this extra time on my bill, of course."

"If it will make you happy, certainly. Of course, you know this is something my secretary is responsible for. I am not one for figures in the way you are, Miss Jacobs, I can assure you.

"Good evening, Miss Jacobs."

"Yes. It is evening, isn't it. Yes. Good evening, Dr. Levy."

End of Tape 5.

Notes Accompanying Tape 5.

As I listened to the beginning of this tape, I could not believe my ears. What could I have been thinking of? I cannot remember in all my days as a Therapist, not even in my beginning years as a student in Medical School, when I was so obviously irritated with a patient and permitted that irritation to be communicated. Why was I so insistent upon having Miss Jacobs tell me about the incident that occurred in the presence of Seymour Cohen? It was obvious she was not ready to tell it to me, but I almost hounded her about it, even to the point of sarcasm. I had to play the beginning portion of the tape several times because it was difficult for me to comprehend that I could behave so unprofessionally. Important points did come out because of it, but that still does not excuse my behavior. I must watch my actions more carefully. What is there about this patient that elicited such a response from me?

However, Miss Jacobs' reaction also indicates the level of the strength of her character. She could have been intimidated and related the incident to please me, or from fear of my position as her Therapist. But she had her carefully thought out reasons, and she was determined to stick to them. This indicates also a degree of self-confidence that is admirable. Yet, amazingly, she still thinks of herself as merely a fat and ugly teenager, revealing her lack of awareness of her own potential. She could not have changed so profoundly since her teenage years, and I still believe if I were to ask her opinion today, she would describe herself unfavorably.

She continues to apologize profusely for the slightest act she considers to be a mistake on her part. It's as if she is asking to be excused for being alive, for having any thoughts of her own. How interesting it is to have this in juxtaposition with her determination to tell her story in her own fashion. Could these apologies be an affectation? A ploy to divert attention from her strength of character? Many women of independent thought are forced, by our society, into such role-playing. These are interesting contradictions in her character, which require exploration.

This determination to tell her story in her own way was not simple obstinacy, for, as it turns out, it appears that she was correct in her thought processes. It does seem now, to make much more sense for me to hear about this incident <u>after</u> I had learned about this game that Harry had involved her in.

What kind of man was this Harry? What was his motivation for involving her in this so-called game? What did he want from this child? Despite her lies, he certainly must have realized, as an adult male, how young she really was. He probably knew and decided to ignore the fact of her age. Was he using her? It certainly seems so, on the surface, although she would vehemently deny it, I suspect. She obviously worshipped him then and now. But for what purpose was he using her? Did their relationship become sexual? And is Miss Jacobs being objective in her description of Harry and his abilities? She herself indicates he was a ballplayer who was not well-known to the general public, although he apparently was respected by his peers and by sportswriters. Was he really as profoundly intelligent and introspective as she believes? She may want to see and romanticize him as a mysterious misunderstood unique individual, when he may simply have been a mid-Westerner who had little to say or think about.

Was Harry psychotic? Miss Jacobs indicates he had problems dealing with his combat experiences in the War. Only God knows what horrors those poor men faced in that wretched brutality. But that in itself would not mean he was psychotic. Was he psychic? Did he have psychic abilities which he recognized in Miss Jacobs, although she was still just a child? There is considerable literature in the field to indicate that poltergeist phenomena are more prevalent among young teenage females.

Again the question must be faced: are we dealing here with psychosis or psychic phenomena?

Was her hearing Harry's voice in her mind an auditory hallucination or extra-sensory perception? Thought-transference?

There is a certain irony here, in resolving these questions. Typically, those who are psychotic loudly protest they are sane and are convinced that what they are experiencing is reality. On the other hand, here we have Miss Jacobs, whose behavior is obsessively rational, who fears she may be psychotic. Her eyes are steady and straightforward, there is no darting and furtiveness. Her speech and mental reactions are not scattered, but reveal a superior intellect; rational and logical - far from hysterical. Her appearance, as previously described and noted, is personable and professional. Even when she telephoned that first morning, although highly agitated, she was still in control enough to be aware of the time, to apologize, and to organize her thoughts in explaining her need to make the call. Were it not for that particular incident, I might never have heard from her, as she apparently was dealing with these strange incidents (which she has yet to tell me) in her own way, although she was beginning to believe she was losing the battle. But what battle? The battle for her sanity, it appears.

She does not seem to be psychotic. Obsessive-compulsive? Neurotic? Possibly. The loss of her parents at an early age, then learning of the death of this man who was possibly a father-figure for her, could exacerbate any complexes she might harbor. Yet she is aware enough of the workings of her psyche to accept the fact that she used (and still uses?) the cloak of rationality to hide her emotions.

Miss Jacobs is a woman with a wide variety of interests, and no sense of embarrassment about acknowledging them. She is <u>definitely not</u> pretentious. She spoke of her initial dream of being a concert musician, then of liking Science Fiction, watching television programs, and made several references to literature and metaphysics. She obtained her degrees and Certificates in the Accounting profession. Then there was her interest in baseball, obviously a manifestation of rebellion for a teenage girl of her generation. What contradictions exist in this woman: strength, independence, yet apparent lack of awareness of these very qualities in herself.

A fascinating woman, a mysterious man. This is by far the most unusual case I have encountered in all my years of practise. I may have noted this reaction previously, but this case has become, if anything, even <u>more</u> complex and intriguing as it progresses.

***

TAPE 6

April 8, 1981

4:30 pm

"Good afternoon, Miss Jacobs."

"Dr. Levy."

"Please sit down, Miss Jacobs."

"Yes."

[Silence - then both begin speaking at once.]

—"I suppose you..." — "Do you want to..."

[Laughter. Sounding forced.]

"Miss Jacobs, when you mentioned this incident involving Harry at which Seymour was present, I perhaps interpreted it to have more significance than..."

[Interrupting.]

"No, Dr. Levy. You were correct. The incident IS very relevant to the discussion of my relationship with Harry, but it just seemed to make more sense to have you learn about it as it occurred chronologically, so that you could appreciate its true significance."

"Does it still seem that way to you now?"

"Yes."

"Then please go on with the development of your relationship with this man Harry, as it led to the incident."

"I'm sorry I even mentioned it now. It has taken on perhaps more meaning - no, that's not true. It IS significant. In fact, when I learned of Harry's death, this incident was one of the first things I remembered, when I thought about the time I had spent with Harry.

"But I'll go on.

"I told you about the time Harry and I went to the Stadium and the candy store and it

68

started to drizzle. The next day it was the same, and there was some doubt as to whether the game would be played. Still, I went to the Polo Grounds, because I wanted to see Harry any chance I could get.

"When I arrived, both teams were sitting in their respective dugouts, and the umpires huddled together, obviously deciding what to do.

"Pretty soon it began to rain heavily, and the umpires called the game because of rain. The teams ran to their respective clubhouses, but not Harry. He still took those same big strides and walked briskly and confidently to the clubhouse. By that time he was alone on the field. No one tried to get autographs from the players this time, as it was raining too hard.

"Everyone had left the bleachers but me, as I was waiting to see Harry enter the clubhouse. When he got there, he looked up at me, somewhat seriously, and communicated to me, through thought, that I should wait for him in the subway station. I smiled back at him. I thought it was really neat that he didn't have to bother to yell to talk to me this time; he just let me know what he wanted to say through the use of our minds.

"Anyway, I waited for him in the subway station. Sitting on the bench - it was safe then - and was certainly preferable to standing outside in the pouring rain. By the time he arrived, the rest of the fans and players had left, and I was virtually alone on the station. When he joined me, I noticed the strange combination of clothing again. I don't remember if I told you, but I used to make notes, as soon as I left him, of what he was wearing. Usually it was weird color and pattern combinations.

"I'll always remember that day. We sat silently on the bench together, as if we were strangers who did not know one another. All our communication was through thought. He explained more, what I'll call 'rules' of the 'game'. He told me that he believed it was possible, through reading he had done, that if both he and I were to think very hard and very intensely about something, about the same thing I mean, we could make that thing happen. As I look back at it now, I didn't hesitate for even a moment of disbelief. If Harry said it, it had to be true.

"He suggested we try it on something minor at first, like when the next train would come. We had sat and watched several go by, and one had just left. He suggested that we try something improbable, to lessen the possibility of chance; so we decided that the next train would come in one minute - something totally unusual for that time of day at that station."

"And?"

"It worked. In exactly one minute, another train came and we got on. He smiled and I was so excited I could barely stay still. He sat in one place and suggested where I should sit, away from him facing the opposite direction. Of course I did exactly as directed. He then told me, mentally, from where he was sitting, to meet him at the 59th Street station. I did.

"When we met there, he spoke aloud. He told me he had somewhere else to go before returning to his hotel, and that I should go home. He said that it was fun playing our game together, and he looked forward to it the next time we would see each other. We did not know

70

when that would be, as the Cardinals were
scheduled to go to Brooklyn. But he told me
again that it was fun playing this mind-game
and it helped make him feel less lonely when
on the road. He liked his teammates, but did
not share many of their interests. He never
said it, but I read in a St. Louis paper at
the time that he and his roommate were not the
typical rowdy ballplayers who liked to get
drunk, fight, pick up women, stay out past
curfew, and all that sort of thing. Perhaps
that was why he was alone so often."

"You read a St. Louis paper? How was that
possible?"

"I found out about this newsstand on Times
Square where they sold papers from all over
the U.S. and the World. My aunt would give me
milk money, and I would drink water at school
and use the money to buy the St. Louis paper
and to pay for the subway fare to get to Times
Square and home.

"I found that when I was not with Harry, or
somewhere I could see him in person, I missed
him so very much - I guess like he missed his
wife. So I read all I could about him from the
St. Louis papers - there were three of them as
I remember, and I cut out any reference to
Harry to put into a special red scrapbook I
had for articles about the Cardinal team."

"And when did you see Harry next, please."

"Well, first I should say that I told just
about anyone at school who would listen, about
how I had become friends with this Cardinal
ballplayer. My stock rose really high with
kids who were baseball fans and knew who Harry
was, and generally higher with the regular
kids who thought it was neat that I should
have this older good-looking ballplayer pay
attention to me. Of course, there were the

71

really serious kids who never paid attention to me anyway, so nothing I did made any difference to them."

[Pause.]

"Until my last year in high school, I see now."

"And what happened the next time you saw Harry, please."

"Well, it was the next time the Cardinals were at the Polo Grounds. I managed to talk one of the Art students in my school to go with me. She was very good at sketching, and when I showed her photos of Harry from the St. Louis papers, she agreed to see if she could do a sketch of him for me. Honestly, I forget if I had to do anything for her in return – I didn't have any money except for the subway and the milk money I used to buy the papers, so I couldn't have paid her. Maybe she came just for the heck of it, or maybe I did her some kind of favor in return.

"Anyway, we were in luck. When we got to the Polo Grounds, Harry was sitting in the bullpen, right near the bleachers. We went down to the railing, and I started to call his name; but then I remembered our 'game,' and I decided to see if it still worked, or if I had imagined the whole thing. So I called him in my thoughts, and sure enough, he turned around and looked up at me. He smiled, a big broad grin, as if he were really glad to see me. Then, again, through thought, he told me that if the girl next to me was someone I had brought along, we had better talk out loud. So I yelled his name, and he walked over to where we were standing.

"I introduced Carolyn to him and like a true gentleman, he took her hand and bowed. I thought she would faint. Funny, [Pause.] I think I knew what she was thinking and feeling then too. [Another pause.] But maybe that's my imagination. I tell you Dr. Levy, with all this stuff that's going on now, it's hard for me to know what to believe anymore.

"Anyway, I told Harry, out loud, as he had asked, that Carolyn was an artist and I had asked her to do a sketch of him for me. He said he was very flattered, and agreed. Carolyn was quite taken with him. He spoke slowly, with this mid-western drawl, like Henry Fonda. He even looked a lot like Henry Fonda. I remember at the end of the 1947 season, when the players returned to their homes for the Winter, I missed Harry so much that I saw one particular Henry Fonda film 14 times, because he reminded me so much of Harry. Funny too, now that I think of it, this film was about a disturbed World War II Veteran."

"Do you think Harry was disturbed?"

"No. Not in the normal sense of the word. But I did learn, after his death, how emotionally shattered he had been by the War, how what he had seen had troubled him so deeply that it haunted him up to the time he died. For example, he was the first GI to enter one of those horrible Concentration Camps - but I can tell you about that later."

"Yes, do, please. I want <u>very much</u> to hear about this experience of Harry." [These words of Dr. Levy were spoken with more emotion than usual.]

"Anyway — about that game — Harry went back to sit on the bench. I can still see him so clearly as he was that day. He sat with his right foot resting on his left knee and leaned back somewhat with his arms folded. Carolyn started sketching and got quite a ways before

Harry was told to warm up. He was called in to relieve a pitcher, so Carolyn never did get to complete her sketch, but I still have the unfinished drawing and it is really quite fine.

"It was so sweet, Dr. Levy. As Harry left to go into the game, he turned to us, removed his cap, and bowed again. For the heck of it, Carolyn actually blew a kiss at him. You know I would <u>never</u> have had the nerve to do that, even though I knew Harry. But Carolyn was very spontaneous and a lot of fun, and I was always so shy. Then he turned and walked that wonderful beautiful fast walk of his to the Pitcher's Mound."

"It's difficult for me to think of you as being 'shy', Miss Jacobs. In fact, you give the impression of being an extrovert."

"I know what you are saying, and I can explain that. Yes, I <u>WAS</u> actually <u>VERY</u> shy. I could barely speak to anyone in that school because I felt so out of place, and I was <u>terrified</u> to be called on in class to speak for any reason. But as Harry made me feel more at ease, I began to loosen up. I didn't see that then, but I realize it now.

"Also, I realize that this is the way Harry was, too. On the outside, he seemed quite gregarious. I think I told you. But in reality, he was rather shy, and introspective. I would not say that I am shy now, but I do not actively seek the company of others."

"Do others actively seek your company?"

"Yes. And I think that is true of Harry, also. I suppose it is because we appear to be gregarious on the surface."

"Are you aware that you spoke of him in the present tense just now?"

"I did? If I did, I guess it's because I am no longer sure of the meaning of death and the passage of time, after all the things that have happened.

[Pause.]

"Anyway, Harry went into the game and retired all the hitters. No one ever got on base during the entire time he pitched. After the game, Carolyn and I waited for him outside, because we wanted to show him the sketch, but this time he was with the other players and I told Carolyn that we shouldn't interfere. Actually, Harry had told me that - that if he were with the others, I should stay away and we would communicate through our 'game.'

"This time, something Harry said made me feel a little creepy. As he walked past us with his teammates, I heard him say in my mind something like: 'You see, it worked. You and I both wished that no one would get a hit and no one even got to first base.'"

"Why did this make you feel uneasy, Miss Jacobs, please."

"I don't know if I can really say. It seemed like a lot of power for a kid my age to have, and then I really wasn't sure if it was just a coincidence or what. I would have preferred it to be a coincidence rather than an indication that we had the power to effect the outcome of events."

"And how do you feel now, Miss Jacobs? Would you rather that these events that you say have occurred were coincidences rather than examples of another form of communication? Would you prefer to think that you are delusional rather than that you are experiencing phenomena for which Science as yet has no explanation?"

"Please, Dr. Levy. Those are very difficult questions. [Pause.] But I guess that is why I decided to come to see you on a regular basis - because I need to know the answers to those very questions."

"Tell me, Miss Jacobs. During the period that you have been coming to my office, have you still been having these experiences that you describe as weird or bizarre?"

"Yes. Only not as often and not as weird."

"All right. You will tell me about them, of course. But for now, go on with what happened next with Harry. Did you and your friend go with him on the same subway train?"

"Yes."

"Did Harry communicate with you through thought?"

"Not exactly. I guess he was too involved with his friends, and also Carolyn was talking to me."

"What do you mean, 'not exactly'."

"I knew what he was thinking in his mind even though he wasn't talking directly to me. He was thinking about how hot he was and how he was going to insist on pitching tomorrow's game. [Pause.] Then the next day things really escalated."

"What do you mean, 'escalated'?"

"By the time I got to the game, it was about the third inning or so. That was usually the way it was when I arrived after school. But what was unusual with this game, was that Harry was the starting pitcher. Usually, after a pitcher pitches several innings of relief, he does not start a full ballgame the next day. At least, that was how it was then. As I told you, I know <u>nothing</u> about how the game is played today. Anyway, that showed me that what I thought I heard Harry thinking was true, and

76

actually happened – he managed to convince the Cardinal manager to let him start the next day's game.

"So there he was, on the mound pitching. I asked, as I usually did, what had happened in the game up to that point, and was told that the Cardinals had gotten a run in the first inning, and that one of the Giants had hit a double, but that was all. The score was one-to-nothing, Cardinals. I watched Harry as best I could, but the distance was so far. Still, even from the bleachers, I could see how graceful and elegant his movements were. Seymour referred to him as 'the thinking man's pitcher'.

"Then, I heard Harry's voice, very clearly in my mind. 'No other Giant ballplayer is going to get a hit'. And I felt <u>very strongly</u> the same way. It was – it is so difficult to describe. I <u>KNOW</u> it sounds crazy – there I go again – but when I received Harry's message, I was absolutely <u>POSITIVE</u> this is what would happen. I <u>KNEW</u> that together we would make sure that no player on the Giant ballteam would get another hit off Harry.

"And that's <u>exactly</u> what happened. No Giant player got to first base. The game was what is known as a 'one-hitter'. That is not as important as a <u>NO-hitter</u>, but it is an accomplishment that is duly noted and given considerable attention by the media. In fact, one of the St. Louis papers described Harry's performance as 'brilliant'."

"How did that make you feel."

"I was SO excited. I was SO happy for Harry. [Pause.] And I also felt this strange sense of power."

[Silence.]

"What happened when you saw Harry after the game?"

"Well, I didn't really get to see him. This time he was surrounded not only by his teammates, but by the Press as well, taking his picture and asking questions – you know, all the things reporters did in those days. Of course, there was no TV, nor any of the modern electronic equipment.

"So I couldn't get anywhere near him, not even on the train, but I did manage, somehow in all of this, to hear his voice clearly in my mind: 'We did it, Sandy, we did it.'"

[Silence.]

"Miss Jacobs, are you all right, please."

[Continued silence; then weeping.]

"It's just remembering all this. It comes back so vividly, after I had thought I had forgotten it for so long. 'Repressed', I guess you would call it. It is very emotional for me."

"I was going to ask you about how it felt."

"I remember wanting to cry, I felt so happy for him. [Pause.] Dr. Levy, I can tell you that in my entire life, NO human being has evoked such feelings of emotion in me as Harry Gault. NO ONE. NOT EVER."

"You were in love with him."

"Yes. I know that now. I did not know it then, however."

"What did you think it was then, what you were feeling."

"I don't know. I guess I just thought of it as a schoolgirl crush, or what was called 'puppy love'. I really don't know. I had no understanding of my emotions at that time."

[Pause.]

"Anyway, I rode down in the same subway car, watching as everybody was surrounding him, fans coming up to him for his autograph. And all I could think of were his words, 'We did it, Sandy, we did it.' It was as if I were under some kind of magic spell, or in a trance, or something. Believe me, Dr. Levy, it is <u>very</u> hard to describe, but the emotions were <u>very powerful</u>."

[Pause.]

"Miss Jacobs, I see our time is up. Are you all right, please."

"Yes, I am, Dr. Levy. I will take some of your tissues, though. And I'll see you on Friday. Thank you."

"Good night, Miss Jacobs."

"Good night, Dr. Levy."

End of Tape 6.

Notes Accompanying Tape 6.

The details and circumstances of this "game" that Miss Jacobs describes as taking place between herself and this man Harry are very intriguing. Were the manifestations of their "game" mere coincidence? Or is she tying events together in order to create an appearance of some form of connection - either coincidental or purposeful. Did these events actually occur as described, or are they something she is fantasizing about currently, in order to give more credibility to the recent incidents she refers to as "bizarre." But if these past events did occur as related, is her feeling of "power" - as she herself terms it - an example of magical thinking — the process whereby schizophrenics ascribe to themselves God-like abilities to create and destroy?

It is also interesting that her explanations, for the most part, continue to be related in a straight-forward analytical manner. It is not that she lacks affect; it is simply the kind of narrative one would expect from a person determined to convey facts in an objective fashion. She certainly has done a good job of repressing emotional content (for example - in situations involving school and family life) - except, of course, very noticeably when she talks about this fellow Harry. She is often on the verge of tears or weeping openly as she remembers how he was in those days when she was a schoolgirl. But that is understandable, considering that he may have been the only adult in her life to give her any hint of attention and affection.

A thought: these recent "bizarre" incidents to which Miss Jacobs refers constantly - I have heard only one, the episode she believes occurred in Harry's bedroom (interesting that it should be his <u>bedroom</u> - does that indicate her sexual desire for him?) - could these incidents, whatever they are, have been induced by the ingestion of illegal hallucinogenic drugs? I must remember to ask whether she uses any of these substances. That certainly would provide a simple explanation for her current experiences, although it would not explain the things she describes as having happened in her childhood — for example, the "game." If she were taking these drugs now however, they could influence how she remembers her childhood, as well. I <u>MUST</u> remember to ask her about any possible drug usage.

I am still faced with the dilemma of whether this woman, who seems on the surface at least, to be a mature and rational human being, is neurotic, psychotic, or - merely psychic. I am still of the opinion that she displays none of the typical symptoms of mental illness or even neurosis, except perhaps in milder forms, such as obsessive-compulsive behavior, and of course, her strong sense (complex) of inferiority. She acknowledges her shortcomings in areas when questioned, and even offers her own explanations. She appears to be trying to find indications of mental illness rather than accept what she has come to view as illogical — as if for her, it is more of a problem or illness to be psychic than to be mentally disturbed. She would seem to prefer the latter diagnosis.

For my own curiosity, I would like to know more about Harry's War experiences, in particular his encounter with one of the Camps. Miss Jacobs has made reference, more than once, to how troubled this man was by his combat experiences. I must see what else she knows about this.

As I learn more about Miss Jacobs, her case continues to be intriguing - and we have apparently touched only what is merely the surface.

* * *

TAPE 7

April 10, 1981

4:30 pm

"Oh, it's pouring so hard out there. I'm sorry, but my clothes and shoes are damp, even though I left my coat in the reception area."

"Do not trouble yourself about that Miss Jacobs, unless you are uncomfortable and wish to reschedule your appointment."

"No. Please. I'm all right, as long as you don't mind my sitting on your couch with damp clothing."

"You look as if you might be cold, Miss Jacobs. There is a quilt on that armchair over there, if you wish to put it around you."

"Thank you, Dr. Levy. I think I will, if you don't mind."

"Of course I don't mind. That is why I suggested it."

"Yes. I'm sorry."

[Sounds of movement in background.]

"Why do you always feel the need to apologize for things that you are not at fault for, Miss Jacobs?"

"I don't know. It's something left from childhood, I suppose, when I seemed to be in everybody's way."

"But not Harry's."

"No. You're right, Dr. Levy. Not Harry's."

[Pause.]

"Are you comfortable now?"

"Yes. Thank you. That is much better."

[Silence.]

"I left off, I think, when Harry and I had just begun playing our 'game', and I wanted to tell you more about what happened with that.

We continued to go to the Stadium and Candy Shop, or we would ride separately on the same subway car, if Harry were with some of his teammates. But we would always be talking to each other, either orally, or through this mind process.

"He told me that he was working on controlling psychic abilities he recognized he had as a child. He was a master of magic tricks, and amused his teammates with them in the clubhouse or when they traveled. I think I told you; but I didn't tell you that what he was really doing was hiding psychic ability behind the more acceptable cloak of magic. His teammates just thought of him as a fun guy who liked to do magic tricks. Also, one of the reasons he went into baseball was, sure because it was fun, but also because he soon realized, when he became a pitcher, that he could sense what the batter was thinking and tailor his pitches accordingly. One season, his last in the Minor Leagues, he actually won 22 games and did not lose even one; he had mastered the skill so well. But of course, it was a lot different in the Majors, where he faced the best players in the Nation. Still, he had this unique style of pitching, which he varied according to what he could read from the mind of the batter."

"As you know, Miss Jacobs, I do not understand anything about baseball, so provide a bit more detail, please."

"Of course. I'm sorry, Dr. Levy."

"There, you have done it again. Why are you sorry? What have <u>you</u> done wrong, Miss Jacobs, simply because <u>I</u> do not understand the game of baseball."

"You're right. I've done it again. I'm sorry. Ooops." [Nervous Laughter.]

84

"Anyway, When Harry would face down the batter, that is, the player who was to hit the ball, he would stare at the batter and most of the time could sense what the guy was thinking. Then he would tailor his pitch exactly the opposite from what the batter expected. Most of the time, Harry was correct, but if he was mistaken, there'd be a LOT of homeruns hit off him. The other team would get big scores. What Harry <u>especially</u> liked to do was let the batter think he, the batter I mean, was getting the best of Harry, and Harry would <u>deliberately</u> maneuver himself into difficult situations. This would drive his manager nuts, and he would be furious with Harry. The two never really got along, because, of course, the manager never understood Harry – not that any of the players did.

"Anyway, Harry would get himself into these tight situations, and then miraculously get out of them. It might have seemed miraculous to anybody watching, but Harry knew <u>exactly</u> what he was doing. That, to him, was the most rewarding challenge of all, and the most fun.

"And then, when he got <u>me</u> involved in this kind of magic, or psychic stuff, whatever you want to call it, he was convinced that the two of us, acting in unison, could influence the outcome of the games he pitched."

"And you think that you did?"

"I realize this sounds crazy, but somehow I <u>know</u> that we did. I told you about the games that he won right after we started on this plan, and there were many others, although not as dramatic. The plan even worked long distance, and I can give examples of that, too; like when I was listening to a Cardinal/Dodger game on the radio coming from

85

St. Louis - I always listened to <u>all</u> the Cardinal games on the radio, if I was not at school or at the Polo Grounds."

"How could you hear the games from the other cities?"

"Oh, I'm sorry - oh - well, I mean, you see, if the Cardinals were playing New York teams, then the games would be broadcast either from New York or from the location where the New York teams were playing, usually St. Louis.

"Anyway, this one game, the Cardinals were behind 10 to 4 at the bottom of the ninth with two out - oh, well, you won't appreciate it - I'll just say that the Cardinals came from behind against impossible odds, once Harry entered the game in relief."

"And you were listening to this game on the radio."

"Yes. And when Harry entered the game, I concentrated all my thoughts and emotions on him. Actually, I probably would have done that anyway, even without his suggestions about our 'game', as he called it.

"But the best, or worst, I should probably say, example of the effect of our combined Will upon the outcome of a ballgame was the incident Seymour witnessed. Well, no, there was - well, let's just say it was the most dramatic and certainly the most distressing."

[Pause.]

"I guess that means I am ready to tell you about the incident that had such an effect upon Seymour and me. Did Seymour ever discuss it with you?"

"Miss Jacobs. Shame on you. You should know that I can not discuss even whether someone is in therapy or not, much less what they talk about. You know that Seymour is in therapy with me only because <u>he</u> told you; I never would."

"I'm sorry. Ooops. I shouldn't have said I'm sorry, I suppose."

"No. That would be an appropriate time to apologize."

[Laughter.]

"Proceed with the incident then, if you are ready, Miss Jacobs."

[Audible deep breath.]

"Excuse me, Miss Jacobs, but before you begin - you have spoken many times about this incident, and always about the effect it had upon you and Seymour. Do you know, did it have any effect upon Harry, please."

"I'm sure it did. I never really knew how much, though, because one thing I didn't mention before, and that is that Harry could, if he wished, block any access to his thought processes. He could read <u>my</u> thoughts - I don't think I was ever able to deny him access to <u>my</u> mind; but there were times when I could not read anything at all from him. It was as if I had come upon a barrier."

"Did you ever consider that he simply had no thoughts at that particular time?"

"Harry? NEVER. It is impossible to conceive of a time when Harry would not have something percolating in his mind."

"Forgive the interruption. Continue, please."

"See! Now <u>you're</u> apologizing."

"Yes. But again, I see this as a situation where it is appropriate. [Hint of irritation in voice.] Continue, please."

"OK. Anyway, a few months after all this began with Harry, I managed to convince my Aunt that since my birthday was coming up soon and I would turn 14, it would be OK for me to go to a ballgame with Seymour. That way, I could get a chance to see Harry pitch in Brooklyn, and Seymour would want to go because he was a Dodger fan and would want to see Jackie Robinson in action. It was Summer vacation and I wasn't able to go to the Polo Grounds after school, and I would have had to pay full admission, plus the fare to get there, and my Aunt didn't have the money for that. But if Seymour took me to a Dodger game – then it would be free for me; and I figured my Aunt would approve of my going with Seymour, as our families had been close friends since before the two of us were even born.

"I was right. My Aunt actually let me go with Seymour. This was a big deal to her. It was like my first date, even though she had previously said I could not date until after I turned 16. Of course, since I had cooked up this plan in order to get to see Harry, I actually had to fill Seymour in on it and get him to ask permission to take me out on a "date" to a Sunday afternoon baseball game at Ebbett's Field. And who knows? Maybe my Aunt thought that going to Ebbett's Field would put some sense into my head and make me a Dodger fan instead of rooting for those prejudiced Cardinal players.

"So, both families agreed, and Seymour, who was a bit older than I, got to go on his first date, taking me, on my first date, to this ballgame at Ebbett's Field. You'd think we were getting married or something, the way our families reacted.

"Anyway, Seymour and I went. I remember every moment of that wretched game. It was a beautiful Summer day. It was warm, somewhat humid, but not uncomfortable, just pleasant.

There wasn't a cloud in the sky. At least not then.

"Harry had been scheduled to pitch, but something must have happened to change the schedule, because someone else, I forget who, started the game. Almost immediately, things started getting rough, and players on both sides were getting runs all over the place. I remember that the scores were high and pitchers were being removed on both teams a lot. That's when Harry and Ed, one of his good friends, were sent to the Bullpen to warm up.

"I remember there was so much excitement with this game. I even got to see Jackie Robinson steal home. Oh, I'm sorry. You probably don't know what that means. Let me just say that this was unusual and thrilling and something Robinson had great talent for. Anyway, the fans were going wild. The scores were not only high, but very close, so there was no way to tell who would win.

"Somewhere around the seventh inning, yes, I remember now, it WAS the seventh inning, because I had been standing in support of the Cardinals, and I thought I would be lynched or something - anyway, the Cardinals had gotten some runs and had gone ahead by just a little bit, and the manager signaled for BOTH Harry and Ed to warm up, in case the Cardinal pitcher got into trouble.

"Well, sure enough, he did. The Dodgers had the bases loaded and nobody out. Uh, that means the Cardinals were in big trouble if they wanted to hold onto their slim lead. So, of course, the manager signaled to the Bullpen for another pitcher to come in to relieve the one who had caused the problem. Now I KNEW this was exactly the kind of situation Harry thrived on. He was well-known and respected by the entire sports community as an <u>excellent</u> relief pitcher. And <u>he</u> loved the challenge of it because it gave him the opportunity to use his psychic skills.

"But the manager signaled for Ed to come, instead of Harry."

[Silence.]

"I can still see it all so clearly. I can even <u>feel</u> it, as if I were there this minute. The sky had begun to cloud over, you know, the way it does in Summer when a thunderstorm is brewing. I was still standing, and Seymour had just brought me a hot-dog. I had maybe taken a bite or two when the guy announced over the loudspeaker that Ed was coming in to relieve for the Cardinals.

"I could see Harry from where I was standing. He had seen me earlier, and winked, but had not communicated with me - perhaps because he guessed Seymour was with me, I don't know. Anyway, I looked at Harry as Ed walked to the mound. He stopped warming up and just stood there as Ed left the Bullpen. Harry was furious. He <u>KNEW</u> he could get the side out without any damage. But the manager - there was this discomfort, this unpleasantness between them, although it was never acknowledged - because of Harry's unorthodox ways of handling situations. The manager never knew what to expect from Harry. But he knew, he could predict exactly what Ed, a very good and very reliable pitcher, would do, and so I guess he felt more comfortable sending Ed in. I can see that now as an adult, but I certainly didn't see it that way as a kid.

"I watched Harry look at Ed as he lumbered down to the mound - there was certainly nothing graceful about the way Ed, a big square-shouldered guy, carried himself. I was so angry. How dare the manager send in Ed instead of Harry. Was he crazy or something? All kinds of hateful thoughts went on in my mind.

"I remember Seymour saying something to tease me about the Cardinals sending in everyone else BUT Harry, and that I would have come to Ebbett's Field for nothing, except to see the Cardinals lose. But I looked at Seymour, and I was still chewing on the hot-dog, and I said, and these were my exact words, because Seymour keeps throwing them in my face so I can <u>never</u> forget them:

'It doesn't matter, because the first pitch Ed throws will hit him in the head and Harry will come in to pitch anyway.'[1]
[Pause.]

"The sky clouded over and hid the sun. Ed warmed up a little on the mound and while he was doing so, I took another peek at Harry. He was still standing there, as if he couldn't believe he hadn't been chosen, and had bitter, hostile thoughts, mostly against the manager. Harry should have been warming up also, but he was just standing there.

"When Ed was ready, he threw the first ball. The batter swung and it was a line drive that hit Ed directly in the head. [Pause.] There are two things I know I will never forget as long as I live: the sound of that ball hitting Ed, and the feel of how that hot-dog in my mouth turned to sawdust. That's exactly what it tasted and felt like - sawdust.

"The crowd became silent. The umpire halted the game. The Cardinals were all around Ed; even the Dodger players ran to the Pitcher's Mound. Medics were called and a stretcher was

---

[1] Italics added, in an attempt to convey the emphasis and serious tone of the words spoken.

brought out. Seymour stared at me. Oh yes. That's another thing I'll always remember. The incredible expression that was on Seymour's face, as if he couldn't believe what had just happened."

"And how did <u>you</u> feel at that time, Miss Jacobs."

"Numb. I just was numb. I think my primary sensation was how the hot-dog felt — like sawdust in my mouth."

"Go on, please."

"Then I turned to look at Harry. He had started warming up again. I don't know if anyone had signaled for him to do that, or he just did it on his own. He had a strange look on his face. Ed was his friend, yet there was this expression that was almost like: 'I told you so!' Or maybe that's what I sensed in his mind; I just don't know anymore. All I know was that I was numb.

"But there was also this other feeling, now that I think of it. It was one of power. That's it. Power. Like: 'See what you caused? This is what happened because you didn't send in Harry like you should have.'"

[Pause.]

"Were you glad that Ed had been hurt? By the way, what happened to him? How seriously was he injured?"

"Quite seriously. He survived, and was eventually able to resume his career, but not for some time. But to answer your first question, no, I was not glad that he had been hurt. All I wanted was for Harry to get into the game."

[Silence.]

"It was so strange. It all seemed surreal. Ed was taken away on the stretcher and Harry was called in to pitch, just as I had said."

"Do you think you predicted it?"

"No."

"Then, how do you explain this incident, please. Do you think it was coincidence - euh, clairvoyance - euh, some form of psychokinesis, perhaps?"

"I KNOW you will think this is crazy, but that's what I'm coming to you for — to find out if I'm crazy. But you asked how I explain this incident, and I'll tell you."

[Words spoken very slowly and deliberately.]

"I WILLED IT."

"You 'willed' it? Is that what you said, Miss Jacobs?"

"Yes, Dr. Levy. That's exactly what I said."

[Pause.]

"What do you mean, please."

"I mean just what I said. [Pause.] I WILLED it. I don't know whether it was me alone, or Harry in combination with me, but it was a WILLED act that was accomplished so that Harry could get into the game."

"I see."

[Extended silence.]

"What happened next, please."

"Harry walked that beautiful walk of his to the mound. I remember thinking that this was the only time that I did not derive pleasure from seeing him make that beautiful walk to the mound.

"As expected, at least by me and by Harry, Harry got the side out. But it didn't much matter, because the clouds had become very dark, the sky darker, and it began to rain.

"There was an eerie atmosphere over everything. Seymour just sat speechless. I think I stood for the rest of the game. I never finished the hot-dog. I don't even remember swallowing the part that turned to sawdust in my mouth. The crowd remained silent. I think all that was on everyone's minds was whether Ed would survive that terrible blow to the head. You know a ball hit with such force -"

"Yes, I understand. Go on, please."

"The sky was so dark. The ballpark was so quiet. After Harry got the Dodgers out, it started to rain hard, and the umpires huddled together and called the game. I think they just wanted to get it over with because no one's heart was in it anymore. Except maybe Harry's."

"Why do you say that, Miss Jacobs."

"Because it came to me just now. Maybe that's what we both wanted, but especially Harry, and I was his accomplice in the matter. [Pause.] I don't know how to think about this, except that whenever Seymour throws it in my face, I always have the sensation of that hot-dog turning to sawdust in my mouth."

"Why do you think Seymour brings this incident to your attention so often?"

"I really don't know. Perhaps because he can't understand it. [Pause.] Maybe he viewed it as some kind of psychic phenomena and thought that I had some sort of special powers or something. I don't know. He has never been able to erase it from his mind, and perhaps he hopes I'll have an explanation. But I don't. I know that I WILLED it, but I don't know anything beyond that."

"Did you tell Seymour you 'willed' it, as you say."

"I didn't have to. He was there. He <u>knew</u>. He just needed to understand how or why it happened."

"And you do not know?"

"I can only surmise it was because of the – because of our game, I suppose. You know. [Voice trails off.] What I told you we were doing, Harry and I."

[Pause.]

"What happened after the ballgame was canceled, please."

"After the accident – I don't know how else to call it – I don't think I said another word. I <u>know</u> Seymour didn't. But when the game was called, I <u>knew</u> I had to see Harry. Without even saying anything to Seymour, I started running to get out of the ballpark, to find where the players were leaving from.

"I was unfamiliar with Ebbett's Field, and I remember running around in the rain like a crazy person, but eventually I found the Players' exit. A guard was there. I asked if Harry Gault had left, and was told he had rushed off in a cab, like the other Cardinals, to the hospital to see how Ed was doing. I had just missed him."

[Pause.]

"I can remember standing there in the rain. Rain pouring down my light summer clothes that didn't fit because they were too small. Rain dripping from my braids. And because I wanted Harry, <u>wherever</u> he was at that time, to hear me telepathically – to receive what I wanted him to hear, I started screaming mentally. I screamed his name over and over in my mind. [Voice level raises dramatically.] 'Harry, Harry, I'm so sorry. I didn't mean for Ed to be hurt like this.'

"Dr. Levy, I swear, I really didn't understand the force behind a baseball being hit so hard, the damage it could do. So I stood there, in the pouring rain, to the rest of the world seeming silent, but actually

<u>screaming</u> over and over again in my mind, 'Harry. I'm so sorry. I didn't mean it to happen this way. I'm so sorry'."

[Silence of extraordinary length.]

"I know what you're thinking, Dr. Levy."

"You <u>do</u>, Miss Jacobs?"

"Yes, I do, and of course you're right. I never realized it before, but all these years that I've been saying 'I'm sorry' - sure, I can imagine having to say that as a child living in the homes of different Aunts and Uncles - but it appears to me now, that what I have really been doing all these years, is apologizing for what I did to Ed."

[Pause.]

"Yes, Miss Jacobs, that <u>was</u> the thought that came into my mind. I am pleased you have gained that insight, and I hope you will be able to make use of it. A therapeutic environment is much more productive when the patient realizes the source of a problem, rather than the doctor explaining the cause."

[Pause.]

"However, I am still uncertain as to why you felt <u>you</u> were responsible for the injury sustained by that ballplayer to the extent that you had to keep apologizing for it all these years."

"Because I view it as part of the game that Harry and I had been playing. [Almost frantic pleading.] Don't you see that, Dr. Levy? My act of will was part of our plan to get Harry what he wanted. I am aware of how crazy that sounds, but I don't know what else to say."

[Silence.]

"What happened next, please, after you were standing in the rain mentally screaming for Harry to tell him you were sorry for, as you believe, causing the serious injury to his friend."

[Pause; then heavy sigh.]

"Somehow Seymour managed to find me and took me home. We barely spoke; maybe we didn't speak at all. I'm not sure.

"Seymour knew how I felt about Harry, although, of course, he didn't know about our game. I've sensed that he felt this incident was an example of the very strong emotional ties between me and Harry. I think you have to ask Seymour, because I'm not sure myself why he keeps bringing it up every time he sees me."

"Is it really 'every' time, Miss Jacobs?"

[Response defensive.]

"Yes, it is, Dr. Levy. Although we talk on the 'phone a lot, Seymour and I do not see each other that often now because of his concert schedule; but whenever we do, YES, he brings it up. It is almost the first thing that comes out of his mouth after 'hello'."

"We will need to talk about this incident at greater length, Miss Jacobs; however, I see we have gone over our allotted time again. We will talk next at the usual scheduled hour, unless you wish to come in sooner."

"I'm not sure about that, but I do need to ask you now, Dr. Levy - how would you explain this incident."

[Pause.]

"I need to think about it for awhile, Miss Jacobs. We will talk about it at our next session. If you feel you want to see me earlier than our regular time, call my secretary and see what can be arranged."

"Yes, thank you, Dr. Levy. Goodbye."

Tape 7

[Sounds of movement in background; possibly returning quilt.]

"Good evening, Miss Jacobs."

End of Tape 7.

Notes Accompanying Tape 7.

Her words echo in my ears. How <u>would</u> I explain this incident?

Typically, Miss Jacobs began relating even this significant episode in her life, with her usual objective, dispassionate narrative tone; except whenever she made references to this man Harry. But then, as the events began to escalate, her speech pattern actually became faster, and although she tried to narrate her actions in a detached manner, I could sense, through her voice, the panic she must have felt, running around in the rain, as she described it, "like a crazy person," trying to find Harry. He was the one person who could have helped her in this situation, but of course he was not there.

It wasn't until she described her crying out to him for help, or really <u>absolution for her sin</u>, that the full range of emotions, repressed for so long, came out in her voice.

<u>What a remarkable breakthrough and insight! What a dramatic moment every therapist hopes for</u>! But what did she mean by her comment that <u>she knew what I was thinking</u>? Of course, I'm sure she only sensed, intuitively, that I realized, by her constant use of the words "I'm sorry," that her pleas for forgiveness have remained with her as a direct result of that particular incident. I agree with her also, that some of it came from her unfortunate childhood, but I am convinced her constant apologies are a transference directly connected to this event, which must have had an enormously devastating effect upon such a young girl.

It is unfortunate she has carried this guilt with her for so long. Perhaps if she had been able to talk to this man Harry, he might have managed to reassure her and explain that his friend's injury was not her fault. However, from her description of his character, it is hard to know what he was thinking or feeling at the time. Guilt also, possibly? Could he have thought they were responsible for the incident? Would it have seemed like part of their psychic game (if such it truly was) to him as well? Or was he the type of individual who was incapable of experiencing guilt? It becomes increasingly obvious that he was using this poor young girl who worshipped him, whether or not he did possess what she felt were "psychic" powers. He certainly convinced her that he had them, and he definitely was manipulating her emotions for his own purposes. She has never mentioned whether her relationship with this man Harry developed into sexual intimacy; although I believe that was his ultimate goal.

What kind of amoral character was this Harry, to lead such a vulnerable young girl to wish harm upon his own friend? In many ways, he reminds me of Molnar's "Liliom."[2]

It is unfortunate that I cannot question Seymour about the incident, as he would be the one person who could supply a more objective view, since he was at the scene and aware of Miss Jacobs' attachment to this man Harry.

As for the event itself, was it coincidence? Jung spoke often of synchronicity[3] - perhaps this is just such an instance. Or was it

---

[2] "Liliom, A Legend in Seven Scenes and a Prologue;" by Ferenc Molnar. Hungarian drama, translated and considerably modified as the American Musical, "Carousel."

[3] Synchronicity - a Term used by the Swiss Psychoanalyst Carl Jung to describe what he considered to be "meaningful coincidences." In Jung's view, it was possible for psychic or mystical experiences to coincide with events occurring in the world of physical reality.

simply Miss Jacobs' overactive imagination, which she herself has admitted to having? Our sessions have certainly revealed her ability to over-dramatize the events of her life somewhat, as if she were narrating a novel.

Could the incident have been accomplished through telekinesis? Because Miss Jacobs was a very young teenager at the time, could this have been an example of Poltergeist activity, as young girls her age are primarily responsible for such events when authenticated.

Or again, is she psychotic? Is this an example of magical thinking – where the individual feels all-powerful and is convinced he or she causes the events that happen in this world?

But my impression is still not one of psychosis in her case – nothing else in her outward behavior fits the diagnosis; and she would have to be very controlled to have hidden such symptoms from me in the several sessions we have had thus far. No. I believe, although tentatively, that I can rule out a diagnosis of psychosis.

Neurosis? I still do not see much of that either, except for her hyper-sensitivity, always excusing herself for things for which she has no responsibility. However, I believe we have reached a significant break-through on that issue today, and additional positive gains may be anticipated.

Paranoia? Thus far, there is little evidence to support this diagnosis. Delusions? Of course, she is still at the point of describing what I believe to be background subject-material, and she has yet to relate the incidents she believes involve this man Harry contacting her after his death. Perhaps if she does have indicia of mental illness, they will be revealed then.

As I have never had a patient present such problems or symptomology before, I hesitate to even attempt to speculate on the nature and origin of her experiences, which definitely require consideration by an objective and impartial mind.

* * *

TAPE 8

April 13, 1981
7:00 pm

"Dr. Levy, it was so kind of you to agree to stay late to see me, but after talking to you about that incident, it's been all I could think about, and I just couldn't wait until my next regular session. And you did seem to indicate, if I remember correctly, that it would be OK to call for an earlier appointment if I needed to see you before then."

"Yes, that is correct Miss Jacobs. And I was already working late, so it is not a problem. What is troubling you about the incident, please."

"Well, for one thing, after I left you, I called Seymour. I asked what he remembered about the incident, only this time I had specific questions. And guess what! For the first time in his life, ever since this happened, he refused to talk about it."

"Really? That is interesting."

"INTERESTING! INTERESTING? After throwing it in my face every time he sees me for almost 35 years, for him to suddenly refuse to talk about it - you call that INTERESTING! I can't believe this!"

[Pause.]

"Miss Jacobs, I have been intending to ask you, but somehow something has always interrupted my intention - and that is, explain, please, what you mean when you say that Seymour has been, as you put it, "throwing" this incident in your face each time you see each other."

[Tone agitated.]

103

"He keeps bringing it up. He never lets me forget it."

"And did you <u>want</u> to forget it, Miss Jacobs?"

"Yes. Of course I did. It was one of the most important things about my prior psychic experiences that I wanted to forget. I was concentrating on a life of Logic, remember?"

[Pause.]

"And in what way would Seymour bring this incident to your attention when he was with you?"

"The most usual way would be if he did something to displease me, he would make some kind of comment about being sure not to do that again, otherwise something like what happened to Ed could happen to him. [Pause.] Ways like that. And it really was every time we were together - I'm <u>not</u> exaggerating!"

[Pause.]

"Did Seymour provide a reason for his refusal to discuss the incident?"

"None. [Pause.] Dr. Levy, did YOU tell Seymour not to talk about this to me?"

[Voice solemn, with hurt, almost scolding tone.]

"Miss Jacobs. Come, now. Is that something you really think I would do?"

"No. No. Of course not. I realized almost the moment I said the words how ridiculous they sounded, and I apologize. And I can also tell you that I think it is appropriate at this time for me to say I am sorry."

"Very good, Miss Jacobs, very good. You have retained your insight from our previous session. [Pause.] But I see you are obviously quite upset, so let me ask again. Do you have any idea why Seymour would refuse to talk about this incident, particularly when you specifically asked him to do so?"

"No. Except perhaps for sheer perversity. He knew how involved I was with Harry, and maybe he was jealous and now won't give me the satisfaction of talking about it when I want to. [Pause.] Or maybe the whole thing really frightened him too much. I tell you, Dr. Levy, I just don't know what to think."

"Is that why you wanted to come for an earlier appointment?"

"Oh good grief, no. It was just that remembering the incident was very upsetting. Things I had forgotten for so many years came back to me, along with a flood of emotion, all the feelings I had, and still have for Harry. I know I have yet to tell you about the things that really brought me to see you on a regular basis, and I wonder if I am taking up too much of your time by going into all this childhood stuff."

"But you yourself made a very logical case as to why I needed to know this background information in order to understand the total situation. And, as you are probably aware, discussion of childhood incidents is a prominent feature of psychoanalysis. However, if you feel it is more important now for you to discuss your current experiences, that does not present a problem for me."

"Was I apologizing unnecessarily again?"

"No, Miss Jacobs. You are far too hard on yourself. I can tell you are more upset than I have ever seen you. [Pause.] What is the trouble?"

[Silence.]

"Is there something else? Have you had another experience with Harry, another incidence of post-mortem contact?"

[Pause.]

"Yes. First, he's been, well, what I call 'hanging around' a lot more than usual. Then, the night when I came home after talking about the incident, I took off my wet clothes, took a hot shower, and was relaxing on my couch, listening to WQXR, when I felt this terrible ache in my heart. I don't mean it as a physical condition — it's very difficult to describe — but as an emotional state, a feeling of deep anguish. Then something made me understand it was Harry's emotions I was feeling, the way I used to when I was a teenager, and I got up and went into my bedroom, where I keep my clippings and photos concerning Harry, and somehow knew to take out the one involving Ed's 'accident' - for lack of a better word.

"And then, it was so strange. I didn't see Harry - in fact, I've <u>never</u> seen him, like the way Mrs. Muir saw the Ghost, or the way people typically see Ghosts in films, like in 'Blithe Spirit,' for example. [Pause.] Funny I should mention that. This one sports writer used to refer to Harry as a 'blithe spirit.' But maybe I told you that already.

"Anyway, although I didn't see him, I felt his presence <u>so</u> strongly - now I <u>know</u> this is going to sound absurd - but I felt his presence <u>so</u> strongly next to me that I actually moved over so that he could see the article more clearly. Isn't that ridiculous? As a ghost, he could probably see through me to read the article. But then what do I know about how ghosts operate? Maybe my instincts <u>were</u> right. Maybe I <u>did</u> have to move over to let him see it better. Anyway, that's what I did."

[Pause.]

106

"This sounds so crazy. I can't believe I'm saying all these things to you."

"But this is why you contacted me originally, Miss Jacobs, remember? Because you felt you needed help in determining the status of your mental health."

"Yes, of course, Dr. Levy. I'm sorry. Ooops. Anyway, I read the sports article coverage of the incident where Ed was injured – and possibly Harry did also."

"Excuse me, Miss Jacobs, but I have two questions. First, did this emotional pain that you described subside after you took out the article about the incident so that you, and perhaps Harry also, could read it? And second, how did the sports writer relate the incident?"

"Yes, Dr. Levy, I can answer both questions. After I took out the article and moved over – that seems so ridiculous to say that – but after I took out the article, the aching pain disappeared almost immediately. In fact, I almost forgot I ever felt it.

"As for the article itself, it was very straight-forward, and actually devoted what I thought was VERY little space to the incident involving Ed. The writer concentrated on what a wild game it was, about how both teams got so many hits and runs, and how Robinson stole home, and how so many different pitchers were called in as replacements, and how one of them, poor Ed, actually was <u>literally</u> knocked out of the ballgame. You see, Dr. Levy, it is a typical phrase in baseball – at least it was then — when a lot of runs are scored against a pitcher, to say he was "knocked" out of the game when he is replaced by another pitcher. So, in a way, to answer your question, I got the feeling that the writer was more concerned with how clever he was in stating Ed was literally knocked out of the game, than he was about the actual injury and how it happened. Although later, at the end of the article, he added that word had been received from the hospital that Ed was expected to recover."

"So, if I am to understand you correctly, the sportswriter did not attach too much significance to what happened to this ballplayer, Ed. Could that be because such injuries are to be expected in a ballgame?"

"Well why should the writer be concerned. He wasn't the one to put a curse on Ed, like I did."

"Is that what you think you did, Miss Jacobs? Put a curse on this man?"

"Well, it just seemed to fit into what was going on with this 'game' that Harry and I were involved in. That's what I meant."

[Pause.]

"When you saw Harry again, did you speak of it with him? And I mean at the time following the incident, not recently."

"Harry and I NEVER, NOT ONCE, talked about the incident involving Ed. NEVER."

"And this time, after reading the article, was there any indication of Harry's feelings concerning the incident?"

"No. Unless it was the pain that I felt, the emotional pain that made me get up and go to the bedroom and retrieve the article. It's entirely possible that my talking about the incident with you, and recalling everything about it so vividly made Harry remember and feel sad about what happened."

"Is this man Ed still alive?"

"No. And that's another strange thing. Ed died the same year as Harry, and on Harry's birthday, as well. Isn't that a strange coincidence?

"You know, Dr. Levy, I was also thinking that perhaps Harry never knew I put that curse on Ed and found out about it only when I told you, and that's what made him feel sad."

[Pause.]

"No, that doesn't seem right. Because Harry knew everything I was thinking. At least I think he did. Maybe he didn't. Maybe his own emotions were so strong at that moment that he wasn't paying attention to mine. But then again, maybe if we were both thinking about the same thing at the same time, that is why it happened.

"Honestly, Dr. Levy, I don't know what to think anymore. Perhaps now that I've told you, about both the incident and what happened when I got home after I left your office, I've said all I can about it now. Maybe I should go on to what happened next in my teenage years, if there is still time now and it's all right with you."

"Yes, we still have time, and yes, it is all right. But do you feel ready? Are you really ready to leave this subject now? It was very emotional for you, and apparently still is."

"Yes, but after talking to you tonight, I feel much better, and crazy as it may seem, after reading the article with Harry, I felt better. I still am confused about why Seymour won't talk to me about it anymore, but I feel that is _his_ problem now, not mine."

"That is a reasonable response. [Pause.] All right, Miss Jacobs. If you feel comfortable with proceeding, please do. Remember, we can always return to a discussion of this incident, if you wish."

"Well, there is one thing more. At the end of our last session, I remember asking what you thought of the incident involving Ed. Are you able to tell me now?"

"I am sorry, Miss Jacobs, but I still have not formulated an opinion. It is still an isolated incident for me. Perhaps, with further details of what transpired between you and Harry, particularly after his death, I will be able to view the incident as part of a larger focus, and give you my opinion then. I hope that is acceptable to you, but it is all that I can say at this time."

"I understand, Dr. Levy. [Pause.] I'll go on with my connections with Harry when I was a teenager.

"At the time the incident involving Ed occurred, the baseball season was almost over, so I think I saw Harry only one more time at the Polo Grounds that year. It was as if the Ed incident never happened. We talked about our lives—-"

"Excuse me, Miss Jacobs, but when you say 'talk,' do you mean aloud, or via mental communication."

"Both, actually. He told me about his family, and I told him about school. I don't even think we mentioned our 'game', now that I think of it.

"Then came the time for separation. It was almost unbearable for me."

"What do you mean by 'time for separation.'"

"Well, the baseball season ended and Harry went back to his family in Missouri and resumed his work as a carpenter in his brothers' business in the off-season."

"Did you communicate with him, either through mail or through thought?"

"I <u>know</u> for sure that I never received any letters from him, as we never exchanged addresses. And I don't think we communicated telepathically, either."

"Was distance a problem?"

"None whatsoever, but I guess he had too many other things on his mind to think of me. And I remember now, it just came to me - that it was almost as if there were some sort of unspoken, unverbalized even by thought, agreement between us that we would not communicate with each other between the Baseball seasons."

"Which is?"

"Well, Spring Training starts in March I believe - at least it did then - and the World Series is over in October usually, so I would say the season is March through October."

"And you had no contact at all with Harry then, from October to March, is that correct?"

"Yes."

"And what years are we talking about please, again?"

"In 1947, I saw Harry last in September and not again until May 1948."

"Miss Jacobs, I don't think I asked you, but when Harry was traveling with the St. Louis team and not playing any New York teams, were you still in contact with him?"

"Yes, Dr. Levy. Yes. Even though I could not see him in person, and of course baseball games were not televised at the time, and I could not listen to the games on the radio if he was not playing a New York team, I managed to know how he was doing through telepathic communication. Also, I might add, through reading both the local and St. Louis papers. And if there happened to be a special article or interview of Harry in some other paper or

111

magazine that I was unaware of or couldn't afford, friends who knew how much I cared for Harry would give these to me. I really have quite a collection of articles about him, which I saved to this day."

"What were these communications about?"

"Well, at first they seemed to be just testing, to see if it could be done. But then it broadened to the point where it was like having a conversation with a friend you bumped into on the street or in school, whatever."

"Would these thoughts just enter your mind at random, or did you have some pre-arranged type of schedule?"

"That question makes it seem so silly, but at the time I was so young and so naïve, to me it seemed that this is what happened when you fell in love – that everyone who was in love communicated this way. We just had these conversations, I'll call them, and if one of us wasn't free to talk at the time, we'd say so. Whatever."

"When you say you thought all people who were in love communicated this way, did you believe that this man Harry was in love with you?"

"Oh no, never. NOT EVER. I knew he loved his wife very much and I was so happy for him that he had this love with her. I loved him, that was all that mattered to me, and all I ever wanted was for him to be happy. That was all I ever wanted. Then and now."

[Sounds of weeping.]

"Here, Miss Jacobs." [Sounds of tissues being pulled from container.]

"When you are ready, Miss Jacobs, tell me, it is true then that you had none of these communications, nor any letters from this man

Harry during the period September 1947 through May 1948?"

[Sniffle.] "Yes, that is correct."

"Miss Jacobs, what was it that made you cry then? Was it remembering that you had no contact with Harry during this time period?"

"No. It's just that I become very emotional whenever I think of my feelings for him. I had buried them so deep for so long and now they are overwhelming me."

"Are you able to go on, or would you like to stop and continue this discussion at our next session."

"No, I'm all right. Thank you, Dr. Levy. Is there anything else you want to ask about that time period before I saw Harry again?"

"Do you remember how you felt during his absence? Did you lapse into depression? Did you cry often? What do you remember?"

"I was depressed, but I don't think in the sense of the clinical term. I just was very sad. I missed him so much. I would read my clippings and look at pictures of him whenever I could. And there was a particular film starring Henry Fonda that I saw 14 times. I think I used my milk money or something, since I wasn't buying St. Louis papers anymore. I went to every Brooklyn theater where it was playing and saw it as many times as I could."

"And why was that?"

"Because Henry Fonda reminded me of Harry in so many ways. He was tall, thin and muscular. He had the same dark hair and complexion, and blue eyes. They both had that slow mid-West way of speaking. The film was about a troubled World War II Veteran. And I've since learned that Harry was deeply troubled by his experiences in the War, as probably every Veteran was who saw combat. So that film had a

113

deeper connection with Harry than I realized
at the time. [Pause.] But I think I may have
told you about this before, already."

"Indeed, you did, Miss Jacobs. [Pause.] And
when you no longer could see the film?"

"I just went on with my life. But Harry was
always in my mind."

"Tell me what your first meeting was like in
May of 1948, please."

[Pause.]

"Dr. Levy, I just remembered something. It
really was quite important to me at the time.
I don't know how I could have almost forgotten
to tell you."

"Yes?"

"As the 1948 season approached, I started
getting the St. Louis papers again in order to
find out about the Cardinals' Opening Game and
when Harry would be pitching. Well, as it
turned out, Harry was pitching the Opening
Game for the Cardinals in St. Louis, and I
remember on that day, even though I was busy
with school and other activities, I placed all
my powers of concentration on Harry winning."

"Excuse me, but had he contacted you about
this Opening Game?"

"No. That's interesting, now that you
mention it. He didn't, as far as I can
remember. But I knew about it, and put all my
thoughts on Harry winning."

"And did he?"

"Yes. I can remember reading the score in
the New York paper, and then I went to get the
St. Louis paper as soon as I could.

"It was such a marvelous write-up. I still
have it, of course, in my collection. Harry
pitched a three-hit shut out. That means the
other team, I forget who it was now - not a
New York team of course, because then I would

have been able to hear the broadcast - only got three hits and no runs. The Cardinals won something like 5 to 0, I think."

[Pause.]

"After the game, this one particular writer, the one who referred to Harry as a 'blithe spirit' or the 'Merry Magician of the Mound' because of Harry's love of magic tricks - I mean, little did this guy know - anyway, it was <u>this</u> writer who interviewed Harry after the game. And although I didn't understand when I read it as a teenager, the article is actually rather poignant.

"Harry was sitting in the clubhouse alone. All the other players had left, but Harry still had not changed from his uniform, and was listening to a Blues ballad on the radio. As the reporter sat with him, Harry was running his dirt-stained fingers through his thick black hair, and wondering aloud about his happiness and success and how fleeting it could be. [Pause.] I believe now that his experiences in the War were still preying on his mind."

[Pause.]

"But best of all, there was also a photo of Harry taken right after the game, while he was still in uniform, and he was holding his baby girl in his arms. There she was, just like he said, with the two braids. I cried when I saw that picture. I could feel the love between them. [Voice tone very emotional.] She had one arm around his neck, hugging him hard, and the other arm outstretched with the winning baseball in her little hand. It must have been hard for her to hold. But, the warmth and the love - I could feel it so strongly from the photo."

[Silence.]

"And do you remember when that took place?"

"Sometime in April 1948, I imagine."

"And did you hear from Harry in any way before you saw him in May?"

"No. I had not heard from him before then, so I even wondered if he had forgotten about me during the off-season. But then, as I sat in the stands at the first game the Cardinals played at the Polo Grounds, I heard this voice loud and clear in my mind, as if someone had turned on a radio. He said, 'Hi, Sandy. See you at the elevated station after the game.' I was so excited I thought I would wet my pants. Ooops. Sorry, Dr. Levy."

"That's quite all right. Continue, please."

"Anyway, I was so excited, I forget the outcome of the game. It didn't really matter to me anyway, as Harry wasn't pitching. I just ran as fast as I could, as soon as it was over, and practically flew up the stairs to the train station. It seemed like forever before he arrived, but there he was, the same as ever, only he seemed better looking than I remembered, and he was still wearing those bizarre combinations of color and patterns that were his trademark, and the same tan shoes.

"He smiled, but didn't say anything. He just stood there on the platform, hands thrust deep into the pockets of his pants, chewing gum, rocking back and forth on his heels. Every once in a while, he would turn, look at me and wink, then smile that little crooked grin I loved so much."

"Did he communicate with you in any way?"

"Not in words, but there was so much, I see now, in the way he looked at me that said more than I was capable of understanding then. Do you know what I mean?"

116

[Pause.]

"Yes. Go on, Miss Jacobs, please."

"When we got to the next stop, we walked down the stairs and stood by the Yankee Stadium, and then he grabbed my hand. He spoke out loud this time and asked how I liked his Opening Game shutout, or if I knew about it. I told him that of course I knew about it and was so excited and had concentrated real hard on having him win. When he heard that he smiled a really great big smile, and told me he had something special for me, something magical. He said that he had wanted to wait to give it to me when we got to that 'soda-joint', as he called it, but that he was too excited and wanted to give it to me right then."

[Pause.]

"What happened next?"

"He spun me around, and said fake phony magic words like 'hocus-pocus' whatever, and... [Voice trails off, then resumes choked with tears.] … and when I turned around to face him, he pretended to pull an envelope out of nowhere. I asked if it was for me, and he laughed and said something like, 'Of course, silly', and I was almost dizzy, both from being spun around and from the excitement of being with him again after so long. I loved him so much."

[Crying, then resuming with choked voice.]

"Anyway, I opened the envelope, it was 8½ by 11, and in it was that photo, the one of Harry holding his baby girl. I pulled it out. The pose was slightly different from the one in the paper, but it was still the two of them at that interview after the game. I started to cry."

"You mean you cried then, when he gave you the photo."

"Yes. And he told me not to cry, but to turn the photo over, because there was more to see. I did as he said, and he had written a special message for me, that the photo was for his 'best fan' – 'To Sandy, my best fan, from Harry' were the exact words. And of course, I started to cry even more."

[Sounds of sobbing; then prolonged silence.]

"What made you weep now, Miss Jacobs, please."

"I don't know if I can get anybody to understand. Seymour, any other friends I try to tell this to -- nobody understands. But I know now how much I loved him and he's gone and I'll never see him again. And when I was telling you about this – I could see so clearly how he looked that day, hands in his pockets, rocking back and forth, glancing over to look at me and grin impishly – I can see it all now, and I miss him so much. I want it back, the way it was."

"But how was it then, Miss Jacobs, in reality? He was much older than you, a married man with a little girl, and you were 14 years old and still in school. And, from what you have told me, the rest of your life was not that pleasant. So, what is it you <u>really</u> want?"

"Harry, I guess. I – since he's come back, I mean after he died, I've had all these strange experiences that I haven't told you about yet, that made me see and feel how much more was going on then that I did not understand before."

"Yes. Perhaps I will understand when you tell me about these things. Now, one more question and then it will be time for our session to close. Do you know why you cried at the time Harry handed you this photo?"

"It's just that I was overwhelmed with emotion. I don't think I understood then why I cried. It just was a spontaneous reaction. Perhaps women understand these things better than men, I don't know, but my guess is that I cried because I was overwhelmed by his presence and the thoughtfulness of his gift. I had loved that photo so much when I saw it in the paper, and then to have my own copy with my own personal message from Harry."

"Really, Miss Jacobs, it was fairly typical, and not unique in any way."

"Perhaps. I might say that now, but I certainly did not feel that way then. I didn't have much that was personal and special to me in the way of gifts then, and having this photo, which meant so much to me, having my own personally for me from him, I just reacted spontaneously with tears."

"I understand. Did anything else happen after he gave you the photo."

"No. He wiped my tears with a handkerchief he had in the pocket of whatever wild pattern jacket he was wearing, and put the photo back in the envelope for me saying something like, 'before it dissolves from my tears'. Then he took my hand and we walked silently to the candy store. We had our usual drinks and he talked about the games he had pitched, but I could barely pay attention. All I could think of was having that photo and the message in Harry's own handwriting. After we finished, we walked back to the station and went home the usual way."

"Nothing special happened."

"Nothing."

"All right, Miss Jacobs. That will close this session. You are returning for your regularly scheduled appointment, is that correct?"

"Yes, Dr. Levy. That is what I had planned."

"Good. I will see you then. [Pause.] Oh, let me escort you to the door, as my secretary has left by now."

End of Tape 8.

Notes Accompanying Tape 8.

What is there in this patient that makes me react in ways that are so unprofessional? It was hard for me to believe, once again, that it was my own voice making those insensitive remarks. Perhaps it is my irritation at this man Harry, and his treatment of this naïve young girl. He really does remind me of Molnar's Liliom, even to the point of returning after death. But, like Liliom, would he have had a special reason for returning?

Still, that is not really relevant to why I acted so unprofessionally and so insensitively toward this woman and the obvious turmoil and grief she is suffering. Once again, she put me to shame by responding properly and not being offended. But, as she has talked about her childhood of neglect, perhaps she is used to being treated with insensitivity. That would also explain why the gift of this photo, with its simple message, would have meant so much to her. As she said in her own words, she had not had anything that she could call her own before. In addition, it was from this man for whom she cared so deeply. I should never have attempted to minimize the importance of this gift, nor its significance in her life.

But why, after all these years, is she still so upset just remembering her time spent with him? She can barely talk about him without weeping. But perhaps she is right - she has not told me yet about all the experiences, the contacts she has supposedly had with him after his death. Still, the depth of emotion conveyed by Miss Jacobs for this man Harry is extraordinary. It is more than substitution of a father-figure - and this emotion has

apparently been continuous since 1947. Is it
love? But she was so young.

What is there about Miss Jacobs that causes
men to react so strongly in response to her?
Obviously this man Harry found something in
her to captivate him. And Seymour's reported
response of refusing to discuss the incident
at the ballpark after so many years of
revealing the enormous impact it had upon him
is a particularly unusual reaction. Perhaps
Miss Jacob's analysis of his refusal is
accurate. Then there has been my own
inappropriate impatience and insensitivity
with her on more than one occasion. Is she
overly-imaginative — creating dramatic
incidents with which to manipulate men in
order to gain control? Has she been
manipulating Seymour all the years she has
known him, and is she now attempting to
manipulate me? Fascinating.

Her description of her sense of the presence
of this man Harry, now deceased, is
astounding. On the one hand, she relates this
unusual experience as having disturbed her to
the point of questioning her sanity; yet on
the other hand, she analyzes the situation
with complete logic - again like a detached
observer. In that respect, she makes an
immensely reliable chronicler of post-mortem
contact; because, although she claims to be
upset and frightened by these incidents, she
still manages to subject them to the scrutiny
of logical analysis.

No. I am convinced this woman is not
psychotic in any way. Schizophrenia is
definitely ruled out. Nor do her thought
processes indicate Paranoia - at least not as
revealed thus far, although her intimating
that it was I who coached Seymour not to talk

to her about the incident at the ballpark is certainly a paranoid reaction; however, this may be an isolated example. I will need to watch for other indications before I can completely rule out this diagnosis.

I must also remember to ask Miss Jacobs about her constant references to the problems this man Harry suffered during combat in World War II. I need to be sure she provides relevant details of his experiences.

***

TAPE 9

April 15, 1981
4:40 pm

"Good afternoon, Miss Jacobs."

"Dr. Levy. [Out of breath] Please forgive me for being late for my appointment, but you know I _am_ a CPA, and I have a number of Income Tax Returns I must complete before midnight. In fact, after our session, I'll be returning to my office. [Pause.] I really don't understand how some people can wait until the very last minute to face their tax consequences. They _know_ when their Returns are due. [Pause.] I'm sorry, Dr. Levy. That is a pet peeve of mine and really of no consequence to you, except as a justifiable excuse on my part for keeping you waiting."

"I understand completely, Miss Jacobs, in particular because I am one of those persons of whom you complain. And now that I can appreciate the situation from an accountant's point of view, I shall try to do better next year."

[Sounds of indistinguishable chatter and laughter.]

"Miss Jacobs, tell me please, have you had any further experiences with the presence of this man Harry since our last meeting."

"Nothing other than the routine."

"Routine? And what do you mean by that, please."

"I know we haven't gotten into a discussion of the substance of my contacts with Harry since I learned of his death, mainly because I've chosen to provide you with background material first so that you could better

124

understand the nature of these contacts. But let me just say that a day does not go by when I don't have some kind of contact with him – it's become almost expected. It's just when something SO bizarre happens, like the incident when I called you so early in the morning, that I feel I cannot cope. In the beginning, when it first started, I panicked, and was on the phone to Seymour and other close friends almost daily. But now, except for the unusual incidents, I've gotten sort of used to these things."

"And what things are those, please."

[Pause.]

"Oh, for example, I'll be thinking of something and a song will play on the radio that deals with the same subject, sometimes even providing solutions to problems I've been worried about. [Pause.] I guess because of my intense involvement with music, Harry chooses that way to keep in touch with me."

"Would you like to talk about some of those incidents now?"

"No. I'm almost finished with what happened in the time I was with Harry when he was alive, and I honestly do believe it will help you to understand what has been happening recently."

"Ah, Miss Jacobs, I wonder why you still wish to come to me, as there seems to be little that I can do to be of assistance for you. You seem to feel confident about your contacts with Harry – that they are real and not imaginary – and have conducted your own investigation, rather professionally I might add, very systematic and orderly. Therefore, I can not help but inquire as to why you believe it necessary to continue our visits. I'm not trying to discourage you, understand that please. It is just that you do not -"

"I know. You are remembering how frantic I was the first time I contacted you. Well, I might SEEM calm and rational, but that could be a carry-over from my work environment. After all, when I come to your office, it is after a day of dealing with facts and figures, and I think it could be that I am just continuing that mode of confidence that I have to exude for my colleagues and clients. But believe me, Dr. Levy, when some of these experiences with Harry occur, I am anything but calm. I have come to you, not just because Seymour insisted ever since this began for me, but because I have my own doubts from time to time as to my sanity."

"Is it helpful then, for you to proceed in chronological order with the story of your childhood experiences with Harry? In addition, is it calming to postpone, for as long as possible, a discussion of the more unsettling aspects of your communication with him now?"

"No. I don't know. No. I honestly believe that it will be more comprehensible to you if I tell you about things as they happened, so that you will understand why Harry chose certain methods and ways of contacting me after he died. And also, why he chose to contact me, period.

"But before you think I am the only one who is aware Harry is around me, I can tell you there are many synchronistic experiences - I no longer think of them as mere coincidences - where friends have been present when they occurred, or were actually the cause of their occurrence, if that makes any sense."

"Very interesting. All right, Miss Jacobs, proceed with your chronological narrative, please. I believe the last session ended with you discussing how you felt after Harry gave you the photo with its personal message."

"Yes. Well, we walked back to the station and went our ways home. I saw him the next day, when he sat in the Bullpen, but he never got to pitch, and a day or so later, the team went to Brooklyn to play against the Dodgers."

"Did you go to see any of those games?"

"No, I couldn't. I was going to school in upper Manhattan and so, with the exception of that one game, when that horrible incident occurred, I never saw the Cardinals play at Ebbett's Field."

"Excuse me. Go on, Miss Jacobs, please."

"After the team left Brooklyn, they went on to play other East Coast teams before heading back to St. Louis, where the other teams would come and play against the Cardinals at their home field. Then another strange thing happened. Very strange. Involving Harry and me in one of those concentration-wish games."

"Go on, please."

"This is another incident I will ALWAYS remember. The Giants were in St. Louis playing against the Cardinals, and I listened to one of the games on the radio, as it was played at night. I got up to go to school the next morning, and that day's game wasn't of much interest to me, because Harry wasn't scheduled to pitch. Then without any warning, I became violently ill. Now that was unusual for me, as I was generally a pretty healthy kid. But it came on so unexpectedly. I ran into the bathroom, and I was really very sick. My Aunt didn't have the money to get a doctor, and she guessed her own convenient diagnosis that it must have been something I ate, or whatever, and told me to go back to bed and sleep until

I felt better. So I did just that. It was probably about 6:00 am or so, as I had to get up very early to get to school on time.

"I woke up later and it was already afternoon. I realized then that I had slept straight through. I called my Aunt but there was no answer. I got up and staggered around, but no one was home. I felt a little better, but still somewhat woozy. Then I remembered the Giants were playing the Cardinals and the game would be on the radio, so I turned it on. My bed, if you want to call it that, was a couch in the living room, so the radio was right nearby.

"When I turned on the game, I was surprised to learn that Harry was pitching. It was already the third inning or so, and the Cardinals were ahead by a few runs and the Giants had zero. I listened carefully and as the game progressed, soon it became the sixth inning, and the Giants' announcer commented that so far the Giants hadn't gotten any hits off Harry. Boy, then I really sat up and paid attention. I know you don't understand baseball Dr. Levy, but a No-hit ballgame is something a pitcher always dreams of. It is really a display of skill.

"Also, there's a certain mystique about a No-hitter. When it begins to be obvious that no one has gotten a hit off the pitcher, it is viewed as bad-luck to talk about it, at least it was back then. So this crazy kind of double-speak goes on, where the announcer knows that there is the possibility of a No-hit ballgame, but doesn't talk about it for fear of putting a jinx on the pitcher.

"Well, at that point I started becoming extremely agitated. I knew how much a No-hitter would mean to Harry. I remembered the fuss they made about his one-hit ballgame, but a No-hitter means mention in the Baseball Hall of Fame. I was almost hysterical. All I could do was summon all my emotions and focus, concentrate heavily on every move that Harry made. I was at a fever pitch - no pun intended.

"It was so bizarre. I remember my poor Aunt. I can still see it all so clearly. She must have been out shopping or something, and she was really concerned about me, because she probably saw how asleep I was - how I was really out of it, after suddenly being so sick. She came into the livingroom, where I was sitting up with covers wrapped all around me like some kind of Indian Chief[1] or something, because I had a bad case of the chills. I don't know to this day whether that was because I was sick or because of the excitement of the moment. In fact, I'm not even sure about that sickness - but I'll tell you about that later.

"Anyway, my poor Aunt asked how I was, and I was absolutely panicked, because she broke my concentration and focus on Harry's pitching. I remember screaming at her, REALLY screaming, at the top of my lungs, telling her to get out of the room and leave me alone. The poor woman must have thought I was delusional or in intense pain or something, and she meekly left the room.

"By that time it was the eighth inning, and the Giants still hadn't gotten a hit off Harry. The announcer could not hide the excitement in his voice. Even though he was the announcer for the Giants, still a No-hit

---

[1] Apologies are offered to Native American readers of these transcribed tapes for the stereotypical imagery used by Ms. Jacobs.

ballgame was pretty rare in those days, and to be able to be present, and especially to be announcing one, was really a thrill. He commented on how skillful Harry was, with his weird assortment of pitches that confounded the batters as they faced him.

"Then came the ninth and final inning. Harry had only three more outs to go. My Aunt yelled something about going down to get the mail, but I scarcely heard her. Then she came back into the apartment, and apparently I had received a letter from my penpal in England, and my poor Aunt must have thought that would put me in a better mood, as she came straight to the livingroom to tell me I had gotten a letter from overseas.

"Now that I look back at it, I can really sympathize with my poor Aunt. She meant well. After all, she had the six children of her own to cope with, plus her husband, her mother-in-law, and me, and I KNOW I was a handful. Anyway, she came into the livingroom, so cheerful, telling me about this letter, and all she got in return was my wrath. I swear, I was like a crazy person. I can remember yelling and screaming at her to 'GET OUT', and the poor thing was almost in tears as she put the letter down meekly and left her own livingroom.

"I turned up the volume on the radio as far as it would go. A player had walked to first base. I know you don't understand that, Dr. Levy, but it meant there could be trouble for Harry, although he still had not given up a hit. But then I remembered how he liked to dramatize things, and I smiled as I thought: 'I bet you're doing that just to liven things up - you have NO INTENTION of giving up any hits'.

"I can remember almost shaking with emotion and nerves, and really, being semi-hysterical as I put all of my mind, closing my eyes and focusing on Harry on the pitcher's mound, on his getting that final out. And he did. It was over and Harry had his No-hitter. Even the Giants' announcer was thrilled and excited, and was heaping praise on the way Harry had pitched the game. He described the Cardinal players rushing to the mound and carrying him off the field in triumph. Even Giant players came up to congratulate him.

"And when it was over, all I could do was shake and weep. I couldn't do anything else but weep, weeping and sobbing, hysterically."

[Pause; then very impassioned voice, choked with emotion.]

"What is it? I don't understand. What is it about this man? I have shed more tears over him than any other human being who ever lived on this earth. Why? I don't understand."

[Sounds of weeping.]

"Here, Miss Jacobs. Take this box of tissues, please."

[Pause. Nose blowing.]

"I look back at that game now, and I wonder."

"Excuse me, Miss Jacobs, but what is it that you 'wonder', please."

[Pause.]

"Now that I've been trying to understand these incidents that have occurred in my life since I learned of Harry's death, I've read material that has led me to believe that what happened that day was no coincidence. I don't know how to explain it, but I KNOW none of what happened was a coincidence."

"Explain, please."

"Well, for one thing, I was a kid who <u>never</u> got sick, and then suddenly, for no reason, I become violently ill and have to stay home from school. If I had gone to school, I never would have listened to the game."

"And?"

"And, without my listening to the ballgame, I would not have been able to add my part to Harry's pitching his No-hitter."

"What do you mean by your 'part'?"

"Well, it's obvious. I'm sorry. I mean, it was part of our 'game,' Harry's and mine, where I would concentrate on the outcome of a ballgame with him to help him win. And the strange thing, which really confirms this hypothesis for me, was when Harry was interviewed after the game."

"Explain, please."

"Naturally, as you can expect, the reporters and announcers were all over Harry in the clubhouse when the game was over. Everyone was heaping praise upon him; even the Cardinal manager who never really understood what Harry was all about.

"Anyway, the announcers from both teams were there talking with Harry. It was so interesting to hear him. I know every sound and nuance of Harry's voice. Yet, when he would speak on the radio for an interview, he would put on this 'aw shucks' kind of just plain ole country boy kind of talk."

"I'm not sure I understand what you mean, Miss Jacobs."

"Well, his voice, when we talked, either orally or mentally, was very strong and clear. Yet, when he would talk in public, his tone became softer, more countrified, like he was acting the part of some plain ole country farmer, just simple country folk."

"How can you be sure that he just wasn't shy when he had to speak in public?"

"Because I <u>know</u> this man, and he was anything <u>but</u> a simple country boy. I think this was just something else he liked to do to fool people, to mess with their minds. It was <u>all</u> a game to him.

"Anyway, one of the reporters made this comment that has stuck with me all these years, and seems especially relevant to what has been happening and what I've learned lately. He had apparently tried to interview Harry as he was warming up before the game, and Harry had smiled enigmatically and told the reporter to come back <u>after</u> the game was over, as they would <u>really</u> have something to talk about then. The reporter asked Harry pointedly if Harry had a 'premonition' that something like this No-hit ballgame would happen. Harry laughed in response, and it was – what a marvelous laugh. It was this kind of 'aw-shucks' Mortimer Snerd laugh. [Pause.] Do you know who that character was, Dr. Levy?"

"No. I do not."

"Well, Mortimer Snerd was a ventriloquist's dummy who was a stereotype of what we would call a 'country bumpkin' – someone who is really from down deep in farm country, with not too much smarts. Anyway, Harry laughed a kind of Mortimer Snerd laugh, and replied, with a slower, thicker drawl than usual, and in a real farm-boy kind of voice, something like 'nope,'t weren't nuttin' like 'at.' And I thought to myself, 'you liar you' – 'you <u>really</u> have these folks fooled, taking them for suckers'."

"But you are sure, Miss Jacobs, that this was not just nervousness on his part, that made him revert to his country upbringing?

After all, he had just completed a major accomplishment, and all these announcers, reporters, photographers, etc., were surrounding him. And he did not make his living from public speaking, but from playing baseball."

"Well, you'll just have to trust me on this one, Dr. Levy. It's something I <u>know</u> with all my heart. This was part of the 'game' that Harry was playing. [Pause.] And I wonder too, if he cast some sort of spell on me, in order to get me sick so I would be sure to be home to hear the ballgame and help him win it. [Pause; as if contemplating the possibility.] And to <u>actually</u> tell this reporter to see him <u>after</u> it was over, because he would really have something to talk about then. Of course, you could say it was just a coincidence, but—"

"Excuse me, Miss Jacobs, but could Harry have said that just to send the reporter away so he could concentrate on preparing for the game?"

"It's possible, I suppose, but it all fits so well: my unexpected illness resulting in my listening to the game, my fierce and intense concentration on Harry's every move – except, of course, for those interruptions by my Aunt, Harry's telling the reporter that there would be something they could talk about <u>after</u> the game – it all fits too well. Don't you see?"

[Pause.]

"And something else I just remembered."

"Yes?"

"The reporter also commented to Harry about how remarkable it was that the wind, which was blowing in a way that should have had an adverse impact on the direction and velocity of the balls Harry threw, had no effect upon them whatsoever. And Harry responded with something like — and I can see in my mind the subtle smirk he must have had on his face — 'Yep, 'twere a might strange, weren't it.' The bastard!"

"Miss Jacobs! I'm surprised. Not at your use of language, please do not misunderstand me, but that you should refer to Harry in this way. Do you know why you called him that just then?"

"I didn't mean it with malice. It's just that, as I've gotten older, I can see moral implications for messing with people's minds the way Harry and I were doing. He <u>knew</u> we were controlling the outcome of this game, and yet he was acting so humble and innocent."

"And you are convinced it was an act. You do not believe that he may have been genuinely puzzled by the lack of effect of the wind upon his pitching skills."

"Absolutely. I <u>know</u> it was his simple country boy routine."

"But then Miss Jacobs, that means that not only were you and Harry controlling the behavior of the opposing team members, but also the forces of nature and the laws of physics, as well."

"I realize it sounds insane, but as I tell this to you I can remember it as vividly as if it were happening now. I <u>KNOW</u> we were responsible for the outcome of that game, but I don't know how to explain it, just like I don't know how to explain what happened to Ed, and all the other things that happened when I was focusing on Harry's pitching."

[Extended silence.]

"And how long did it take you to recover from whatever illness you suffered that day?"

"After the game — after I finished weeping and listening to Harry being interviewed, I wrapped myself up in the blankets and went back to sleep. I slept like a baby, and when I woke the next morning I felt fine, and went back to school as if nothing had happened.

"Of course, Harry's No-hitter had happened and that was ALL I could talk about that day in school. Even kids who weren't Cardinal fans were talking about it, both because they knew of my association with Harry, and because in those days, No-hitters were very rare."

"Did that make you feel important in the eyes of your schoolmates, your friendship with this sports figure who had just —"

"Not really. I was not concerned about what the others were thinking about me, all that was on my mind that next day was sharing my joy and excitement over Harry's triumph. He was all that I could talk about at school then. Do you know that when I attended my 30th High School Reunion and walked into the room where my classmates were gathered, when they saw me, they actually screamed out Harry's name, not mine. Some of them couldn't even remember my name, but they remembered my association with Harry. And they all rushed over to talk to me about him and ask how he was doing."

"How did that make you feel?"

"Well — now I realize this will sound surprising — but I was actually annoyed. Here I had received Scholarships, supported myself through College, had worked myself up through the rigorous procedure of becoming a CPA and being the first woman to be hired by the prestigious firm where I am now employed, and all they could think of was my association with some has-been ballplayer I hadn't seen in over thirty years. Of course, they had no way

136

of knowing any of that, but you asked how I felt, and that's how it was."

"This is fascinating, Miss Jacobs. I have never heard you speak of Harry in this way before, or to place your own self and existence ahead of his."

"Yes, but that was how I felt at the Reunion, which was in 1980. I hadn't seen Harry since 1949, and the circumstances of our last meeting were something that had been difficult for me to deal with. [Pause.] But I realize now that I had to have the experiences of that evening in order to get to the path I am on now."

"That sounds somewhat mystical, Miss Jacobs. Do you mean it that way?"

"Yes, I do, Dr. Levy. I wouldn't have understood that at the time of the Reunion, but I know it now."

"Explain, please."

"Part of it involved one of the most uncomfortable - no, that's too mild a word - unsettling, terrifying? I'm having trouble finding the word.

"Anyway, these people I hadn't seen in thirty years came rushing up to me, and were asking me all kinds of questions about Harry: was he still a carpenter, was he a coach or manager of some team somewhere, what became of his baby girl - of course I had shown them that photo—. And all I could do was try to explain that I hadn't seen him in a very long time."

"And what was so unsettling about those questions, please."

"It was merely annoying until someone, one of the gals, said to me that she wondered if Harry was even still alive, as he was older then we were. And then someone else asked how old he would be."

[Pause.]

"Dr. Levy - [Pause] - it is very difficult for me to describe how I felt when this woman asked if Harry was still alive. It was as if - and the only way I know how to say it is - as if someone plunged an icicle deep into my heart. A frozen dagger might be more accurate, but what I want to convey is the absolute icy cold stabbing pain in my heart."

"What did you do when you felt this pain?"

"I tried to respond to the question about how old he would be, but I remember feeling so panicky about this question of whether he was still alive, I couldn't calculate properly. ME - a CPA - and I couldn't perform a simple subtraction. I remembered he was born the same year as President Kennedy, and I tried to remember when that was, and I was fumbling with words, while trying to act logical about figuring how old Harry would be.

"I remember vaguely someone coming to my rescue and saying something like 'he's probably in his early 60s', and my feeling relieved by that response, and confirming that I thought that was about right.

"Anyway, they probably could sense how uneasy I was, and they started to change the subject, or - I remember now. I said something like I hadn't seen him for awhile, and I must remember to look him up and find out how he's doing - something like that. And so they dropped it, and either walked away, or stayed and talked to me about something else."

"And did you look him up then? Is that how you found out Harry had passed away?"

"No, Dr. Levy. I didn't look him up then. It wasn't until months later."

[Pause.]

"Dr. Levy, I see it's almost time for us to stop and I <u>REALLY</u> do not want to talk about this now. It is too painful. If I get started in the direction I see we're heading — how I found out about Harry's death, I know I won't be able to handle it in the short time we have left. Can we please put this off for another session? I'm almost finished telling you about my relationship with Harry when I was a teenager, and I can go on from there about how I found out. I didn't expect we would - I'm just not prepared to open it up now in the short -"

"I understand, Miss Jacobs, and it is not a problem. And in general, I would say it is better that, even if there were a vast amount of time available, someone not talk about an issue that would be disturbing for them until they are ready to face it."

"Thank you for understanding."

"Good night then, Miss Jacobs."

"Good night, Dr. Levy."

End of Tape 9.

Notes Accompanying Tape 9.

   Although I am somewhat displeased with
myself for some of my remarks to Miss Jacobs,
which I consider to be inappropriate, I still
consider this to be the most revealing session
I have had with her to date.

   She spoke more about her feelings than
before, and did much more than simply relate
what appeared to be an objective narrative
about someone other than herself. (Displace-
ment) She was lively and animated, and reached
into the heart of what has been effecting her.

   If she is <u>not</u> psychotic (as I have virtually
ruled out), nor even neurotic, then her
experiences and her objectivity in reviewing
and analyzing them, should be very helpful to
serious researchers of the paranormal. I
wonder if she would be amenable to submit to
such research, for example, what is going on
now at Duke, or if she would consent to
discuss her situation with members of the
Society for Psychical Research. She seems to
have done considerable research of her own in
this area, and by her frequent use of the word
"synchronicity," I am wondering what degree of
familiarity she has with the work of Jung, who
would, incidentally, find her a fascinating
patient, as do I.

   She has raised the question, which of
course, recurs after almost every session: are
these events which she relates the result of
an over-active imagination, or are they events
for which there are no known explanations at
this time. The majority of my colleagues, I am
afraid, would perhaps even consider her to be
psychotic, in view of what can easily be
described as her tendency toward "magical
thinking." Her narration is filled with

references to the casting of spells and curses, which she seems to accept now as fact. In addition, she is <u>absolutely convinced</u> that she was the <u>direct cause</u> of the injury to that unfortunate ballplayer. She also believes, without a doubt, that she is directly responsible, not only for Harry's exceptional victory, but also for the lack of effect of the forces of nature upon his performance!

However, despite what the majority of my colleagues might think (and I certainly know what that is, in view of their reaction to the radio program!), I see no other signs of psychosis in this woman, and this is now our 9th session.

I am concerned however, about her relationship with this man Harry, both then and now. The objectivity and rational analysis which she applies to almost every experience of her life, is completely abandoned whenever she talks about him and his abilities. To me, it seems she is exaggerating his intelligence and talents. But why would she do this? Is she blinded by love? Or is it more? Is it that she found him physically attractive, which was not enough to satisfy her expectations in a relationship, so she therefore ascribed to him attributes of intelligence and talent which he did not possess?

He is larger than life, like a God to her. He was good-looking, perhaps had certain abilities as an athlete, but to her he had this God-like power almost of life and death. Whether directly or indirectly through her, Harry caused serious injury to a teammate, and even caused her to become ill, in order to carry out his plans. Then she ascribes to him the ability to alter his patterns of speech, in order to deceive and mock members of the

Tape 9 (Notes)

Media. (Sometimes I wish I could do that myself!) If there is neurosis in Ms. Jacobs, it definitely can be found in her relationship with this man Harry. Even the thought of the possibility of his death caused her to experience what can only be termed a panic attack. This existence (or not) of neurosis will become clearer as I hear the details of her alleged post-mortem contacts with him. Perhaps I have been too impatient with her to get to that part of her life. I can hear, from the tape, the slight hint of power struggle between us as she continues to insist upon presenting her situation in chronological detail, so that, as she claims, I might understand the alleged paranormal activities better. She may be right, but I am not sure if she is postponing what may be too frightening or painful for her, or just being her logical self. Then too, am I annoyed because I am impatient to get to the "meat" of the matter, and am growing tired of hearing how magnificent this man Harry is? (perhaps even jealous, for not being the focus of her attention?)

In today's session, however, she did not stick to straight chronological order, which I, personally, view as a sign of improvement. She was less rigid and more flexible in her willingness to proceed to the heart of what is disturbing her. Although, perhaps the teenage experience was also disturbing, with this man having such complete control over her. I was surprised when she referred to him as a "bastard," thereby revealing inner moral conflict she has developed as an adult to what she perceives as their interference with the natural outcome of events, and the inflicting of harm upon others.

142

It was also VERY INTERESTING when she actually revealed annoyance with her peers for connecting her solely to Harry, without recognition of her own accomplishments. She actually referred to him, in her own words, as a "has-been ballplayer." She appeared to have broken his hold over her, that is until the suggestion was offered that he might be deceased. Then it seemed to start for her again. I am most interested to know what happened that resulted in Miss Jacobs not seeing Harry after 1949, and why she would have such a strong reaction, over 30 years later, to the possibility of his death.

There is the continued strong reaction she has almost every time she talks about him, which, if anything, has become exacerbated. Then there was that tearful outburst when she, herself, questioned why she reacts so emotionally to everything about this man. Perhaps that, too, will be revealed once she discusses the nature of these post-mortem contacts, which will be, in a way (at least I think so at this time), like discussing dreams with a patient.

It is obvious that the subject of Harry's death is very disturbing to her. It will be interesting to see what she will be able to discuss at our next session.

What is presented in the case of this patient is MUCH MORE than just neurotic ramblings. Are these events mere coincidences, or are they examples of verifiable synchronicities? (She claims to have witnesses to these events - certainly the incident of the injury at the ballgame was witnessed by Seymour. I am curious as to whether he will discuss this at one of his future sessions.) And her intimation that the events of her life

143

were happening for a purpose – as if there were some kind of "Divine Order." If this woman is to be believed, there may be deep metaphysical significance to these experiences. Her case would make a marvelous subject for a Treatise.

***

Tape 10

April 17, 1981

4:30 pm

"Good afternoon, Miss Jacobs."

"Dr. Levy.

"I think you'll be relieved to know that I think I can finish the story of my teenage years with Harry, including our last meeting, by the end of today's session, and then get to the experiences that made Seymour, most of my other friends — then eventually me, decide that I needed your help."

"Forgive me, Miss Jacobs, but before you provide the details of your experiences, can you summarize why Seymour and these other friends felt you needed the help of a psychiatrist, please."

"Seymour knew of my relationship with Harry, not just because of that one incident at Ebbett's Field, but because he knew about my feelings for Harry and the times I spent with him when we were kids. Of course, Seymour has been seeing you for his own problems of neurosis, and seems to think I have some sort of neurotic obsession with Harry, possibly because of the early loss of my parents, and he felt you could help me sort things out.

"As for the others, they were so used to seeing me as Miss Logic, that they were puzzled and I think also frightened by the changes I was undergoing because of these experiences involving Harry. I think they felt I might be losing my mind, or at the very least, having a nervous breakdown."

"What changes were you undergoing, Miss Jacobs, please."

"Well — I would talk to them about some of the synchronicities, or the sensing of Harry's presence - things like that — none of which was like anything they had heard before from the person they thought they knew. However, none of these people - - -. Seymour was the only one who knew what I was like when I knew Harry, so he didn't see these experiences as being that unusual for me. But the others actually believed, I think, based upon what I was telling them, that I was losing my mind. I mean, to them, normal sane CPAs don't go around talking to someone they sense is in a room, but can't be seen, especially if that person is deceased. So these friends felt I needed to see a psychiatrist before I had to be committed to an institution involuntarily. [Pause.] There were only two friends, women I've known since College, who accepted the changes I was experiencing for what they were."

"Let me ask you again Miss Jacobs: do you think you are losing your mind? Do you think you need to see a psychiatrist, or need to be committed to an institution for treatment of symptoms of mental disorders?"

"No, I don't think I need to be committed to an institution — but I did not think I needed to see a psychiatrist either until the experience that made me call you so early in the morning."

"And how do you feel about it now?"

"I need answers. I have studied metaphysical literature and read books about psychic phenomena, and have even been to a few Psychics. But after that one incident, plus some almost as disturbing, I felt reading what others had written would not provide answers to the specific problems I was facing. I knew

146

I needed to talk to someone with knowledge of mental disorders, because if I was deluding myself about what was happening to me, I should find out what was <u>really</u> going on in order to do something about it. Also, as I believe I told you before, these experiences were consuming my life, they were <u>all</u> I could think about, and when it got to the point that they were beginning to interfere with my ability to concentrate at work, then I KNEW I needed professional guidance. That one experience became the precipitating factor that compelled me to act upon something I had been considering for some time.

"Does what I said answer your question, Dr. Levy?"

"Yes, thank you. [Pause.] Now continue, please, with your meetings with Harry. You had been talking about his No-hit ballgame, and how excited you were, because you felt you contributed to his victory. What year was this again, please."

"It was 1948. And it wasn't just that I felt I had contributed to his victory that I was so excited - it was mainly because I knew how proud and happy he would be, and all I really wanted out of life was for him to be happy."

"And you mentioned how you went to school the next day and talked to all your friends about it. But you did not say anything about your own role in his victory, is that correct?"

"Yes. Of course. I would never have mentioned anything at all like that to them. It would have seemed way too strange. Perhaps not as much then as now though, because the kids who knew me at school were aware that I had a rather vivid imagination."

"And what was their reaction, please."

"Well, of course, whenever there is a No-hitter, baseball fans always talk about it, but this was something even more special, because I was someone who actually knew the pitcher who had done it. So everyone who knew me and my association with Harry, was very excited, and kids who didn't know me, but were told about my friendship with Harry came over to talk to me. It was all very exciting."

"And what was Harry's reaction the next time you saw each other? How much time was there before you met again?"

"You know, I really can't remember, because it seemed like an eternity. But when we did see each other after a game at the Polo Grounds the next time the Cardinals were in New York, we were both very excited and happy. I remember wanting so badly to hug him, but I was too afraid. I thought I would seem like a silly kid to him, and also my Aunt's words about fooling around with a married man were somewhere in my mind, and they also held me back. Now I would give anything, ANYTHING, to be able to give him that hug, hold him tight and tell him how happy and proud I was for him."

[Pause, and sound of tissues being pulled from box.]

"This time, I seem to remember that we spent the entire time talking aloud, talking about the No-hitter, and specific details of the game. [Pause.] You know, now that I think of it, I don't remember once him asking me if I had heard the game. [Silence.] I see now. It was as if he already knew I had, even though I would ordinarily have been in school that day, so he had no need to ask if I actually heard the game. [Pause.] Very interesting."

[Pause.]

"After that day, things returned to normal, if you can consider anything between Harry and me as being normal. For the rest of 1948, I saw him after each of the Cardinal/Giant games at the Polo Grounds. Oh, I DO remember something else a little unusual."

"What was that, Miss Jacobs, please."

"It was rather strange, and I'm not sure why I did it. But there was this bizarre ballgame that Harry was the pitcher in. The Cardinals won by one of the largest scores ever in baseball history at the time, I think the final score was something like 25 to 2, if you can believe that. Harry got a homerun, and a triple, and made one of the most outstanding fielding plays that earned yells from even the Giant fans. It was a crazy game.

"And after it was over, of course I waited for Harry to leave the Clubhouse, but this time he was surrounded by all the famous ones again. The players were really excited and boisterous, and once again, Harry was the center of attention as they listened intently to whatever he was saying. He really was quite a story-teller."

[Pause.]

"I know I mentioned that several times now, I think, about how Harry was such an effective story-teller. Well, I came across a poem that describes exactly the kind of ability Harry had. May I read it to you please, Dr. Levy? It's very short, I promise, and I'll even skip some of it. I made a copy so you could read it in its entirety later if you want, because it sums up Harry's talent far better than I can."

"Proceed, Miss Jacobs, please."

"It goes like this: 'There are two kinds of human beings in the world... firstly, those who even though they were to reveal the secret

149

of the universe... would fail to impress you with any sense of the importance of the news; and secondly, those who could communicate... that they had just purchased ten cents worth of paper napkins and make you thrill and vibrate with the intelligence.' [Words emphasized with emotion; then pause.] Harry was that second kind of story teller - he could thrill and involve you in every element of what he was saying. [Pause.] Here, Dr. Levy. I made this copy for you."

[Pause.]

"Anyway, I watched as Harry and the other ballplayers walked by. I don't think Harry even saw me, and I know he didn't send me any messages. Also, what was different this time was that there were a whole bunch of other kids outside waiting for the players. I don't know where they came from, as it was a school day, but there they were, all boys of course, waiting for the players to come out. And when they saw the famous ones, they ran up and got their autographs. But no one bothered to ask Harry for his. I think they probably had no idea who he was. He was never really famous; the appreciation of his unique style was mostly from adults who enjoyed the chess-type aspect of the game.

"When I saw that, I felt sad, although I really had no reason to believe Harry noticed or even cared, and I did something crazy. I ran up to him, the way the boys had run up to the other players, and asked for his autograph - and his only. I think I wanted the other players to see that someone would want Harry's autograph also. My actions surprised Harry, and I'll always remember the look on his face when I gave him my scorecard to sign."

"Can you describe this expression, please."

"It's a little difficult, although I can still see it so clearly in my mind. It was such a different look, almost one of - and I know this sounds strange, but almost one of sadness."

"Why do you think he would have had a sad expression on his face?"

"I don't know. Maybe sadness isn't the right word to use. But it was a special look, maybe wistful - I really don't know how to convey it to someone else, even though I can still see it so clearly."

"Continue, please."

"Anyway, we all rode down on the subway together. And by 'we', I mean the boys and I and the ballplayers. Although I was having an excited conversation with the boys - they were about my age or so - all the time I was looking at Harry, who was having his own excited conversation with the other ballplayers, who were still focused solely upon him and whatever it was he was telling them."

"Did you exchange telepathic communications?"

"No. And I wondered about that also."

"Did you see him again, after that?"

"Oh yes. There were a few more games before the season ended when I had a chance to visit with him. These were routine, once again. We took our usual ride to the Stadium, walked to the 'soda joint', as he called it, had our drinks, and went back to our respective homes. We communicated both orally and telepathically.

"And I have another vivid memory of him. Once when we were on the elevated station, waiting for the train to arrive, he got on one of those huge scales, you know, the kind -

<u>really</u> huge — where you put a nickel or a penny in, I forget which, and you weigh yourself. I remember, partly because of the wild combination of clothing colors and patterns he was wearing, but also because of the way he smiled at me and handed me a coin for me to get on and weigh myself. But I had seen his weight on the scale - 155 pounds, and I <u>knew</u> I weighed more than he did at the time, and I was too embarrassed to have him see that, so I refused his offer of the coin and the chance to weigh myself.

"It's little things like that. Isn't it funny? You spend time with a person and years later it's the little, tiny inconsequential things that stand out more than anything: the broad smile, the crooked grin, the wink, the way he rocked back and forth on his heels, that beautiful fast joyful walk - [Pause.] Even the way he lit a cigarette, or had it dangling from the corner of his lips as he talked - I thought it looked so sexy; and now I hate myself when I think of that, because it was what ultimately caused his death."

[Lengthy silence.]

"Anyway, [Sounds of sniffling.] the season came to an end, and I didn't see him again until 1949."

"And that was the last year you saw him."

"Yes. That's correct."

"And if I remember, that is also the last year in which you attended a baseball game, is that correct?"

"Yes, it is."

"And how did you spend the time between the end of the 1948 season and when you saw this man Harry again in 1949? Were your emotions the same as at the end of the 1947 season?"

"It's strange that you should ask, because my emotions were definitely <u>not</u> the same. Funny. [Pause.] Harry and I had talked about school and about my lack of dates and not having any boys paying attention to me, and he had told me to be patient, that sooner or later the boys would wise up to what I was really about and I'd have no trouble after that. And he told me about how he met his wife and how they had been childhood sweethearts and had gone together all through high school.

"Then that Fall, after the baseball season ended, things began to change for me. I got a little part-time job, and was finally able to buy some clothes that actually fit. I still was overweight, but I had lost a bunch of what I call 'baby fat'. My hair was still in braids, but somehow I felt differently about myself. A lot of changes took place in my life. Suddenly boys were flocking all over me, including the most sought after boys in the school. My grades skyrocketed and even the teachers began to notice me. I seemed to have gained a sense of self-confidence I never had before. As I say this to you, I wonder if Harry had something to do with it - you know, like remote control, almost in the same way I worked on his pitching that No-hit ballgame."

"Are you saying that he may have cast some kind of spell or performed something similar to alter the course of your life?"

"Well, I hadn't thought of it before in that way, but now I'm beginning to wonder. I would never have thought of it before because - well for two reasons: one, is that I had made my mind accept only logic and that idea would have seemed too preposterous, until now, that is; and two, I <u>never ever</u> felt that I had any meaning in Harry's life. I always thought in terms of what <u>he</u> meant to me. The possibility never dawned on me that I could have had <u>any</u> effect or meaning in his life whatsoever. In fact, I believed, until recently, that he never even once gave a thought to me after he returned to his home in Missouri."

"What do you mean by 'recently', please."

"Well, when Harry began to contact me after his death, one of the very first things he did was to let me know, not only how much I loved him, but how much he cared about me, as well."

"And how did he do that, please."

"Dr. Levy, I'd like to tell you about our final meeting first, if you don't mind, as it will help you appreciate what Harry wanted me to understand about the nature of our relationship, what <u>really</u> was going on."

"Yes, Miss Jacobs, all right. Please continue."

"I'll always remember how we met that last year – 1949 – after the first game the Cardinals played against the Giants at the Polo Grounds. He was the same Harry, dressed in the same weird combinations of colors and patterns, with those same old darn tan shoes of his; but I must have appeared different to him, because he stopped and looked at me intently, and also – well, differently. I suppose to him, I must <u>not</u> have looked the same. I still had the same braids, but I had lost weight, and I had clothes that fit properly for a change. I was dressed more like a regular girl my age, for the first time since he had known me. I realize that now, but I didn't then, I'm sure.

"When he saw me and stopped like that, I stopped also, although what I really wanted to do, of course, was run straight to him. And he said, out loud, he actually spoke my real name

- I remember being surprised that he still knew it - he said, 'Sophie?' - only it was more like a question than anything else. And I was kinda taken aback, because he had always called me by his special name for me: 'Sandy'.

"So I yelled back, 'Sophie? What do you mean, 'Sophie'? It's Sandy, remember?' And I waved my two thick red braids up in the air to emphasize the point."

"What was his reaction, please."

"Well, he just kinda stood there. He kept looking at me in this strange way, then smiled that big warm wonderful smile of his that could light up a room, and stepped up close to me, tugged at my braids, and said in that slow country drawl he could put on when he wanted to, something like: 'Well, I guess it is my Miss Sandy after all' - then, back to his regular voice: 'C'mon, race you to the train platform.' And off we went, running up the stairs to the elevated station, as usual."

[Pause.]

"You know Dr. Levy, now that I think of it, in those last few days we were together, not once did he ever communicate with me telepathically. Not once."

[Silence.]

"And why do you think that was Miss Jacobs, please."

"I don't know. [Pause.] I really don't know. [Pause.] Could it have been because he didn't want me to know what he was thinking and so did not want to open up that means of communication at all? Honestly, Dr. Levy, I really don't know."

[Pause.]

"Were there any other differences in this first meeting of 1949, please."

"Well, we were more silent, for one thing. We stood by the Stadium, which I remember that day seemed more desolate than ever. I don't think we said much, and then we walked on to the candy store and had our drinks. This time, it seemed to me that we talked more about baseball, and less about life in general. Then went back to our homes, as usual.

"There were two more games, as I remember. Harry pitched one of them, and won easily, nothing spectacular, but still a solid victory. After that game, he was with some of his teammates, and so I didn't get to go with him to the Bronx.

"Then came the last day we were together. It started off as usual. We met after the game, but instead of going up the stairs to the train station, he said something about why not have coffee and a soda at his hotel, where they had a snack place as well as a restaurant. Well, I was real excited about that. I had never been inside a hotel before, and to go inside the very hotel where the Cardinals stayed, that was really something for me. So I went with him to his hotel. I remember that we talked very little on the subway going down there, and as I said before, there was no mind communication going on."

"What happened when you got to his hotel, please."

"Actually, I had been to that hotel before. I never went inside, but I had gone to it and stood outside a few times, just to see what it was like and with the hope I might get a chance to see - well, first it was Howie Pollette, then Harry.

"This time I went inside with Harry, but we didn't go to the Coffee Shop. He plopped down on one of the big sofas in the lobby, and

motioned for me to sit next to him. I did, but
he seemed somewhat different to me, I
remember. He talked small talk, nothing at all
in particular, that I can think of - unless,
of course, I'm blocking it out. But I don't
think so. Also, he was nervous, fidgety. He
always was like a wound-up spring, coiled for
action. When we would stand on the elevated
station platform, and I would watch him out of
the corner of my eye, he would be rocking back
and forth on his heels, and I always felt he
was a tightly wrapped package covering a
coiled-up spring."

"That's a rather strange and strong analogy,
Miss Jacobs. Could you elaborate a little
more, please."

"I don't know if I can, Dr. Levy. It was
that he was probably the most <u>intense</u> human
being I have ever known. There was so much
depth to him, so much inside. Later, when I
learned what happened to him in the War, I
understood so much better. But back then, of
course, I had no way of knowing. And that day,
in the late afternoon, as we sat on the couch
in the lobby of his hotel, he seemed even more
intense than ever. He was silent for awhile,
then lit a cigarette."

"What did you do in reaction to this
behavior of his, Miss Jacobs, please."

"I didn't really know what to do because I
didn't understand it. [Pause.] I began to feel
rather strange being in the hotel lobby. I was
probably the only teenager. I watched some of
the Cardinals pass by; some of them waved or
winked at Harry, and he just kinda grinned,
and nodded back. My Aunt and I had had some
fierce arguments about my seeing Harry, so
much so to the point that I had to make up
stories about where I had been rather than

telling her I had been with Harry. I knew she was exaggerating her worries, and that she didn't understand the time I spent with Harry was totally innocent, and that ballplayers were not all wild guys who got drunk, gambled, and fooled around with so-called loose women. But I did feel a little uneasy, because this was so different from what we normally did after a game."

[Silence.]

"Then what happened, Miss Jacobs, please."

"He took a few drags of the cigarette, then stood up. He looked at me; it was such a different look this time, almost sad, really. He was quiet for awhile, then held out his hand to me. I'll never forget that moment, what happened next. He said, 'C'mon Sandy. Let's go. I'll get a cab and send you home. C'mon, I'll walk you'.

"I took his hand and got up from the sofa. We walked out of the hotel in silence, holding hands. I remember the contrast of the busy street, so noisy and busy, while we were so quiet. Harry hailed a cab, and when it pulled up, he opened the door for me. I remember how serious he looked, the cigarette dangling from his lips. He took it out of his mouth, threw it to the ground, stepped on it, as he told me to give the driver my address. I did, and Harry made arrangements with the man for the fare and the tip and gave him some money. I hadn't gotten into the cab yet, but was about to, when Harry pulled on my braids, turned my face to his and kissed me gently on the lips. And then he said, [Voice breaking up, difficulty speaking while sobbing.] 'Goodbye, Sophie.'"

[Lengthy silence, interrupted by weeping.]

"'Goodbye, Sophie.' He never said 'goodbye' to me before. It was always something like: 'Solong, Sandy' — 'Be seeing you' — 'See ya next time' - something like that. Never 'Goodbye'. [Pause.] And calling me 'Sophie'. I had always been 'Sandy' to him, never Sophie until this season. I didn't understand what was happening, but I could tell it was serious from the expression on his face and the look in his eyes."

[Pause.]

"And that kiss. That sweet, gentle kiss. It was so soft, so tender, so sweet."

[Pause.]

"And then I got into the cab, and he closed the door, looking at me so intently. And as the cab drove away, I turned to watch until I couldn't see him anymore. He was headed in the direction of his hotel, his hands thrust deep into the pockets of his pants, and for the first time, the bounce was gone from his tan shoes. I never saw him again — I never saw him again."

[Lengthy silence, interrupted by sounds of weeping; then voice resumes filled with emotion.]

"I keep thinking: 'Touch her soft lips and part'."

"Henry the Fifth."

"Actually, Dr. Levy, I was thinking of the very lyrical music of Sir William Walton. [Pause.] But in the long run I suppose it's the same, isn't it?"

"Here, Miss Jacobs, please help yourself to these tissues. And why don't we close this session now, it's almost time anyway; in fact, we are actually quite a bit over. Please take your time in the reception area, if you wish, and use the facilities if you want to freshen up. I will see you at the usual time next week, unless you want an earlier appointment. Also, as you know, if you are seriously troubled and need to talk immediately, you can reach me at my private number."

"Thank you, Dr. Levy."

"Yes. Goodnight, Miss Jacobs."

End of Tape 10.

Notes Accompanying Tape 10.

As Miss Jacobs left the office, I could see she was still quite upset about the subject matter discussed during our session; particularly her last meeting with this man Harry. I had gone home for the day, but after supper, something unknown inside me, a gnawing feeling, came over me to return to the office and listen to the tape of her session and make my notations and evaluation.

I was in the process of doing this when the telephone rang. Instinctively, I answered it, and it was Miss Jacobs. Her voice was frantic. She was calling from a telephone booth, and it sounded as if she said she was on the corner of 45th Street and 9th Avenue. Although she disclaimed any suicidal feelings, she related, hysterically, that she had just intentionally walked in front of a large delivery truck, not caring whether she lived or died. I ordered her to find a taxi immediately and come to the office. Fortunately she agreed to do so.

I could not in good conscience tell this woman, in such obvious distress, to come and see me in the office tomorrow to discuss her problems. Only God knows what she might do to herself if left alone all night without talking about whatever it was that made her so distraught that she was oblivious to the danger in which she placed herself. If she does as promised (which I certainly hope), given the distance from the office, she should be arriving fairly soon. In the meantime, I will continue reviewing the tape of today's session, but I think I will not make any separate notes, but will wait until tonight's session (assuming there is one) is completed, and make notes from the two tapes, which most surely will have overlapping subject matter.

It is possible that the memory of her last meeting with this man Harry was much more painful to her than I realized, and we will have to delve into it more deeply.

It is also possible that if I feel she <u>is actually suicidal</u>, I may have her hospitalized for observation.

(What puzzles me is WHY, after hours, she would call me at the Office telephone number. Why would she not call me at home on my private line, where patients know to call me in an emergency after the Office is closed. She has done so in the past. Why would she, on this night when I felt drawn to go to the office for reasons I do not comprehend - why on <u>this</u> night would she call me at the Office when normally no one would answer the telephone.

I find I must acknowledge that the paranormal implications of this example of synchronicity are <u>more</u> than somewhat disturbing!)[1]

* * *

---

[1] The drawn line, intervening space, and parenthetical sentences have been retained from the original handwritten notes.

162

takes talent[2]

there are two
kinds of human
beings in the world
so my observation
has told me
namely and to wit
as follows
firstly
those who
even though they
were to reveal
the secret of the universe
to you would fail
to impress you
with any sense
of the importance
of the news
and secondly
those who could
communicate to you
that they had
just purchased
ten cents worth
of paper napkins
and make you
thrill and vibrate
with the intelligence
                    archy

from **archy does his part**; <u>**the lives and times of archy and mehitabel**</u>; Don Marquis; Doubleday, Doran and Company, Inc.; New York, 1940.

---

[2] A copy of this poem was fastened by paper clip to Dr. Levy's Notes. Obviously, this is the poem from which Ms. Jacobs read portions during her Session. The lower case used for both the poem and the title of the book from which it was excerpted is as appears in the original.

Tape 11

April 17, 1981

9:10 pm

"Miss Jacobs, please come in."

"This is very kind of you, Dr. Levy, to offer to see me at this late hour. I hate to have you do this. I know I'm taking you away from time with your family."

"Do not worry yourself about that, Miss Jacobs. It is thoughtful of you to be concerned, but by now, with my profession, my family is used to situations which arise unexpectedly. Besides, my wife is a physician and my son is a psychologist, and he has his own practise and his own family now. And my little granddaughter, already she is talking about wanting to be a doctor when she grows up."

"You sound very proud of them, Dr. Levy."

"Oh, indeed I am.[1] But I did not tell you to come here tonight to talk about my family, Miss Jacobs. Here, let me take your jacket.

"Please sit down Miss Jacobs. I can prepare some tea for us, if you would like, and you can tell me what happened after you left my office this afternoon."

"Thank you, Dr. Levy. Yes, I would like some tea. I need something to calm my nerves."

[Recording machine paused; presumably while Dr. Levy prepared tea for himself and Miss Jacobs.]

"Thank you so much, Dr. Levy, this is really very soothing."

---

[1] This comment was remarkable, considering the emotional detachment Dr. Levy normally exhibited towards members of his immediate family.

"You are welcome, Miss Jacobs. Now tell me please, what happened after you left here this afternoon."

[Pause.]

"I was really upset when I left. Remembering so many things about Harry, especially our last meeting, was very emotional. [Pause.] I walked around for the longest while. It was aimless walking. I had no idea where my feet were taking me, and I'm not even sure how much time passed. I just kept walking, mostly with my head down, crying. Every once in a while I would stop to wipe tears away, or blow my nose, but I never really paid attention to where I was. I needed to walk to clear my head – yet all I could think of were the things that had gone on and are <u>still</u> going on with Harry in my life.

"The strange thing was that one of those times I stopped, I looked up to see where I was and found I was directly across the street from the hotel that the Cardinals stayed in when Harry was on the team. I'm sure they no longer stay there now, as the hotel and the area around it has become quite seedy and run down."

"Where was this please, Miss Jacobs, do you remember?"

"Yes. By 42nd Street and 9th Avenue."

"Excuse me, continue, please."

"Yes. [Pause.] I saw the hotel, it was almost eerie, how different it was from the way I remembered it from the late '40s. Anyway, for reasons I <u>do not</u> understand, I found myself walking into the hotel lobby and up to the Registration desk. I stood there. The man behind the counter paid absolutely <u>no</u> attention to me.

"I looked around the lobby. It was rundown and shabby. I felt so strange, being there. I saw the sofa. I recognized it. It had patches of tape on it, and its colors were faded and pathetic — that very same sofa where Harry and I sat the last time I ever saw him.

"And from then on, my behavior became very weird and foreign to me."

"Explain, please, Miss Jacobs."

"That's really difficult to do, Dr. Levy. It was as if I were a spectator to what I was doing and saying. I knew what was happening, but it was as if I were watching it happen from somewhere else.

"I turned to the man behind the counter and told him I used to stay in this hotel in the '40s. I asked him all kinds of questions about what had happened to the hotel in the interim and what was going on with it now. The man had worked there for quite some time and brought me up to date with information about the hotel. Mostly transients and Welfare recipients were staying there now, but a Japanese or Middle Eastern corporation - he wasn't sure which — recently purchased it with the idea of renovating it, and perhaps restoring it to its former glory.

"Then I said the strangest thing to him, and I wondered at my own words as they came out of my mouth. I told him that I had spent some of the happiest days of my life in this hotel in the '40s, and he responded that he could believe it. Then he told me that this new corporation was slowly renovating the old rooms. He wished he could show me the room I had previously occupied, but he couldn't under the circumstances, and I replied that I understood and thanked him for his time. All this was <u>so</u> bizarre to me, Dr. Levy, believe me."

"Yes, Miss Jacobs. Continue, please."

"I felt very depressed, and I walked out onto the street. Then I realized this was the very same street that Harry and I walked on while he called the cab for me that last time we saw each other. Suddenly, it was as if all Time froze, and I could see the young girl Sandy getting into the cab, and the young man pulling on her braids, turning her face to his, kissing her gently on the lips."

[Silence; then voice resumed with thinly veiled, but controlled emotions.]

"I started to cry. Tears were streaming down my face and I began walking again. I got as far as across the street and down to the corner. I turned around, like Lot's wife, to take one more look at the faded hotel. Then I looked in the direction I was going, I think I had it in my mind to walk home, you know I live on 54th Street, and saw that the light had just turned red. I waited for the light to change, and after a few moments, somehow, and I'm not sure what made me aware of it, but somehow I noticed that I was standing with my hands deep into the pockets of my skirt, rocking back and forth on the heels of my walking shoes.

"That's when I snapped. I literally snapped. I really thought I had lost my mind, that I was completely and totally insane. And I thought of a *Dybbuk*,[2] and I wondered if that was what was happening to me. What other explanation could there be? The whole thing became too much for me - WAY too much for me, and at that point I didn't care whether I

---

[2] In Jewish folklore, a *Dybbuk* is the soul of a dead person, which enters and takes control of the body of a living person.

167

lived or died. So I crossed the street against the light. I saw this big truck barreling down on me. I was right in his path but I didn't give a damn. I'm sorry -—"

"Please, Miss Jacobs, continue. Please."

"I just couldn't take it anymore. You don't know what it's been like. [Voice tone rising, almost to point of hysteria.] All of this — so bizarre, so overpowering - - nothing like the careful calm ordered life I've lived from 1950 on - - there was no way my mind could handle anything else. I really didn't care whether I lived or died, so when I saw that truck barreling down on me, my thought was 'Que sera, sera' — whatever will be, will be. But the truck swerved and missed me and I just kept on walking and was oblivious to all the things the driver was screaming at me as he sped past.

"I kept on walking a block or so more, and that's when I knew I had to call you, because I honestly didn't trust myself anymore. I had no confidence in my own behavior. After all, what I had just said and done was nothing that belonged to me. I certainly never spent happy days in that hotel - why should I say such a thing to the man behind the counter. My only memory of being in that hotel was a tragic one, one of the saddest days in my entire life, certainly not a 'happy' time.

"And then, to rock back and forth on my heels with my hands deep into the pockets of my skirt - NEVER in my life, I can assure you, Dr. Levy, have I done anything like that."

"What are you trying to tell me, Miss Jacobs? That Harry has taken possession of your soul, or your body? Is that what you meant when you used the term 'Dybbuk'?"

"Honestly, Dr. Levy, I don't know what I mean anymore. All this is far beyond anything I've ever dealt with. I'm not sure which is more bizarre - this or the bedroom light incident that I called you about at two in the morning."

[Silence.]

"Miss Jacobs, when you said - I think your words were 'all Time froze,' - or something similar —what did you mean by that?"

"It's hard to explain. Very hard. You would have had to experience something like that in order to understand."

"Try, Miss Jacobs, please."

"It was as if everything around me went from normal speed to slow motion, and then the rest of life, what was happening in the present, became a faded backdrop. I KNOW, I AM aware, that I was not seeing flesh and blood people, but it was as if a movie machine had projected the images of 1949, in black and white, of the young girl getting into the cab.

"I saw the taxi pull up, I saw him, Harry I mean, putting out the cigarette, and I felt inside what I felt then, so young, so frightened and confused. I was a bystander, almost like someone in a theater watching a movie, as I saw the images of the girl and then the young man pulling on her braids and turning her face to his. [Pause.] And then the kiss."

[Sounds of sobbing.]

"Miss Jacobs, is it possible that the reason you walked in front of the truck was that you were very upset remembering your last meeting with Harry?"

"OF COURSE I was upset at the memory of the last time I saw Harry." [Tone of voice bordering on anger and/or hysteria.] "But that was NOT the reason for my not caring whether I lived or died. What can I do to get you to understand? There I was, I had just left this hotel where I had said strange things, things that had NO reference whatsoever to MY life, and then I find myself standing on a street corner with my hands thrust deep into my pockets and rocking back and forth on the heels of my flats —. WHAT DO YOU think? I mean, WHAT WOULD YOU have thought if that had just happened to you?"

"I would have been distressed, I am sure, but I do not believe I would have deliberately walked in front of a fast moving truck."

"Yes, but that's easy for you to say because you haven't had so many other weird things happen to you for almost a year."

[Extended silence.]

"How do you feel now, Miss Jacobs, please."

"I don't feel like committing suicide, if that's what you mean." [Tone approximating contempt.]

"That indeed was one of my major concerns, and I am relieved that you do not contemplate that as a solution to your disturbing experiences."

"I told you that from the beginning, Dr. Levy, from my very first 'phone call. I told you that sometimes I don't care whether I live or die, but that I've never considered suicide as an option. [Pause.] I suppose I am too curious to find out what all this means, and I can't do that if I'm dead. [Pause.] Although – [Pause.] – perhaps that might be one way.... [Voice drifting.] Oh don't worry, Dr. Levy, really. I have NO intention of taking my life."

"Then explain what you mean by not caring whether you live or die, and why you intentionally walked in the path of an oncoming truck."

[Silence, then words spoken with careful deliberation.]

"At the time it happened, my thought was not of ending my life, but of not caring. Right then, it made no difference to me whether I was alive or dead. It was like a crapshoot - I told you: 'Que sera, sera.'"

[Silence.]

"Do you feel this way because Harry is dead? Do you think you might be able to be united with him if you were no longer alive?"

[Pause.]

"I'm not sure. Perhaps."

[Pause.]

"Miss Jacobs, it is quite obvious that we have much to discuss in future sessions. I realize it is important to you to proceed in a particular order, and I have respected your judgment, but I hope it will not be too much longer before we reach this material that you have been telling me is so bizarre."

"Do you think I have been deliberately avoiding discussing this material?"

"I'm not sure. Have you? Have you considered that as a possibility?"

[Pause.]

"Perhaps. But if so, it no longer matters, because I believe that I will be able to finish the background material by the next session."

"You have told me about your last meeting with Harry. What else remains before we can discuss these experiences?"

"How I learned of Harry's death, and how, after more than thirty years, Harry reentered my life and the experiences began."

[Silence.]

"How are you feeling now, Miss Jacobs, please."

"I told you. I'm fine."

"Do you think you can return home and be all right?"

"I told you. I don't contemplate harming myself."

"Would you like me to write a prescription for some medication to help calm you or to help you sleep tonight? I would write a temporary dosage only — something to assist you if you feel you need it for tonight."

"No. I want to have a clear head to be able to think about all of this. If I don't sleep, well, that's not unusual since these events began."

"It is late, and if you feel that you will be all right alone — you do live alone, is that correct?"

"Yes, I do. But I will be all right, Dr. Levy, believe me. I am not trying to deceive you. I called you from Ninth Avenue because I was so unnerved at what I had almost done to myself. But I'm OK now, honest. And despite how I may have acted tonight, I am glad that I was able to come here and talk to you. I KNOW we have a lot to discuss. And perhaps you are right. Possibly I have been postponing the inevitable, but we're almost there, I promise."

"I appreciate that, Miss Jacobs. And you have convinced me that you will be all right by yourself tonight. But if you are not, or if you want to see me before your regularly scheduled session, please DO call me. Also, let me arrange a taxi for you now, if you will allow me please."

"Yes, all right, thank you, Dr. Levy."

End of Tape 11.

Notes Accompanying Tape 11.

What is there about this woman???[3] Is she a seductive manipulator, in addition to having an intense need of being in control? Does her need for control extend to controlling others?

When she called from 9th Avenue, she was hysterical; yet when she arrived at the office door, she was calm and acted as if she had merely dropped by for a social visit. Obviously, she had time, while in the taxi, to arrange her appearance (apply make-up, straighten her hair and clothing, or whatever else she needed to do to make herself presentable) and also arrange her thoughts, so that she could be in control once again. If only I could get to her during her moments of hysteria, before she has a chance to hide its effects upon her psyche. Unfortunately, I missed the one opportunity I <u>did</u> have. If I had only known, when she called that first morning after 2am, that it would be <u>this</u> difficult to break through her resistance, I would have listened to her right then. But how was I to know?

She may not be beautiful by Anglo-American standards, but she is every bit a seductress of the mind. More than once now, she has managed to divert my attention from my primary duty as Therapist. When she arrived, looking as if she was keeping a social engagement, I fell into her trap and reacted accordingly, talking about the family and sharing tea with her. <u>NEVER</u>, in all my years of practise, have I done anything like this before.

(But perhaps I am being too hard on myself. Perhaps I instinctively discerned her state-

---

[3] The three question marks appear in the original text of Dr. Levy's handwritten notes.

of-mind, her <u>real</u> state-of-mind behind the facade, and wanted to calm her with talk of family in a social setting with tea.)

It is odd, but she spoke about seeing this vision of herself as a teenager with Harry as if she were watching a film being projected. That is <u>exactly</u> the way she narrated what happened to her tonight – as if she were telling the plot of a film or play she had just seen. I have noted this elsewhere, this tendency to mask her problems by organizing them into a sequential narrative that would seem to be a study of a character – someone other than herself.

Fortunately, I was able to regain my professional distance and point out things to her that she needed to confront.

Now I should return to my analysis of the tape of our earlier meeting of this day, which I was listening to at the time I received her telephone call.

It is obvious that reliving the memories of her last meeting with this man Harry had a devastating effect upon Miss Jacobs. I am not convinced, as she apparently is, that her mere identifying with his nervous habits was enough to compel her to walk in front of an oncoming truck. It is almost as if she <u>wants</u> to believe that she has been possessed by him— that her body has been taken over by Harry as a "Dybbuk" — could this be a sublimated sexual reference? (This is something that might be of interest to Singer[4]. I should perhaps discuss this with him, without disclosing identities, of course.)

---

[4] Isaac Bashevis Singer (1904-1991), a noted Jewish writer in the Yiddish language, a Nobel Laureate, and close friend of Dr. Levy. Singer was known for his interest in Jewish mysticism.

Perhaps her disregard for her personal safety (it is interesting that she continues to deny any suicidal intent) – is a result of many factors: such as guilt over what she feels is her responsibility for the injury to that other ballplayer; inability to deal with her grief over the death of this man Harry, and <u>particularly</u> her failure to come to terms with losing his "friendship" when she was such a young girl.

Despite my initial characterization of this man Harry as another "Liliom", I must acknowledge that it took a sense of decency and moral fibre on his part to resist the temptation to take advantage of her sexually – which was surely his intent when he took her to his hotel. He probably was well aware of how she worshipped him — she would have done anything he asked, including, most likely, any sexual activity.

But to her, as a girl of 14 or 15, his behavior must have seemed like an ultimate rejection. Not only had she lost her parents, not only was she treated as Cinderella in the home of relatives, but now she had lost her Prince Charming — the <u>only</u> adult who ever paid any attention to her and provided her with any affection. And at her age, how could she have understood that his motives, rather than cruel, were in reality, noble and a sign of <u>true</u> caring for her best interest. This was probably the reason for her hostile reaction when her classmates remembered her association with Harry before they knew her own identity. She still harbored feelings of anger and resentment because of what she believed to be his rejection of her.

However, as an adult, after learning of his death, she obviously re-evaluated their relationship and understood the motives behind his actions the final night they were together. That would be further cause for grief. Not only was he no longer alive, but all those years she had misunderstood his motivation and judged him harshly, when in fact, she should have appreciated his noble act of sacrificing their friendship for the sake of her well-being. This re-evaluation would be cause for guilt as well as grief.

Then there is the larger issue, which I have touched on briefly in many previous Notes, of whether her behavior and experiences indicate advanced neurosis or psychosis. Although I have avoided going into these lengths of detail before, it appears inevitable that such an analysis must be made.

1. Her intellect does not seem impaired, nor does she exhibit signs of disorientation. Her ideas and explanations may be unorthodox, however, she is oriented as to time and place, despite the fact she claims to have had experiences involving current contacts with past events in different locations.

2. She has not exhibited signs of confusion and disorganization which have interfered with her skills of communication. On the contrary, she <u>insists</u> on maintaining sequential order of the events she relates during her sessions. If anything, this would reveal an obsessive-compulsive neurotic tendency.

3. She has had a history of difficult interpersonal relationships in childhood; however, these tragic early events have neither prevented her from obtaining nor maintaining a successful career. Indeed, they may have provided the motivating

force behind her achievements. She appears to be capable of sustaining friendships and has been married, which at least provides a surface indication of normal social and sexual relationships.

4. There have been no indications of a perception of the World and its inhabitants as hostile, nor have there been indications of delusions of persecution. Indeed, she has exhibited sufficient trust to discuss her experiences not only with friends, but to seek my assistance in determining the status of her mental condition.

5. There have been episodes of what can be categorized as auditory and visual hallucinations, depending on how her contacts with the deceased, Harry, are analyzed. However, she herself has acknowledged the possibility of these classifications and has indicated an ability to accept medical intervention, if necessary.

6. There have been episodes which can be described as harmful to self, such as deliberately walking in the path of the oncoming truck. In addition, she has alluded to other occasions when she has not cared whether she lived or died. In some ways, there has been an indication that Death has an attraction as a means of reuniting with the deceased, Harry. However, she is aware of these self-destructive tendencies and is cooperative in discussing them and their implications, and has shown willingness to accept precautionary measures.

7. Lastly, she appears to be cooperative, although perhaps manipulative (a device

she may had learned in order to survive, considering her childhood); and is aware of the importance of maintaining good physical health and hygiene, and the continuation of acceptable behavior in her working and social environment.

Based on all of the above, it is clear, at least in the absence of other behavior and data to the contrary, that at this time Sophie Jacobs is <u>NOT</u> psychotic – at most, she is neurotic with a flair for the dramatic and imaginative.

But then, a final diagnosis must await whatever information she provides in terms of the many experiences she has had which she describes as "paranormal." As noted previously, perhaps the medical persons she should be speaking with are those at Duke University, rather than myself.

* * *

Tape 12

April 21, 1981

5:45 pm

"Good afternoon, Miss Jacobs."

"Thank you so much, Dr. Levy, for agreeing to see me today."

"That is quite all right, Miss Jacobs. As you know from when you came to my office Friday night, I said it would be all right if you wished to arrange an appointment before your regular visit."

"Yes, and I called the very next morning, and your service worked this out for me. Thank you very much. I really appreciate it."

"It is not a problem, Miss Jacobs."

[Pause.]

"And tell me, how have you been feeling since that very dramatic incident the night you came to my office."

"Dramatic? Well, I guess it must have seemed dramatic. I suppose everything in my life has become dramatic now.

"But today is different — today I am feeling rather high, uh, excited, enthusiastic - well, you know what I mean."

"Actually, Miss Jacobs, I do not know what you mean when you say you are feeling rather 'high,' as you put it. In fact, that expression reminds me that there has been something I have been meaning to ask you ever since your initial visit."

[Pause.]

"What is that, Dr. Levy?"

"Miss Jacobs, I want you to respond with complete honesty to what I am about to ask. Remember, please, that everything [word spoken forcefully and slowly] that is said between you and me, whether in this office or on the telephone, or any other place where we might have a discussion pertaining to the substance of your therapy, is **COMPLETELY CONFIDENTIAL."** [Words spoken with extreme emphasis.]

"Yes, I am aware of that, Dr. Levy. [Pause.] What is it you want to ask me?"

"Miss Jacobs, do you now, or have you ever, taken any drugs for any reason other than medicinal purposes. I am sure you understand what I am asking. Do you take drugs for recreational or —"

"Let me stop you right there, Dr. Levy. [Tone of voice incensed, to the point of outrage.] NO. NEVER. I do not believe in the use of drugs for anything other than medical purposes, and I have NEVER, NOT EVEN ONCE, taken any hallucinogen, not even marijuana, which some of my friends use, and I think you know — well, maybe I shouldn't say anything more about that. Anyway, I can tell you with absolute conviction, so that you will understand my reasoning: it is not because of any puritanical morality or holier than thou reason, it is because as a child, I saw too much death and dying from medical illnesses, and I chose to preserve my health to the fullest extent possible. I have never even smoked one cigarette in my life, much less experimented with any illegal drugs. I don't take prescribed medicine unless I feel it is an absolute necessity. If you'll remember, you offered to write me a prescription for sleeping pills, which I refused."

[Silence.]

"Yes, I do remember, and I regret that my asking this question is so disturbing to you. But surely, Miss Jacobs, you must understand

180

the need and the logic behind my asking. You have related experiences which you yourself describe as 'bizarre,' and I wanted to rule out the possibility that you might be suffering flashbacks or delayed reactions from hallucinogens."

[Lengthy silence.]

"Yes. All right. I do understand, Dr. Levy, and I'm sorry if I sounded off at you, but I DO NOT take any substance which I feel might be harmful to my health, and I feel very strongly about that, although I don't condemn others if they choose to do so. [Slight laugh.] If I did, I might not have many friends left." [Another laugh.]

"My dear Miss Jacobs, you have no reason to apologize to me for your anger. It was an appropriate reaction under the circumstances. [Pause.] In a way, it is I who should apologize to you, since I interrupted your mood of elation. You were just beginning to tell me about something that made you feel very excited, and I hope I have not entirely spoiled your happy emotions."

[Pause.]

"Well, not really. I'm actually so happy about what happened today that nothing could spoil it, although that is not why I called originally for this extra appointment. But I was so excited, I felt I just had to share my good feelings with you, so you could see something positive happening in my life for a change."

"Ah. It is good to see you smile again, Miss Jacobs. In fact, I have not seen you smile very often. [Pause.] But then, in my profession, my patients are not usually in situations where they feel like smiling. [Pause.] Tell me, please, why did you call for

181

an appointment originally, and what has intervened to make you feel so elated."

"Well, when I called to make the appointment, I was still very confused and depressed, and I felt I <u>had</u> to see you to talk about it. I still was not sure I could trust myself.

"But then, late yesterday afternoon, I got this telephone call, and today has been a simply marvelous day for me." [Voice very excited with positive enthusiasm.]

"Explain please, Miss Jacobs."

"I BOUGHT A HOUSE! ME! SOPHIE JACOBS. I ACTUALLY OWN A HOUSE." [Words spoken with extreme emphasis and excitement.]

[Pause.]

"Can you provide details, please."

"Well, you know how I've told you about my childhood of absolute poverty. After High School, I tried to make a career in music, but that didn't work – and I can explain why later. Actually, it was rather sad, but that is another story.

"So then I took an exam and got into college, where I majored in Business and later went on to my current profession. This meant good money for the first time in my life, and I was finally able to obtain proper medical care. I had my teeth fixed – do you know I actually had <u>13</u> cavities! I bet that must be some kind of all-time record. Our family had been so poor I never received medical attention as a child. In other words, I finally started to live a comfortable life. Still I never thought I would own my own home!"

"Go on, please."

"When all this stuff started going on with Harry – and I know, I have to tell you about it, and I will - but anyway, when all this stuff started, as I think I told you before, I talked to Seymour about it whenever I could. At the time it first happened, Seymour was in the process of having a vacation retreat built in the Berkshires, near Tanglewood, where he performs often in the Summer, and he suggested I do the same."

[Pause.]

"At first the idea seemed totally insane. [Pause.] Funny I should use that word, considering what has <u>really</u> seemed to be insane in my life. Anyway, never in my life did it ever enter my mind that I could own my own home."

"And why is that, Miss Jacobs, please."

"I don't know. [Pause.] Maybe because I had become so used to poverty. [Pause.] I don't know. Also, maybe because my family was so into Socialism, that owning a house seemed too bourgeois. [Pause, then softer tone.] Maybe I felt I just didn't deserve one. I don't know."

[Silence.]

"Anyway, you know that famous architect, LaRossa? Well, he and Seymour are friends because LaRossa's wife went to our school. He personally worked with Seymour on the design of Seymour's house, and Seymour got the idea that I should have a house in the Berkshires, too."

"Do you know why Seymour felt this way?"

"Well, part of it was, I think, to have a friend nearby. But mostly, dear Seymour, I guess he was thinking of what was best for me. We talked about it a lot, metaphysically. Seymour had the idea, and I agree with it, that Harry interacts with me in places where we both have been. For example, in New York, where I live, or in Missouri, where he lived.

But if I had a place in the Berkshires where neither of us had been before, chances are strong that Harry wouldn't be around because that was not a place he had ever been."

"How could Seymour be certain of that?"

"Well, for one thing, it is brand new construction out of forest land, and also, I don't think Harry was the type to wander around a place known for classical music.

"Anyway, Seymour's idea made sense to me.

"At first, I was worried about the finances, but when I sat down with Seymour and the LaRossas - we talked over dinner at their apartment in Manhattan - absolutely gorgeous - anyway, when we talked about the design of the house and what I could afford, everything fell into place as if by magic."

"You never spoke of this before, Miss Jacobs."

"I know. I was more concerned about these psychic events. Those were all I could concentrate on. And, after all, that IS why I am coming to you, right?"

"Right. [Pause.] Continue, please."

"Anyway, Seymour pressured me. I guess he could sense my doubts and fears. We've always understood each other so well. We've known each other since infancy, probably even from the womb!

"Anyway, Seymour's house would be next to mine, but 'next to' definitely does not mean within walking distance. The houses would be separated by considerable wooded land in between. But we would be within close driving distance, and there would be no other houses around. Seymour seemed to think that I would benefit from the serenity of nature, and would be able to escape the turmoil I was experiencing from these encounters with Harry.

"So, I took his suggestion, signed on the dotted line, *et cetera*. Every so often, Seymour and I would drive there and watch the houses as they were going up. We continued to confer with LaRossa. Seymour's house was completed before mine, and he had a fabulous party."

"Ah. Yes. I remember. He invited me and my wife, but we were unable to attend. I remember now. Go on please."

"Anyway, my house was finally finished, I went through the final inspection, and this morning, I signed the documents that made it mine. All mine. I STILL can't believe it!

"On the times when we would drive up there, Seymour and I would be like a couple of kids. He insisted that I buy all NEW furniture. That was another way he felt I could be rid of Harry. Also, it just seemed appropriate to have brand new furniture in a brand new house. LaRossa's wife helped with the decorating. It was just a simply wonderful experience. And I think Seymour knew that, as well. He knew that I needed something to bolster my spirit, excuse the expression, and to get my mind on to happier things."

[Pause.]

"You know, Dr. Levy, I was so poor for so long, that I've lived rather frugally ever since I began working. I have quite — well at least for me, at any rate - a tidy sum put away, and Seymour bugged me to take it out and spend it on myself. Enjoy myself. You know. Well there's that song - it's later than you think.

"Anyway, I took his advice all the way. I liquidated some of my investments - not all - and used the funds for the down payment, LaRossa's fee, which by the way, he reduced substantially, as a favor to Seymour, and all the furniture and other miscellaneous items associated with buying a new house. Of course I have a mortgage. But still – my OWN HOME! What a kick!"

"I can see why you are so happy, Miss Jacobs, and I'm surprised you did not cancel this extra appointment so you could go and celebrate."

"Oh we will, believe me, Dr. Levy. I'm taking Seymour and the LaRossas out to dinner after our session. [Pause.] But I wanted to talk to you. I felt there were loose ends left from the last night when I saw you, and I wanted to clear those up."

[Silence.]

"Yes, Miss Jacobs. Continue whenever you are ready, please."

[Silence.]

"Actually, Dr. Levy, you're right. I really DO feel so good and so excited that I don't think I want to go on with a discussion that could make me feel sad or somehow dampen my spirits. Do you understand what I mean?"

"Of course I do, Miss Jacobs, and that is why I said what I did. [Pause.] Would you like to conclude our session at this time or --"

"Well, I'm not sure. If there's something you want to ask me or anything you want to tell me about that you —"

"In fact, there is, Miss Jacobs. There is something I've been meaning to ask you, but have never found the time, or the moment when it would be appropriate. Also, I must confess, what I want to ask may be more from a motive of curiosity than from any concern about the progress of your therapy."

"Go ahead. It's OK. You picked the right time, because I'm in such a good mood, I'll probably answer even if your motive is just plain curiosity. Fire away."

"Thank you for indulging me, Miss Jacobs. [Pause.] I'm curious about the ring you wear. I have seen you with it every time you have been in my office, even on those occasions when you have arrived without prior planning. Do you wear this ring every day?"

"Yes."

"Do you ever remove it?"

"No."

"I notice that you wear it on the third finger of your left hand — the finger Americans usually reserve for engagement or wedding bands."

"That's true."

[Silence.]

"That ring is somehow associated with this man Harry, isn't it?"

"Yes."

[Silence.]

"Miss Jacobs, please forgive me. It was never my intention to dampen your mood, and if it is painful for you to discuss this ring, please accept my apologies, and skip the rest of today's session. We can talk about it at some future time, if you wish."

"No, no. It's OK, Dr. Levy. Really, it's OK. [Pause.] Actually, it's rather interesting about this ring. I can tell you a little about it now, and maybe fill in more details later."

"If that is what you wish, Miss Jacobs."

"Yes, I'll fill in the blanks to satisfy your curiosity, and then, if there's anything to discuss relating to my therapy, you can bring it up later. How's that, Dr. Levy?"

"That is agreeable to me, and I appreciate your resolution of an awkward situation, for which I again apologize. It is very gracious of you to satisfy my curiosity, and astute of you to suggest that if I <u>do</u> find anything of relevance to your treatment, we can discuss it at a future session. [Pause.] Now continue, please, with what you feel comfortable revealing."

"Well, you're the one who's astute — but I guess that goes with your profession — to notice the ring at all, and of course to associate it with Harry.

"The story behind this ring is rather strange, actually. I knew for a long time that this ring was special to me, but I never understood <u>how</u> special until I had one of my communications from Harry."

[Pause.]

"When I knew him, Harry always wore an extremely unusual ring, quite similar to the one I have on that you asked about. I never saw anything like it before, and I used to stare at it often. It wasn't until I began exploring all this metaphysical stuff after Harry's death, that I learned it was an occult Celtic ring, which Harry had made especially to order.

"I don't know if I can tell you the story about this ring so that it makes sense. It makes perfect sense to me, but I don't know if anyone else will see it as I do. I've never told anyone about what started me wearing it permanently — not even Seymour, and I'm not sure I can go into detail about that right now."

"That is all right, Miss Jacobs. Please continue only with what you feel comfortable in revealing."

[Pause.]

"When I was in college, several years after I last saw Harry, I did something very unusual for me. I went to the first showing of a new film. Now that was something I <u>never</u> did for 2 reasons: one, it was very costly, and two, I was used to waiting until a movie came around to the local theater. But something made me go to this film shortly after it opened in a major movie house on the East Side. It was the strangest thing. I couldn't afford it, but I felt somehow compelled to go."

"What was the film, Miss Jacobs?"

"It was 'Lili'." [Pause.] And <u>now</u> I understand why I <u>had</u> to see it. But I didn't then."

[Silence.]

"Please, Miss Jacobs, I didn't mean to make you cry. Please. Here, take some tissues. Please — go and enjoy your dinner. Go, freshen up and —"

"No, Dr. Levy, I started this, and I need to finish it; otherwise it will be an open wound and I really won't be able to enjoy the evening — it's just that — I guess I should have known how emotional this would be."

[Pause.]

"Anyway, I saw the film, 'Lili.' Did you see it, Dr. Levy? Do you remember what it's about?"

"Yes, I did see it, but it was so many years ago, I can barely remember. Please tell me about it, and especially why it has such emotional meaning for you."

"I didn't realize it then, but I do now. You see, it's about an orphan girl, right after the War. She falls in love with this magician — remember? Harry was often referred to as 'The Merry Magician of the Mound,' not just because of his pitching style, but because he used to amuse his teammates with magic tricks. This magician, played by Jean-Pierre Aumont,

189

was tall and handsome, but blonde and blue-eyed. Then there was another man who befriended Lili, the orphan girl. This was a man who had been crippled by combat as a soldier in the War, and who suffered and was very bitter about his experience, which ruined his creative career. This man, played so sensitively by Mel Ferrer, was dark and brooding, the way Harry could be at times. But you see, back when I was a kid, all I saw was the side of Harry that was the Merry Magician. It wasn't until after his death that I learned that he, too, had suffered because of his combat experiences in the War.

"Anyway, Lili, the orphan girl, thinks she's in love with the magician, but at the end, after the one she calls 'The Angry Man' sends her away, she realizes that it is he she loved all along, because of the true nature of his sensitivity and caring, and she rushes back into his waiting arms. [Pause.] It really is a beautiful film.

"But back then, when I saw it, I just thought of it as a nice sentimental story. I never saw the parallel between my own life with Harry — not until after his death."

[Pause.]

"I bet you're wondering what all this has to do with the ring. But it does, you see, Dr. Levy, because when I left that first-run theater, right beside it, as soon as I turned to walk to the subway, was a Silversmith's shop; and on display in the window was this ring. [Pause.] I remember how delighted I was when I saw it, because it was the closest I had ever seen to the ring which Harry had made especially for himself. And I knew I had to have this ring. I didn't have the money to buy it then, but I was on such a high — oooops, sorry, let's not go into that again! But anyway, I had enjoyed the film, I had treated myself to a first-run showing, my first ever, and then, to top it off, here was this ring almost exactly like Harry's.

"Anyway, I boldly went into the shop — which was very pricey, because of its location and the type of people who live in that area — well, like yourself for instance — anyway, I went in, and I told the artist that I had to have that ring, and that I didn't have much money, but I would pay for it in weekly installments — anything, as long as he would hold it for me.

"Fortunately, because he was an artist who just happened to work in silver, well, I guess he understood my starving student-slash-artist type and he actually went along with my plan. So, I put whatever I could — I had a part-time job as a Governess then — into weekly payments to him, and eventually the ring was mine.

"I didn't wear it that often, only on special occasions, and despite the fact that the only reason I bought it was because it reminded me of Harry's ring, I never thought of it in that connection until after I saw the movie 'Lili' again."

[Pause.]

"And then I remembered, and I put all the pieces together. [The next words are spoken slowly and deliberately, as if giving a lecture.] You see, Dr. Levy, nothing is by chance. When I saw that film, 'Lili', it laid out the story of my life as an orphan, who fell in love with Harry — who was both the magician and the disillusioned Combat Veteran. [Pause.] Strange, too. The War Veteran was dark haired with dark complexion, and the

Merry Magician had sparkling lively blue eyes. I just realized that now.

"And it was not by chance that I was compelled to see 'Lili' on its first run, because that set the stage for me to be next to the Silversmith's, where I found this ring — the ring that will <u>always</u> keep Harry in my mind and in my heart.

"When I saw 'Lili' again, after Harry's death, all this came together. [Pause.] And then another psychic experience happened — and I <u>definitely</u> do <u>not</u> want to talk about that now — which made me realize I am to wear this ring forever, at least while I am alive on this plane. And <u>please</u> don't ask me to go into that either, because that is part of my metaphysical research, which I can tell you about later if you wish. [Pause; then heavy sigh.] There. Does that answer your curiosity about the ring? And did anything I said about 'Lili' and the ring make sense to you?"

"Yes, Miss Jacobs. I <u>do</u> understand — both about the significance of this film for you, and about your need to wear this ring in remembrance of your feelings for this man Harry."

"Dr. Levy — now may I ask <u>you</u> something?"

"Certainly, Miss Jacobs."

"Why do you always refer to him as 'this man Harry'? I mean, why don't you just call him 'Harry.' Why do you de-personalize him so much. He really wasn't that bad a human being, you know."

"I'm sorry, Miss Jacobs. I meant no disrespect. I wasn't even aware I had been doing that. I promise to pay more attention whenever I refer to this — [Pause, followed by laughter.] — to Harry. Touché; Miss Jacobs.

"Thank you for satisfying my curiosity about the ring. And I do think there is more to discuss about it — I believe you agree as well. But that is for another time. Right now, go, and enjoy your evening.

"And please accept my congratulations upon the purchase of your new home. You should be VERY PROUD of your accomplishments, Miss Jacobs. You have come a long way with your life, and I hope you realize that."

"It's still so new to me, Dr. Levy. It still is difficult for me to realize I can have a good life if I want to, or that I'm having a good life now. It's still hard to accept. But I'm trying, believe me I am."

"And that is also something to be proud of. And with that, I say, have a very enjoyable evening, Miss Jacobs."

"Thank you. Good night, Dr. Levy."

End of Tape 12.

Notes Accompanying Tape 12.

I feel very good about this session with Miss Jacobs. She was happy for the first time that I have seen, and she was able to express her happiness. Furthermore, she did not want to dampen her feelings of happiness, and was able to exercise control when she felt close to dissipating her joy — control both over me as well as herself!

What makes this case so fascinating is the juxtaposition of her very logical mind with these experiences that she refers to as bizarre. I must admit to impatience at her reluctance to discuss them thus far, but perhaps they are too painful. Too threatening for her sanity (?), which she continually expresses fear of losing, despite the lack of evidence indicating any degree of mental illness.

It was also interesting how she challenged me on the way I referred to this man Harry. Ach! I did it again. I wonder what could be the reason — she describes it as "depersonalizing" him. Do I really think of him as a villain? Was "Liliom" a villain?

It is interesting that her very analytical mind was able to discern that not only was she the orphan girl in this film, but each of the men the young girl was involved with was older than she and each represented Harry in her subconscious mind. Although she claims not to have realized the brooding veteran was Harry until after she learned of his death, part of her subconscious mind undoubtedly sensed this upon seeing the film initially.

We are back to synchronicity again. Surely it was mere coincidence that the Silversmith shop was just outside the theater. However,

Miss Jacobs claims it was an event that <u>had</u> to happen, in order that she should have this ring, as a symbol of the love she bore for Harry, which was expressed by the film she had just seen.

Fascinating.

***

Tape 13

4:30 pm

"Good afternoon, Miss Jacobs."

"Dr. Levy."

[Pause.]

"Dr. Levy, I know you are probably anxious for me to get on to the incidents I've been telling you have been so bizarre lately in my life. I believe —"

"I am not sure 'anxious' is the appropriate -"

"I'm sorry, I just —"

"There is no need to apologize, Miss Jacobs. Continue, please."

"I just wanted to say that now that I've told you about my last meeting with Harry, I can probably finish with the events that led to these incidents — or maybe preceded is a better word to use."

"As you wish, Miss Jacobs."

[Pause.]

"I believe I already told you about how I went to my 30th High School Reunion — at least I think I did, and how my classmates all screamed Harry's name when I entered the room. Also, about how, when that one gal asked if he were still alive, it felt as if an icicle had been plunged deep into my heart — like a frozen dagger."

"Yes, I remember you discussing that incident. Your description of it was very vivid."

"But that's <u>exactly</u> how it felt to me. And I became so disoriented that I couldn't respond to their questions, all those questions they

196

were asking about Harry. [Pause.] Anyway, I managed to call a halt to it by telling them I would have to look him up to see how he was.

[Silence.]

"But I didn't do it right away. It was as if — well, almost as if I knew, or had some kind of intuition as to what I would find out. So I kept putting it off."

[Pause.]

"Then, one day — and it was <u>months</u> later — I ran into one of the gals from <u>my</u> class. It was so weird. She was in town from California, where she lives — I think she was here for a concert — she's a violinist — and we just happened to meet on 57th Street, near Carnegie Hall.

"But I can't really say it was weird, can I? Because, I think I've told you, after all that has happened to me, I no longer believe there are such things as what people refer to as 'coincidences'. Everything is part of a larger scheme. Synchronicity. Right?"

[Pause.]

"Anyway, Doris and I went for lunch together, and of course we went over old times. She hadn't been able to attend the 30th Reunion, so she too, had to ask about Harry. And once again, I said something like, 'Oh, I guess I have to look him up' — something like that.

"So because of that lunch date, that so-called 'chance' meeting, I looked up his name that very afternoon. We have all kinds of computer data bases at work, and when I keyed in his name, the word 'Obit' kept popping up, and I knew, without need for any further research, that he was dead. [Pause.] That Harry Gault had died."

[Extended silence, after which sounds of weeping and pulling of tissues can be heard. When her voice resumes, it is apparent Ms. Jacobs is struggling to control a steady tone, often unsuccessfully.]

"I remember distinctly that I didn't cry. I really didn't feel much of anything. I just thought in my mind something like 'Oh, he's dead, how sad,' and then went on to read the articles. They were all the same, actually, an AP release. I found out he died the year before. I think Harry would have been pleased to know that Notice of his death appeared in the New York Times. [Pause.] Well, I guess he probably does know, right? Oh don't bother to answer — that was just a rhetorical question.

"Anyway, the obituary said that he died from complications of emphysema. And I'll never forget the words used to describe that he had been living alone — the exact words were 'virtual recluse.' That came as a shock to me. [Pause.] And it said he was survived by his daughter, Diana. There was no mention at all of his wife, Betty. And that made me curious, too. Reading the Obituary left me with more questions about Harry's life than I had before. The only thing I knew for sure was that he was dead. [Pause.] That's a joke. I can't even be sure of that anymore. Well, I know he's dead medically — you know what I'm trying to say, don't you, Dr. Levy?"

"Yes. I do. Continue please, Miss Jacobs."

"I remember that day so clearly. It was mid-afternoon when I finished reading the Obituary, but I felt no particular strong emotion, and was able to continue with my work schedule as if nothing of any significance had occurred. Then I went home, and did my usual activities, fixed dinner, fed the cats, watched TV — my normal stuff."

[Pause.]

"I remember getting ready for bed, it was about 11:00pm or so, and deciding to glance at the baseball clippings I had in a scrapbook from the time I was a teenager. It was then, seeing the face of the young Harry, that the flood of memories came back, and I started to weep hysterically. And I don't think a day has gone by since then when I haven't wept over Harry for some reason or other." [Sounds of uncontrolled sobbing.]

"Here, Miss Jacobs, these tissues please."

[Pause.]

"But that was almost a year ago, if not more, isn't that so? [Pause.] I see you are nodding your head, so I will assume that means yes. Do you mean literally, or is it perhaps an exaggeration, that you have actually shed tears over the death of this man Harry every day for almost a year?"

[Pause; then shaky voice tone.]

"Yes. [Pause.] At first it was because he was dead. Also, I remember that as I was reading those old clippings, all faded and yellow, I had the radio on WQXR and the Copland Clarinet Concerto was playing. And now, I can't hear that piece without crying, no matter where I am or what I'm doing. [Pause.] And then these things started happening, and I wept because of them, as well."

"What 'things', Miss Jacobs?"

[Pause.]

"And it wasn't just the clippings, either. I found the photo of Harry holding his baby girl, and the sketch that Carolyn made of Harry that time I took her to the Polo Grounds

199

with me. [Pause.] All those memories came flooding back, all those times seeing and being with Harry."

"What things, Miss Jacobs, please."

"All these things that have been so bizarre. [Pause.] I know they're not meant to frighten me. Actually, most are beautiful and so tender and loving — but it's — at times it's more than I can handle."

[Pause.]

"Also — it's their cumulative — you see, each incident has its own exponential effect. It may be so lovely that it causes me to miss him more and multiplies my feeling of loss — emphasizing repeatedly that he is no longer here for me to touch, embrace, or even tell how much I love him.

"And after these incidents occur, I not only remember that Harry is dead, but I realize again that I'm still receiving communications from him. [Pause.] Is it really so difficult to believe that I can cry every day because of what has been happening? Can you possibly understand what I'm trying to say, Dr. Levy?"

"I think so, Miss Jacobs. [Pause.] Describe such an incident for me, please."

"Yes. But first I need to tell you about what happened the next night."

"Yes. All right."

"The next morning I went to work as usual, and I was fine. I think I just felt I was reacting normally, weeping over the loss of someone I had been fond of when I was a child. I remember that everything was as usual for me at the office that day.

"And when I got home, I started my typical routine, fed the cats, and while I was preparing my supper, I had this very strange sensation."

"And what was that, Miss Jacobs, please."

"It's so difficult to describe — that is, unless you've had it yourself."

[Silence.]

"Dr. Levy, please don't mind, but I really <u>need</u> to ask this question: have you ever had any communication from a person who is deceased?"

"Not that I'm aware of, Miss Jacobs."

"Well believe me, Dr. Levy, if you had, you'd remember it. I can assure you!"

[Pause.]

"Anyway, I had this very strange sensation. I was preparing some vegetable or something. I was standing at the stove — when somehow I <u>KNEW</u>, without looking, that Harry was standing to my left by the kitchen counter. I turned to look, and I knew he was there."

[Silence.]

"What do you mean you 'knew' he was there, Miss Jacobs. Could you see him? <u>Did</u> you see him? And by that, I mean, did you see him as a three-dimensional person, alive, as you are seeing me now, for instance."

[Pause.]

"It's so difficult to explain."

"Try, Miss Jacobs, please."

"No. I did not see him as I am seeing you now. But it might as well have been. It's so hard to describe. But I could see him like an image on a movie-screen. That's the best to describe it that I -"

"Was it the way you described seeing the vision of the taxi-cab pulling up and the young girl Sandy getting in while —"

"No. I remember telling you about that. That was like watching a movie, yes, but this was more like reality. Yet it was not as if I could touch Harry, or feel his body — it was

201

more — oh, this is so god-damned frustrating. [Pause.] I'm sorry, Dr. Levy."

"No need. Continue, please. Wait, describe how he appeared to you. How did he look?"

"Well, that was another strange thing. He looked — that is <u>really</u> strange. It was Harry I saw. I <u>know</u> that. But he was not the young Harry, the way he looked when I saw him last. And it wasn't the Harry who had died, either — by that I mean, he wasn't a man in his sixties, as Harry would have been at the time of his death. He appeared to be, well, the way I would imagine Harry to have looked in his mid-40s.

"And he was standing <u>exactly</u> the way Harry would have been standing. He was leaning against the kitchen counter, with his hands thrust deep into the pockets of his pants — something that was so typical for Harry. [Pause.] And his head was bent down, as if he was — as if he felt very sad about something.

"And it was as if he was reading my mind again, the way it was when I knew him. It was as if he knew that in my mind he had heard me ask, 'What's wrong, Harry?'"

[Silence.]

"And then I heard him -"

"You <u>heard</u> him? What do you mean, Miss Jacobs, when you say you 'heard' him? Did you hear his voice? Did you hear it aloud?"

"No. <u>Definitely</u> not. Of <u>course</u> not. But you don't understand. How <u>could</u> you, since it's never happened to you. It was just like when I was a child, and we read each other's minds. Remember how I told you about our 'game' — the game Harry and I used to play, where we read each other's thoughts? Well, it was like that. I heard his voice in my head."

"What did he say, please, Miss Jacobs."

[Pause. Then crying.]

"He told me he was 'not at peace'. Those were his exact words — he was 'not at peace'."

[Silence.]

"Did he explain <u>why</u> he was 'not at peace'?"

"No. But I <u>knew</u> it was my job to find out."

"Your 'job'? What <u>exactly</u> do you mean by that, Miss Jacobs."

"I <u>knew</u> that somehow something was wrong, and that I had to help make things right for Harry, so he could be at peace. [Pause.] There were so many unanswered questions. For example, what happened to Betty, the wife he loved so much. Had they gotten a divorce? Had she passed away? And what about his daughter? Why was he living, as the article stated, in an isolated cabin in the Ozarks, as a 'virtual recluse'? There was so much that didn't make sense, and I could <u>never</u> turn away from helping Harry — NEVER. If he was not at peace, then I <u>knew</u>, I <u>knew</u>, that I had to find out why and make things right for him."

"Did you communicate that to Harry, Miss Jacobs?"

"Yes, I did. And thank you for not referring to him as 'this man'. Yes, I did. And before you ask, yes, it was the same way we communicated back then. I let him know that there was <u>nothing</u> I would not do for him, alive or dead, and that I would do <u>everything</u> that I could to help him find the peace he apparently never found in life <u>or</u> death."

[Silence.]

"And I couldn't help but wonder what went wrong? What happened to the Harry that I knew — the young man who so loved life — whose every step had a bounce of joy at being alive."

[Silence.]

"But you see, I didn't know about the War then. I didn't understand the toll it took upon Harry's life. I was so young, how could I understand. Also, he never talked about it, so how could I know. I remember some things from articles I had cut out of the paper, but it meant nothing more to me than that he had been a soldier and now he was back pitching again. [Pause.] There was just so much I didn't know about what went on in Harry's life. But I knew that after that incident, after his appearance to me, I was going to find out and do everything in my power to help him find the peace he seemed to need so desperately."

"You have no doubts as to the reality of this experience, Miss Jacobs?"

"None then. It wasn't until later, when I kept being bombarded by more and more unusual episodes, that I began to wonder if I was in fact, losing my mind. You know, like the incident that made me call you."

"And how long did Harry remain in your presence that evening, Miss Jacobs?"

"It was all very quick. Once he understood that I would do everything in my power to help him find peace, he was gone. It was as if he appeared, we had this little talk, and then he departed. [Pause.] I guess I really understand now what that term 'the dear departed' means."

"Ah, it's good to see you smile again, Miss Jacobs. [Pause.] I see our time is about up. But first I want to ask: how did your dinner party go with Seymour and the LaRossas?"

"Very well, thank you, Dr. Levy, very well."

"I'm pleased to hear that. And now, good evening, Miss Jacobs."

"Good evening, Dr. Levy."

End of Tape 13.

Notes Accompanying Tape 13.

Asking about the dinner party! Indeed! As if any amount of social pleasantry could make up for the coldness with which I responded to this woman's most intimate experiences.

Why do I do this? I listen to the tape of this session and I can NOT believe I can sound so harsh. The tone of my voice is brusque, insensitive almost to the point of cruelty.[1]

Obviously I was impatient for her to get on with examples of these "incidents," which she keeps postponing in our discussions. But I view myself as a skilled therapist, and even smugly pride myself that I am better than the majority of my colleagues, who are reluctant to express any degree of emotion in sessions with their patients.

I MUST analyze my feelings about this woman to find why she elicits these atypical responses from me. But I think I have written that before in my Notes; still I have yet to do so. And WHY haven't I? Is it because I am afraid of what I will find in my own subconscious?

I continue to be impatient with her for her reluctance to get to the heart of the matter — these incidents she can only describe as "bizarre." But this is a familiar, typical, problem with patients. Something that is painful to them they are reluctant to discuss. There is nothing new about that — I see it all the time with my patients — in fact, I would be surprised if I did not! Then WHY am I so impatient only with Miss Jacobs?

Is it because I am determined that she face what is painful to her and get on with it so

---

[1] Dr. Levy's analysis is correct. The tone of his voice on the tape can indeed be described as "brusque" and "insensitive."

that she can make progress in her treatment? Or is it because I, myself, am overcome with such curiosity that I can not restrain my impatience.

Or is it something else?

Do I sense (perhaps "intuitively," as Miss Jacobs herself would put it) that her postponing the discussion of these incidents is not from fear, but from coyness?

She has spoken of Harry as a master story-teller. Is she, like him (who she so admires and loves), a story-teller who enjoys building suspense in her listener? Does she enjoy being center-stage, the way she described Harry to be? And here am I, her captive audience! After all the neglect she suffered in childhood, is it worth it to her to pay a high-priced therapist in order to receive undivided attention? She admits to having a vivid imagination. Is she using this now to entice me into her fantasy-world? But if so, that STILL does not excuse my reactions. **WHAT IS THE MATTER WITH ME IN MY DEALINGS WITH THIS WOMAN!!** [2] And, since I have noted this same problem before, WHY have I done nothing to correct it!

Her story IS genuinely engrossing and intriguing. I probably should consider myself fortunate to have such a patient.

One thing I must admit she was correct about. It was a more logical approach to learn of her background experiences with this [word crossed out] — I was about to write "this man Harry", when I remembered how she took me to task for that, and rightfully so! AND THIS IS ANOTHER THING! WHY DO I CONTINUALLY EXPRESS, in one form or another, HOSTILITY TOWARDS TH—

---

[2] This sentence was written with very bold strokes of the pen, with every word capitalized and punctuated exactly as transcribed.

HARRY! At this point, I am almost driven to wonder <u>WHO</u> needs therapy here, Miss Jacobs or <u>myself</u>???

What continues to impress me is her ability to exercise logical analysis coupled with experiences that in other persons, less in control of themselves and their emotions, might result in involuntary commitment. What she described, in her first encounter with the "deceased" Harry, could easily be analyzed as both visual and auditory hallucinations. Yet she very carefully stated that these sights and sounds emanated from within her mind, or were similar to projections therefrom.

Could these things <u>be</u>? I MUST retain an Open Mind to the possibility that her experiences ARE exactly as she describes them, and are NOT figments of a deranged mind or vivid imagination.

I know only of that one experience, the one in Harry's bedroom. I think there may have been some others she related, but as I can't recall them immediately, they must not have been that significant — at least to me. But what <u>are</u> these others — the ones she describes as "tender and loving"?

And she keeps referring to the War and its effect upon Harry. I wish — I <u>need</u> to hear what it was that so effected him. Perhaps he suffered from PTSD[3] — a term evolving out of the War in Vietnam, but which most certainly can be applied to those soldiers who saw prolonged vicious combat in the Second World War. Perhaps this stress was latent in Harry. Perhaps it was buried, not only by Harry, but by ALL Veterans of that horrible Conflict, who went to War as soldiers and were expected to

---

[3] Post Traumatic Stress Disorder; associated with an individual's reaction to an event of overwhelming personal tragedy.

return to civilian life as if nothing had happened. They were just "away" for awhile.

I must remember to ask her to discuss what she means when she refers, as she has done several times now, to the effect the War had upon Harry.

And may God help me, I MUST remember to be more professional in my dealings with this woman. It does not matter how manipulative SHE may be. It is I, as Therapist, who must be in control, so that I can provide whatever treatment is appropriate for her condition.

* * *

Tape 14

April 24, 1981

4:30 pm

"Good afternoon, Miss Jacobs."

"Dr. Levy."

"How are you feeling, Miss Jacobs?"

"Fine, Dr. Levy. Why do you ask?"

"I was concerned about any reaction you may have had to our last session, when you told me about your first encounter with the spirit of the deceased, Harry."

"Well, at least I see he's graduated from being called 'this man' to 'the deceased'. [Tone indicating sarcasm.] I haven't walked in front of any trucks, if that's what you mean."

"My dear Miss Jacobs, I did not have any such worry, I can assure you. When a patient has had a prior emotional session, I want to know about any important reaction. Believe me, that is <u>the only</u> reason for my inquiry about your state of being."

"I've been fine, Dr. Levy. In fact, I feel better now that I have given you all the preliminary background facts and can go on to the experiences that followed after I learned of Harry's death."

"Good."

[Pause.]

"Tell me, Miss Jacobs, what happened next after the vision of Harry's presence disappeared."

[Pause.]

"That's an interesting way to describe it. [Pause.] I think I like that — 'the vision of Harry's presence'. Yes. That seems to fit. That seems to be about the best way to

209

describe it. Perhaps YOU have psychic abilities of which you are unaware, Dr. Levy!"

[Uneasy laughter.] "Thank you for the compliment, however I seriously doubt it, Miss Jacobs. [Pause.] But tell me, what happened next, please."

"Nothing happened that night. I went to bed — wait, something DID happen. My God! How could I have forgotten. My God!"

[Silence.]

"What is it Miss Jacobs, please. You look so-"

"How could I have —. It was — I had gone to bed, and sometime much later, I awoke to a frightening sensation. I was in a bed, NOT my own, and it was as if dirt were being shoveled on top of me, or as if I were lying under piles of dirt, mounds of earth-soil. I tried to breathe, but I could not. I felt what it was like to suffocate. I realized I was going to die. I thought, or else I said aloud, I'm not sure which, but the words came: 'I'm dying. I'm going to die.' And there was NOTHING I could do. NOTHING. I couldn't move and I couldn't breathe. I KNEW I was going to die. And then I think I passed out."

[Silence.]

"And when I came to, and after realizing I was really in my own bed, for some reason I looked at the clock. It was 6:37 am. [Pause.] And then the title of William Faulkner's work, As I Lay Dying, came to me, and I understood that this is what it felt like for Harry as he took his last breath. [Pause.] And you know what?"

"No. What, Miss Jacobs, please."

"I learned later that the time assigned to Harry's death was 5:37 am — the difference being merely between the time zones."

"I see."

"You see? Do you? Or are you saying those words as the typical trained therapist response?"

"Miss Jacobs, I —"

"No. Listen to what I am actually saying for a change. [Voice fraught with emotion.] Can you truly appreciate the significance of what I am telling you? I actually experienced Harry's death. I knew what it felt like as he took his last tortured breath. How could I go back to sleep after that. It felt to me as if I had taken my last breath, as if I was the one who had died.

"Believe me Dr. Levy, if you had known me in those days, you most likely would have had me committed."

"Miss Jacobs, please, I -"

"I was, or at least it felt to me, as if I was totally out of control. I don't know how I managed to get through the next few months. I know I got up and went to the office each day. I know I must have produced some meaningful work, as no one spoke to me about poor performance or lack of productivity, or expressed any concerns — but I went through the motions like an automaton. The only time I experienced any emotion was when I was doing something connected with Harry's life — like writing letters, making telephone calls, reading books and newspaper articles. I HAD to learn what happened to him in the years since I had seen him."

[Silence.]

"You see, Dr. Levy, I never went to another baseball game after the night Harry put me in that cab. I never followed the sport, even to this day. At school, my grades and personality had improved so much, that I became part of the "in" clique, possibly even because I had known Harry, and I no longer hung around with friends who were baseball fans. I started on my path to total and complete intellectuality — and when I embarked on that path, there was no looking back. I graduated with all kinds of honors, both in High School and College. Sometimes I was the only female enrolled in certain technical classes at College, but that was the way it was. [Pause.] And I forgot that I ever knew any man named Harry Gault — but I expect that <u>you</u> would describe the process as 'repressing' rather than 'forgetting'."

"Miss Jacobs, please do —"

"NO. <u>YOU</u> listen. [Pause.] I poured myself into learning everything I could about Harry from the moment I last saw him. But the strange thing was that even before his death, there were events, almost like road markers, that indicated Harry's continued presence in my life.

"For example, I went with one of my older cousins to a Race Track. It was something on a dare, I think — I don't know, I can't remember. But there was a horse in one of the races, and that was the ONE AND ONLY time in my life I EVER went to a Race Track, and there was this horse named 'Harry G.' I swear to God, that was the name of the horse — 'Harry G.'

"And then, in 1967, I had a student intern assigned to me in the office. I remember him so well. His name was Doug, a dear young man, very intelligent, courteous and conscientious. Anyway, it was October and everyone BUT me in the office was watching and talking about the World Series. The Cardinals and Red Sox were playing. When Doug asked why I wasn't watching, I told him I <u>used to be</u> a baseball fan, but that was a long time ago, and that in fact the very last World Series I paid any attention to was in 1946, between these same two teams — the Cardinals and the Red Sox. Doug kept questioning, and I mentioned that I had known someone who was on the Cardinals at that time. I'll make it short by telling you it turned out that Harry and his family had been Doug's next door neighbors when Doug was a child before moving to New York, and Doug remembered playing with Harry's daughter, the little girl with the long red braids.

"And then there was the time I was sent on assignment by my firm to Sacramento, California to work on a tax case for a multi-national corporation. I needed to remain in that location for several months, almost a year in fact, and so, rather than stay in a hotel, I rented a charming little house in a rural town on the outskirts of Sacramento. The town is Galt — spelled 'G - A - L - T'. Later, in an edition of their local paper, marking an anniversary of its founding, something like that, there was an article about how the original settlers were farmers from Missouri, a family whose name was actually spelled 'G - A - U - L - T', but somehow, when the town was placed on the map, the name was misspelled and has remained that way ever since.

"So you see, Dr. Levy — even though I had no direct contact with Harry since early 1949, there were these reminders that kept turning up in my life — like signposts so I could never forget him, despite my attempts."

[Silence.]

"Anyway, I don't really remember how I got through those next few months after learning Harry was dead. I was a zombie at work, functioning on autopilot, and came alive only when I was pouring over the substance of Harry's life. And it was such a sad life. I don't understand that, really — why one person should have so many sad things happen to him.

"First, his wife Betty, who he loved so much, developed a long and painful stomach cancer, and he had to watch as she suffered and all he could do was get her the best medical care he could afford. Then, when she passed away, he was still playing ball — he was so good he played until he was 40, something really rare for a pitcher in those days — anyway, because he was on the road so much, he felt he had to send his little girl to live with his sister — who was almost old enough to be the child's Grandmother — in California, and — there went his family. Gone. Just like that. I learned his daughter became very bitter and remained estranged from him until his death. [Pause.] And I look at that photo, the one of Harry and his baby girl holding the — [sounds of sobbing]..."

[Lengthy silence.]

"How did you manage to obtain all these details of Harry's life, Miss Jacobs?"

"I read back issues of the local newspaper of the tiny town he lived in in Missouri. He was the only celebrity around and everything that happened to Harry was news. I also wrote and called different people who would have known him. Eventually, I went to visit his gravesite in Missouri, and while there, I spoke to some of Harry's friends and family members."

[Silence.]

"Miss Jacobs, earlier in today's session, you said something to the effect that if I had known you during this period I would have had you committed to a mental institution. Why do you think that — or did you mean it as a figure of speech, or a slight exaggeration of your mental state at the time?"

"No. I meant every word of it. [Pause.] I felt so out of control."

"It <u>is</u> important to you to be in control, isn't it, Miss Jacobs?"

"Yes. But under the circumstances, is that unusual? Would YOU want to see YOUR life taken over by an obsession with the life of another human being, Dr. Levy?"

"We make choices in our lives, Miss Jacobs, and —"

"That's <u>precisely</u> my point, Dr. Levy. We make choices. And <u>I</u> made the choice to become obsessed with learning everything I could about Harry's life. [Pause.] I'm sorry, you wanted to know why I felt I was certifiable. Mostly because I was manic. If I were to give myself a diagnosis in that time frame, I would say I was clearly manic-depressive."

"Explain, please, Miss Jacobs."

"Well, during the day, at work, or when I wasn't doing anything associated with Harry's life, I was truly depressed. Sometimes, on weekends, when I didn't have to go into work, I remember just sitting on the edge of my bed for hours at a time, unable to move.

"Then, when I would be doing something involved with Harry and his life, I would be all manicky, working furiously, long hours, delving deeper and deeper. In fact, I'm <u>still</u> hoping to find out more about what happened to him, not just in the time period since I saw him last, but in his entire life."

[Silence.]

"In order to be committed to an institution involuntarily, Miss Jacobs, you would have to meet certain criteria. Nothing you have told me today, or in previous sessions, indicates that you are or were anywhere near meeting that criteria. You may have been obsessed, yes; even to the point of being depressed or hyperactive. But somehow you managed to maintain enough control to continue to be productive at your office, where apparently no one observed any symptoms of serious dysfunction. And, despite being 'obsessed', as you stated, with the concerns you had about the life of someone who had been very dear, you managed to meet your needs of food, clothing, and shelter, and gave no indication of inflicting harm upon yourself or others. Therefore, although this period of your life may have been VERY stressful to you, Miss Jacobs, and I mean no disrespect for your judgment, in my opinion as a professional, from what you have told me, you were by NO means certifiable."

[Silence.]

"I'm curious, Miss Jacobs please, did any of these incidents you term as 'bizarre' occur during this time period when you felt you were 'certifiable'."

"Well, I should think that the incident of experiencing Harry's death might qualify as 'bizarre'."

"No, no, Miss Jacobs. Certainly I meant after that experience, when you returned to work and began what you describe as your obsessive research into Harry's life."

[Silence.]

"You know, that's very interesting, Dr. Levy. I never realized it before. [Pause.] That's fascinating. No. Nothing. Nothing bizarre happened. At least not during that specific time period. But there were lots of synchronicities."

"Can you give some examples, Miss Jacobs, please."

"Well, actually, most of those happened when I took my trip to Missouri. But there was one that was — well, like I've said before, tender and touching, and that happened here in the City."

"Tell me about it, Miss Jacobs, please."

"Sure. [Pause.] I have this friend, Sarah. We've known each other since College. Sarah is one of the few friends I have who shares an interest in psychic phenomena. She and one other woman are about the only friends, besides Seymour of course, who I can trust to tell anything about this whole Harry experience."

"Go on, Miss Jacobs, please."

"Anyway, one day when I came home from work, I found this package by my apartment door. It was something wrapped in newspaper inside a plastic bag. At first, with all that's been going on in the City lately, I was almost suspicious it was a bomb, but that was only for a moment, and I picked up the bag and brought it inside.

"Well, of course, as soon as I got into my apartment and put my things down, I had to open the package. Wrapped inside this newspaper was a beautiful statuette of a Cardinal sitting on a treebranch, but there was no card, no note, nothing to indicate who it was from, or why."

[Pause.]

"I must say, Dr. Levy, that for some reason, even though they don't believe in this psychic stuff, as they call it, almost all my friends, including Seymour, have been giving me presents of all kinds of things with Cardinals. I have Cardinal night lights,

217

Cardinal refrigerator magnets, Cardinal letter openers, Cardinal wine corks, Cardinal drinking glasses — even a Cardinal alarm clock that wakes you with the actual recorded sound of a Cardinal in the wild. I must admit though, that some of these I bought myself — but MOST have been gifts. [Pause.] But even the ones I bought myself were almost thrust in my path — as if to say: 'Here. Buy this in memory of me!'

"Anyway, I had no clue as to who gave me this lovely statuette, but I was thrilled to have it, as it was quite delicate and exquisite. I called Sarah to tell her about it, and to my surprise, she sounded rather annoyed. When I tried to find out what was bothering her, I learned that she was the one who had given it to me.

"I knew her Mother-in-law had recently passed away. Sarah told me about how she would be driving out to Long Island to pick up some of the items that her Mother-in-Law wanted her to have. Well, apparently the woman had a collection of bird statuettes. Sarah had always loved the Cardinal most, because it was so delicate, with such beautiful red coloring in contrast to the green leaves on the branch. Naturally, she picked it up along with the other items that had been left to her.

"But she felt uneasy about keeping it. She knew — Sarah more than anyone, except Seymour, of course — how much I loved, and still love Harry. She told me she actually drove around Long Island and the City with that Cardinal statuette in her trunk for five days, because she couldn't decide what to do with it. She wanted to keep it, she had admired it for many years, yet she knew how much I would love it. Finally, and believe me, Dr. Levy, when I tell you how disgusted she sounded with herself, she decided it really belonged with me, so she left it by my door while I was at work."

"That was very thoughtful and considerate of her. She sounds like a very good friend."

"Yeah, but that's not all, Dr. Levy. It gets even better. While she was telling me the story, I noticed a little curvature on the bottom of the pedestal of the branch. I told Sarah about it and she seemed not to know at all what I was talking about and started asking if it had gotten damaged while rolling around in her trunk.

"I told her I wasn't sure if that was the case, and when I went to touch it, all of a sudden it started to play music. It was a MUSIC BOX, for crying-out-loud! And you know, that in all those years Sarah had been admiring that statuette, she never once knew it was a music box.

"And can you guess what it plays, Dr. Levy?"

"No. I'm afraid I can't even begin to speculate."

"It plays the theme from the film "Love Story."

[Pause.]

"This just blew our minds away! Then Sarah suggested that this was another gift, not from her, but from Harry. She has often said that whenever I get one of these Cardinal chachkas,[1] it's actually Harry showing that he loves me. And what better way could there be than a music box that plays the theme of 'Love Story'."

[Pause.]

"You are right, Miss Jacobs. That incident can definitely be described as loving, both on

---

[1] Yiddish word, difficult to translate into English, but loosely meaning knick-knack, or bauble.

219

the part of Sarah as well as Harry. It certainly was generous and unselfish of her to give what she had cherished to you, because she felt you needed it more than she. And of course, if she is a believer in psychic phenomena, then she would also consider it as being a gift from Harry to you, as well."

"But don't you think it strange Dr. Levy, that in all those years she never knew it was a music box? And that it should play the theme from 'Love Story'? A Cardinal music box playing music called 'Love Story'? Come on, please, gimme a break here!"

"All right, Miss Jacobs. I <u>will</u> admit that it is a rather strong coincidence. Perhaps even an event of synchronicity. But, as — "

"OOOh. Dr. Levy. Look at the time! May I leave a little early please? I'll be supervising the opening of my house next week, and I want to get an early start with the arrangements. I'm not sure, but I may have to cancel my appointments for next week so I can take care of all that needs to be done. I'll call and leave word with your receptionist."

"Ah. So your house is ready then. Of course. Leave now if you wish, and I will check with my secretary to see when your next appointment is scheduled.

"Good luck, Miss Jacobs."

"Thank you, Dr. Levy. I'm sorry I have to rush like this, but I'm glad you understand. Good night."

"Good night, Miss Jacobs."

End of Tape 14.

Notes Accompanying Tape 14.

The almost immediate sarcasm shown by Miss Jacobs today can almost surely be defined in reaction to my cold, unfeeling behavior of our previous session. I really can't say that I blame her, and in a way, I had it coming.

The experiences she relates are astounding, yet she manages to absorb them into her daily functioning. Even when she felt her worst, she apparently exhibited no symptoms of behavioral disorder at her office, and remains a successful professional in her field. She continues to have close relationships, as demonstrated by casual references to the many gifts received from friends, who, despite the fact that they may not accept her beliefs, care enough to give her presents associated with the subject of her psychic obsession.

NO. There is NOTHING here that suggests any clinical dx.[2] Yet, despite that, NEVER, at least that I can recall, in ALL the many years I have been in practise, have I had a patient who is almost BEGGING to have a dx of mental illness placed upon their behavior and belief system. She would rather be labeled mentally ill, than to be considered in possession of abilities she can not comprehend - or worse yet - control! To her, mental illness is a concept readily understood by all persons of rational mind, controllable through treatment, medication, and even hospitalization. But how can she be perfectly sane and still have the experiences she has related thus far. That is the issue she has not been able to resolve. Nor have I.

---

[2] Medical abbreviation for "diagnosis."

It goes far beyond her vivid imagination — a simplistic explanation which in itself leaves many unanswered questions. For example, apparently others, including Seymour and her friend Sarah, have been involved in some of these incidents. I need to learn more in order to understand what is happening here.

In the absence of any readily identifiable symptoms of mental illness, it is difficult to know <u>what</u> to treat or <u>how</u> to treat it. Yet, her situation is SO intriguing that were Miss Jacobs a complete pauper, I would take her case and treat her without charge.

* * *

Tape 15

12:30 pm

"Miss Jacobs."

"Thank you so much, Dr. Levy, for agreeing to see me at this time. [Voice tone very rushed and excited; out of breath.] I realize it's probably your lunch or rest period – I know you usually don't schedule patients at this hour, but I really felt I needed to talk to you before I go into my office."

"Yes, I understand, Miss Jacobs. Sit down, please."

"I don't know when this will ever stop. There doesn't seem to be any getting away from these experiences; and they keep getting more and more intense."

"My secretary told me you sounded very upset and that you urgently needed to see me as soon as possible."

"Yes, that's right. I couldn't stay in that house another minute, at least not right now; and I thought it would be better for me to drive back to the City and see about getting some work done in the office. I have the rest of the week off, but I just couldn't face staying in that house – I <u>had</u> to get out."

"Miss Jacobs, are you aware that you have called me many times, sounding very desperate and unable to face a particular situation, and then by the time you reach my office, the problem seems to have resolved itself? Are you aware of this?"

[Silence.]

"And is this one of those times?"

"I don't know what you mean."

"Is this one of those times when the problem has decreased in urgency, so that you no longer have the same feeling of desperation?"

[Silence.]

"All right. Now I think I understand what you mean. I am overwhelmed by an experience, but by the time I reach your office, it has not seemed as crucial, or as threatening to my sanity as at the time I placed my call to you."

"Exactly. Or even if it is as critical, you behave as if it is not."

"But you don't know what it is like from my perspective, Dr. Levy. At the time I call you, I really do feel totally desperate, but by the time I reach your office, I probably do appear much calmer. But I can think of several reasons for that - or at least, a few.

"First, there is the fact that time and space have intervened. Like - I'm no longer threatened by the situation because I am away from it. Also, when I am with you, I don't feel Harry's presence - at least he is not doing anything that I am overtly aware of, so that helps to calm me down. And also, just being with you is reassuring - having someone to talk to who can accept what I am saying without thinking I am completely insane. Wait - you DO think I am sane, don't you? I mean, you don't think I am insane - that is correct, isn't it?"

"My dear Miss Jacobs, if I had thought you were insane, as you state it, I would have treated your situation quite differently, you can believe me. As it is now, you come and talk to me about these experiences that have occurred which are troubling to you. We discuss them in the time allotted, and then, hopefully, you think about the experiences in the light of our discussion. I will say frankly that the only time I had any real concern for your mental stability was the time you telephoned and told me you had just deliberately walked in front of a speeding truck."

[Pause.]

"Now, tell me what it is that made you feel that you needed - first, to get away from your new home, and second, to see me before you could go to your office to work."

[Pause; then sigh.]

"You probably remember that I left here Friday dashing to make arrangements for the opening of the house."

[Silence; voice agitated when resumed.]

"The whole reason for having this house was to have someplace quiet and peaceful in the country, isolated from the mainstream hustle of the City - and also, a place where I could find peace from Harry's psychic assaults."

[Pause.]

"That wasn't fair. I shouldn't have used the word 'assault.' Many of these experiences have been quite tender and loving. It's just that they're so unexpected that I don't know how to react. The only thing that is predictable is that they are unpredictable."

[Pause.]

"Anyway, when I left the City Sunday morning - my God! - that was only two days ago! - today is Tuesday, right? - I was so happy and excited as I drove my convertible up the Taconic. But then it started to cloud over, and by the time I reached the Berkshires, I had to stop and put the top up, and managed to get drenched in the process. It was later than I planned when I arrived, which caused something of a problem, because there was no electricity in the house at the time.

"My original plan was to get there Sunday afternoon, unpack my most precious items, which I had brought up in the trunk of my car, and stay the night, so I could be there when the movers arrived early the next morning with the furniture I had selected for the new house. It really wasn't too much of a problem that I arrived later than I planned, except that I missed most of the daylight hours I had counted on, and had to do a lot by candle light."

[Pause.]

"Now that I think of it, it's funny. It's actually funny. The only candles I had with me were "Jahrzeit" candles.[1] [Nervous laughter.]

"Anyway, I parked the car in the garage. There was still some sunlight remaining, enough for me to unpack my valuables. I had a special jewelry case built into the closet of the Master Bedroom, and I placed those items away, by candlelight. I had brought a sleeping bag with me, and I placed it on the bedroom floor. I took out the Cardinal Alarm Clock and the Cardinal Music Box and placed them by the sleeping bag. The Music Box was to help me sleep, like a lullaby, and the Alarm Clock was to make sure I got up in time to be ready when the furniture was delivered. I had Harry's radio with me also, but of course there was nothing I could do with it, without any electricity.

"And to be sure, I checked the switches that I could see. Nothing worked. So I lit candles in every room I would be in. I had brought a folding chair with me, and sat on it and ate a

---

[1] A Memorial candle, used in Jewish ceremonial rites to commemorate the death of a loved one.

picnic lunch I had made before leaving my apartment.

"It's funny, well, I suppose I mean strange, but there I was, sitting in clothes that were still damp, eating a sandwich and drinking tea out of a Thermos. I almost didn't notice that my clothes were damp — I had this - it was as if I were some sort of robot, going through all these acts mechanically.

"I had brought a suitcase with me, with my pajamas and jeans and T-shirts and other stuff - you know what I mean, as I had taken the week off to get the house in order, and generally to relax - - supposedly away from Harry and all that has been happening."

"Tell me again why you felt these experiences would not occur in your house in the Berkshires, please."

"Well, everywhere they <u>had</u> occurred had been places where either I had been with Harry, like New York, or where <u>he</u> had been, like Missouri. There was nothing at all to associate Harry with the Berkshires, so I could think of no reason why he should be around me in my new house. [Pause, followed by sarcastic tone.] And it wasn't built on any Indian[2] Burial Ground either, like Harry's cabin.

"Anyway, it was almost 9pm by then, so I decided to get ready for bed. I blew out the candles, except two in the Master Bedroom Suite. I set the Alarm and planned to take a shower upon getting up the next morning. I'm a

---

[2] Apologies are again offered to Native American readers of this chronicle, who, it is hoped, will not take umbrage at the term "Indian," which, when used by Ms. Jacobs, was not meant as offensive terminology. In addition, the reader will learn that Harry, of part-Cherokee descent, deliberately built a cabin on land that was known to be the site of an abandoned Native American Campsite and burial ground. (Tape 20, page 309.)

person who likes showers. I really don't appreciate baths - they bring back too many memories of a childhood of being the last person in a large family to use the water in the tub, which by the time I got to it, was almost always cold and dirty. So I take showers, definitely NOT baths. But this night it was different. I felt compelled - [Pause.] - that's the word — compelled to take a bath. And what was so strange about that was, not only do I hate baths, but there was no hot water, as the electricity wasn't on to heat the water. The serviceman was supposed to come the next morning to turn everything on. Taking a cold shower in the morning is one thing, but a cold bath at night - ugh!

"But somehow I felt drawn to do that. I rationalized by thinking that I was soaked through and sweaty and tired, and even sitting in a small amount of tepid water - it was really very humid with the rain and all - would be good for me, and would help me relax. Sure.

"So I took off my wet clothes and started the bathtub water running.

"I think I should describe my bathtub - well maybe if I describe the whole layout of the Master Bedroom and Bathroom, you will appreciate how important it is to visualize what happened next."

"Yes, but spare any unnecessary details, Miss Jacobs, please."

"OK. Sure. I understand. Anyway, the Master Bedroom is really a Suite. It is a HUGE room, with a large bay window overlooking a deck which extends the length of that side of the house. It is almost the size of my Aunt's entire apartment from when I was a kid.

"Anyway, attached to this huge bedroom is a GIGANTIC bathroom. It is so luxurious, it is almost sinful. You should see this bathroom - [Pause.] - well I don't mean you should <u>really</u> see it --"

"I understand. Go on, Miss Jacobs, please."

"This bathroom is really incredible. It's every woman's dream. It has two long counters, lots of drawers, lots of mirrors, two sinks, an <u>actual</u> W.C., a toilet in a separate little room of its own - I mean, it's actually adorable!" [Light giggles.]

"Miss Jacobs, continue —."

"OK. Anyway, it has a HUGE separate shower — a work of art, like some kind of Roman decadence. And so is the bathtub. I really didn't care <u>what</u> was done with the tub, or even if there was one, but both Seymour and LaRossa insisted that a Master Bathroom would NOT be complete without a bathtub, and who was I to argue with them.

"It was Seymour who insisted on the design of the tub. You know how Seymour is about those things - I KNOW you know what I mean, Dr. Levy. It seemed OK, and looked good in the designs, so I agreed to it, since I didn't care one way or the other as I knew I would never be using it."

"What is so unusual about your bathtub, Miss Jacobs?"

"Well, it <u>really</u> is Roman decadence. It is completely round - can you believe that? A round bathtub? It is beautifully sculpted, and looks gorgeous in the general configuration of this huge bathroom. The darn thing looks palatial to me, considering my childhood. I'm perfectly satisfied with the bathroom in my apartment. But this thing is monstrous and definitely palatial.

"Anyway, I took my clothes off and ran the tub water. The practical consequences of a round bathtub had never dawned on me before, until I had to get in and use it.

"Without electricity, there was no hot water - I think I said that before. But it was hot enough outside to make the water tepid as it ran into the tub. It was just about the same temperature I can remember having as a kid, when I was the last one to use the bathtub. I placed a Jahrzeit candle on each of the two counters and stepped into the tub. My sleeping bag and the Alarm Clock and Music Box were nearby in the adjacent bedroom.

"I didn't fill the tub, because the water started to run cold after awhile, so I had barely enough water to cover my bottom. I stepped into the tub, and sat down. That's when I realized the problems of having a circular bathtub."

"Explain, please, Miss Jacobs."

"Well, I guess I have to be graphic. I'm five feet eight, and that's pretty tall for a woman. Seymour's shorter than I am, so maybe that explains part of it, in addition to the almost Roman orgy appearance of the thing. Anyway, as soon as I got into it, I could see where I would have problems. The only bathtubs I've been used to are the long rectangular kind, and I can stretch out in something like that. But this - this was something else.

"I had to scrunch into virtual contortions in order to fit. I arranged myself into an almost pretzel position, with my knees touching the sides of the tub, exposing my genitalia - I'm sorry, but it was awkward and uncomfortable.

"Anyway, I decided to make the best of a bad situation and use the soap, washcloth and towel I had brought with me, and with the little bit of lukewarm water in the tub, began to give myself what I call a 'sponge bath'. I was almost ready to get out of the tub, when this strange feeling came over me. It's so hard — it's so difficult to explain. It's so - so —"

[Silence. Sounds of sniffling.]

"Try, please, Miss Jacobs."

[Deep sigh, then voice softer, gentler in tone.]

"There came over me, little by little, this feeling of sexual desire. It was like nothing I had ever known or experienced in my life. It was as if I were enveloped - almost as if I were in a cocoon, of tender feelings of love and sexuality. This was <u>not</u> - please understand me, it's important that you <u>do</u> <u>understand</u> - it was not what people call 'horny' - nothing like that.

"It seemed to come out of nowhere. But little by little I was enveloped in this sensation of love, tenderness, sensuality, —- I'm sorry - I --"

[Silence.]

"It's all right, Miss Jacobs. Please. It's all right. Take your time."

[Silence. Voice resuming, choked with profound emotion and stifled tears.]

"And then, as I was drifting deeper and deeper into this tender sensation of intimate love, -- [Pause.] — a light went on."

[Silence.]

"What do you mean, Miss Jacobs, 'a light went on'."

"Just that. And I have no explanation for it, believe me, Dr. Levy - I <u>have</u> no explanation."

"Tell me more about this light, please. I do not understand."

"Neither do I. [Pause.] A light, recessed in the ceiling, directly over the bathtub, went on, and it illuminated my body as I lay naked in the tub."

"Did you do anything?"

"Nothing."

[Pause.]

"I remained in the same position and surrendered to this intense feeling of sensuality, love, and passion."

[Pause. Voice resuming with depth of emotion.]

"It was so unlike anything I have ever known before. It was uniquely beautiful. The light remained on, and I succumbed to this enrapture - - bliss and enrapture."

[Silence.]

"The feeling gradually subsided, and the light went off as strangely as it came on. I let the water drain out of the tub, and just sat numbly in the same position. Then I got out of the tub, dried myself with the towel, and walked - I remember how numb I was, as if in a trance - walked into the adjoining Master Bedroom."

[Silence.]

"Did anything else happen that night."

"Yes. How did you know?"

"By this time, Miss Jacobs, I have come to expect that anything is possible in your experiences."

[Pause.]

"Yes. I blew out the Jahrzeit candle I had on one of the counters and took the other with me so I could see when I went into the bedroom. It was still hot and muggy, so I didn't get inside my sleeping bag; rather, I

232

lay on top of it, still naked. I checked the Cardinal Alarm Clock, then blew out the candle. The room was completely dark.

"I turned on the Cardinal Music Box. I lay on top of my sleeping bag, still somewhat numb from what had just happened, and listened as the music to 'Love Story' played. Then it happened again."

[Silence, broken briefly by the sound of crying.]

"What happened, Miss Jacobs?"

"The light. [Crying.] The light in the bathroom went on again. At first I couldn't believe it, since I had extinguished all the candles; but I could see from where I was lying that the bathroom was flooded with light. One moment the bathroom was totally dark; the next moment, as I lay listening to the music of 'Love Story', the bathroom was filled with light.

"I got up — the music box was still playing — and I walked, again as if in a trance - who knows - maybe I really was. I walked into the bathroom and that same light, the one directly over the circular bathtub, was on again. I almost could not believe my eyes."

[Pause.]

"Go on, please, Miss Jacobs. What happened next."

"I stood there, naked, the music box still playing the theme from 'Love Story'. I stood there under the glow of the light, until the music box ran down. Then the light went out also. After that, I just walked, in the dark, back into the bedroom and lay on top of the sleeping bag."

"Were you able to sleep that night?"

"No. Not very well. I might have had a few short naps. Actually, I don't remember very well."

"What is <u>your</u> explanation for this incident, or I should say, <u>these</u> incidents, Miss Jacobs."

"I don't know what to think. Actually, I was hoping you could tell me. Was I hallucinating? Was I dreaming? Sleepwalking?"

"Miss Jacobs, you will forgive me if I ask, but did you indulge in any sexual self-gratification during these incidents."

[Very firmly spoken, almost to the degree of anger.]

"No. I did not. I could not. I was too overwhelmed by what was happening to me to even think in those terms - of doing anything like that. No. And besides, I tried to tell you, but how can I expect you or anyone else to understand - it was as if I were enveloped from outside of myself by these feelings of tender love - covered by a cloak of warmth and intimacy."

"Did you obtain sexual gratification from this experience in the bathtub?"

"No. It was nothing at all like that. It was a form of ecstasy, of sensual desire and passion that comes from purity of <u>love</u>, not lust. <u>Why can't I make you understand?</u>"

[Pause.]

"All right, Miss Jacobs. I accept your explanation, as much as I can. But you did not telephone me that next day. What happened to make you decide you could not stay in your country home — to feel you <u>had</u> to see me and return to work in the City before the end of the week?"

[Pause.]

"You know, it seems silly now. [Muffled tears.] It seems silly and stupid. Sometimes I don't understand why I act the way I do. As my friend Midge, one of only a few people who possibly understands what is happening - as Midge says to me so many times - why am I not enjoying this and savoring every moment? Why am I so fearful anytime something like this happens? Why must I feel that I am losing my mind, instead of just taking it for what it is and being thankful that Harry is able to communicate his feelings of love to me.

"I'm sorry. I'll answer your question. It just seems so stupid to me, now that I look back on it.

"Anyway, Monday, that next morning, I got up to the sound of the Cardinal Alarm Clock, and pretty soon the men arrived with the furniture. Also, the utility serviceman came and we had this long discussion about the bathroom light. He flat out told me that there was NO way that any lights could have come on without the power, which he himself turned on only that morning. The power that had been used during the construction of the house had been turned off during the process of transfer of title. I guess he must have thought I was nuts, or high on drugs or something.

"I spent Monday, arranging what I could, planning to do a little each day, so that by the end of the week, I would have my lovely new furnishings in order in my lovely new home. I didn't set the Alarm that night —I had no need to. Whatever time I got up would be fine. No one was expected, and I could work as I pleased. I plugged Harry's radio in, and listened to it as I went about the house. The events of the night before were still with me, but I was so busy arranging things, that what had happened was less on my mind - except there was a residue of warmth, a tender loving form of afterglow, that stayed with me and carried a sense of sweet remembrance.

"Then, this morning, Tuesday, — right?"

"Yes. That is correct, Miss Jacobs. Today is Tuesday. But did anything happen Monday night?"

"No. Not a thing. Monday was normal both day and night. Anyway, I woke this morning to what I thought was the Cardinal Alarm Clock. But I <u>knew</u> I hadn't set it the night before. Then I thought it was another one of those experiences like I had with that same clock before."

"What experience with the clock, Miss Jacobs? I don't remember you —-"

"I didn't tell you? Well, that's something for another session, I suppose."

[Pause.]

"Anyway, I thought it was the Cardinal clock alarm, and went to turn it off, only it WAS off! It had never been turned on. But the Cardinal sound continued - then I realized it wasn't coming from the clock at all.

"Monday night I had gone to sleep in my pjs, so I felt no problem in stepping out onto my deck. And there, like in Missouri, was the most beautiful Cardinal redbird - you know, the male cardinal. It was perched on the deck railing. I walked carefully up to it, but it was not the slightest disturbed by my presence. It seemed to welcome me. And it sang the most beautiful birdsong. It was almost as lovely as the sounds of the recorded nightingales used in Respighi's 'Pines of Rome'. It let me get really close to it. And somehow I knew it was Harry, welcoming me to my new home. It was as if I were being carried over the threshold. Do you know what I mean – do you know about that custom, Dr. Levy?"

"Yes, Miss Jacobs, I do. [Pause.] But why should such – surely it was not the bird singing that made you leave your home in such a hurry."

"But it WAS. It was the realization that the bird was Harry. I have never heard of Cardinals in the Berkshires, have you? I mean, those are mid-West birds, aren't they? And he is not leaving me alone. There was even a song that played on his radio –I think it was Peggy Lee singing – something like: 'Where can I go without you?' And the idea that he has such control over my life – making lights go on when there is no power, arousing in me feelings of such tenderness and desire, and then serenading me – I guess it was just the cumulative effect.

"Now that I talk to you, Dr. Levy, I really don't understand why I panicked the way I did. But after the bird stopped singing and flew away, I wept, then I stood by the railing, again as if in a trance."

[Pause.]

"I think if I stayed in that house I would have done nothing but be a slave to Harry's love. If I had given in and stayed there, I don't know if I could vouch for my sanity, because it was so tempting to remain, and be with him and see what happened."

[Silence. Voice, when resumed, choked with emotion.]

"I remember that after Harry kissed me and said 'goodbye,' so many years ago, I was totally devastated. I went into a deep depression. I really lost weight and slimmed down. And I kept reading love poetry, especially the poems of Sara Teasdale, who, as

I learned recently, was also born in Missouri. Another 'coincidence', of course. [Words spoken with bitter irony.] I memorized those poems back then, and I've been reading them again, with all that's been happening.

"There's one in particular, although so <u>many</u> of them are appropriate to our situation, mine and Harry's, but there is one, one I thought of this morning when I stood at the railing after the bird serenaded me:

[Pause.]

> I would live in your love as the sea-
> grasses live in the sea,
> Borne up by each wave as it passes,
> drawn down by each wave that recedes;
> I would empty my soul of the dreams that
> have gathered in me,
> I would beat with your heart as it
> beats, I would follow your soul as it
> leads.

[Lengthy silence.]

"That's what I meant when I said I had to leave. I knew if I stayed I would have surrendered completely to my feelings of love for Harry.

"Don't you understand, Dr. Levy? <u>I'm being courted by a Ghost!</u>" [Words spoken with profound emotional emphasis.]

[Silence.]

"Miss Jacobs – euh - why do you think Harry is doing this? But before you answer, tell me please, do you know what an Incubus is?"

"Yes. I have read about it in psychic and metaphysical literature. An Incubus is the spirit of a deceased male making love to a living woman. Is that what you think Harry is?"

"Do you, Miss Jacobs?"

"I don't know. I don't think so. I think the intent of an Incubus is something evil. I don't get that from Harry. I get the feeling that he wants me to know how much I love him and that he loves me as well. It's all about love and remembrance[3]. He wants to be sure that I love him and remember him. And I do, I do." [Uncontrolled weeping.]

"Miss Jacobs, forgive me, but it IS time for my next patient. Tell me when it is you would like to see me again, and I will work something out and have my secretary give you a call."

[Pause.]

"Are you all right, Miss Jacobs?"

"Yes. [Sounds of tissues being pulled from box.] I think I will just sit in your waiting room for awhile until I decide what to do next. Now I'm not sure whether I want to return to my house, to work, or to my apartment. I'll sit for awhile. Maybe I'll see if Midge is home and visit her. Anyway, thank you Dr. Levy, for seeing me on such short notice. I will come at whatever time is convenient for you to see me again, although perhaps I can just wait until my regular appointment tomorrow."

"As you wish, Miss Jacobs; however, I do think it is a good idea for you to sit for awhile and think about things before you decide what to do next."

"Yes, Dr. Levy."

"Goodbye, Miss Jacobs."

"Goodbye, and thank you again, Dr. Levy."

End of Tape 15.

---

[3] These words have been underlined, to alert the reader that this is where the title for this compilation of therapy sessions was derived.

Notes Accompanying Tape 15.

Now I am beginning to wonder who is seducing whom at this time. I think I may have noted before that this woman is a seducer of the mind. Now I wonder if she is a seductress such as Circe, or even Medea.

Is Harry truly an Incubus here? Or, assuming that his Spirit is in contact with Miss Jacobs, is he the victim of her seduction? It was she who undressed and lay naked first in the tub, and then on her sleeping bag, not in it.

Of course, the entire episode can be explained as her own sexual fantasy – her sexual desire for Harry, which was never fulfilled when they were together in her teenage years.

According to Miss Jacobs, she was ugly and unattractive, and Harry felt something akin to pity when he began a friendship with her. But for all I know, she could have been as enticing as Nabokov's "Lolita," EVEN if she looked as she described. Given American standards of what is beautiful, she might have believed, as a neglected child in a family of beautiful, slender women (again, according to her description) that she was fat, when in fact, she was merely Ruebenesque. As an adult woman, she has an air that would be seductive to any man of imagination – the more intelligent man who sees beyond the stereotypical beauty worshipped in this country.

Although it is possible to believe that her current state of allure came as a result of the confidence she gained from the attention of this man Harry, it is more likely that there was something seductive about her even as a young girl. It is possible Harry had very good reason to put her in that taxi. I have only Miss Jacobs' description of her unattractive appearance to accept.

Is she a reliable historian? She seems to be. The way she tells her story, as I have noted before, is like a narration – straightforward and factual, objective and detached. Except this time, when she spoke of her unusual sexual experience, the tone of her voice and the appearance of her face conveyed an expression of warmth and tender emotion.

Was what she told me truly an objective description of events as seen from her perspective, or a narrative of something she had scripted, like a play. But there are some philosophers and metaphysicians who believe that all aspects of our lives are scripted by ourselves. And of course, there is Shakespeare's "All the world's a stage…"

Then there was the Cardinal with its song the next morning. If every word of her story is to be believed, perhaps Miss Jacobs and the Spirit of this man Harry are truly Lovers who are united beyond Time and the appearance of Death.

But if that is so, why, as she herself asks, do these experiences, if meant for love and not evil, continue to disturb her? Perhaps it is the possibility of loss of control to something she cannot understand which <u>truly</u> terrifies Miss Jacobs.

Extraordinary!

*   *   *

Tape 16

April 29, 1981

4:30 pm

"Good afternoon, Miss Jacobs."

"Dr. Levy."

[Pause.]

"I seem to remember that before I went to my house, I was going to give you examples of some of the things that happened to me that I believe go well beyond the realm of coincidence. Little did I expect to provide you with such dramatic incidents as what prompted yesterday's visit."

"Yes — but Miss Jacobs, tell me first, please - what happened after you left my office yesterday. You are here, therefore I assume you did not return to your country home."

"No. But I plan to this weekend."

[Pause.]

"Did you go to your office? Did you return to your apartment, or visit your friend?"

"After I left here, I went to work at my office. I told them I was able to take care of things quicker than expected, and since I'm viewed as somewhat of a workaholic anyway, no one seemed surprised at my early return."

[Pause.]

"So then, these occurrences have not resulted in any adverse opinion about the characteristic nature of your work per-formance, at least as far as your office management is concerned, is that correct, Miss Jacobs?"

[Pause.]

"I guess you're right, Dr. Levy."

[Silence.]

"I was thinking. Talk about synchron-icities,[1] I was in such a rush last week, making arrangements to go up to open my house — you know, it still seems so strange to refer to 'MY' house — anyway, I was in such a rush that I completely forgot to cancel my appointments with you for this week. Now isn't that convenient!"

"And, I take it, Miss Jacobs, that you consider your act of forgetting as another example of synchronicity, rather than mere coincidence."

"Well, what would YOU say, Dr. Levy."

"I don't know how to answer that, Miss Jacobs. My immediate reaction, if you were any other patient, would be to assume you were, so to speak, making a mountain out of a molehill, in order to fit your own theory or belief system. But in your case — [Pause.] — in your case, I can not be sure."

[Pause.]

"Why do you say that, Dr. Levy?"

"Because, my dear Miss Jacobs, you have had so many strange events happen in your life, particularly after you learned of the death of this man Harry. [Pause.] Further, there comes a time when the number of coincidences, if significant, becomes, of itself, statistically beyond the realm of mere coincidence. [Pause.] Do you understand what I am saying, Miss Jacobs?"

"I think so. [Pause.] I think, if I understand you correctly, you mean that if the number of coincidences is so large, then that number, of itself, places the events outside the statistical probability of coincidence."

---

[1] See explanation, Tape 7, fn. 3.

"Exactly. [Pause.] And in your case, Miss Jacobs, as you continue providing me with more examples of these so-called coincidences that have occurred in your life, we may rapidly be approaching such a number, if it has not been passed already."

"And if it <u>has</u>?"

"If it has, then we are into the realm of synchronicity, and I am uncertain of my ability to treat such episodes in patient therapy. [Pause.] So, to return to what you asked originally, I can not be sure, in your case, whether your forgetting to cancel your appointments with me this week was coincidental, or one more example of synchronicity in your life."

[Silence.]

"Tell me about the events that occurred when you went to Missouri, which you believe are examples of synchronicities, Miss Jacobs, please."

"Yes. You know, it was as if that entire trip was to Synchronicity Land. [Pause; then voice excited with tone of teasing.] Say, that's a MARVELOUS idea for a New-Age Theme Park. Synchronicity Land. [Laughter.] I LOVE IT!"

"Miss Jacobs. Sometimes I believe you have the strangest sense of humor."

"I can understand why you say that. [Pause.] And so did Harry — have a weird sense of humor, I mean. That's why we fit so well together with each other. We talked the same way, we joked the same way — we understood each other so well, and could be so at ease with each other."

[Silence.]

"Miss Jacobs, I do not understand why you are continually reduced to tears almost every time you talk about this - euh, — Harry. Can you possibly convey to me why it is that almost every time you talk about him, even when it is with pleasant memories, you start-"

"**I DON'T KNOW!** [Voice loud, semi-hysterical.] I swear to God, Dr. Levy, **I DON'T KNOW**! I wish I <u>did</u> know. Don't you think I've asked myself that same question a million times? I DON'T KNOW, I tell you, but I wish I did. [Pause.] Sometimes I find myself asking over and over, what is it about Harry that makes me weep whenever thoughts of him come into my mind, or events happen involving him or memories of him. I can be alone, I can be here in your office, or worse yet, I can be with friends or strangers, and if thoughts or events occur that are somehow related to Harry, I start to cry. I've told you Dr. Levy — I have shed more tears over this man than over any human being I have known in my life. I know I love him. I believe now that I've <u>always</u> loved him. But I am being honest with you, Dr. Levy, I can't explain it either."

[Silence.]

"When you feel ready Miss Jacobs, please continue with what you have indicated was a most eventful trip to Missouri. In fact, can you tell me how it was that you came to make this trip — the circumstances leading up to it."

"Yes. All right. Actually, you're right. The circumstances leading up to it are themselves significant."

[Pause.]

"I have this friend Midge - I believe I may have mentioned her name to you before."

"Yes. Perhaps."

"Anyway — Wait! I just remembered what it was that triggered this whole conversation with Midge I was about to relate to you."

"And what was that, Miss Jacobs, please."

"I was listening to WQXR, the way I always do — it's always there in the background for me, and I usually don't pay that much attention to what's playing, unless it's something I know and like, or something I've not heard before, but really grabs my attention. This time, fortunately I was not at work, they were playing a beautiful rendition of some folk singer singing 'Danny Boy,' and for some strange reason — but of course it's NOT strange, is it — I was meant to hear it. Anyway, it made me think of Harry, almost like it was 'Oh Harry Boy', instead of 'Danny Boy.' Of course, as you can well imagine, I started to cry, and stopped whatever it was I was doing and sat down and listened to the words. [Pause.] The singer went on to the second verse. I swear to you, Dr. Levy; I had <u>never</u> heard the second verse before in all the years of my life. It goes on about 'Danny Boy' being dead — and I remember how the singer actually accented the word 'dead', as if to specifically call it to my attention. Anyway, it goes on about how his beloved will find the place where he is buried, and how, even though he is dead and in the ground, he will be comforted by her words of love for him, and will be able to sleep in peace until she dies and they are together again."

[Silence.]

"That's very moving. Indeed. [Pause.] Miss Jacobs, are you aware that 'Danny Boy', although a song that's been around most likely for centuries — that these particular words were written in connection with soldiers who were fighting in the First World War?"

"No. Oh my God, no. I didn't know that."

"It would seem as if we have revealed an example of another so-called coincidence, would you agree Miss Jacobs?"

"I guess I would. [Voice very subdued; then pause.]

"But from what I knew at the time, and I didn't know about it being a song in memory of fallen soldiers in a World at War, I still was crying, and I felt so blue, I had to call Midge. She's been such a good friend to me, Dr. Levy. I can call her any time, well almost any time, as her husband put a stop to my middle-of-the-night calls. Midge may not have to go to work, but <u>he</u> does."

"I'm pleased to see you smile just then, Miss Jacobs. [Pause.] Excuse the interruption. Continue, please."

"Anyway, Midge and I talked for hours that night. Her husband was watching some TV special, so he didn't mind. He's really a good sport that way, very supportive — except for those mid-morning calls, for which I can't blame him."

"And what did you and Midge talk about for so long?"

"First, after I told her about the words to the second verse of 'Danny Boy', which I had never known, she <u>insisted</u>, and I really mean <u>insisted</u>, that this was a direct message from Harry that I was supposed to go to where he is buried and tell him how much I love him. She asked if I had ever told Harry, during the time I knew him, that I loved him. When I told her I hadn't, because actually I did not think of it then as love, that made her even <u>more</u>

insistent, if possible, that I was supposed to visit Harry's gravesite.

"Then she asked where Harry was buried. I told her it was a tiny little town somewhere in Missouri. And then she became all excited and asked for the name of the town, so I told her. She said she would call me back, because she wanted to look something up on the map. So I told her OK, and in a few minutes she called back, and was almost hysterical with excitement. [Pause.] Dr. Levy, did I tell you that Midge has psychic abilities?"

"No, Miss Jacobs. I don't believe you did."

[Pause. When voice resumed, tone softer, contemplative.]

"Dr. Levy, what do _you_ think about psychic abilities? I mean, do you think they exist and that people can actually possess them."

[Pause.]

"My dear Miss Jacobs, that is a _very_ complex question, which I think requires an answer that would take too much time to be appropriate in your hour."

"How can you say that, Dr. Levy? If there was ever a patient for whom a discussion of the subject of psychic phenomena was appropriate, I would think it would be me, and would not be a waste of my time. [Pause, followed by tone of indignation.] Besides, it's my money, and if I feel like wasting my time on a discussion of something that's important to me, shouldn't I be entitled to it?"

"Miss Jacobs, the purpose of therapy is not to indulge patients in discussions of abstractions which interest them, but to deal with and resolve issues that trouble them. It is not whether _I_ believe in psychic phenomena that matters, but how YOU feel and think about them that is at issue."

[Silence.]

"But to respond briefly to your question, because I can understand why it is important and relevant to you, I can state honestly that my mind is not closed, but remains open to the possibility that these phenomena do occur and that some persons have abilities which can not be explained within the traditional definitions of human behavior. I'm sorry, Miss Jacobs, but that is the best I can offer within the professional therapeutic setting."

"I understand, and I am grateful for what you just told me. That reply was actually more than I had hoped for."

[Pause.]

"Why was your friend Midge so excited when she called back, Miss Jacobs, please."

"Because of what she found out about where Harry had lived and was buried. [Pause.] It seems Midge has had an interest in metaphysics and related subjects ever since she first discovered she had these abilities. She, unlike me, was never disturbed by them, but accepted them as part of her nature and keeps berating me to do the same. Of course, she and I are different people, with different experiences, different backgrounds, and so —. [Pause.] But, I DO wish I could accept them as easily as Midge does.

"Anyway, for years Midge has been subscribing to literature from an obscure Metaphysical Institute somewhere in Missouri, and when she called back, it was to tell me that the place where Harry is buried is very close on the map to the location of this Institute. She showed the map to her husband during a TV commercial break and he estimated that they were about an hour apart, maximum.

"At that point Midge became absolutely merciless and eventually convinced me that the only logical thing for me to do was combine a visit to Harry's grave with a visit to the Institute's library, which apparently has an extensive collection of books, magazines, research papers, etc. on metaphysical and paranormal subjects.

"And so that's what I did. I took a week's vacation and went to Missouri, where I devoted a full 8 days to indulging my need for learning more about Harry and about psychic phenomena. [Pause.] And metaphysical subject matter in general, I might add. Because once I started reading about paranormal phenomena, of course it followed that the whole subject of what constitutes — quote, reality, unquote — came into question."

"And now it's my turn to ask. Did you reach any conclusion as to what constitutes reality, Miss Jacobs."

[Laughter.] "Now it's my turn to be evasive. And I apologize if I sounded off at you before. I understand why you could not respond to my earlier question in any way other than as you did. I can not — well how can ANYBODY answer that question, even in the space of an hour! OK. Touché, Dr. Levy. And to answer simply, there is NO WAY I can answer that question, because — well, perhaps that actually is why I am coming to you for therapy — to find out more about what is the nature of reality. If it is as most of the people in the world think, then perhaps I am mentally unbalanced. But if reality encompasses more, then my experiences are not symptoms of mental illness."

"Do you think you can really learn the nature of reality through therapy, Miss Jacobs?"

"Maybe not, but if I were really nuts, you'd be able to tell me and give me the help I need. [Pause.] Seymour recommended <u>many</u> times before I actually made that first morning call, that you could help me, because you had an open mind and were a compassionate listener. That's why I came to you, and I'm grateful you've been patient enough to put up with me."

"Thank you for the kind words, Miss Jacobs. And tell me, what does your friend Midge think of you seeing a psychotherapist, assuming you've told her."

"Of course I have. And she's a very outspoken person. She <u>definitely</u> thinks it's a waste of time and money. She keeps saying — 'there's nothing wrong with you; it's all in your head' — and I keep telling her — 'yeah, you're right; it's all in my head and that's why I need to see a shrink'!"

[Laughter.]

"Good for Midge. I can tell she is truly a good friend to you, Miss Jacobs. [Pause.] And with that, I see our time is up, and I look forward to hearing about this eventful visit to Missouri."

"Thank you, Dr. Levy. Good-bye."

"Good-bye, Miss Jacobs."

End of Tape 16.

Notes Accompanying Tape 16.

There are <u>definitely</u> times when I have reason to wonder about this "active imagination" Miss Jacobs possesses. She claims this man Harry was a "story-teller." She has stated that several times. She has also often referred to how much they were alike — she did so at this day's session. Does she also have that story-telling ability? To exaggerate — to "stretch" the truth — but, as <u>she</u> would say: "What is Truth"!

How many times has she told me in distress that these occurrences have interfered with her ability to function, and effected her performance at work. Yet, when she was in such apparent distress after the incidents at her new home, where does she go for solace? To the home of her friend Midge? No! To her office!

This act conveys several possibilities to me. First, it could be she has such need to be in control, both of herself and others, that she knew the work environment would offer structure and returned to it as a known, familiar source of peace and comfort. Second, she was not <u>really</u> in distress at all, but was manipulating me with more tales — a veritable Scheherazade! But <u>why</u> would she do that? Again, I must ask myself, why would she spend her time and money to tell me stories? Simply for attention? I find myself returning to that possibility so often in this case.

Is it possible she feels <u>so</u> inferior, <u>so</u> inappropriate in her new home, that she "conjured" up this incident in order to have a reason to leave it? (Now it is <u>I</u> who am referring to "conjuring" — still, it <u>is</u> appropriate in this case with a magician and a woman with alleged psychic abilities!) So often she has spoken about how unbelievable it is that she, POOR Sophie Jacobs (because, in many ways, she <u>still</u> sees herself as that poor orphan girl), could have such a magnificent house for herself. Yet she <u>did</u> state she intends to return to her home at the end of the week.

And those compliments she heaped on me! I have such an "open mind" and am such a "compassionate listener." HAH! And I am so "patient" to "put up with" her! INDEED!

Now it is MY turn to wonder about my own ability to judge what is happening here! What if this woman is indeed telling me <u>everything</u> she sees and understands. What if these events are occurring <u>exactly</u> as she has narrated and her reactions to them are <u>exactly</u> as she has described. Perhaps I should take myself to task for not accepting what she says for what it is — the "Truth" (whatever that may be). I have ruled out Psychosis in this case. Compared to the rest of my patients, she bears almost <u>no</u> traces of Neurosis! Unless, of course, she is fabricating all of this — and so here I am, full circle.

Why can I not believe? Am I not, then, like Miss Jacobs, as well? Am I searching too hard for an answer to her concerns within the realm of Science, when the answer is indeed somewhere else? And that glorious speech I gave! Am I such a hypocrite! Is my mind <u>truly</u> open, as I told her it was!

Perhaps, after hearing more of her experiences, which she keeps leading to believe are copious, particularly during her trip to Missouri — perhaps as we delve deeper and I attempt to analyze something that may lie beyond our current capability of analysis

— I will discover that she is <u>truly</u> someone who possesses abilities beyond those of most human beings. Can, or even, SHOULD, someone like this be in analytical therapy? Is it ethical for me to take money from her to hear her story, or is it <u>I</u> who should be paying her for the knowledge I gain about psychic experiences which occur to particularly sensitive individuals.

***

Tape 17

"Good afternoon, Miss Jacobs."

"Hi, Dr. Levy."

"I can't help but notice that you seem in an exceptionally cheerful mood this afternoon — indeed, more cheerful than I've ever seen you since we first met."

"Probably so. In fact, I have to be absolutely sure that I leave on time today, because I know we sometimes take longer than usual since I am your last scheduled patient."

"And why is that, Miss Jacobs. Do you have what is called 'a heavy date'?"

"Dr. Levy, shame on you! No. That isn't it at all. Besides, why do you think I would be dating?"

"And why not? You are an attractive, intelligent woman who happens to be single and unattached. Why shouldn't you be dating?"

[Pause. When voice responds, tone is somber.]

"Dr. Levy, you of all people should know the answer to your own question. I appreciate your kind comments about my good qualities, but I am NOT unattached — and I don't understand why you would even <u>consider</u> that I am."

"Miss Jacobs — I'm sorry. I apologize. First, because I dampened your good mood, and secondly, because I apparently offended you in some way. If I understood correctly from one of our earlier sessions, you are divorced, is that not right? Or perhaps I misunderstood and your divorce is not yet final."

"You did not misunderstand, Dr. Levy. My divorce was final many years ago. But apparently we have a <u>very serious</u> misunderstanding of another kind here."

"If that is so, Miss Jacobs, then I need to have you explain what that misunderstanding is, please."

"<u>I can't believe this</u>. How could YOU, of ALL people, Dr. Levy, believe I am unattached. [Pause.] How <u>could</u> you, when I have sat here in this very office, week after week, crying my eyes and my heart out over 'this man Harry' [tone very sarcastic here] as you refer to him time and time again — how <u>could</u> you even <u>consider</u> that I am 'unattached', as you put it."

[Extended silence.]

"Miss Jacobs, I can see we have something very serious to discuss here. <u>Very</u> serious. [Pause.] Before this, I have not believed that you displayed any symptoms of neurosis — none at least that warranted any form of treatment. We have concentrated our sessions on your reaction to the unusual events in your life. But <u>now</u>, if I am to understand you correctly, you are letting me know that you cannot have a normal dating relationship because of your devotion to the memory of a man who died almost two years ago, and who you have not seen in over 30 years."

[Pause; then intense, almost angry response.]

"You <u>are</u> right, Dr. Levy. We <u>DO</u> have a <u>VERY</u> serious problem here. Let me see if I can set you straight about some things.

"First of all, you <u>DID</u> understand me correctly. <u>Yes</u>. I <u>am</u> letting you know that I <u>can</u> not, and <u>will</u> not even <u>consider</u> the possibility of dating. Let me explain, although by now it should be obvious."

"Yes, Miss Jacobs. I want very much to hear your explanation."

"You acted surprised that I would not consider dating. Haven't you been listening to anything I've been saying in these sessions. It's not as if I've been keeping secrets from you. You've known since our very first meeting, that — I think I even stated it to you as such — that I'm being — I think my words were: 'courted by a Ghost'. I've told you, and you'll hear much more about it, believe me, when I tell you what happened in Missouri, how Harry has been letting me understand both how much I love him and how much he loves me.

"I distinctly remember our discussion about the ring I wear. In fact, you were the one who initiated that particular discussion because you noticed that I wear it on the finger women usually reserve for wedding bands or engagement rings. And I also remember that I told you that I wore that ring in remembrance of Harry and that I would wear it for — I think I said something like — 'for the rest of my life on this particular plane' — or words to that effect."

"Yes. I remember. And I also remember that we had left that discussion unresolved. I believe that you had more to tell me about why you would never remove that ring from your finger for the remainder of your life. And quite frankly, Miss Jacobs, I also remember feeling somewhat troubled by the fact that this decision seemed to me to be almost like a wedding vow, and I wanted to discuss it further with you. [Pause.] I presume we are at that point now."

"I believe so. Yes."

[Silence.]

"Tell me, Miss Jacobs please, why have you decided never to remove this ring for the remainder of your life. And I would also like to know whether this decision is irrevocable, or subject to change."

"Believe me, Dr. Levy, it is irrevocable."

"Then explain, please. Without an explanation you see, it appears almost as if you have become a Nun, retreating from the secular world of the living to be a bride of the Holy Spirit."

[Pause; then tone of sarcasm.]

"Well, that's an interesting way of putting it. I never quite — [Pause.] I'll have to give that concept some thought."

[Silence.]

"I ask you again Miss Jacobs. Tell me, please, why have you decided never to remove this ring for the remainder of your life."

"Because Harry Gault is the one man, the ONLY man I loved before, am in love with now, and will ever love. Now and Forever. Truly, madly, deeply. [Pause.] I trust that answers your question, Dr. Levy."

[Silence.]

"Miss Jacobs, I have told you more than once that I have not seen any indications in your behavior that lead me to believe you have problems of a serious mental disorder, and that sometimes I believe you would rather be diagnosed as such rather than deal with the possibility of the validity of your unusual experiences. However, now I am wondering whether it is possible that, because of your unfortunate childhood, you feel so unworthy of receiving love, that you would shun it from a living human being thereby risking rejection, and would prefer to indulge yourself in this inter-dimensional love relationship which theoretically can continue forever.

"Furthermore, I am wondering whether you feel yourself so unworthy of love that you would prefer risking a diagnosis of mental illness rather than surrender this relationship with a man who is deceased."

[Silence. When voice resumes, tone softer.]

"Perhaps what you are saying is true, Dr. Levy. I don't know. That's why I came for your help in the first place — to find out what meaning all this has in my life. [Pause.] But please, let me tell you about this other related experience, after which you can consider whether or not I have a problem of mental instability. I will accept your judgment, whatever it is."

"Yes, Miss Jacobs."

[Pause.]

"I had told you how, when I saw the film 'Lili' again after learning of Harry's death, I realized this ring was irrevocably associated with him in my mind and heart."

"Yes. I remember."

"And I told you that I had another psychic experience that made me realize I was to wear this ring for the rest of my life here on earth."

"Yes. I remember that, as well."

"So now I'll tell you about that experience."

"Yes, Miss Jacobs, please do."

"I had been on assignment for my job. I was auditing the books of a multi-national corporation in Southern California. I remember that I had decided to wear the ring at a dinner party the CEO was giving when the audit was completed. I was all dressed and set to go to the dinner when I could not find the ring, which I had seen last on the dresser. I panicked. I remember calling the front desk and asking if anyone had turned it in. I reported it as lost or stolen, but later I found it in the most bizarre place. It was under one of the pillows in the bed I was using in my hotel room. Interesting that the room was equipped with two double beds, and that the ring was under <u>not</u> the pillow <u>I</u> was sleeping on, but the other, ostensibly, unused pillow of this double bed. <u>I</u> certainly did not put it there. To this day, I do not know how it got there — although I could offer a psychic explanation. I found it only as I got into bed that night, with acute gastric pain probably caused by being so upset over what I considered to be the loss of the ring. I decided to use both pillows to elevate my head, thereby minimizing the possibility of gastric reflux. It was only when I lifted the other pillow that I found the ring, nicely centered beneath it.

"Of course, I put the ring on immediately. And I put it on the finger on which you see it now. But it was not then that I made what I refer to as my solemn vow to wear it forever. That happened after the experience of the next morning."

"And what was that, Miss Jacobs, please."

"I was at the front desk of the hotel, in the process of checking out. I can remember it so clearly. I was fiddling nervously with the ring, moving it back and forth on my finger, as the clerk computed my bill. Then suddenly — in a way it was somewhat similar to how I described the walls of my bedroom disappearing when I had what I refer to as my 'vision' — suddenly the scene around me began to fade away. I could still see the clerk working on my bill, and I could still make out the lobby and people in it, but they all seemed unreal, as if they were part of a movie backdrop — that's the only way I can think to describe it. They were still there, but hazy, almost transparent."

"Then Harry was beside me. Before you ask, no, he was not three dimensional the way you and I are at this moment. In fact, and I <u>know</u> this will REALLY seem crazy, but I'm not sure if <u>I</u> was three-dimensional at that point. It was as if we were together on some other plane, perhaps in some other dimension, as you stated earlier — I don't know — but what I <u>DO</u> know is that wherever it was, Harry and I were together, while all this other stuff was there as haze in the background — a background without sound.

"Harry took my hand, and held my finger with the ring, and slipped it gently but firmly on my finger. He said, 'Wear this in memory of me', and then he was gone. [Pause.] What happened next was in some ways even stranger."

"And what was that, Miss Jacobs, please."

"Everything went back to normal, the people in the lobby, who had previously been part of this flimsy backdrop, came to life again, and the clerk was talking to me about my bill — going over it with me and verifying the charges. Apparently, as far as he was concerned, I had not disappeared nor had any lapse occurred in the sequence of time — it was as if I had been engaged in a conversation with him during that interval, of which <u>he</u> was fully aware, but <u>I</u> was not, because the <u>I</u> which I know as myself, was somewhere else with Harry.

"Are you following me, Dr. Levy, or have I lost you yet?"

"No, I am able to follow what you are saying, Miss Jacobs. Continue, please."

"It was what happened next which unified the entire experience. It was probably the strangest of all. I became conscious of music playing in the background, as the desk clerk was talking to me about my bill. It was from 'West Side Story'; the song in which Tony and Maria exchange their vows of love. [Pause.]

Now it begins,
Now we start,
One Hand,
One Heart –
And then:
Even Death won't part us now."

[Prolonged silence, broken only by sounds of weeping.]

"I'm sorry you are so upset, Miss Jacobs. But I must ask you. Was that music actually playing in the lobby, or was it something that came into your mind, appropriately at that time."

[Voice weak with effort of controlling emotion.]

"No. It was music that was being piped into the hotel lobby. Usually I just block that sort of thing out, but this time it was inevitable that I should hear it."

[Another prolonged silence.]

"What did you do next, Miss Jacobs, please."

"Initially, I had the same doubt you just expressed. It was as if I couldn't believe what I was hearing. So to confirm that the song could be heard by people other than myself, I <u>actually</u> asked the clerk something like: 'Oh, what's the name of that lovely song that's playing now, it's on the tip of my tongue'. And he replied something like: 'I don't know the name, but it's from "West Side Story". Isn't it beautiful?'"

[Silence.]

"Dr. Levy, I swear to you to this day, I do not know how I was able to conduct a rational conversation with that desk clerk. Apparently, not only did I conduct one with him while I was going crazy in my mind over what had just happened with Harry and what was happening with that song in the background, but it would seem that I had conducted one with him while I was, in my own mind, somewhere else with Harry, pledging undying love. And when I say, 'in my own mind,' I don't mean imagination. It was as real as the exchange that is going on between you and me at this moment."

[Silence.]

"Miss Jacobs — [Pause.] — I truly do not know what to say to you. I have never dealt with such experiences before, and I do not know how to address them in the exercise of my profession. [Pause.] It would be simple to say that you were obviously delusional. The majority of my colleagues would be quick to jump to such a conclusion. But I cannot, in good conscience, make such a rash judgment. [Pause.] I suppose it would be easiest for me to say that I need more time to think about everything you have just told me — and that would <u>definitely</u> be true — not a lie. But I <u>am</u> not, I <u>can</u> not, be sure if given even 100 years to think about what you have said, that I would be able to come up with an explanation for these circumstances.

"If this had been an isolated incident, I probably would have taken the easier road that most of my colleagues would choose — that is, to say you were definitely suffering from delusions, in combination with visual and auditory hallucinations. But, considering everything you have told me thus far, plus the things you indicate you have <u>yet</u> to tell me — again, I am at a loss to know what to say or do. [Pause.] It is <u>I</u> who must ask <u>you</u> to bear with me, please, Miss Jacobs."

[Silence.]

"And, after what you have just told me, I can only offer a belated apology for my humorous reference to a 'heavy date'. I meant no disrespect — I simply did not understand. [Pause.] And I also withdraw what must surely seem like a very insensitive remark about you living the life of a Nun wedded to the Holy Spirit."

[Pause.]

"However, as a therapist, I still have concerns that continuing along this path may lead to difficulties in your outer World. Continued preoccupation with Harry and your devotion to him, no matter <u>how</u> appealing or compelling, may impact your daily existence, and eventually effect your professional life as well, even though there are no apparent problems at this time. I feel it is my duty to tell you this, because I am worried that if you are unable to maintain a balance between your fascination for the World of Spirit and the requirements of performing in the World of the Living, it may eventually result in a situation where you <u>will</u> require psychiatric assistance. [Pause.] And that is another reason why I have suggested you seek the guidance of one of my colleagues with experience in working with paranormal phenomena. I apologize that I have not yet provided any names to you, but I will do so at my earliest convenience."

[Silence.]

"Ah, Miss Jacobs. I feel sad that not only have I destroyed the cheerful mood in which you entered my office, but I have also kept you later than you wanted, when you had specifically requested we end our session early today."

"That's all right, Dr. Levy. I share part of the responsibility by coming so unglued over what basically was an innocuous statement meant to tease me. It's just that I'm so sensitive about everything having to do with Harry, because what you just told me is what all my friends — except Midge — have been telling me."

"Even Seymour?"

"Especially Seymour."

[Pause.]

"Now that you're already late, Miss Jacobs, can you possibly spare a moment to tell me what it was that had you so elated when you came in for your appointment?"

"Midge is sitting in your outer reception area. She is going to spend the weekend with me at my house so I don't have to worry about being alone if anything else strange happens. We're going to drive up to the Berkshires as soon as we leave your office."

"Oh."

"Good-bye, Dr. Levy. [Pause.] I plan to keep my regular appointment schedule next week. I'll be back in the City."

"Yes. Good-bye, and good luck at your house, Miss Jacobs."

End of Tape 17.

Notes Accompanying Tape 17.

This session may have been one of the most confrontational between this patient and myself thus far. It began innocently enough, but what a STORM my remark about "dating" provoked.

This woman never ceases to amaze me. She is like no one I have ever known or treated before. I still can not, in the exercise of my professional judgment, attach any definition of mental disorder to her behavior. And, once again, she herself seemed to indicate she would even accept the diagnosis of neurosis resulting from a love-starved childhood, if it would provide an explanation for the phenomena she is experiencing.

And WHAT experiences! And to think that there are many more which she has yet to tell me.

But let me consider the possibility that she is inventing everything she has told me. If such were the case, then she indeed has a fertile imagination and should perhaps be writing a book about her fantasies, rather than spending time and money to see a psychoanalyst. I realize she has a flair for the dramatic, but unless I have been completely deceived by her manipulative behavior, she appears to be genuinely troubled by the lack of rational explanations for what she relates as happening in her life.

One thing is clear beyond doubt — and that is the fierceness of her protective love for this man Harry. Can it be that he has returned, as Liliom, to set things right? But these experiences seem to continue, even as she sees me for treatment. I never know, when she appears, if some additional experience has

266

occurred in the few days that separate our sessions. And if they are continuing — what is their expected duration? For the remainder of her life? Or will there ultimately be some resolution to the relationship between Miss Jacobs and her Spirit-Lover.

What is also so fascinating about this woman is the strength of her analytical mind. She continues to question — and perhaps that is the nature of the entire problem. She seeks logical answers to events which are without explanation in this stage of knowledge of Mankind, and steadfastly refuses to accept that there may be phenomena for which there are NO logical answers. What is that famous line in Shakespeare?

"There are more things on heaven and earth than are dreamt of in your philosophy."
or whatever the words.

How <u>extraordinary</u> that she had enough purpose of mind to actually make inquiry of the desk clerk to learn if the music was being heard by others. What powers of concentration and analysis! Surely, if she were merely delusional, such a tactic would not be necessary, nor would it have meaning or purpose. But she <u>needed</u> to be sure — to find out for herself if what she was hearing was her own imagination, or if it could be heard by others who had not shared her experience. And <u>such</u> an experience! If I am to accept it as related, it is not surprising that she feels wedded to Harry for life!

But before I DO accept this incident without question, perhaps I should consider other explanations. Could she have imagined this romantic episode with Harry <u>after</u> hearing the love song in the lobby? But to believe that would be to doubt her veracity, and thus far,

I have nothing to indicate she has not been a reliable historian. And if she did imagine it after hearing the song, the way this woman is in pursuit of logical explanations, she would never have brought the matter to my attention. Moreover, it is NOT just a question of this incident in isolation. It is this incident PLUS all the others which she has related and has yet to relate.

Could the missing ring have been found by a cleaning person? Assume for the moment that it had fallen to the floor — but why would a cleaning person place the ring and center it carefully under a pillow, as Miss Jacobs described she found it. The more normal reaction would be, assuming they did not keep it for themselves, to place the ring on top of a piece of furniture, or take it to the front desk. Nor is it plausible to assume that a maid would place it under the pillow for sentimental reasons, as the ring bears absolutely NO resemblance to a wedding or engagement band.

How Jung would loved to have had this woman for a patient! Yet here I have her, and am at a loss to know what to do, other than sit back and be fascinated by what I hear. Whatever I seem to offer in analysis, she seems to have already considered. Moreover, she is far too quick to seek an explanation of illness where none is sufficient.

Sometimes I have to ask myself why this woman continues to see me. She certainly has no need of my assistance, as I can not believe I am providing any to her.

And something else I have noticed, but do not believe I have noted previously. There are times when she has anticipated the next question I was about to ask — however, that could simply be explained as another example of her analytical or even intuitive mental processes. Or again, as mere coincidence! Yet somehow it goes beyond all that. And what is more, she does it naturally, without even realizing she is doing it!

Could she actually possess psychic abilities? Can she read minds? Not just Harry's, which she freely acknowledges, but the minds of others, including my own? Unfortunately, ethical considerations prevent me from asking Seymour if he has observed any such ability in Miss Jacobs.

I have never considered the possibilities of this alleged mind-reading game played between Miss Jacobs and Harry when she was a child. Could it actually have occurred? At the time she was relating these experiences, I was concentrating on the <u>nature</u> of her relationship with Harry, not the <u>content</u>. Does this woman have psychic powers that have existed <u>throughout</u> her life — not just in the form of pubescent Poltergeist activity — which <u>continue</u> to exist to this moment?

Sometimes I wish I had Miss Jacobs organizational abilities — then I would remember the many things I want to follow through with in her case. I should make a list of things to ask her. Certainly one of the primary questions at this time is whether she is aware, or believes, that she is able to read my thoughts during our sessions.

Absolutely fascinating!

***

Tape 18

May 6, 1981

4:30 pm

"Good afternoon, Miss Jacobs."

"Hi, Dr. Levy."

"Ah. I notice again that you seem very cheerful. I trust that means you had an enjoyable and also uneventful weekend with Midge at your country home."

"Actually, it WAS an eventful weekend, but, thank God, not those supernatural or however you want to call them, events."

"Do you want to tell me about it, Miss Jacobs?"

"Sure. It was really terrific. Unknown to me, Midge — she's so thoughtful — knowing how under stress I've been, and how nervous I was about returning to my home, arranged a surprise housewarming party for me."

"That really *is* thoughtful."

"You bet. That's why she was in such a hurry to get up there. She had told me it was because she wanted us to beat the weekend traffic, but actually Seymour — you <u>know</u> how he loves to cook — was preparing a gourmet meal for us. Renato and Ariana, that's the LaRossas, were there also. Seymour had the diningroom set with his own fine china and lit with candles when Midge and I finally arrived. I walked into the house, and there they were, yelling 'SURPRISE!' I really <u>was</u> surprised of course, and, like an idiot, burst into tears."

"That is perfectly understandable, considering what you had just been through in our session, Miss Jacobs."

"They seemed to understand, and we had a <u>marvelous</u> evening. We talked and enjoyed this fantastic meal that Seymour prepared. After, we sat around the fireplace, and Seymour even played one of the Bach Unaccompanied Suites that he'll be performing at Tanglewood this Summer. When he and the LaRossas left, Midge even cleaned up for me. It was an incredible evening. I felt like some kind of Duchess in a palace or something. It's still hard to believe that all this was happening in <u>my</u> house!"

"You have worked hard for everything you have, Miss Jacobs, and you deserve such enjoyable evenings. May you have many more of them."

[Pause.]

"I assume then, that you had no experiences involving Harry this weekend."

"That's true. But Midge and I did spend all our time talking about Harry and the things that have happened to me. [Pause.] But what's strange, Dr. Levy, is that when these things do <u>not</u> happen — if there's a period of time without any such incident, I find myself panicking, wondering if it means that Harry has left and is no longer with me."

[Silence.]

"That's bizarre, isn't it? I am panicked when these events happen, but also panicked when they don't because I'm frightened it means Harry's no longer around."

[Silence.]

"It's like I would be losing him twice. [Pause.] Actually, maybe <u>three</u> times. First, when he put me in that cab; then, when I learned he was dead and I could never see him again; and then — if he were to leave me now. [Pause.] So I find myself in the ambivalent

271

position of both fearing, and yet wanting these incidents to occur."

"That is a <u>very</u> interesting and perceptive insight, Miss Jacobs. Did you discuss that at all with your friend, Midge."

"No. [Pause.] Actually, it just came to me."

"Do you wish to explore it further and discuss it now?"

[Tone emphatic.] "<u>No</u>. I would <u>not</u>."

[Prolonged silence.]

"Miss Jacobs, I believe before you left for the weekend, you were going to tell me about the very eventful visit you had to Missouri. Do you feel ready to discuss it now?"

"Yes. I do. This is probably a good time for it."

[Pause; then deep breath before resuming.]

"I had made reservations at a Motel in the tiny town where Harry had lived most of his life, and where he and his wife, Betty, are buried side-by-side. There only one Motel there, and of course it's not listed in any of the Guide or Travel books, so I had to be a detective to find it. It's not bad, actually. It was clean and cozy, and the owners were an older, very friendly couple. It has a Diner attached to it also, and the food was real down home and delicious.

"I found myself quite charmed by the Midwest. I had never been there before, and I found the people to be very warm, very friendly, and very polite. [Pause.] Of course, there was another cynical part of me that realized they could all have white sheets with three holes hanging in their closets, but at least they were friendly and helpful to me during the daylight!"

"Miss Jacobs. Sometimes your sense of humor — I believe I —"

"Yes, I know. Somewhat warped. [Pause.] Anyway, I made reservations at this little Motel and also contacted the Metaphysical Institute Midge told me about. I made arrangements to visit their campus and library.

"I was all set to go when about two days before I was to leave, I suddenly developed Flu-like symptoms. Naturally, I suspected either supernatural forces or my own mind playing tricks to prevent me from going. Still, I was determined to make this trip even if I had to go in an ambulance and stretcher!

"So, the next day, the day before I was to leave, when I was no better, I went to the doctor and learned I indeed had not only the Flu, but an inner-ear infection as well. When I told the doctor about my trip planned for the next day, he advised strongly against it; but when I insisted I was going regardless, he gave me prescriptions for heavy-duty med-ication, with detailed instructions about how to use them properly.

"That entire trip was so strange, Dr. Levy, from beginning to end. I know it will take several sessions to tell you about it. First, there were the experiences in the Cemetery where Harry is buried. Then, there were the extraordinary events at the Institute — although, the way these things have been happening to me, THEY have in fact, become what is ordinary, and perhaps I should just accept them as part of my life experience."

"Perhaps you should, Miss Jacobs. Perhaps you should. [Pause.] But continue, please."

"Then there were my visits to Harry's Brother-in-law and Harry's friends, and a visit to the cabin where Harry lived in isolation for so many years."

"It must have been an extremely emotional experience for you, Miss Jacobs — almost like a Pilgrimage, I would suspect."

"That's true, Dr. Levy. That's probably the best way to describe the entire trip. It was <u>indeed</u> a Pilgrimage. There was, looking back at it, probably not even one minute that was not in some way heavily connected to Harry's life."

[Pause; then another very deep breath before resuming.]

"You know me well enough by now to know that I prefer to have things in organized form, so I think the best way for me to relate these incidents is by the way I just indicated — according to the place where they occurred. So I'll begin with all the Cemetery experiences."

"Miss Jacobs, it never ceases to intrigue me how, in relating experiences that are very unusual or even painful, you insist on placing events in sequence. I've not seen too many other indications, or I might be inclined to provide a diagnosis of obsessive-compulsive character disorder."

"Now Dr. Levy, I believe it is <u>you</u> who is showing a warped sense of humor!"

"Not entirely, Miss Jacobs. Not entirely."

[Pause.]

"Anyway, when I arrived at the airport in St. Louis, I remember feeling so strange. Here I was, actually in St. Louis, the home of the Cardinal team that I had so adored as a kid, and that Harry had played with when I knew him. Never in those days could I have imagined that I would be standing in an airport in St. Louis in the future. <u>Never</u>. [Pause.] Anyway, I rented a car, and I knew, because Midge had insisted — she had experienced psychic vibes or something — that the first thing to do, even before checking into the Motel, was go straight to where Harry is buried and tell him how I feel, like the words of 'Danny Boy'.

"So I got the car and I turned the radio to the first classical music station I could find, and made the long drive to the tiny town. As I neared it, I thought I'd better stop and ask for directions to the Cemetery. I went to a local Market, found out the Cemetery was fairly close, and then bought flowers to place on the graves of Harry and his wife.

"When I returned to the car, I placed the flowers on the passenger seat. I started the engine, but when the radio came on, the classical station had a discussion program, so I turned the dial. And then it happened. This was the song I heard, with these words, as I drove along the winding country road to the Cemetery:

[Begins singing:]
    It's very clear,
    Our Love is here to stay.
    Not for a year, but ever and a day.
    The radio and the telephone
    And the movies that we know
    May just be passing fancies,
    And in time may go.
    But, oh my dear,
    Our Love is here to stay.
    Together we're going a long, long way.
    In time the Rockies may crumble,
[Voice begins to falter with emotion.]
    Gibraltar may tumble,
    They're only made of clay, but
    Our Love is here to stay.
[Sounds of sobbing; then silence.]

"My dear Miss Jacobs, I had no idea you had such a lovely voice. It is truly beautiful."

"That was my original training when I went to that special High School. Thank you, Dr. Levy. But believe me, Ella Fitzgerald does it far better than I ever could, and that's what I heard as I was driving to the Cemetery."

"And I suspect you believe that it was a message from Harry."

"Of course. What else. [Pause.] And then I found the Cemetery. It wasn't difficult at all — what was <u>really</u> hard to find was the location of Harry's grave. [Pause.] The sky was cloudy and misty, but the sun was still trying to come through. I was feeling — I'm not sure how to describe it — overwhelmed by everything. I felt detached — spacey — emotional — all at the same time. I wondered if the medication I had taken might be having some effect upon me. But I kept wandering around, looking at all the gravestones, looking for Harry's name. It began to drizzle a little, and I think my eyes were teary, which made it even more difficult to see the names.

"And then something really strange happened. I <u>know</u> you are going to think I'm making this up — in fact, it was so unreal, maybe I <u>am</u> making it up. Maybe I was on so much medication that I was actually hallucinating."

"What happened, Miss Jacobs, please."

"A man came up to me. An elderly man. I just assumed he was the Caretaker of the Cemetery, and I asked if he could help me find a particular grave. When he asked for the name and I told him 'Harry Gault', he replied, and I <u>swear</u> to you Dr. Levy, these were his exact words: 'Why are you looking for the living among the dead?'. He frightened me with those words and I tried to look at him carefully. He grinned and turned and walked away into the mist with both hands in the pockets of his overalls.

"I remember being terrified, and I called out Harry's name and fell to my knees on the ground. And of course, that was the exact spot where Harry's gravemarker was, with Betty's beside it."

"Fascinating."

[Pause.]

"Their graves were not well cared for at all. It was quite obvious it had been some time since anyone had visited. It continued to drizzle. I was still on my knees, and I placed the flowers in urns that were by the markers. I remember feeling no particular strong emotion then, but tears started to flow. I began to pull weeds from around their gravestones and then I really started to cry.

"I didn't want to leave. It felt so peaceful. The drizzling had slackened and the sky turned into a beautiful sunset, with an unbelievably gorgeous rainbow. And I thought, as I knelt there by Harry's grave, how strange Life is. I had this picture of Harry in my mind, how he looked that first afternoon, as he leaned out the Clubhouse window with only a towel around his waist, and called to me. Who would have imagined then, would either he or I, that over 30 years later I would be sitting in Missouri at his grave, pulling weeds from around the marker and wondering if he was at last at peace?

"I sat there as if in a trance. Then I remembered two things. One was what that strange man, the one I had at first assumed was the caretaker, said to me. And I wondered whether in fact Harry was truly dead. Had he not shown his continued existence to me in so many ways? And then I remembered the words of

'Danny Boy' and I realized I needed to bend and tell Harry that I loved him. And so I did. I told him: 'You are alive in my heart because I loved you then, I love you now, and I love you always — always and forever'."

[Pause.]

"I continued to sit there as it became twilight. Then I realized I had better be going so I could find the Motel. But I didn't want to leave; so I promised that I would return the next day and stay with Harry until it became dark. And then I left."

[Pause.]

"Dr. Levy, did I tell you that as it worked out, the time I had planned to go to Missouri, the soonest I was able to have time free from work, coincided with the anniversary of the date of Harry's death?"

"No. Believe me, you did <u>not</u>, Miss Jacobs. Something as significant as that I would <u>definitely</u> remember."

"Well, it's not as if I was trying to hide it from you or anything, it's just that, with so much that's gone on, it's hard to remember what I've told you and what I have not."

"I can understand perfectly, Miss Jacobs, and you can believe it never occurred to me that this is something you would not wish me to know. Quite the contrary."

"Actually, perhaps I didn't tell you about it was because that day, the anniversary of Harry's death — it was the day before I left Missouri — was in itself such a separate and significant adventure — and that's the only appropriate word I can use to describe it — that perhaps I felt it needed a session all to itself. At <u>least</u> one — if not more."

"As you wish, Miss Jacobs."

"So I think I will save that one for another time. [Pause.] Anyway, I found the Motel, which was not difficult, believe me, as the entire town has a population of less than 300 people, at least according to the sign. I also drove past the house where Harry had lived, according to my student intern, when he and Betty and their daughter were together. It was such a charming house. Harry and his brothers, all carpenters, built it themselves after Harry returned from the War.

"Although I was occupied with some activity every day, I made sure I returned to the Cemetery each evening. During the weekdays, I went to the Institute; the other days I either visited people or looked at back issues of newspapers from when Harry was with the Cardinals."

[Pause.]

"I remember the next evening when I returned after that first visit to the Cemetery. I had promised Harry I would stay with him until dark — and I remember specifically — orderly person that I am - that I had defined 'dark' as when I was no longer able to see his name on the marker.

"Well, what happened next was actually comical. I suppose, when a person is dead, if they somehow return, they maintain their same character traits, and I've told you about Harry's mischievous sense of humor. Anyway, it never became so dark that I couldn't read his name. It was so funny, I even had to laugh aloud. First there were all these fireflies. They came en masse and actually hovered over Harry's marker as if to put a beacon on it. And then the moon came out. It was hilarious. So, in order to keep my promise, I would have had to stay almost 24 hours, because first there were the fireflies, then the moon lighting up the marker, then, the sun would come up."

"So how did you resolve that situation, Miss Jacobs."

"I think it was almost 11:00 pm when I left the Cemetery."

[Pause.]

"You're right, Miss Jacobs. That <u>is</u> both humorous <u>and</u> touching, as I'm sure you felt it to be. [Pause.] Tell me, Miss Jacobs, please. Did you ever see that Caretaker again?"

"No. Never."

"And do you suspect that this was the ghost of Harry — or whatever term you would use to signify the presence of someone who is known to be deceased?"

"I don't know, Dr. Levy. I don't know. But I remember how frightened and bewildered I felt. [Pause.] But at the risk of sounding insane, yes, I would 'suspect', as you put it, that this was Harry in some form."

"And was this person three-dimensional; and by that I mean, did he appear as you and I do now in this room."

"Yes. He was. But then, when he walked away into the mist, he was not. [Pause.] Oh my God. That was so strange and unbelievable. Please. I don't want to think about it. It gives me shivers."

"But why not, Miss Jacobs? Shouldn't it bring you happiness to know that Harry was actually able to manifest in human form and tell you himself that he was not dead?"

"But wouldn't that be insane? I mean —"

"My dear Miss Jacobs. We go over this time and time again. Why are you so afraid for your sanity? Do you not trust my judgment in making a proper diagnosis? If you do not, and insist upon being classified as mentally ill, there are MANY of my colleagues to whom I can refer you, who would make such a diagnosis quite easily if you wish."

[Silence.]

"Are you ready to continue, Miss Jacobs?"

"Yes." [Tone best described as "sheepish."]

"But first, I'm also curious: were the fireflies and moon out in such force every night you were at the Cemetery?"

"Yes, actually they were. Except for the night before I left — the one I was telling you was an adventure all by itself."

"And how long did you stay at Harry's gravesite each night?"

"Until almost eleven. It was so peaceful, and somehow I felt so comforted to be there."

"And what did you do there, at Harry's gravesite, each evening until 11:00 pm?"

"Most of the time, just sat quietly, remembering all the times we were together, picturing how he looked, wondering what had happened with his life. Sometimes I spoke to him, even to his wife Betty, reassuring her about how much Harry loved her."

"Yes, Miss Jacobs. That is one thing that has puzzled me. If Harry loved his wife as much as you say he did, then why is he sending these messages of love to you now? Why is he not reunited in peace with Betty, instead of wandering the earth seeking your love. And believe me, Miss Jacobs, by that question I do not mean to minimize the feelings the deceased, Harry, obviously had for you. [Pause.] If you had told me that he and his wife were in conflict, and were staying together solely for the sake of their little girl, it would be easier for me to comprehend. But you have consistently told me how much he truly loved this woman. And of course, we know he sent you away because he was tempted to become unfaithful to her."

"Believe me, Dr. Levy. I wondered that myself for so long. But I think I have the answer now. I found it through my conversations with Harry's friends, through my metaphysical studies, and mainly, through the messages Harry keeps sending me — mostly through music."

"And what is that answer, Miss Jacobs, please."

"The easiest part to answer is that Betty and I were such different people. She was his anchor, his strength, his port in the storm. She held him to this earth. But he and I together — we were two of a kind. We were a pair. A wild, perhaps even <u>dangerous</u> combination. [Pause.] And, with all the things that went on in our lives, separately and together, perhaps in the Cosmic Order of things, we were not meant to be together. At least not in <u>this</u> lifetime. Which brings me to the other part of the answer. But — <u>PLEASE</u>, Dr. Levy, let's <u>NOT</u> get into a discussion of what I say next. At least not tonight. Our time is probably almost up anyway, right?"

"Correct. But what is the other part of your answer, Miss Jacobs, please."

[Pause.]

"Well, I'm <u>still</u> exploring this part, but it's basically that we — Harry and I — were together in a past lifetime and will be together again in a future existence."

[Pause.]

"Oh. I see. [Pause.] Yes. You are perfectly right, Miss Jacobs. Reincarnation is <u>NOT</u> a subject we should begin discussing at this point."

[Pause.]

"There is one final thing. Something that happened at the Cemetery the evening before the anniversary of Harry's death. [Pause.] I was sitting on the grass by Harry's marker. It was twilight and I had been moving my fingers over the raised letters of his name, almost the way a person without sight does when they read in Braille. And instantly, for some reason, I started to sing, out loud, a song I had known when I was about 5 or 6 years old. I had no reason to sing that song of my own conscious volition. I hadn't heard or thought of it since childhood. And I knew only a portion of it. It goes like this:

{Singing softly:]

    In the Gloaming, oh my Darling,
    When the lights are dim and low,
    And the shadows quietly falling
    Softly come and softly go.

"Anyway, that was all I knew of the song. And for some reason unknown to me, I felt I had to sing it. [Pause.] I remained until my usual time, then left.

"When I returned to New York, I felt compelled to find the sheet music for this song, if I could, to learn the rest of the words. It was as if I knew there was some special meaning, perhaps a message from Harry. I won't go into all the details, Dr. Levy, you'll just have to trust me when I say that finding the words and music to that song involved a whole bunch of coincidences, or synchronous events — whatever. And it turns out that this song is not, as I thought, a simple love serenade, but is actually a song whose words have rather profound metaphysical meaning. In fact, it is about a man specifically telling his beloved how she

283

should react to his death. <u>Can you believe that</u>! He asks if she still loves him as she did — quote, once long ago, quote. Then near the end of the song he tells her that despite the fact that he longed for her greatly, their love was not meant to be. [Pause.] I'm sure you can imagine my reaction when I read the words of that song. In fact, the friend who gave it to me is one of those who thinks I have gone off the deep end with all this behavior concerning Harry, and asked <u>specifically</u> that I leave her home before reading the lyrics. Obviously she did not want me to create a scene in front of her family."

[Silence.]

"Miss Jacobs, once again I see we are over our time; however, what you have to tell me is so compelling that it is almost as difficult for me to terminate our sessions as it may be for you. I do not know. [Pause.] I find everything you say — NO — in fact, I can <u>not</u> find the appropriate terminology at this point. [Pause.] You have given me much to think about. There are NO easy explanations for what has been happening since you learned of Harry's death. I am as much a seeker as you, Miss Jacobs. And with that, I say Good Night, and look forward to our next session and your next installment of what happened on your trip to Missouri."

"Thank you, Dr. Levy. Good night."

End of Tape 18.

Notes Accompanying Tape 18.

I told Miss Jacobs I was a "seeker," as is she. I do not understand why I made such a statement. Has she been sent to me, not by chance, but as an experience of synchronicity for me?

Her explanation of why Harry is actively seeking her love and is not resting in peace with his beloved wife, was not only fascinating, but puzzling. What did she mean when she described herself and Harry as a "dangerous combination." She even gave special emphasis to the word "dangerous." I did not ask at the time because I assumed she was referring to the incident of the injury to Harry's teammate, for which she believes she bears responsibility, along with Harry. But perhaps she also meant what she describes as this "game" they played, or perhaps even their psychic powers used jointly.

And what is this about Reincarnation? She states that she is still "exploring" the concept. No doubt she researched this subject while at the Metaphysical Institute she visited. It will be interesting to hear what opinions she has developed.

There is a very minor point that has puzzled me throughout our sessions. Every so often, and if I remember correctly, it is during some statement attributed to Harry, there are distortions of Biblical quotations — I believe mainly from the New Testament. I find that rather strange. For example, the alleged Caretaker's query as to why she is seeking the living among the dead. I think, although I am certainly not anyone with specific knowledge in this field, that this is almost the identical remark made when the family of Jesus came to his tomb after his Crucifixion. If it is, what a strange remark. Could this be part of Miss Jacob's fantasy — ascribing God-like status to this man Harry? (I remember how she took me to task for my concerns that she was behaving like a Nun married to the Holy Ghost!) Or, if this and the other statements (I can't recall them now, but I <u>do</u> remember there were several) were indeed spoken to her by Harry, perhaps they were a manifestation of his unusual sense of humor to which she often refers.

Once again, she expressed uncertainty as to the status of her mental health. She still seems to prefer logical explanations, even if that includes a diagnosis of what she terms "insanity." Now she is beginning to effect me! Her doubts may become MY doubts, if I am not careful.

Am I indeed missing something? Is this woman truly deranged, but I am so captivated by her stories — under her "spell", as it were — that I am oblivious to manifestations of illness which should be obvious? I do not think that this is the situation, but I would feel much more comfortable, both for myself and for Miss Jacobs, if she were to visit a skilled therapist who is also knowledgeable and familiar with the area of paranormal phenomena. I keep saying I will find a name for her. What is preventing me! I should go to the book right now, before I have an opportunity to "forget" again!

* * *

Tape 19

"Good afternoon, Miss Jacobs."

"Dr. Levy."

"How has everything been lately?"

"Why do you ask, Dr. Levy? It's only two days since I saw you."

"That may be true, Miss Jacobs; however, in your case, I've come to expect the unexpected. I was curious to see if you have had any additional experiences that could be classified as either coincidental or synchronous."

"No. [Tone very casual.] Nothing has happened one way or the other."

"Does that concern you?"

"What do you mean, does it 'concern' me? Why should I be concerned?"

"If I remember correctly Miss Jacobs, the other day you told me that these experiences upset you when they occur, but when they do not occur, you become concerned that Harry is no longer in contact with you."

[Silence.]

"Yes. Of course. I did say that, and I do feel that way. I guess I just prefer not to think about it and that's why I couldn't understand what you meant by your question. I'm sorry."

"There is no need to apologize, Miss Jacobs. Please continue with what you wanted to tell me about your trip to Missouri."

[Pause.]

"Well, let me try to respond to your question first, now that I understand it. Like

I said, I have <u>not</u> had any additional experiences since our last visit, but that hasn't bothered me. I suppose the reason is that I've been thinking so much about what I have to tell you about my incredible trip to Missouri."

"Then proceed, please. I believe you had finished with your experiences at the Cemetery where Harry and his wife are buried — all, except, for something that happened on the anniversary of Harry's death, which you feel is so unique, if I understood you correctly, that it may take more than one session to discuss."

"Yes. That's correct, Dr. Levy. [Pause.] I'll continue and tell you about my experiences at the Institute."

"Please."

"I arrived in Missouri on a Friday, and as you know, visited Harry's grave and stayed in the Motel in his little town. On Saturday, I slept late into the afternoon, probably as a result not only of all the emotions I had felt the night before, but also because of the heavy doses of medication I was still required to take. When I did wake up, I had a delicious meal in the Diner, then walked around the little town. Quaint is about the best word I can think of to describe it. Sunday, I spent the day with Harry's closest friends. That was a very emotional experience.

"On Monday, the Institute was open, and I went there Monday through Friday during the hours it was accessible. On Saturday, the Institute was closed to the public; besides, I wanted to use that day to go to the University Library. I learned at the Institute that the University, which was closer to where I was staying than St. Louis, has an excellent library with an extensive collection of back issues of various Missouri newspapers. So I went to the University on Saturday — the day when all kinds of magic happened. Sunday, I met with Harry's Brother-in-law, and then I left."

[Pause.]

"The Institute is rather unique. I would not exactly classify it and its members as a cult, but it is entirely devoted to research into metaphysical subjects."

"I should believe that would be an ideal place for you to visit, Miss Jacobs. Do they offer classes that you could take?"

"Yes, they do. And I actually did some investigation into that possibility while I was there; however, I became — how shall I put it — disenchanted. Yes — that's actually a pretty good word, considering the subject matter."

"Hmm. Yes, of course, Miss Jacobs. [Pause.] But tell me, what made you become, as you put it, 'disenchanted'."

"The people who founded the Institute in the late 1890s were deeply involved in the study of all areas of metaphysics. They collected an enormous amount of literature on the subject, in addition to their own research and writing. They published Tracts which were quite scholarly. However, through the years, and this is my opinion only, you understand — people like Midge and many others would definitely not agree — but to me, its emphasis has changed. It's become very 'New Age', if you know what I mean. And I never was one for that type of group experience. I would have been more comfortable with the Institute the way it was originally intended by the Founders.

"However, they <u>do</u> have an absolutely <u>fantastic</u> library, and I was there every day it was open."

"Did you find any books that were helpful to you, Miss Jacobs."

"Yes, Dr. Levy. Many."

"And what types of books were these, and how were they of help to you."

"First I read books and or articles about the grieving process, then about the possibility of survival after death, then about psychic phenomena, synchronicity, spirit possession, et cetera, et cetera. I think you can fill in the blanks. And they were <u>all</u> helpful. It's difficult to pinpoint one particular subject area that was more helpful than any other.

"They have a bookstore and gift shop. The gift shop had all kinds of New Age stuff in it. I picked up something for Midge — there was nothing there for me. But I went absolutely wild in the bookstore. I bought all kinds of books, some of which I had already glanced through in the library. And before you ask, they were a mix of the subjects I spoke about before. Now all I have to do is find time to read them!"

"Yes, Miss Jacobs. [Pause.] You were going to tell me about the synchronous experiences that occurred while you were at the Institute."

"I'm not sure whether these are examples of synchronicity or just how to classify them. I don't feel comfortable using the word strange anymore, because when a particular type of event happens often enough, it is no longer strange, wouldn't you agree, Dr. Levy?"

"Yes. I see what you mean, Miss Jacobs. But go on with whatever it was that happened, please."

[Pause.]

"There were three incidents, actually; two of which were somewhat inter-related."

[Pause.]

"On the campus of the Institute, they have a marvelous Cafeteria. Along the walls and the hallway leading to the Cafeteria are works painted by local artists. I ate lunch there each day and when I was on line Monday, I noticed this striking portrait of a Cardinal. It was truly unique. It was not a typical scene of nature, but a stark portrait of a lone redbird standing on a spare branch, struggling to hang on against a strong wind. Of course, to me it symbolized Harry immediately. [Pause.] But did I buy it? No. I was in my one of my super-rational moods and thought that I had so many Cardinal objects at home it would be ridiculous to buy anything else. However, I couldn't stop thinking about this painting. You might say it haunted me. I decided to buy it, but when I went on line to eat in the Cafeteria the next day, it was gone. I inquired at the register and learned it had been sold the previous day. Then, the next day, Wednesday, I stared at the empty space where the painting had been hanging and fantasized that it was still there for me to buy — that's how disappointed I was that it was gone.

"The following day, Thursday, when I was on line again, I looked at the spot where the painting had been hanging, and I couldn't believe my eyes. It was there. Just as I had imagined it would be. [Pause.] Dr. Levy, I know you are aware of how emotional I become when there is something associated with Harry. Actually, I think you've seen me in some of my milder moments. I probably restrain my behavior in deference to you, if you can believe that. The reason I'm saying this is to convey to you that I became semi-hysterical at the sight of that painting. I took it down from the wall immediately and ran outside the building with it. I was weeping, more than you've ever seen me do here, and I was clutching that painting tight to my heart. I remember leaning against a tree that was right outside the Cafeteria door. When I regained my composure, I went back inside the building and bought the painting. I don't even think I ate lunch that day, either.

"What was even more unusual about this incident was what the Manager of the Cafeteria told me when I went to pay for the painting. She told me she felt so sorry for the woman who returned the painting that she took it back and refunded her money, contrary to their general policy.

"Apparently the woman had loved the painting and had bought it on Monday, the day it was first displayed. She took it home and hung it in her livingroom. Everytime she looked at the painting it gave her the creeps. It was like it did not want to be hung there. After three days of anxiety whenever she saw the painting she took it down and returned it.

"You know what I think, Dr. Levy? I think that had it been any place other than this Metaphysical Institute, they would have laughed at the woman and told her tough luck, or words to that effect. But in this place, they took her fears seriously, and not only accepted the painting but also refunded her money. And then I come along, tears streaming down my face, clutching the painting to my bosom, begging to buy it. Now the Manager remembered me from Tuesday, when I first asked about what happened to the painting, and how disappointed I was to learn that it had been sold. And in telling me the story about the other woman's experience with the painting, the Manager took my hand — now remember, this is a Metaphysical Institute, even though it was just the Cafeteria — and said to me, and these were her exact words: 'The Infinite Spirit meant for you to have this painting.' And you know what? I actually believe she was right. [Pause.] What do you think, Dr. Levy?"

"It is indeed fascinating, Miss Jacobs. [Pause.] Now was this incident one which is somehow inter-related with another?"

"Yes. [Pause.] The next one is inter-related in an interesting way to the incident of the painting. I had become friendly with a woman about my age who I met while I was visiting the Institute. She is a full-time student who lives on Campus, and when she graduates, she will be licensed to teach in their branch facilities throughout the United States. When she asked why I was visiting, I summarized my experiences with Harry."

[Pause.]

"You know, in many ways it really was a wonderful experience for me to be there. For once I could talk openly and completely honestly about my experiences, and not only did people not think I was crazy, but they accepted everything I said in complete faith, as if it was the natural course of events. And, to them, it probably is the natural way of the world."

"It is unfortunate then, Miss Jacobs, that you have this distaste for their current value

293

system, otherwise this would seem an ideal situation for you — perhaps to take a sabbatical from your work and enroll in Metaphysical Studies."

"I know. But I just find that New Age stuff a little difficult to swallow. [Pause.] Anyway, as far as the inter-related incident — I had told Shirley, that was this woman's name — by the way, we have kept up our friendship. We exchange letters and 'phone calls."

"I'm delighted to hear that, Miss Jacobs. The more people who can appreciate your situation and offer supportive insight, the better. Now continue, please."

"Yes. Thank you, Dr. Levy. [Pause.] Anyway, I had told Shirley about Harry and the Cardinal painting and how it was gone. Somehow, in our discussion, I also told her that I had never actually seen a real live Cardinal. She sympathized and said that although they are prevalent all over Missouri, this was the time of year when they did something, whatever, and that they would most likely be in wooded areas rather than the suburbs. In other words, the chances of seeing a Cardinal at the Institute were fairly bleak.

"Then, Friday morning, while I was in the library, she came rushing up to me, all excited. I thought it was because somehow she had found out about my good luck with the painting. But no. She had come to tell me that at this very moment, there was a male Cardinal — a Redbird — sitting on a tree right outside. Of course, off I went, and do you know where it was, Dr. Levy? It was on a branch of the very tree that I had leaned against the day before, clutching the Cardinal painting to my heart and crying my eyes out.

"I remember staring at it. It was so very very beautiful. Its coloring was magnificent. And it was so tame. That entire Cardinal episode was incredible. That bird followed me wherever I went on Campus. At times I felt as if I were in a Disney movie, walking along with one of Nature's creatures flying beside me. Shirley told me, when we said good-bye Friday evening, that she had even seen it sitting on a tree looking in at me while I was reading in the Library. Of course, I took photos of it. Now on the wall next to my bed in my apartment are hanging my favorite photo of Harry in his Cardinal uniform, then the Cardinal painting that so symbolizes him and his spirit against all odds, and then a photo of the live Cardinal sitting on a branch of the tree I leaned against with the painting."

"Fascinating, Miss Jacobs. Absolutely fascinating. [Pause.] And what is the final incident that happened at the Institute. I believe you told me there were three."

"Yes. [Pause.] The third has to do with music again. I think Harry likes to give me messages through music because he knows how large a part it plays in my life. I have my radio on WQXR all the time, and when it is not on that station, it is because I am listening to tapes or records. Then I also play the piano. Seymour and I sometimes play together for our friends, and he's currently bugging me to get a piano for my home in the Berkshires. I told him he should give one to me for a house-warming gift, because of course he insists upon it being a Concert Grand!

"Anyway, I think the reason Harry sends so many messages to me through music is because he is aware that there is never a moment in my life which is not accompanied by music. For example, as I sit and talk to you now, I can hear music in my mind, although I would have to concentrate in order to tell you what it is I am hearing."

"That is very interesting, Miss Jacobs. But continue with this next contact from Harry, please."

"Yes. I'm sorry. I seem to be rambling today, and I'm not sure why. [Pause.] Anyway, Shirley told me about how on the Institute campus there is a place that I absolutely had to go to. It's a very special room; a room set aside solely for Meditation, and is open 24 hours, seven days a week. It is always available to anyone who needs it.

"I had peeked into the room once, and it seemed like so much New Age fluff to me — you know what I mean, pillows on the floor, incense, that sort of thing. But finally, that Friday, as I was about to return to the Motel, I decided to go into this room. I went and sat on one of the few chairs available. I became still and tried to free my mind the way I learned once in a Meditation class I attended with Midge. Eventually I was able to relax and let my mind drift. And it did - back to the days when I knew Harry. Shirley told me that the room has an almost spooky reputation for the things that people learn there — the insights they reach, or the answers to desperate prayers. Some say that the Spirit or Essence of the Founders is present in that room."

[Silence.]

"I don't know how to tell you about what happened next. It seems distant now, but at the time it happened, I was overwhelmed - overcome with emotion - so much so, that — can you believe I actually went down on my knees?

[Pause.] I hope I can get through telling you about this without crying."

[Silence.]

"There is a Carillon in the Tower of the building where the Meditation Room is housed. The times that I was at the Institute I would hear it chime the quarter-hours, then intone the hour - sounding like a mid-western version of Big Ben.

"But this time, as I was sitting so still in that room, remembering what it was to be with Harry, it felt so real - I could feel, actually <u>feel</u> the heat and the humidity of the Summer days at the Ballpark, and - it's so hard to describe - but I could also feel the emotions the way I felt them then - as teenage Sandy."

[Pause.]

"And that's when I heard it."

"Heard what, Miss Jacobs, please."

[Voice barely audible through vain attempt to control sobbing.]

"The Carillon was playing 'If I Loved You.'"

[Silence.]

"I know that could be explained as just a change in the Carillon Programming, or merely a coincidence, but I didn't think so, as I fell to my knees. I don't know why I did that -- except to me, of course, it was not a coincidence. [Pause.] Maybe it was the reputation of that room. I don't know. But to me it was a sign. A sign from - I don't know — from, from -- [Voice hesitant; tentative.] - above?"

[Pause.]

"And to hear <u>that</u> song? [Pause.] You know, of course, it's from the American musical version of 'Liliom'; and the words are so similar to Liliom's speech to Julie - the one

in which he tries to tell her he loves her,
but isn't able, because of who he is."
    [Pause.]
    "So often I've thought of how much Harry is
like Liliom and how I was like the young girl,
Julie. She was the <u>only</u> one who understood
him, and he knew it. But <u>still</u> he couldn't
bring himself to tell her how he felt.
[Pause.] The words and music are so beautiful:
    [Begins singing.]
        If I loved you,
        Time and again I would try to say
        All I'd want you to know.

        If I loved you,
        Words wouldn't come in an easy way,
        'Round in circles I'd go.

        Longin' to tell you, but afraid and shy,
        I'd let my golden chances pass me by.

        Soon you'd leave me,
        Off you would go in the mist of day,
        Never, never to know
        How I loved you -
        If I loved you.

    "And when, at the end, he is led off to
wherever it is he is doomed to spend Eternity,
he sings the last words slightly different:

        Soon I'll leave you,
        Off I will go in the mist of day,
        And you never will know
        How I love you.
        How I love you.

    [Silence.]

"I'm trying really hard not to cry. I hope you appreciate that, Dr. Levy."

[Pause.]

"Miss Jacobs, I must say that you have been spoiling me with your beautiful singing. It is very kind of Harry to send musical messages that you can then share with me. Our sessions are turning into concerts. [Pause.] And I mean no disrespect or sarcasm with my remarks. Quite the contrary. I appreciate hearing you sing, and I also appreciate the messages contained in the songs and understand why they have such heartfelt meaning for you."

"I'm not sure why I feel I have to sing the words. I suppose it comes naturally for me. I hear the melodies in my mind, and I guess the music just comes out, so you can hear how it sounds as well as listen to the words."

[Pause.]

"But can you possibly have any idea of the impact all this had upon me? All this happened in only one week — well, actually ten days. But think of it — the things that happened at Harry's grave, the events at the Institute, — strange, isn't it, but I suppose I should say magical — how these incidents each had significant musical messages for me. Then there were the visits with Harry's friends and Brother-in-law. I've yet to tell you about them."

"Yes. Perhaps you can do that at your next session, Miss Jacobs. [Pause.] Tell me, will I be treated to any songs? [Pause.] No? I'm disappointed. But I'm also quite pleased that today you seem much better at accepting these incidents."

[Pause.]

"I hope you're right, Dr. Levy. I do so want to believe in these messages. I just have to work at it."

"We all have to work on our lives, Miss Jacobs. We just have different paths, that's all. [Pause.] And so, on that metaphysical note, I will say goodnight until our next session."

"Dr. Levy - [Mock surprise.] - I'm shocked at that last comment! Anyway, goodnight, and thank you."

End of Tape 19.

Notes Accompanying Tape 19.

I find so little to write after reviewing these sessions with Miss Jacobs. What comments can be made — except, perhaps, something minor or trivial — when the subjects she presents are so profound. What diagnosis can possibly be given within the current regimen of psycho-analysis that incorporates the experiences of this woman? If there were her involvement alone — but indeed, there are often at least one, if not more, witnesses or participants to these occurrences.

In today's session, Miss Jacobs seemed to ramble in her speech even more than usual; however, I sense that was because of the very emotional content of the incidents she was relating.

As emotional as this woman has been in my office, it is extremely difficult for me to imagine that I have seen her in her "milder moments", and that she is restraining her behavior for my benefit. If such is true, then I would surely not want to be anywhere near such manifestation of hysteria — although I might have to, of necessity, in a true emergency!

But then, she is careful to be in control as much as possible in my office. Can it be that her behavior actually is far worse than she presents here, and that is why, aware of the full extent of her actions, Miss Jacobs is convinced she is mentally ill?

But that is difficult to accept. She herself admits she is having no problems at work. Nor does it appear she is having problems with social interactions. Her friends and acquaintances provided her with a recent surprise party. She made new friends while on a trip to another State. It seems she was readily accepted into the homes of Harry's family and friends — something I am sure they would not do if she presented even the slightest hint of mental derangement. Her sense of humor, though unconventional, is obviously still intact. She retains her passion and devotion to music. I am still unable, in good conscience, to discern any verifiable indication of mental disorder.

(I am ashamed to admit that I have yet to provide Miss Jacobs with the names of colleagues who are experienced in the field of parapsychology. I must ask myself again if I have become as addicted to her as a teller of tales as the Sultan was to Scheherazade.)

In addition, her singing voice is enchanting — *comme une vraie chanteuse*[1]. Am I being lured by one of Debussy's *Sirènes*?

It is interesting that Miss Jacobs views the so-called "New Age" movement with such contempt. Her disdain for this belief system is somewhat ironic, considering how her own experiences would be similarly viewed within traditional religions.

Once again, I need to explore for myself, why I have taken so long to provide Miss Jacobs with the appropriate referral. But then, neither has she pursued asking me for the names of other therapists. Still, it is I who should be in control here, and I feel I am remiss, and perhaps even selfish, not to provide this woman with the names of doctors who can be of true assistance to her. I MUST attend to this, and if I do not, I MUST be sure to learn for my own benefit what is

---

[1] French; simplest translation = "a veritable songstress."

preventing me from performing my ethical duty to this patient.

***

Tape 20

May 13, 1981

4:30 pm

"Good afternoon, Miss Jacobs."

"Good afternoon, Dr. Levy. And before you ask, no, nothing else has happened in the way of activities which may be considered paranormal."

[Pause.]

"Miss Jacobs, your last comment brings to my memory something that I have been meaning to ask you for several sessions, but for some reason, have either forgotten, or it has not seemed appropriate."

"Well, you know my Motto, Dr. Levy: 'Nothing by chance'."

"By that I assume, Miss Jacobs, that you mean if it were the right time for me to ask the question, I would have remembered?"

"Precisely."

"Miss Jacobs, I am perhaps as anxious to hear about the rest of your trip to Missouri as you are to tell it — but I feel I must ask this question first before we proceed."

"Dr. Levy, you keep using the word 'anxious.'[1] Believe me, I am not 'anxious' to tell you what happened, but I <u>want</u> to. As you know, at times there <u>are</u> some things I really do feel anxious about and need to talk to you as soon as possible. But I don't believe this falls into that category. I just want to talk about it, whenever the time is there."

[Pause.]

---

[1] <u>Cf</u>. Tape 13, p.196.

"Thank you for that clarification, Miss Jacobs. Now may I ask my question, please."

"As you wish, Dr. Levy."

[Laughter.]

"I see our roles are reversed today, Miss Jacobs."

"Ah. Und it feels *sehr gut* for a change, believe me!"[2]

"*Ach. Sprechen Sie Deutsch, Frau Jacobs?*"

"*Nein, Herr Doktor. Nein.*"[3]

"Ah, but My Dear Miss Jacobs, you do a very convincing job of speaking as if you know the language."

"When I took vocal lessons, I studied many German *Lieder*."

"Ah. I understand. [Pause.] And now may I ask my question, before I forget it this time as well?"

"Hmm. Perhaps it is I who is resisting hearing the question and am therefore preventing you, by whatever means, from asking it."

[Pause.]

"*Mein Gott!*[4] Excuse me, Miss Jacobs, but you are almost fiendishly clever this afternoon. What has put you in such a mood?"

"You'd better be careful, Dr. Levy, or you will completely forget to ask your question this time!"

[Silence.]

"This entire exchange between us, although it began quite enjoyably, is now making me feel extremely uncomfortable. And it is because of the nature of the question I was prepared to ask."

---

[2] "*Sehr gut*" is German for "very good."

[3] Dr. Levy asked, in German, whether Ms. Jacobs speaks the language, to which she replied that she does not.

[4] German for "My God!"

"You were going to ask if I could read people's minds, isn't that true?"

[<u>Prolonged silence</u>, except intermittently the voice of Dr. Levy can be heard indistinctly in the background muttering words that seem to be in German.]

"Miss Jacobs [Voice tone obviously shaken] — for once, in my profession, I am at a loss for words. I truly do not know how to respond at this time."

[Silence.]

"You never really <u>did</u> believe what I was saying about my experiences with Harry, did you Dr. Levy. I don't think it was that you thought I was lying — perhaps merely exaggerating, or using my vivid imagination."

[Silence.]

"What's the matter, Dr. Levy? There's an expression in English — 'cat got your tongue'?"

[Silence.]

"Dr. Levy, please forgive me. I don't know what made me say something so cruel. Can you forgive me, please? It's just that — you can't imagine how <u>frustrating</u> it is for me to try to explain to people what is going on with my life and not have anyone understand. [Pause.] I guess when the situation was reversed, I took my repressed hostility out on you. And you're such a good person, Dr. Levy — you don't deserve my cruelty. Can you please forgive me?"

[Pause.]

"My dear Miss Jacobs, there is nothing to forgive. Indeed, if anything, it is <u>I</u> who should be asking your forgiveness for not understanding, for not fully realizing everything you have been trying to tell me.

"But your tone of voice before, when you spoke about the cat getting my tongue — that did not sound like you, Miss Jacobs. It was <u>very</u> atypical."

"There are two possible explanations, aren't there, Dr. Levy. [Pause. When voice resumes, tone is cold and deliberate.] One is that you do not realize who I am or what I am really about, and never have. The other is that it possibly was someone else speaking through me."

[Silence.]

"And which do you think it is, Miss Jacobs, please."

[Normal voice tone, almost pleading.] "You see, I don't know either. And that's one of the reasons I came to you for help in sorting out what's going on in my life."

[Silence.]

"Miss Jacobs, I implore you. You need to find, you MUST get the help you need from someone who is knowledgeable in the area of parapsychology. I will — I realize I have been negligent in finding names for you, but —"

"Dr. Levy. I'm sorry for what's happened here today, but I really do not want to see anyone else, at least not yet. I've told you so much already, and I don't want to have to start all over again."

"Yes. I can understand. But I still think —"

"I promise you, I <u>will</u> look for someone else when you give me the names, if you insist. But please, not yet. I'm not ready."

[Lengthy silence.]

"Perhaps now you understand, Dr. Levy, why I would prefer a diagnosis of mental illness — <u>anything</u> rather than acknowledge these things I seem to be able to do."

"Yes. Of course, Miss Jacobs. Now it becomes clear."

[Silence.]

"How long have you known, Miss Jacobs?"

"Of course I knew when I was a child with Harry. But after he sent me away, I blocked out everything I could: Harry, Baseball, and especially anything having to do with the 'game' Harry and I played.

"At the time, I didn't fully understand what these abilities were. All I knew was that it was something I could do with Harry. Every so often, however, in the years that passed, something would happen that would bring it back, but I would pass it off with some pseudo-logical explanation or label it mere coincidence.

"I didn't become fully aware of it again, until Harry returned to me. Then everything happened as I related. And, since Seymour spoke so highly of you, I felt if there was any chance that I was truly insane, you would recognize it and have me put away, where I would not be able to hurt myself or anyone else."

"And have you done harm to others, Miss Jacobs?"

[Pause, then voice tone quite subdued.]

"Yes."

"In what way, please."

"The way it happened to Ed."

[Pause.]

"Can you provide an example, please."

"All right. I'll give you one, if you let that be the end of it. I really don't like to think of it or talk about it. I had believed I managed to repress everything, that is until Harry returned."

"And why do you think he returned, Miss Jacobs?"

"I have some ideas, but I'd rather not speculate openly.

"One thing I have come to appreciate with increasing clarity is why Harry felt the need to live totally isolated from civilization. Don't forget, he had already been on the path for many years, and was far deeper into manifesting his abilities than I ever was or ever could be."

"Perhaps that is why he is not at peace, Miss Jacobs."

"Yes. I know. I thought of that as a distinct possibility.

[Silence.]

"You're still wanting me to provide an example of harm to others, but you are reluctant to ask, right?"

"Miss Jacobs, how can we work together if –"

"I'm sorry. I promise not to do it again. I've worked very hard at hiding it, but every once in a while, something would slip through that you would pick up. I need to learn how to control it. I KNOW that was something Harry had been working on. I don't remember if I told you about Harry being part Cherokee. He built his cabin on an abandoned Indian Campsite, near ancient sacred burial grounds. The better to practise his Art or commune with his People, I imagine — although I can't be sure."

[Pause.]

"All right. Here it is. It would happen like this. Perhaps I would get into a heated discussion with someone. Sometime later I would learn of some misfortune that had occurred to that individual, usually in direct proportion to the degree of anger I had been feeling.

"Now, I realize that most of the normal World would consider such events as mere coincidence. Therefore, Dr. Levy, if you wish to conclude that I am suffering from delusions of grandeur – please, be my guest!"

[Pause.]

"You're curious as to how often these events occurred. Often enough that Seymour did not even consider the possibility of lack of causal relationship, especially after having witnessed the episode with Ed. Midge accepted these events as well, and often teased that she wished she had the power so she could 'do in', as she put it, some of her enemies!

"But I never accepted responsibility for these events, as I call them. I always viewed them as mere coincidence and felt that Midge was making use of her active imagination, and that Seymour was still suffering from the memory of that incident with Ed. [Pause.] I was, as you doctors might say, in total denial about any paranormal abilities I might possess. [Pause.] Do you think that these experiences of harm to others are mere coincidences, Dr. Levy?"

"Why do you bother to ask me, Miss Jacobs. Don't you know what my response will be? And I ask these questions, not out of sarcasm, but because I am bewildered. I do not understand what is happening here. At one moment you know exactly what I am about to say, or what I am thinking, and then at another, you ask for my opinion. Are you testing me? Do you want to see if my response matches what you KNOW I will say? [Pause.] At this point, Miss Jacobs, I am almost afraid to speak. I am also beginning to feel somewhat redundant, or superfluous in this situation."

"You mean, I might as well sit here, facing your armchair without you in it, and conduct a question and answer session by myself, supplying my questions and your answers."

"Precisely, Miss Jacobs."

"But it doesn't work that simply, Dr. Levy. [Pause.] Since I'll never be sure what I'll say, then I can not be sure how you will answer, unless you are here."

[Silence.]

"Dr. Levy. You asked about my ability to inflict harm upon others through use of mental processes. I gave you the typical scenario, and I'd really like to know whether you think these are mere coincidences, or if you think I am suffering from some form of grandiose delusions."

"To be truthful, Miss Jacobs — and at this point, I believe I certainly can NOT be anything else BUT truthful — as a trained therapist, I do not have enough clinical information to be able to give a reliable opinion. [Pause.] However, based upon what you have told me about your life experiences, and if the number of these occurrences are beyond a certain level of statistical probability, I would hazard my own personal opinion that these may not be mere coincidences. [Pause.] But as for what they really are, I have NO explanation, I can assure you."

[Pause.]

"As for delusions of grandeur, as you call them, you should know by now what my opinion is as to assigning a diagnosis of mental illness to your behavior."

[Pause.]

"Thank you, Dr. Levy. At least I <u>know</u> you are being honest with me, and that you are not a pretentious snob the way so many other medical professionals can be. That's another reason I'm reluctant to transfer to another psychiatrist. So many of them can be pompous and overbearing. I know because of my association with them as clients during my work duties. [Pause.] I feel I can trust you with my thoughts. I've told you so many personal things already that I have <u>never</u> said to anyone. I'm not sure I want to risk being a laboratory animal for some other doctor's fame and fortune as a researcher into paranormal phenomena. [Pause.] And then there are my emotional feelings about Harry. How many doctors would be able to empathize the way you have. [Pause.] Think about it, Dr. Levy. There may have been a reason why it has taken you so long to come forward with the names of those doctors that you've spoken about so often."

[Silence.]

"And no. I have never demonstrated an ability to predict the future. I'm not sure why. That's an ability that most people who are psychic possess. Midge, for instance, does it; but I never have had any indication that I have this ability. [Pause.] No. I never had any indication that Harry had it either."

"Miss Jacobs, I'm not sure whether this is infuriating or funny, actually. But it <u>is</u> nerve-wracking, to say the least!"

"I'm sorry, Dr. Levy. [Pause.] I must admit to having a little fun with you now that the cat is out of the bag. [Pause.] Ooops. Sorry. I won't mention clichés with cats in them again. I should have been more sensitive!"

"Miss Jacobs!"

"You're right. I guess I was playing cat and mouse with you there for a while!"

"Miss Jacobs — Please! I implore you! STOP THIS!"

[Sounds of laughter from both Dr. Levy and Miss Jacobs. Then silence.]

"You're wondering where we go from here, Dr. Levy, and so am I. I want VERY MUCH to continue my sessions with you. I've said many times how I think you are a kind and compassionate human being, and I trust you implicitly. I want very much for you to believe that I mean those words sincerely. I've come to depend on you to help me work all this through. [Pause.] No. My friends — NONE of my friends, including Midge, know anything about the FULL extent of what I am capable of doing. The only one who knew was Harry."

[Silence.]

"Please don't ask what I mean by the 'full' extent. It's really difficult for me to discuss. I've tried for so long to deny the existence of these abilities, like I said before — calling them coincidences, or ignoring any connection to my personal life."

[Silence.]

"You're still wondering how our sessions can possibly proceed after today. [Pause.] I have a suggestion. Suppose we pretend this session never happened."

"Miss Jacobs, how could that be —-"

"Please, Dr. Levy. Bear with me. And NO. I'm not going to put you under some kind of spell or into some kind of trance to make you forget!"

[Laughter.]

"Seriously. Let's pretend this session never happened. Please make an appointment for me tomorrow, as I do not think too much time

313

should lapse, because then you might not want to see me again at all. But if you see me tomorrow, I SWEAR to you on all that's holy, that I WILL NOT do this to you ever again — well, I can't be 100% certain, since I <u>did</u> make those tiny slip-ups that made you suspicious — but I will place it under control. I really <u>do</u> want to tell you about the rest of the things that happened in Missouri. I need someone with patience and compassion to listen, someone who will try to understand what I have been, and am <u>still,</u> going through. And for me, that person is you, Dr. Levy.

"Then there's always the hope that you will find I am delusional and will treat me with something that will make all this go away."

[Pause.]

"Yes. I really <u>DO</u> want it to go away. I never understood it in the first place, I don't know why I have it, and I certainly don't know what to do with it. And yes. Perhaps these abilities <u>were</u> the reason Harry was not at peace — although honestly, I believe it had more to do with the cumulative effect of the War, his wife's death, and the loss of his daughter."

"And the loss of you, too, Miss Jacobs."

[Silence.]

"Isn't that interesting, Dr. Levy. That is one thought I <u>absolutely</u> could not read!"

"Yes, that <u>is</u> interesting, Miss Jacobs. You still <u>do</u> have difficulty finding yourself worthy of love and good fortune."

"A condition serious enough to merit a treatable diagnosis, she asked?"[5]

---

[5] This question has been transcribed <u>exactly</u> as spoken by Miss Jacobs, <u>including</u> the words "she asked."

"Miss Jacobs. Enough mocking me today, please!"

[Silence.]

"All right, Miss Jacobs. We have an agreement. You will not usurp my function and I will continue to listen to your experiences. But sincerely — I DO want you to keep your promise to select a practitioner with skills in parapsychology as soon as I provide you with some names, and as soon as you feel secure about it. And I swear to you, that I will look only for those who will be sympathetic — even empathetic — to your situation. As you most likely realize, I do not feel comfortable taking your valuable time and money when I can offer nothing more than a sympathetic ear."

"First of all, Dr. Levy, a sympathetic ear is of itself worth any sum of money. But secondly, you give much more than that. I value your thoughts and insights. They provide much for me to think about."

[Pause.]

"So we're agreed then. And you'll have your secretary 'phone me with the appointment time?"

"Why Miss Jacobs, I'm shocked. Don't you know the answers to those questions already?"

[Laughter.]

"Is it even necessary to say good night?"

"But that is our tradition, Dr. Levy."

"All right then. Good night, Miss Jacobs."

"Good night, Dr. Levy. And thank you for everything — your patience, your kindness, your understanding. Thank you."

"Enough, already. You're welcome, Miss Jacobs."

End of Tape 20.

There are NO Notes Accompanying Tape 20.

* * *

Tape 21

May 14, 1981

11:30 am

"Good Morning, Miss Jacobs."

"Good Morning, Dr. Levy."

"As another example of your belief that there are no coincidences, it just so happened that my 11:30 appointment canceled and his time became available for you."

"I'm not surprised, are you, Dr. Levy?"

"As I have said often, nothing that happens concerning you is a surprise to me, Miss Jacobs. Sit, please."

[Pause.]

"Are you ready to tell me more about your trip to Missouri?"

"Yes. I'm ready to tell you about the time that I spent with Harry's closest friends."

"Proceed then, please, Miss Jacobs."

[Pause.]

"The strange — no — I shouldn't use that word, remember? Particularly in this instance. You see, I met Harry's closest friends because I was at the Cemetery.

"I had talked and written to several of his relatives and friends before I went to Missouri, but no one seemed to know much about his later years, after he retreated to his cabin in the Ozarks. Some never bothered to answer, but the responses I <u>did</u> receive were fairly unanimous: what a fine, decent person Harry Gault was, how much he had suffered because of the War, topped by the loss of his wife and daughter, to whom he had been devoted. No one seemed to understand why he made such a drastic move, so far from everyone

317

and everything, totally isolated, but they guessed it was because Life had dealt him so many cruel blows. And that was it. No one readily agreed to meet with me, and no one indicated to me that they knew the location of Harry's cabin. Each person kept referring me to someone else, from whom I would receive almost the identical response."

"Do you think they were trying to protect Harry's privacy?"

"I'm not sure, Dr. Levy. It may have seemed weird to them that an outsider, a woman at that, would want to know so much about Harry, and they did not want to volunteer too much information. On the other hand, once Harry left the area, perhaps these people actually did not know anything more."

"How many years did he live in isolation, Miss Jacobs, if you know?"

"More than ten years, Dr. Levy."

"And how old would Harry have been during this period?"

"I'm not sure. Somehow I learned he was born the same year as President Kennedy, so that would have made him ages 50 through 61, I believe."

"And in what year did Harry die, Miss Jacobs."

"He died in 1979."

[Pause.]

"You were saying, Miss Jacobs, that when you were at the Cemetery you met someone who knew Harry?"

"Yes. It was another example of nothing being by chance."

"Explain, please."

"As I told you earlier, I arrived on a Friday evening and went straight to the Cemetery. Then on Saturday, I slept late and took a leisurely stroll around the tiny town. After an early dinner, I went again to the Cemetery. As I approached Harry's grave, I heard deep heavy sobbing. I looked around and saw a small frail woman kneeling and weeping by a gravesite that was beautifully and lovingly decorated. Something about the way she was weeping made me want to go and comfort her — perhaps because I understood so much of what she was going through.

"So I went and put my arms around her and unfortunately startled the poor woman. I know I spoke words I hoped would be comforting to her, but I really don't remember what I said. I DO know that I told her I thought the grave she was attending was so lovingly cared for, and she explained that her only daughter — she had three sons, was buried there. Then she told me the story of her daughter coming home from college for Christmas, and how the young woman was killed by a drunk driver when she went to buy ice cream on Christmas Eve. [Pause.] What can you say to people who go through something like that? What senseless tragedy."

[Silence.]

"We talked some more and because it was obvious I was a stranger in town, it was inevitable that the woman would ask whose grave I was visiting. When I told her 'Harry and Betty Gault', she almost fell over! It seems that she and her husband were best friends with the Gaults since childhood, and wasn't it terrible how poor Harry had suffered so much in the War only to lose his beloved wife and be forced to separate from his little girl. Then all those years alone in that cabin in the wilderness! As it turned out, this couple were the only ones who kept in touch

319

with Harry and helped him get medical attention in the final months of his life. They also arranged all the details of his burial and funeral and disbursal of his worldly goods, of which there were very few. We were talking in the Cemetery for so long, that eventually the woman decided it would be best to invite me to her house to meet her husband, who had known Harry even better. And so I accepted her invitation for Sunday Brunch, which, when I visited, became the entire day, lasting well into the night, because we actually drove to Harry's cabin."

[Pause.]

"That must have been very emotional for you, Miss Jacobs."

"Yes, Dr. Levy, it was — more than you, or anyone probably, can possibly comprehend."

[Pause.]

"Go on, please, Miss Jacobs."

"Yes. [Pause.] Anyway, the next day I drove out to where this couple — George and Lil — live on a large farm, the kind you typically visualize when you think of the Midwest. They were more than gracious. We've formed our own friendship now, and keep in touch regularly. In fact, I'll be visiting them again this year when I go to Harry's grave on the anniversary of his death."

"Is that what you plan to do, Miss Jacobs — visit Harry's grave each year on the anniversary of his death?"

"Yes. And I think you'll understand why after I tell you what happened that following Saturday."

"All right. Continue Miss Jacobs, please."

"Sure. [Pause.] At first things were somewhat awkward, but it didn't take them long to warm up to me. I told them about being this ugly fat teenager that Harry befriended, and they readily accepted my explanation because, as Lil said, that was <u>exactly</u> something Harry would do. He was always looking out to help or protect the 'underdog,' — which was how she put it.

"They knew Harry and Betty since childhood, all going to the same schools. George even played Semi-Pro Ball with Harry when they were in their late teens, but while Harry went on to become professional, George had to return to the family farm to keep it running during the Depression.

"George enlisted to fight in the War, and saw action early on in Africa and Sicily. He was what was called a "Runner," and would deliver information from Post Headquarters to the troop commanders — probably information obtained from Recon jeep drivers like Harry.

"George didn't see Harry from about 1942 until after the War ended. He never knew about Harry's combat experiences, until some time later when they went duck hunting and Harry brought it up. George could relate to what Harry went through because he also had one of the more dangerous combat assignments, and knew just how horrible everything had been.

"One of the things George remembered they talked about was how hard it was for them to adjust to civilian life after discharge. They could speak about this to each other, but couldn't talk about it with their families. In fact, it's only now that George is beginning to feel able to say anything about the War, and he thinks that's because he's older and so much time has passed."

"Did George tell you about the problems they faced in adjusting to civilian life, Miss Jacobs?"

"Yes - at least some of it. [Pause.] When George was discharged, he came back to the farm. It was not an easy transition after what he had been through, but at least he could ease himself into the chores that needed to be done. But when Harry came back from Europe after serving in the Army of Occupation, he spent some time in a military camp before being discharged, and had only a little over a month before he had to report back to work. Harry found it difficult, after what he had experienced, to relate to how people who had not been in the War could become agitated and upset over little things - but he didn't say anything. [Pause.] George felt the same way, and also didn't say anything. They knew their families didn't want to hear, and even if they did, they could never really comprehend that what seemed so important to them was, to guys like Harry and George, so trivial and inconsequential. I guess these kinds of feelings probably added to Harry's sense of separation from people."

[Pause.]

"Then there were the nightmares, and the cold sweats and memories of fear, memories of what they had witnessed - things they could never talk about, not even to their wives, who knew something was wrong, but were probably afraid themselves to bring it up for fear of the guys' reactions. [Pause.] It was stuff like that they talked about this one time they went duck hunting, and then never talked about again. [Pause.] George could tell the effect the War had on Harry because it had the same effect on him. Only George had Lil who was patient and caring, but after Betty died, Harry had no one."

[Pause.]

"They told me how devastating it was for Harry to watch Betty suffer. Apparently she had a long lasting painful Cancer, and as you can imagine, treatment in the early 1950s was not what it is today, even though Harry could afford the best for Betty."

"In what year did Harry's wife die, Miss Jacobs, if you know."

"In 1953, Dr. Levy. Why do you ask?"

"Because I was interested to know what medical treatment would have been available at that time, and you are right. Go on, please."

"Anyway, after Betty passed away, it was then that Harry had to make what was probably one of the most difficult decisions of his life — one which, unfortunately, had even more tragic repercussions for him. Because he was still playing professional baseball, he was on the road often and away from home. He made what he thought was the best decision for his daughter by sending her to live with his sister, a woman old enough to be the child's Grandmother, in California. Apparently, according to what I've consistently been told, the girl never forgave him. George told me that once Harry even said, after they had been drinking together, that Diana, Harry's daughter, actually 'hated him.' And Lil said she was surprised that Diana even bothered to show up for Harry's funeral. Lil showed me a photo of Diana she took after the Service. Dr. Levy, this young woman is stunningly beautiful. What is so strange is that she has Harry's face. She looks just like him, only female with bright red hair. Tall, thin, and very beautiful. I understand she's an attorney in California. It was so strange and so emotional for me to see her as an adult in that photo. All that I have ever remembered about her was that loving photo of her as a toddler in Harry's arms, holding that ball in her tiny -"

[Sounds of sobbing, then voice continuing choked with emotion.]

"How could she hate him so much? He loved her with all his heart. As an adult, couldn't she realize why he did what he did? I'll never understand it."

"Have you ever tried to contact this young woman — Harry's daughter, Miss Jacobs?"

"No. I've been tempted, but each time I think better of it. She has her reasons for her feelings, I'm sure, and who am I to interfere. It just is so sad, especially when I think of that beautiful loving photograph from when I knew Harry. [Pause.] I only hope he got to learn how beautiful and successful she became as an adult."

[Silence.]

"I'm sorry, Dr. Levy. I'll get on with what happened. [Pause.] Anyway, George filled me in on the rest of Harry's life. After he retired from baseball, he worked as a carpenter, which was his regular off-season employment, and then decided to quit at age 50. Apparently, the way George understood it, Harry had some investments, and after paying off all of Betty's enormous medical bills, went to an attorney, made arrangements to liquidate all his remaining assets, set up a Trust for his daughter, so that her living and tuition expenses for advanced education would be met, and with what was left, bought this property in the middle of nowhere, but on ancient Indian land by a beautiful lake, and retreated from the World as we know it."

"Miss Jacobs, before I forget — but perhaps I have asked this already — did George or <u>any</u>

of Harry's friends have knowledge of his psychic abilities and his fascination with the paranormal."

"No, I'm pretty sure they did not. Harry certainly never told any of his team mates, and probably used the same explanation with his friends and family — he was an amateur magician who loved to experiment with magic tricks."

"Thank you. Continue Miss Jacobs, please."

"According to George, Harry lived very — what's the word I want — well, he sort of went back to Nature, almost. Perhaps primitive is the word — but even that does not supply the full feeling I wish to convey.

"He apparently had modest pensions from his years as a ballplayer and from the Carpenters' Union, and used those for whatever expenses he incurred. But primarily he hunted and fished for his major meals, and basically lived the life of a hermit. He did a lot of reading. George found many books about occult and paranormal phenomena. He didn't know what they were until he went to sell them, and I still don't think he understands what the subject matter dealt with.

"Apparently George and Christy — Betty's younger brother — and their wives were the only people who did not give up on Harry during his ten plus years of isolation. Harry and his own brothers had little in common, and I'll explain that to you some other time, maybe when we have that discussion about Reincarnation we've been postponing.

"Anyway, George and Christy would go out to the cabin and if Harry was there, they would go hunting or fishing together. It would be a nice break for George and Christy, and Harry always seemed to enjoy their company."

"Excuse me, Miss Jacobs, but what do you mean by, 'if Harry was there'. Where would he have gone?"

"Well you see, Dr. Levy, in all those years, Harry never had a telephone, and so George could never be sure if he'd find Harry. Sometimes Harry would go into town for business purposes, like getting his checks, buying essentials, picking up mail at the Post Office — things like that. George knew he had missed him if Harry's truck wasn't around. But if it was there and Harry didn't answer, George knew Harry was off somewhere in the woods, and so he would simply turn around and go home, as there was little chance of finding him.

"Once, and I don't know if I dare say it was a coincidence, or if it was planned because Christy had a suspicion of how ill Harry might be; but about a year before Harry died, some of Betty's relatives from another State came and they all surprised Harry at the cabin. They only stayed the afternoon, because, of course, Harry had no accommodations for them, and there were no Motels nearby."

"Miss Jacobs, excuse me — Harry's illness — how was that taken care of, since he was so isolated, and without a telephone."

"I often wondered that myself, Dr. Levy. [Pause.] Apparently, George and Lil were very devoted. Because of Harry's location, each Winter George would go out with one of his huge pieces of farm equipment, and plow a path through the snow from the cabin to the main road, so Harry would be able to get his truck out. And it was on one of these occasions, that George found Harry quite ill. With great difficulty, he managed to get Harry to go with him to a doctor.

"I don't want to go into it all, but let me summarize, Dr. Levy, by saying that Harry was diagnosed with Emphysema, yet he continued to smoke and ignore his condition, which, naturally, all things considered, only got worse. George became so concerned he went out weekly, and eventually had to have Harry admitted to a Nursing Facility for round-the clock care. [Pause.] It broke George's heart to have to do this, and it's breaking mine to think of it and talk about it."

[Silence; then voice filled with intense emotion.]

"I keep asking myself, why didn't I know? I — the one who had felt his every emotion — why didn't I experience his pain then? Why wasn't I aware of his suffering? And worst of all, why couldn't I have done anything to help? Believe me, Dr. Levy, I would have done anything for Harry — anything."

"I do believe you, Miss Jacobs. [Pause.] But did it occur to you that perhaps Harry deliberately did not want you to know about his suffering, and made sure you did not know so that you could get on with your own life, uninterrupted?"

[Pause.]

"Yes, Dr. Levy. That did occur to me. Yes."

[Pause.]

"Anyway, when Harry died, George notified his relatives, including his daughter and sister in California. His family notified the Press, and the News Services picked it up, because Harry had been a respected player during his career. And that's how I was able to read his Obituary.

"After the funeral, Harry's daughter and sister returned to California almost immediately. What surprised George, who had agreed to go through the Cabin and work with Harry's attorney in getting everything turned over to his daughter, his only legal heir — anyway, what surprised George was that Harry still had a sizable bank account, even after having liquidated everything before moving into the cabin. Apparently he spent very little of his Pensions, and the account just kept growing. Harry ate mostly what he got from hunting and fishing, and bought very little in the way of food. Other than that, his needs were few. It was as if he had everything he needed in that cabin."

"Except perhaps for <u>you</u>, Miss Jacobs."

[Silence.]

"I beg you, Dr. Levy, please, please don't say anything like that again. Please. It's difficult enough for me. I don't need a thought like that to confuse me even more."

"I see we have reached that same tender spot again, Miss Jacobs. Why are you so reluctant to acknowledge the feelings that Harry obviously had for you? Again, I have to ask if you feel yourself unworthy of Harry's love."

[Silence.]

"No. You're right. You reminded me, it's — well, once again, there are no coincidences — something that happened later that evening."

[Pause.]

"I'm not trying to dodge the issue. But let me get to that first, please."

"As you wish, Miss Jacobs."

[Pause.]

"Anyway, George went through Harry's things. Apparently, unfortunately, after the news of his death hit the papers — it was, of course, front page news in his little home town — someone managed to locate the cabin and ransacked it. Most of Harry's prized baseball memorabilia were missing, as were many of his hunting rifles and War souvenirs. However, George sent what was left to the Baseball Museum, and all the family photos, letters, *et cetera*, to his daughter. George kept a few things for himself and Christy. He particularly wanted the War souvenirs because of his own memories from being in Patton's Third Army. And somehow I think it pleases Harry that George has these, don't you, Dr. Levy?"

"I would agree based on what you have told me about the close relationship between the two men. It seems only fitting, yes. This man George was indeed a devoted friend to Harry. We should all be as fortunate to have such friends."

"But Dr. Levy, that's what I've been trying to tell you about Harry all along. To know him was to love him. And this is a perfect example of that love."

"Yes, but Miss Jacobs, even <u>you</u> must acknowledge that Harry's daughter does not feel the same way."

[Pause.]

"Of course, you're right. I suppose I'm too close to the circumstances of Harry's life to view it objectively."

"Don't be so hard on yourself, Miss Jacobs. [Pause.] Continue, please."

"Anyway, after we had talked and they showed me the souvenirs George kept in memory of Harry, George asked if I wanted to see the cabin. Apparently he and Lil purchased the property from Harry's daughter. She was glad to unload it, as she wanted no part of it, and they were afraid she might try to develop it into Lakeside Condos or something. Now George and Lil use it for a vacation get-away, along with Christy and some of their other friends, for hunting and fishing."

"That must be of some consolation to you, Miss Jacobs, to know that the way Harry wanted his cabin to be used is still continuing, and by the people closest to him."

"Dr. Levy, I don't think I will <u>ever</u> be able to convey to you all the emotion I felt, first at being with Harry's dearest friends, then at seeing all those items of memories associated with Harry — even from the War. But to go to his cabin? That was beyond belief!

"I cried several times when I saw some of the memorabilia, especially photos of Harry the way I remembered him as a young man. George also had plenty of photos of his own, from when he and Harry played Semi-Pro Ball together. There were even photos taken at their high school graduation, including a lovely photo of Harry and Betty, in cap and gown, arms around each other. They look so happy and so much in love.

"And there was another photo I'll always remember."

[Pause; sniffling.]

"What was that Miss Jacobs - it must have been rather special in view of your emotional reaction."

"It was, Dr. Levy. [Pause.] It was from the year Harry won 22 games and lost none for his Minor League Team. The Cardinal Management presented Harry with a car. As George told me about this photo, tears started to run down his face, and pretty soon Lil and I were crying also. It's a photo of Harry, his brother-in-law Christy, and George, standing by this car, all smiles and grins. Betty took the photo. At the very last minute, just before she snapped the picture, Harry grabbed

George's big farm hat off George's head and put it on his own. [Pause.] I swear Dr. Levy, Harry looks so much like Henry Fonda in that photo - like Henry Fonda in 'The Grapes of Wrath.'"

[Pause.]

"Anyway, George and Lil took me to the cabin. It was twilight when we arrived. It was so peaceful. [Pause.] Christy had taped the family reunion, and when one of Betty's relatives commented on how beautiful the location was, Harry replied softly — his exact words were: 'That's why I'm here'."

[Pause; then resumption with voice barely controlling emotion.]

"I can still hear his voice — his gentle voice so soft, saying 'That's why I'm here'."

[Weeping.]

"And it was after that, after those very words, that Harry said he was there because he needed to get away from the War. And I remember being surprised and puzzled, because the War had ended almost 35 years before. I couldn't understand what he was talking about. But now I do. And, God help me, understanding it for Harry has helped me to understand what it must have been like, and still is for men who went through that Hell and do not talk about it to this day!"

[Silence.]

"Perhaps, Miss Jacobs, you can put your new found insights and compassion to some useful purpose, such as volunteering your services in a Veterans' Hospital. Are you aware that there are still men from the Second World War — casualties who, for reasons of the nature of their injuries, will never be able to lead normal lives, and who will remain institutionalized until their deaths?"

331

[Sounds of weeping.]

"Forgive me, Miss Jacobs. I didn't mean to upset you. I merely meant to offer a suggestion. Your services could be of considerable value, I can assure you. I have visited such hospitals, and I know whereof I speak."

[Silence.]

"Tell me, if you are able now, Miss Jacobs, what were your emotions upon being at Harry's cabin. Did you go inside?"

"Yes. [Pause.] It was such a beautiful peaceful twilight. We walked in the area Harry had cleared around the cabin, then we walked a little in the woods, then to the lake. We were only in the cabin briefly, as it has no electricity, and we had to leave before dark. There were only the minimal necessary pieces of furniture, a table, a few chairs and a couch that I guess serves as a bed. The funny thing though was that it has a basement, and when I asked George about that, he said Harry very wisely dug that because of tornadoes.

"Can you imagine? I had forgotten all about tornadoes in that area. Somehow, and I know I wouldn't feel that way if I lived there, the thought of a tornado basement in a cabin in the wilderness seems a little funny to me."

"And what were your primary emotions, upon being in Harry's cabin? Did you feel his presence?"

"My primary emotion, which surprised me, because I was prepared that I would make a fool of myself by weeping hysterically — but I did not — because my primary emotion was one of feeling numb. That is the only way I can describe it. I felt numb, washed out, drained."

[Pause.]

"Then you asked if I felt Harry's presence — and the answer is yes. I did. [Pause.] Have I told you about how I can tell Harry is with me by the smell of cigarette smoke?"

"I don't believe so, Miss Jacobs. Please continue."

"It's true. [Pause.] I remember reading in books about the paranormal, that often you can tell if a Spirit is present, because a fragrance associated with the deceased can be smelled."

[Pause.]

"I remember too, as a kid, how sexy I thought Harry looked when he smoked, the way he had with a cigarette dangling from his lips — how sexy he looked. But those damn things were what ultimately caused him to die, and I used to think how sexy he looked when he smoked!"

"My dear Miss Jacobs, do not be so harsh on yourself for a number of reasons. First, in the days when you were a child, practically every adult male smoked, isn't that true?"

"Yes."

"And the dangers of cigarette smoking were not known to the general public at the time, isn't that correct?"

"Yes."

"Nor was the danger of asbestos. Didn't you say that Harry was a carpenter whenever he was not playing baseball? How do you not know that his work with asbestos might not also in some way contributed to the medical problems with his lungs?"[1]

---

[1] As Dr. Levy was an inveterate smoker, these words were most likely his means of rationalization of a habit he knew was self-destructive.

"All right, Dr. Levy. I understand what you're saying, and of course, you're right, as usual."

[Pause.]

"Anyway, I <u>did</u> feel Harry's presence when I was in the cabin. I distinctly smelled cigarette smoke. I remember being startled because it happened so suddenly. I even looked to see if George or Lil were smoking, but they weren't. In fact, I don't remember ever seeing George or Lil smoke when I was with them.

"But I <u>did</u> smell cigarette smoke when I was in the cabin. Absolutely."

"Did the possibility occur to you that it might have remained there from someone else, one of the friends who might have visited?"

"Yes. But by this time, I was completely familiar with the way it is when Harry is present, and that's what it felt like — not the remnant that clings to furniture or clothing.

"In fact, Dr. Levy, let me digress for a moment to tell you how hard I've been working at trying to find rational explanations for what has been happening to me. Of course, Midge thought I was nuts for doing this, but do you know that I actually went to a specialist to learn if I might have some form of illness or allergy that was causing me to experience the sensation of the odor of tobacco?"

"Actually, Miss Jacobs, that <u>is</u> rather humorous. And of course, the specialist could find nothing, correct?"

"Correct. [Pause.] Actually, I'm surprised he didn't recommend that I seek psychiatric help at the time. Who knows? Maybe he noted it in my chart, or something."

[Pause.]

"Anyway, I sensed the smell of cigarette smoke in the cabin as I walked through the rooms, and I still remember how numb I felt. Then we left and returned to George and Lil's place."

"Did anything else happen, Miss Jacobs please."

"Yes. And this is where I <u>did</u> break down."

[Pause.]

"One of the things George showed me that he had taken from Harry's cabin was a radio. It was in rather poor external condition, the knob was gone, and a corner was damaged, but what made it so special was the Plaque on the top. It was a special engraved Plaque commemorating the 25th Anniversary of the 1946 World Series between the Cardinals and the Red Sox, and Harry's name was on it, because he was a member of the Cardinals at the time."

[Pause.]

"Anyway, I'll make this fast so that I don't become hysterical the way I did at George and Lil's place. George decided to give it to me as a gift. He said that it would be nice if I had something to remember Harry by, and since I had known Harry around that time, this would be a fitting memory. [Pause.] You know, Dr. Levy, I almost didn't accept it?"

"But my dear Miss Jacobs, why not? [Pause.] Or are we back to your feelings of unworthiness again."

"I don't know how to answer that. I don't think it was unworthiness. It's just that I felt George and Lil had been such good friends to Harry that they were the ones who should have it, not I."

"But did the possibility occur to you that this was just one more example of the very kind and generous nature of these people that

335

they would want to make such a gift? [Pause.] And did it not occur to you that Harry would have wanted you to accept this gift?"

[Pause.]

"Yes. The first possibility occurred to me after I got through weeping and could control what I was saying. I said something like 'oh, I couldn't', but they <u>insisted</u>, and as they had been so kind to me, I did not want to insult them by refusing. And besides, as you can imagine, I <u>REALLY did want that radio</u>!

"As for the second possibility, that Harry wanted me to have it — well, that occurred to me shortly after I turned the radio on when I got back to the Motel. And that's one of those examples that are best characterized, in my opinion, as synchronicities."

"Explain please, Miss Jacobs."

"I thanked George and Lil profusely and left after a little while. They're farmers and get up real early, so I knew it was well past their bedtime. As soon as I got back to the Motel, I called Midge and told her about the day's events — especially the radio. The first words out of her mouth were, 'This is a gift from Harry. You are meant to have it.' Well, that's typical Midge, and I was so happy to have the radio, I didn't question what she said.

"Then she asked if I had turned it on yet. Well, of course I hadn't. For one thing, it was so beat up looking, I assumed it wouldn't play. For another, the first thing I did upon entering my Motel room, was to call Midge. So she told me to turn it on, and then call her back. She had a feeling that not only would it play, but that it would have a message for me from Harry."

"And was she right?"

"Of course. Yes. She was ABSOLUTELY RIGHT!"

"Tell me about it, Miss Jacobs, please."

"I've told you about my last moments with Harry, and how he placed me in that cab and sent me home."

"Yes, Miss Jacobs."

[Pause.]

"Touch her soft lips and part."

[Pause.]

"Yes, Miss Jacobs."

"Yet I never understood what he was doing at that moment. I had always, despite the sweet gentle kiss — I had always assumed he was getting rid of me in some way. That he was rejecting me."

"Miss Jacobs, forgive me for interrupting, but there is something important which I do not want you to lose sight of."

"Yes, Dr. Levy. What is it?"

"I believe you no longer feel that Harry was trying to get rid of you when he sent you away in that taxicab, am I correct?"

"Yes. Correct."

"And you now realize that what he was doing was motivated by a nobler purpose, is that true?"

"Yes, that's true."

"But you did not realize this until after you had these experiences, is that correct?"

"Yes, that's correct."

"Now — can you possibly understand how Harry's daughter might have felt when he sent her away to California?"

[Pause.]

"Oh. My God."

"Can you understand that to her, it would have felt like rejection, as it did to you — when in fact, the poor man was doing only what he felt to be in the child's best interest, whether she understood or not."

"Oh, my God. I don't know what to say, I -"

"Miss Jacobs, my purpose in bringing this to your attention is so that you could have some basis for understanding why Harry's daughter has retained such bitterness all these years. From what you have told me, the parallel between the two situations is strikingly similar."

[Silence.]

"Then why can't he go to her and let her see how he really felt and why he did what he did?"

"It would seem to me, Miss Jacobs, that the poor soul is having enough trouble getting you to understand, and you are someone with whom he shared psychic abilities. Imagine what it would be like for him to try to convince his daughter. I think it would be safe to assume that even if she possessed those abilities, as yourself, she has chosen a profession, the law in her case, where the use of logic overrules any such aptitude. And perhaps, like yourself, if she suspected she had these abilities, she would want to repress them — particularly in view of her hostility toward her Father."

[Silence.]

"I don't know what to say, Dr. Levy, except that of course you are right. I'm grateful that you helped me to understand his daughter's feelings — I really am."

[Pause.]

"Forgive the interruption, Miss Jacobs. Continue with what happened when you turned on Harry's radio, please."

"Dr. Levy, there is no need for apologies. I needed to hear what you just said. I really did, and I thank you for it."

[Pause.]

"Anyway, I turned on the radio, and I remember thinking that it could have been on the very station that Harry had last listened to when -"

"That is, assuming his friends hadn't listened to it in the time they had it since Harry's death."

"That's true, Dr. Levy — unless they, like I, assumed it wasn't working."

"You're right, Miss Jacobs. Forgive the interruption again and continue, please."

"Anyway, I turned it on and a song called 'Go Away Little Girl' was playing."

"WHAT!" [Voice tone and level indicating intense surprise.]

"Yes. Exactly. [Pause.] The words are something like, and I won't attempt to sing them, but they're something like: — go away little girl, you're much too young to be alone with me — much too young for me to be in love with you — it hurts each time you're near — it's hard for me to resist — your kiss may be sweet, but our lips must never meet, because I belong to another and I must be true — and it ends with the man telling the young girl she has to go away — and these are the exact closing words of the song: 'Go away little girl, before I beg you to stay.'"

[Sounds of heavy sobbing.]

"Tell me, Miss Jacobs, did you call Midge that night?"

[Pause.]

"Yes, I did. And, as you can imagine, she could hardly control how she gloated."

"I wonder why you feel the need to see a Psychoanalyst when you have your friend Midge, Miss Jacobs."

[Laughter.]

"Thank you for that, Dr. Levy, I —"

"That was <u>indeed</u> a very dramatic example of a personal message of love from Harry, in my humble opinion, Miss Jacobs."

"And it was <u>then</u>, <u>only</u> then, for the first time, after hearing that song, I understood, <u>for the VERY first time</u>, why Harry reacted to me the way he did when he saw me in 1949, why he took me to the hotel and acted so strange while we were sitting on the couch, and then of course, why he sent me away in that cab."

"I hope you understand now how he felt about you, and why I stated you were probably also one of the losses he felt in his life."

"Please Dr. Levy — why do you have to say that!"

[Sounds of sobbing.]

"Miss Jacobs, at some time you are going to have to face the reality of being someone worthy of love and that this man Harry had true feelings for you upon which he acted like a decent human being. I thought you had reached the point of accepting this love, but your doubts apparently still remain."

[Pause.]

"We spoke earlier of Harry's Spirit visiting his daughter to let her understand why he did what he felt was necessary. Has the thought occurred to you that this is why he has come back into <u>your</u> life? So that he can let you know how much he cared for you. [Pause.] But I think you <u>are</u> aware, because of your characterization of 'being courted by a Ghost', as you put it. The problem arises however, that despite the poor soul's efforts, you are <u>still</u> struggling <u>not</u> to believe him."

[Pause.]

"Permit me to suggest the following hypothesis, Miss Jacobs. You are deeply troubled by your possession of abilities you do not understand, because they are not accepted in the World of Logic to which you have retreated in order to deny the existence of these abilities. Then when you are bombarded by these experiences for which the only explanations lie outside the realm of Logic, you would prefer a diagnosis of mental disease rather than accept the experiences for what they are. However, the experiences continue, and I believe they will keep continuing, until you are forced to acknowledge their truth and validity."

[Extended silence.]

"I don't know how to respond to that, Dr. Levy. [Pause.] In a way, what you just said sounds a lot like what Midge has been telling me."

"The woman should hang up a shingle and I will refer the very next person who comes to my office with problems like yours, Miss Jacobs!"

[Pause.]

"I see we are well over time, in fact, well past my lunch time. If you will excuse me, Miss Jacobs, I do need to terminate our session."

"Thank you so much, Dr. Levy. And see, it was possible for us to get through a session after what happened yesterday."

"Please do not remind me of that, Miss Jacobs. You make me think that I have to be careful of everything I say to you, because you will know if I am telling a fib or not!"

[Pause.]

"Good-bye, Dr. Levy, and thank you again."

"Good-bye, Miss Jacobs."

End of Tape 21.

Notes Accompanying Tape 21.

It was certainly comforting for me, at any rate, that Miss Jacobs was able to keep to her word, and let today's session continue without the use of her "extrasensory abilities" — for lack of better terminology. Indeed, today was more typical Patient/Therapist than most other sessions Miss Jacobs and I have experienced.

It never ceases to amaze me how she applies investigative techniques to analyze if there can be a rational basis for her experiences. Apparently she even went to a specialist to see if there was a medical explanation for her sensing the smell of Harry's cigarette smoke. Incredible!

I feel I am on the verge of understanding something, but I am not clear if I am able to verbalize it —- I will try to be analytical, as is Miss Jacobs.

Hypothesis:

She continually presents the problem of feeling unworthy of Harry's love. Therefore, Harry keeps trying to convince her both of his continued existence beyond his physical death, and of the depth of emotion he felt for her while living, and apparently still feels for her.

She has said that she fears both the manifestation AND the loss of these contacts. She has admitted, I believe even more than once, that if time goes by without any communication from Harry, she becomes concerned.

What more must Harry do to prove his love to her?

Perhaps the REAL reason Miss Jacobs is reluctant to acknowledge Harry's love, is NOT because she feels unworthy of it, but because, once she acknowledges it and receives it, Harry will no longer need to prove it to her. Perhaps what she <u>REALLY</u> fears is the loss of the constant communication, his continued demonstration of devotion and eternal love. She fears that once he knows she believes in his love, his earthly assignment, like Liliom's, will be finished and she will lose him yet another time.

I need to think about this more. Perhaps I should even suggest it to Miss Jacobs and see what is her reaction. On the other hand, she may know right now that I am thinking and planning this.

There are times when I wish I could strangle Seymour Cohen for suggesting that Miss Jacobs call me. But then the World would lose such a marvelous musician! (I hope Miss Jacobs never gets angry at Seymour so that <u>he</u> suffers an untimely misfortune! Although there was that one Concert Series that was canceled — but NO. I MUST stop here!!!!)

* * *

Tape 22

May 15, 1981

3:30 pm

"Miss Jacobs?" [Tone indicating surprise.]

"Hi, Dr. Levy." [Tone of almost child-like teasing.]

"But your usual appointment hour is at 4:30."

"That's true."

"But how —?" [Genuinely puzzled.]

"You know I've been telling you that the last day I spent at the cemetery in Missouri was very emotional — I know, they ALL were, but this day REALLY more than the others. Anyway, I always felt that we might need more than the usual fifty-minute hour, although our sessions go over that many times, which is one good thing about being your last patient, and —"

"Get to the point, Miss Jacobs, please. It is not that I am displeased, but I am surprised and somewhat mystified."

"Earlier today, I had this peculiar feeling that if I called right after lunch, you might have a cancellation, and I might be able to have more than one session in a row. And guess what happened when I —."

"Miss Jacobs, are you placing some sort of 'spell' on my other patients? It seems to me that this is not the first time something similar has occurred. And as you probably know, I am only half-teasing when I ask."

"Honestly, Dr. Levy, I am not doing anything that I am aware of. If I _am_ doing something, it is without my conscious knowledge, and that's probably even scarier."

"Believe me, Miss Jacobs, I could not agree with you more. If you are capable of influencing the acts of others without awareness of your own conscious volition, then this is a situation far more serious — ...."

[Interrupting. Speaking simultaneously, words difficult to distinguish.]

"— circumstances way over our heads."

[Silence.]

"All right, Miss Jacobs. Make yourself comfortable, and proceed to tell me about that eventful last day at the cemetery. But first, you will permit me to have my usual break before the 4:30 hour, I trust?"

"If you're a good boy, Dr. Levy. Only if you're a good boy."

"My dear Miss Jacobs — I think I denote a sinister tone in your voice."

"You may be right, Dr. Levy. [Pause.] But then, you might not even want to take that break, if my story is so spellbinding, right?"

"As I have indicated many many times — with YOU, Miss Jacobs, anything is possible."

"How true."

[Silence.]

"And now, I will begin the story of Sophie's Magical Mystery Tour."

"Proceed, Miss Jacobs."

"In all seriousness, Dr. Levy, it was a day, from beginning to end, that I shall never forget as long as I live. Everything about this day was magic. It had all the elements of true drama: love, suspense, mystery, storm, fear, beauty, and passion. Really. It did."

"My dear Miss Jacobs. I can see why this man Harry and you got along so famously. You are as much a born story-teller as you said he was. It makes me think of two things — -"

345

"Yes, I know. Harry really WAS a lot like Liliom, in so many ways, including how he has come back to me. And I love that story of Jan de Hartog also. Sometimes I DO think that Harry and I were each 'born liars'."

"Miss Jacobs. [Tone indicating both surprise and disappointment.] You really spoil things for me when you do that. Besides, you gave me your solemn word."

"I'm sorry. Perhaps I meant it to apply only to serious things in our sessions. And honestly, when I am as relaxed as I am with you, it just seems to happen before I can stop it. [Pause.] I'm truly sorry. And I won't do it again. At least I hope not.

"Where was I?"

"Beginning to narrate The Adventures of Sophie and her Magical Mystery Tour."

"OK."

[Pause.]

"It happened on the anniversary of Harry's death. I went to the Cemetery early so I could be there with him at the time I knew he took his last breath."

"Why was that important to you, to be there then, Miss Jacobs?"

"I really don't know. [Pause.] You see, I don't know if anyone was there with him, to comfort him, to hold his hand, or even just to be in the room with him. I just know I needed to be there at that time."

[Pause.]

"And I think you'll be interested in this. I had copied the page from Liliom, where Julie stands over his dead body, and says her beautiful love speech. And on that Saturday, at the anniversary of the moment of Harry's passing, I started reading, by the dimmest light of dawn, Julie's love speech."

"I believe I can remember bits and pieces of it, Miss Jacobs, but if you wish to refresh my recollection —"

"I don't know all of it by heart, but from what I can remember, she tells him something like:

Sleep, Liliom, sleep.
They can't understand how I feel.
I can't even explain it to you.
I never told you before,
I was ashamed.
But now I'll tell you.
I love you Liliom.
Sleep, Liliom, sleep.

[Pause.]

"That's basically what I said over Harry's grave in the very early morning on the anniversary of his death."

[Silence.]

"Then I drove from the Cemetery to the University. It was a good three-hour drive, but I made it in plenty of time for when the Library opened at 10 am.

"The University Library was as good for what I needed as the Library at the Metaphysical Institute was for spiritual literature. They have a magnificent collection of all the important Missouri newspapers for at least 100 years, most of it being on Microfilm, however.

"It was like going to what I can imagine old-fashioned movie shows to be. I sat in this booth-like contraption and turned a handle and watched still figures come to life. At least that's the way it seemed to me.

"And there was Harry, young and alive and well — beautiful photographs and live-action shots and interviews and articles, and snippets of information."

[Pause.]

347

"I stayed in the library until closing time at 4:00 pm. I had read so many articles, especially the ones written by that one reporter who rhapsodized about Harry so eloquently, because of Harry's unique style and personality. I swear, when this reporter wrote about a mere Ballgame, you'd think you were reading a literary essay on a subject of great philosophical significance."

"But isn't that how most Americans view Baseball — as a subject of 'great philosophical significance', as you put it, Miss Jacobs?"

"You may be right, Dr. Levy. You may be right." [Pause.]

"Anyway, when I had entered the Library, the sun was shining and it was a beautiful clear day. The section I was in was underground with no windows, probably to protect the old papers and microfilm; so it was a tremendous shock to me to see such an incredible change in the weather. The sky was dark and menacing.

"Oh, and I almost forgot to tell you one of the most important things. Everytime I would turn on the car radio in Missouri, or <u>any</u> radio, for that matter — like Harry's, remember — there would ALWAYS, and <u>I DO mean ALWAYS</u>, without exaggeration, be some song on that had special meaning for me and Harry. For instance, when I bought those flowers to take to his grave and that song played, and of course as soon as I turned Harry's radio on.

"Anyway, on the long drive to the University that day, there was complete static on the car radio, and I could not pick up a single station. Now that was unbelievable to me. This radio had played perfectly all week and had presented no problems, even in the tiniest of towns. Yet on the highway drive to the

348

University on the anniversary of Harry's death, not a single station came in clearly, even when I passed large metropolitan areas. And the sun was shining without a cloud in the sky.

"However, on the way back from the Library to the Cemetery, the radio was working fine again. First there was a country song about some poor fellow who had passed on and would wait for his beloved until she reached the Gates of Heaven to join him; then there was a song you may have even heard, Dr. Levy — 'What the World needs now, is love, sweet love'. Anyway, it just kept on like that, until I even had to laugh. I felt Harry was being exceptionally clever.

"But then the programs started taking a serious turn. The sky had become increasingly ominous and the music was interrupted by dire weather predictions and warnings. Then I began to grasp the full impact of what it meant to be in Tornado country!

"It was so scary. They were telling people what to do, how to take cover, what precautions to take, *et cetera*. But NOT ONE SINGLE WORD, although I was anxiously waiting to hear it, about what you should do if you were out driving a car on a highway! I then surmised that the announcer felt it was such a hopeless situation why bother to give instructions when the <u>only</u> thing anyone could do in those circumstances was PRAY!

"As I continued to drive the interruptions and reports became longer and more frequent. They named the areas where tornadoes had been spotted: one was a major city which I would reach in about an hour, and the other was Harry's poor little town. Later, as I drove on, there was even a FLOOD warning, of all

349

things, for the county in which Harry's town was located.

"Meanwhile, the sky got worse. The highway was straight and flat so I could see for miles ahead. The sky was a continuous wonder of contradictions. There would be sunshine, then a few miles beyond, huge Thunderheads, then weird yellowish sky coloring, incipient funnel clouds, lightning — you name it. Then, in the midst of all this, the radio resumed with its music, and what does it play? The songs from the 'Wizard of Oz', where The Scarecrow, Tin Man, Lion, and Dorothy sing about what they want most in the World, then are 'Off to see the Wizard'. And I couldn't help but think that I too, was off to see the Wizard, considering how Harry had often been referred to as 'The Merry Magician of the Mound'. And I had to laugh, and compliment Harry on the Magnificent Fireworks Display he was producing and on his marvelous sense of humor about all of this."

"But weren't you afraid, Miss Jacobs?"

"Actually no, Dr. Levy. No, I wasn't. I felt no fear, despite all the ominous forecasts, because I thought it would be a really appropriate ending for my life, to die en route to visit Harry's grave on the same day that marked the anniversary of his death. But I have to tell you it was a pretty grim scene. The radio resumed coverage of the storms, as several tornadoes had touched down in the area, and there were reports of considerable damage. In fact, two ambulances zoomed past as I continued driving.

"When I finally reached the County where Harry's little town was located, I couldn't believe how ferocious the wind was. I went to the same market where I had bought the flowers before, and decided to get a single elegant red rose to place on Harry's gravestone to mark this date. I think the salesclerk thought I was insane, especially when I asked for some tape to hold the rose in place on the stone."

"I can't help notice how quick you are to use that word 'insane,' although I imagine it <u>would</u> seem somewhat unusual, Miss Jacobs."

"To say the least, Dr. Levy.

"Anyway, when I drove to the store, there were reports of winds of up to 100 miles per hour, and quote - <u>baseball</u> size - unquote, hail. I'm sorry, but I really had to laugh at that one; and once again complimented Harry for this magnificent Magic Show."

"I must say I admire your persistence in continuing to drive to the Cemetery under such conditions, Miss Jacobs."

"Would you call it 'persistence', or obsessive-compulsive character disorder, Dr. Levy?"

"Still looking for a diagnosis, are we, Miss Jacobs?"

"I'll pretend I didn't hear that last remark, Dr. Levy. [Pause.] <u>Anyway</u> — as I drove the car up the winding country road that leads to the cemetery, the sky became calmer and clearer. I had turned off the radio when I got into the car with the Rose, because I didn't want anything to spoil what I remembered from the time before with the first set of flowers. And when I reached the Cemetery — did I tell you that it sits on the top of a hill, overlooking the rest of the town and farmland below? Anyway, when I reached the cemetery and parked the car, the sky was absolutely beautiful. Twilight was dimming and the moon was actually beginning to glow. Yet I could see, as I walked to Harry's grave, that in the valley below, there were thunderheads, lightning, and rain."

[Pause. Voice obviously controlling emotion.]

"I sat by Harry's grave and immediately placed the Rose on the marker and taped it in several places, as the wind had not quite died down. And from where I was sitting by Harry's grave, I could still see the Valley below. It was so strange."

[Pause.]

"But it was also deeply intense. I could really feel, strongly feel, Harry's presence beside me. I knew he was there right next to me. So close. So close, that we were touching. It was as if we had front row seats in some Giant Cosmic Movie Theater and were watching a display of Cosmic Fireworks put on just for the two of us.

"Where we were, the moon was shining. A small propeller plane flew overhead. I jokingly referred to it as 'The Spirit of St. Louis'. Yet in the Valley below, the huge thunderheads were still there, the sky was colored a strange yellowish-pink, and there were spectacular bolts and flashes of lightning."

[Silence. Then voice resumed, in subdued but deeply emotional tones, almost weeping.]

"I don't know when I have ever had such feelings of closeness, tenderness and love for another human being as I felt for Harry that night. Nor can I remember ever seeing, nor sensing such a visual display of beauty in Nature around me. Nor can I remember feeling another human being as close to me as I felt Harry was that night.

"I poured out my heart to him, audibly, because I knew he was right there beside me. I can't explain it — I just knew. I <u>felt</u> it, sensed, <u>knew</u> that he was there so close, in spirit, in body, in love. In <u>every</u> way a person can sense the existence of love in another, he was there. So I told him how I had loved seeing those photos of him the way I remembered him; how I had loved reading about all the things he had done. I told him how much I had loved reading about and seeing him age in the photos, but still graceful and always the artful master magician. Always the blithe spirit.

"I told him how much I loved him, although I couldn't understand how or why, but that I knew I loved him more than any human being I had ever known or would ever know in my life. And as I spoke those words, although the storm still raged in the Valley below, stars could be seen from where we were — you see there how simply I said where 'WE' were, because that's how it felt — 'WE' were there together. And the stars and the moon were shining just for us. For us there was only a gentle warm breeze blowing — no winds of up to 100 miles per hour, nor even baseball-size hail. The ground upon which we sat was damp, but not uncomfortable.

"I felt serene — serene in Harry's presence. And I told him that I never wanted to leave this place, and that I would curl up and sleep on the soil surrounding his marker. Then I laughed as I imagined myself being found asleep by Harry's marker and being carted off to some mental institution in Missouri."

"Excuse me for interrupting, Miss Jacobs, but I could not let that reference to involuntary commitment remain unidentified."

"Well, OK. As you wish. [Pause.] Anyway, I also imagined being struck by a bolt of lightning and being found dead beside Harry's marker. And I thought how appropriate that would be — to die on the date of the anniversary of Harry's death, and be found lying beside the remains of his body in the earth.

"And then I wondered — would we be reunited instantly? Would our souls, our spirits walk away into the mist like The Ghost and Mrs. Muir? And if so, who would walk away together? 60 year old Harry and 45 year old Sophie? Or, as with the Ghost and Mrs. Muir, would it be 30 year old Harry and 15 year old Sandy?"

[Silence, broken only by sounds of sobbing.]

"Here, Miss Jacobs, these tissues, please."

"Thank you."

[Silence.]

"Since you are here with me today, Miss Jacobs, what made you finally leave such serenity?"

"I can honestly tell you, Dr. Levy, that I don't know how long I would have stayed there, but almost out of nowhere a car drove into the Cemetery. It startled me. I could hear it, but I couldn't see it clearly. Perhaps it was a Police patrol vehicle. I don't know. But it frightened me out of my reverie and I left quickly. But not before telling Harry once more that I loved him and that I would return the next day before I had to leave for New York."

[Silence; then when voice resumes, filled with emotion, possibly crying.]

"I got into the car, and something strange happened again. When I turned on the radio, the music that was playing — [Pause] —"

"Yes, Miss Jacobs?"

"It was Schoenberg. 'Verklärte Nacht.'[1] [Pause.] I'm sure you must know that piece, Dr. Levy."

"Yes. You are correct, Miss Jacobs. I am familiar with that music. [Pause.] It is one of my favorites."

[Silence.]

"Continue, Miss Jacobs, please. That is if you feel able."

"Sure. I'm OK now, really. [Heavy sigh.] By the time I returned to the Motel, the weather was considerably calmer in the town, which, incidentally did not suffer any damage, despite the warnings and the appearance of conditions in the Valley below. I remember sitting on my bed, fully clothed, but numb. I was too overwhelmed with emotion to move. The entire day had been filled with love for Harry, from beginning to end.

"It began at dawn with the recital of the love soliloquy from 'Liliom,' then continued with the reading of all those articles about him, and the pictures, showing him as he aged. There was even one photo that showed him in his fifties. Somehow, some one managed to coax him away from his cabin, and he pitched in an Old Timers game. Maybe it was when he received the commemorative radio — I bet that was it. [Pause. Then excited tone.] <u>Of course</u>. That <u>has</u> to be it!

"Seeing that photo, of an older Harry, still slim and trim in his Cardinal uniform, made me paraphrase in my mind the Yeats poem: And one girl loved the Pilgrim Soul in you, and loved the sorrows of your changing face."

---

[1] Unlike most of the music of Arnold Schoenberg, "Verklärte Nacht" is romantic and emotional, and is the setting of a passionate interlude between a young couple.

[Pause.]

"Then there was the drive back to the cemetery, and the humor of the songs from 'The Wizard of Oz' — but best of all, there was sitting at Harry's gravesite, feeling his presence so close to me, with the unparalleled beauty in the sky and earth around us, and the sensing of deep shared love, which was repeated by the playing of 'Verklärte Nacht'.

"I shall never forget that day, and shall always be eternally grateful to whatever Force controls our destiny for granting us those moments of love, peace, and beauty."

[Silence.]

"You almost make me want to say 'Amen',[2] Miss Jacobs."

"Then why not say it. If you don't, I will."

"Amen."

"Amen."

[Silence.]

"That was a very touching and beautiful Memorial to Harry's memory, Miss Jacobs. Tell me, did anything else happen while you were still in Missouri? I know you were to leave the next day."

"Yes — actually some other things <u>did</u> happen — the next day when I left — more of those so-called coincidences. Also, that's the day I met with Harry's Brother-in-law."

"Then, as you have more to tell me, this might be a good time for us to take a brief break, don't you agree? [Pause; then teasing tone.] Have I been a good boy? Do I deserve to have my usual break?"

[Pause.]

"Dr. Levy - you smoke, don't you?"

"Yes, I do, Miss Jacobs. Why do you ask?"

---

[2] Both Dr. Levy and Ms. Jacobs give the Hebrew pronunciation of this word — Ah-mayn.

"I KNOW you want your break because you're dying for a cigarette. I'm not sure I should let you have your break if that's how you're going to use your time."

"Miss Jacobs! [Voice agitated.] What is going on here! Enough is enough, already!"

"I'm sorry, Dr. Levy. I didn't mean to lecture you like that, it's just —."

"Yes. Lecture IS the word. [Pause.] You sounded like my wife, or my son - and he is not even a medical doctor!"

"I'm really sorry, Dr. Levy. [Voice becoming increasingly emotional.] It's just that when I think of how Harry died, and I think of you so fondly, and - I'm sorry. Your life is really none of my business, really."

"Forgive me, Miss Jacobs. I should not have reacted the way I did. That was entirely inappropriate and unprofessional on my part, and I ask you to please excuse my behavior."

"Behavior excused. As long as you agree to excuse mine."

"Agreed. [Pause.] And now, may I have my break, please?"

"Yes, Dr. Levy. You may have your break. By now you've earned it."

End of Tape 22.

Notes Accompanying Tape 22.

There are **No Notes** accompanying this Tape. Commentary on the subject matter of the Session recorded on Tape 22 is included within the Notes accompanying Tape 23.

***

Tape 23

May 15, 1981

4:45 pm

"Miss Jacobs, are you ready to resume?"

"Yes, Dr. Levy."

"I have started the tape machine again, and, as they say in Court, we are back on the record."

"[Tone of mischief.] Did you enjoy your cigarette, Dr. Levy?"

"Miss Jacobs! Shame on you. Your promise — remember?"

"I know. I'm just trying to tease you. [Pause.] Everything we say here is always so serious and sometimes I feel — because I spend so much time crying — that I need to do something to lighten things up a bit."

"I understand, and I appreciate your thoughtfulness, Miss Jacobs. Sincerely I do."

[Silence.]

"Tell me, Miss Jacobs, are we still on Sophie's Magical Mystery Tour?"

"I guess so."

"Then ON WITH THE SHOW!"

"Dr. Levy! I'm afraid my bizarre sense of humor has infected you."

"There are far worse things that could happen, believe me, Miss Jacobs." [Tone more serious than words would indicate.]

[Pause.]

"Dr. Levy, do you remember how when I bought flowers to put on Harry's grave, the radio played 'Our Love is Here to Stay'?"

"Yes."

"Well, this time, after I put my luggage in the trunk of the rental car, I got into the

359

driver's seat, turned the ignition on, and the radio started to play. Of course you know what was playing, don't you, Dr. Levy?"

"Let me guess........"

"I simply do NOT know how to explain this, Miss Jacobs. I can find no reason — no logical explanation for this to have occurred. It is now almost 5:20, we have been talking for a little over half-an-hour, and almost <u>nothing</u> of our Session has been recorded.

"In all the years that I have been using this recording device,[1] nothing like this has ever happened.

"I don't understand this. [Pause; resuming with slow thoughtful process of review.] I put in a new tape. I pressed the machine to start, and when you entered and we exchanged greetings, I checked again — as I <u>always</u> do — and it WAS working. Then we resumed our Session. [Pause.] I think I even commented about — something like, being in Court and going on the record. [Pause.] Do you remember me saying something like that, Miss Jacobs?"

"Actually I <u>do</u>, Dr. Levy."

"I can not understand why it stopped, I have no idea <u>when</u> it stopped recording, and I don't know how to explain why it is working <u>NOW</u>, as if nothing was ever wrong with it before."

"Dr. Levy, excuse me, but may I make a suggestion?"

"Of course, Miss Jacobs."

---

[1] It was Dr. Nehemiah Levy who purchased the tape-recorder for his Father, and explained the beneficial uses to which it could be put for the treatment of patients in therapy. Initially, Dr. Eliahu Levy was reluctant to discard his traditional method of making written Notes as his patients spoke. He continued to feel the need for this method of Note taking however, and utilized it while listening to the results of the recorded Sessions. Thus, the Notes after the transcriptions of Ms. Jacobs' Sessions.

"Why don't you rewind it and see what it <u>did</u> record of our Session earlier?"

"But it was not working, Miss Jacobs."

"We don't know that for sure — all we know is that it stopped recording at some point in time."

"All right. I will do as you suggest, Miss Jacobs."

[Sounds of tape machine, then replay of the words spoken from the return of Ms. Jacobs into the office, until Dr. Levy's statement: "Let me guess."]

"Fascinating."

[Pause.]

"And something else, Miss Jacobs. <u>How</u> did you know — I mean, <u>what</u> made you ask me to check if the machine was recording our discussion. This machine has never malfunctioned before. Why did you ask that I check its performance just now?"

[Silence.]

"What do you want me to say, Dr. Levy? What do you <u>expect</u> me to say. [Pause.] Actually, you KNOW what I will have to tell you — and I don't mean through reading my mind, either. [Pause.] This is just one more instance of what I have been going through. [Pause.] Is it beginning to get to you, Dr. Levy? Are you finally beginning to understand?" [Voice tone agitated, bitter.]

"Please, Miss Jacobs. For my sake, then. Explain it to me again." [Voice tone anxious and troubled; unusual for Dr. Levy.]

"It was another of those instances when I <u>knew</u> what would happen — and <u>please</u> don't ask me how, because I DON'T KNOW!"

[Pause.]

"Anyway, I had this psychic — or perhaps you would prefer me to say 'intuitive' — feeling

361

that Harry did not want the things I was telling you to be preserved."

[Silence.]

"But why would that be? What could there possibly have been in our discussion that Harry would not have wanted preserved on tape? [Pause.] The machine recorded our earlier discussion, before we took our break. I know because I checked before changing tapes for the continuation of our extended session."

[Pause.]

"I'm sorry, but I can't answer because I don't know either. I just know he didn't want the machine to record what we were saying."

[Silence.]

"Can you remember, Miss Jacobs, please, what we were discussing when you had this feeling that the machine was not functioning properly."

"But the machine IS functioning properly. There's nothing wrong with the machine. You see it is working now. It just was not taping the things that Harry did not want to have recorded."

"All right. Let us assume for the moment that your hypothesis is -"

"Yes. Let us assume."

"Miss Jacobs, do not interrupt, please."

[Pause.]

"Can you remember at all what it was we were discussing when you had this feeling?"

[Pause.]

"I can't remember."

"Try, Miss Jacobs. Try."

[Pause.]

"Well, we know the tape stopped with you about to guess that the radio was playing 'Our Love is Here to Stay,' and then we -- I think I had just started to tell what happened when

I took flowers to Harry's grave the day I left Mis - -"

[Abrupt stop in mid-word, mid-sentence; pause, shattered by a sudden forceful loud outburst from Ms. Jacobs.]

"THAT'S IT! THAT'S WHAT IT'S ABOUT!

[Pause.]

"I get it now!" [Voice tone very excited. Speech pattern very rapid.]

"I understand! [Pause.] I was wrong before. I had it all wrong. I knew Harry was responsible for the machine not working, but I didn't realize — I assumed it was that he didn't want what we were talking about to be recorded. But that wasn't it at all. [Pause.] I get it now. I see what he was doing — what he was up to!"

"Please enlighten me, as well, Miss Jacobs, if you would."

"Ooops. Sorry, Dr. Levy. It's just that I was so excited to have figured it out — OK. [Pause.] Well, it's like this. Remember I've been telling you about how the car radio, in fact all radios, seem to be under Harry's control whenever I'm around. In fact, it's not limited just to radios — probably all electrical devices. Remember the light in my country home? [Pause.] At the Institute Library, I remember reading books which indicate that Spirits can control electrical energy because that is what they themselves consist of. But of course I'm oversimplifying — -"

"The explanation, Miss Jacobs, please."

"I've tried so many times to tell you that whenever I'm around, Harry basically has control of the airwaves — or at least control over what I hear. And I've given you MANY examples, including today. Correct?"

"Yes. Correct, Miss Jacobs."

"And tell me, please, Dr. Levy, what was your honest reaction to my description of these phenomena."

[Pause.]

"Well, I know by now there is no point in trying to be subtle about expressing my opinions to you, so I will tell you quite frankly, that I did not attach too much significance to these particular phenomena, in view of the other more important areas we needed to discuss within the therapeutic setting."

"So what you mean is that you really didn't believe it was happening."

"That's not what I said, Miss Jacobs. It's just that I have not given it much thought."

"But Dr. Levy, don't you see? It IS central, it IS germane to the substance of my therapy. These songs on the radio, his control of electrical devices, all are an important — are an integral part of this whole paranormal process. I'm sure I've told you how songs on the radio have provided answers to questions in my mind, or have expressed Harry's emotions that were relevant to the moment.

[Tone excited, agitated, almost pleading.]

"THAT IS EXACTLY IT! You did not attach too much significance to this process — so he showed you. He caused your own machine to malfunction to prove his point — and see how that got you to sit up and take notice!"

[Silence.]

"You have never believed, have you Dr. Levy. Part of you thinks seriously about what I tell you, but mainly you think this has all been part of my overactive imagination. I bet you never once put any stock in what I told you about that bathroom light going on in my country house, even when there was no electricity connected. I bet you attributed it to my demented, sex-starved fantasy life. I remember those questions you asked when I told you about that incident."

[Pause.]

"Does any of what I'm saying make sense to you? Do you understand at all what I am trying to tell you, Dr. Levy? Can you possibly understand?" [Tone urgent, insistent.]

[Silence.]

"I have been quiet because I have been trying to put my thoughts in order to explain them carefully with the minimal possibility for misunderstanding or misinterpretation. [Pause.] First, there is something VERY important that I want to clarify immediately. I DO NOT, nor have I EVER, thought of you as 'demented' or 'sex-starved' — or whatever words you used. I have told you <u>repeatedly</u> that I do not believe you suffer from psychosis, neurosis or hysteria, although of course, you know I share your assessment of your active imagination.

"But as far as the workings of this and other machines — NO — I have not paid much attention to them in relation to your experiences with Harry. I have viewed these incidents as rather minor accompaniment — tangential to the more serious episodes. But what you are telling me, if I understand you correctly, is that Harry used my machine today to emphasize the significance of these events by controlling a source of power to illustrate the point."

"**<u>EXACTLY!</u>** [Voice very excited, enthusiastic.] **<u>THAT'S EXACTLY IT!</u>**"

"And Harry wanted me to experience for myself how he does it so that I would believe what you have been telling me."

"Thank God. <u>Yes</u>. <u>YES</u>. **<u>YES</u>.**" [Words spoken with increasing intensity.]

[Extended silence.]

"Dr. Levy, I want to ask you something serious. [Pause.] I <u>know</u> you've said many times that you do not think I'm insane, but what I'm asking now is different: do you <u>believe</u> what I've been telling you. I'm sure you realize the difference. I'm not asking now if I'm crazy, I'm asking if you believe in the reality of these experiences."

"I <u>do</u> understand what you are asking, but as I am sure you realize, I do <u>not</u> know how to answer you."

[Pause.]

"My dear Miss Jacobs. When you first came to see me, you were deeply concerned that you were losing your mind. I have repeatedly attempted to assure you that I was unable to reach that medical conclusion. However — [Pause.] — however, what you have presented anecdotally is <u>so</u> far different from anything I have <u>ever</u> experienced in all my years as a medical professional — [Almost to himself, voice dwindling.] — if only Jung were here for me to consult with —."

[Pause.]

"I realize it is getting late, but there was something that happened when you took the flowers to the Cemetery, the day you returned to New York, is that correct?"

"Yes. [Pause.] And see how well it worked out that I managed to obtain that additional session this afternoon?"

"I am reluctant to respond to that query, Miss Jacobs, for reasons I am sure are quite obvious."

"All right, Dr. Levy. I'll let that pass. [Pause.] At the time I had this feeling about the machine, I remember I was about to tell you what happened when I drove to the Cemetery for one last visit, as I promised Harry I would. [Pause.] Actually, Dr. Levy, this incident is rather raunchy and humorous - -"

"Well then, by all means, please DO continue, Miss Jacobs. [Pause.] Are we still on Sophie's Magical Mystery Tour?"

[Pause.]

"Well, why not!"

[Pause.]

"After my visit with Harry's Brother-in-law, I bought a huge bouquet of flowers, went to Harry's gravesite, placed them in the vase and spoke words of love to Harry. I knew I had to leave soon to drive to the Airport, so I started to get up from where I was sitting on the grass. But I couldn't move. I felt riveted to the spot."

"What do you mean, you could not move?"

"Just that. [Pause.] I could not move. I tried, but something in my mind - -"

"Forgive me, Miss Jacobs, that's what I wanted to ask: did you feel physically restrained from moving?"

"No, Dr. Levy. It was in my mind. Something - somehow, my body was not able to move. [Pause.] So I stayed a little longer, but then I began to become concerned because I like to allow myself lots of extra time to get to airports, especially when I have to return a rental vehicle. So I tried to get up again, and this time got as far as to my knees. I was in a kneeling position."

[Silence.]

"What happened next, Miss Jacobs, please."

"I remained in a kneeling position, my fingers caressing the letters of Harry's name on his marker, when I felt a bug - there were lots of them in the grass and on the gravestone - bite me on my shoulder. [Pause.] I took my right hand and started to scratch where I felt the bite, when, without my control, my right hand started to move downward, groping around my breasts. At that point, I jumped up immediately. I remember being very — indignant I think is the best word. I was angry, indignant, offended.

"I remember I started to storm away from Harry's gravesite, when I realized he was walking quickly alongside me. He was smiling in a teasing way, and asking why I was so upset and storming off like I was.

"I was so angry with him. I felt like I had been used, violated. He was behaving like a dirty old man copping a feel, and I told him so.

"I was livid. I remember I stopped and turned to confront him and said to him directly - and I swear, Dr. Levy, these were my <u>exact</u> words, because I can <u>never</u> forget them - I said: 'For God's sake, Harry. This is a cemetery, for crying out loud. Have you no respect for the dead?'"

[Pause.]

"I'll never forget how he looked. He had a smirk on his face, his hands were in his pants pockets, and he was rocking back and forth on his heels. And, I swear, I'll never forget this - he grinned and then he said, 'Of course I have respect for the dead, Sandy. I'm buried here, you know.'"

[Pause.]

"And with those words, I couldn't help but burst out laughing at the absurdity of it all. And we stood there, the two of us, laughing like anything. [Pause.] And then he was gone."

[Pause.]

"I laughed for a little while longer — but then -- when I realized Harry was no longer next to me, I remembered that he was indeed buried in this cemetery and my laughter turned to tears, and I stood there, on the same spot, only this time crying."

[Silence.]

"I'm not sure how long I stood there, but somehow I managed to pull myself together and walk back to the car. I got in and when I started it, the radio came on, and this time a woman was singing the absolutely most raunchy dirty song I have ever heard in my life. I'm surprised it could even be allowed on a radio station. [Pause.] It was about this woman wanting her man to make love to her right then, there, wherever, and she didn't care who saw or what they thought, *et cetera*, *et cetera*. The song did everything but name body parts - and I'm not even sure about that, either."

[Pause.]

"And then I felt better, I remember smiling and saying something like: 'That's just like you, Harry.' [Pause.] It made me feel better, this little joke, and I drove away and left the cemetery."

[Lengthy silence.]

"Why are you crying now, Miss Jacobs, please."

"Because he's dead, he's not with me, and I love him and I miss him, and I want him with me."

369

"But from what you have been telling me, Miss Jacobs, it seems as if he <u>is</u> with you, and very much so."

"But not in the real sense. Not so that I can hold him close and touch him, and feel his body close to mine."

[Pause.]

"But he seems to be finding ways to touch and stimulate you, Miss Jacobs. Perhaps in time he will be able to initiate ways for you to experience his closeness."

"Dr. Levy! [Voice expressing indignation. Uncertain as to whether it is feigned or real.] You shock me. You sound like a dirty old man yourself!"

[Pause.]

"And with this, have we come to the end of Sophie's Magical Mystery Tour?"

"I'm afraid so, Dr. Levy."

"It certainly has been a <u>very</u> magical tour indeed, with unexpected special effects, as well!"

"Yeah. You're sure right about that!"

[Silence.]

"Miss Jacobs — I know this may seem rather an unusual question for me to ask, but have you ever thought of writing a book about your experiences?"

[Raucous Laughter.]

"No, I am really serious about my question, Miss Jacobs. Surely YOU must know that I am."

"I'm sorry, Dr. Levy. I'm not laughing at you. It's just that you're about the one-millionth person who's said this to me!"

"And I can tell from your reaction that you do not agree with the suggestion."

"For many reasons. Let me summarize a few. First of all, as an accountant, can you imagine what my colleagues and peers would think? Also, Harry was a very private person. I would not wish to do <u>anything</u> that would call attention to him, when what he wished most in life was solitude. [Pause.] I'm sorry, but the list of negatives is so long I don't even want to begin."

"Ah, but Miss Jacobs, we still have some of this extra time you so carefully arranged. Perhaps <u>that</u> is the reason we have it, in order to discuss this very subject."

"Very good, Dr. Levy. You're really catching on. But believe me, with all due respect, I've heard all the possible arguments in favor of writing a book and I just don't agree with, nor can I accept any of them. Case closed."

"My dear Miss Jacobs. I have <u>really</u> hit a nerve. I am sorry, not only because you seem so negative about the possibility, but for the first time since I've known you, you are manifesting a closed mind. That is not like you, Miss Jacobs, and I'm somewhat disappointed, as well as surprised."

"That trick won't work either, Dr. Levy. I'm sorry, but I really don't want to discuss it. Perhaps because I have already, to several persons close to me, and I am tired of everyone refusing to appreciate my feelings on the subject."

"But how can you be sure of what Harry really wants. How can you be sure that what he wanted most in life was 'solitude', as you put it."

[Pause.]

"Don't say it, Dr. Levy. Please."

"All right. I know. And I don't mean to press you against the proverbial wall, Miss Jacobs."

[Silence.]

"Is there anything else you plan to tell me about your trip to Missouri?"

"Yes — about my visit to Harry's Brother-in-law, Christy, remember?"

"Yes, of course. You must forgive me, Miss Jacobs. Sometimes - even dirty old men can be forgetful."

"Then that visit will be next on the Agenda. [Pause, then very deep sigh.] It's been a L - O - N - G [Word drawn out] session, hasn't it, Dr. Levy?"

"Yes, that's true."

"But somehow, I feel it was well worth it."

"So do I, Miss Jacobs. So do I."

"Goodnight, Dr. Levy."

"Goodnight, Miss Jacobs."

End of Tape 23.

Notes Accompanying Tape 23.

What happened in this last session is nothing short of astounding. It could be explained scientifically, rationally, as nothing more than coincidence.

I certainly have no explanation for the failure of this equipment to function properly for only this particular short period. Coincidence?

Then there was also the "convenient" coincidence of the other patient – a man who almost NEVER cancels an appointment – canceling this afternoon's session, freeing the time for Miss Jacobs and I to pursue this much needed lengthy discussion.

Coincidence? What am I to think?

Do these incidents rise to the level of Jung's synchronicity? Jung is not here for me to speak with – I wonder if I should explore the possibility of a Séance – then I could try to reach this man Harry, as well –– but perhaps the next time Singer[2] and I get together – Yes, I think that is what I will do. I will talk about this with Singer. Of course, I will have to frame it as a hypothetical – it has been a while since we have had time to get together – I will give Singer a call.

Even if synchronicity and not coincidence, what then? Does Harry, the Spirit of this man now deceased, actually control the energy of electrical current when it suits his purpose? If so, can this ability be ascribed to all who are deceased? What is happening here?

And WHO has the power? Is it the deceased Harry – or is it Miss Jacobs, herself? I have

---

[2] Isaac Bashevis Singer. See Tape 11, fn. 4.

noted this elsewhere, particularly, I believe, in relation to the injury inflicted upon the fellow team player of this man Harry. I believe I noted the question of whether Miss Jacobs could have had, as a girl entering her teen years, Poltergeist energy, causing the manifestation of movements of matter.

Psychokinesis?

Could this same power have continued for all these years? She herself has acknowledged that she repressed all memory of these phenomena, along with her feelings for Harry, because they were too difficult for her to accept. Perhaps to control?

Can it be that she has the Power, the Psychic Ability, of certain individuals who are studied by investigators in the area of parapsychology? Could it be that she, herself, caused the recorder to suspend operation, so that she could illustrate to me how she believes Harry can, as she puts it, control electrical energy?

Could it also be that, in keeping with her inability to accept her own worth, she would prefer to have it appear as if these unusual acts were caused by the Spirit of her Beloved Harry, rather than her own exceptional Psychic Powers? This explanation would satisfy several of her needs. Ascribing the origin of these unusual events to this man Harry would — allow her to continue to think of herself as insignificant - allow her to continue to think of Harry as not only a God (which she apparently did when she knew him in her teenage years), but an immortal one, at that — - allow her creative, vivid, and romantic imagination to roam free at Will, which, as an accountant, she has had to stifle for so many years.

374

I can state, without hesitation, THAT I HAVE NO EXPLANATION WHATSOEVER for the incident that occurred this evening. Coincidence? Act of Harry? Act of Miss Jacobs? Act of God? Who is to say. I know I can not.

I will have to see if I can talk about this with Singer. I will have to find a time when we both are free for a GOOD discussion at some length.

———

As for the earlier Session, which was recorded without incident, Miss Jacobs revealed several more incidents of synchronicity, most of which involved the communication of love lasting beyond the seeming finality of Death and Time. Although she teased about "Sophie's Magical Mystery Tour", the events she related could easily fall within that description.

If she were to reveal her psychic experiences to the Public, she would perform a valuable service for others who may share her talents, but lack her eloquence and ability to describe these experiences. I would LOVE to have her as a guest on my show, but of course medical ethics prevent such action, and I should be ashamed even to have held such a thought! But if others could hear her for what she is, a SANE (and I find myself needing to capitalize the word because of my need to emphasize it with her), rational person, who has tried every possible traditional means to explain her paranormal experiences — someone who is NOT "crazy" but is a calm, confidant business woman, successful in a Man's World, — if others could hear her story, they might be encouraged to reveal their own. And with that, the entire Scientific Community would be enriched, by a deeper anecdotal understanding of the processes of extra-sensory perception and the survival of the human personality after Death.

But Alas. For some reason which escapes me — she is sensitive to the point of OBSESSION bordering on FANATICISM, in her refusal to write a book about her experiences. What a sensitive nerve I touched! Never in my life would I have anticipated the reaction I received from Miss Jacobs to my suggestion today. And apparently, I am not the first to have made it! (I wonder if her friend Midge, whom she seems to admire and trust so much, also suggested she write a book. And Seymour?) This subject needs to be revisited. It's very sensitivity reveals it must be explored.

This case never ceases to amaze me. Was it just yesterday when I was ready to strangle Seymour for referring this patient to me? Today I am ready to embrace him for it!

and then there was the time when she heard Verklärte Nacht playing on the radio as she was leaving the cemetery. That <u>has</u> to be a coincidence. Just a coincidence that she should mention the <u>one</u> piece of music that has such personal meaning for me — surely a mere coincidence.

***

Tape 24

"Miss Jacobs."

"Dr. Levy."

"How are you, Miss Jacobs?"

"Fine, thanks. I had a nice relaxing time in the Berkshires over the weekend, and now that April 15th is a thing of the past, my work schedule is back to normal."

"Have you thought of what you are going to do about your country home?"

"You mean the one I think I am not worthy of having?"

"I'm not sure I understand your point of reference, Miss Jacobs, although I definitely detect a tone of sarcasm in your voice."

"It's because you are continually referring to my feeling unworthy of so many things in my life. I realize it is standard psychiatric practise to relate the patient's problems to events of their childhood, but I think you've gone overboard in my case."

"Have I, Miss Jacobs? Explain, please."

"Well for one thing, although it <u>certainly</u> is a fact that my childhood was one of poverty, in which I got the little that was leftover from a pot that was very tiny to begin with, as a child I really didn't know anything different, and did not go around feeling sorry for myself or bemoaning my Fate in a situation over which I had no control.

"To me, it just was natural that my Aunt, with her own large family to care for, had little time for me; and that any money the family had needed to go for their own requirements before mine. It was only logical and right, and I felt no bitterness or sense of deprivation. The only time I did feel inadequate was when I first went to my High School and came upon all those kids who were not only rich, but famous as well. I think I told you how frightened I was to even <u>talk</u> in that school because I felt so out of place. But even that changed, after I got to know Harry, and by the time I graduated, I was among the most popular in the school and had been invited to join all the top Honor Societies and participate in the in-group clique activities.

"Then I worked my way through College and up through my profession. [Pause.] What I'm trying to say, I guess, Dr. Levy, is that while it is easy to ascribe feelings of unworthiness to me because of the situation in which I grew up - in fact, to a Psychiatrist such as yourself it would seem inevitable that I would have these. Yet the truth is that I really do not have feelings of unworthiness. Life was just what it was, and I needed to do whatever it took to survive and succeed, so that my situation would be better than the one I was in."

"That is quite admirable, Miss Jacobs."

"And don't think that I'm saying these things only to get you off my back. [Pause.] When I went on about getting this house, it was because I never expected, in my childhood, that I could be in a situation where I would actually own a home. I couldn't see that far ahead into what would become of my life - except to know I had absolutely NO intention of remaining in poverty. And, as I explained to you, there were also political reasons that it seemed unlikely I would ever own a home.

Our family's Socialist beliefs were such that ownership of property was considered theft from the masses."

"I see."

"Do you, Dr. Levy? Or are you still wondering if I'm not carrying on like this in order to hide feelings of unworthiness, as you refer to them - and almost constantly, I might add."

"And that annoys you, Miss Jacobs."

"It sure does, Dr. Levy. [Pause.] I've been patient about it until now, but I think I finally need to bring it to your attention."

"Good for you, Miss Jacobs. I'm pleased to hear you speak out for yourself."

"Now wait a minute. That statement not only sounds condescending, but also as if you still believe I am timid about speaking in my own behalf - possibly because I feel unworthy?"

"Quite honestly, Miss Jacobs, you are going on about this so much that I wonder if the subject is still uncomfortable, despite your protestations."

[Response in anger.] "Well, if it is 'un-comfortable', as you put it, it's only because you keep bringing it up so much."

[Silence.]

"Let me propose this, Miss Jacobs, please. [Pause.] I will not mention it if you promise — and I believe that you are a person of integrity who will keep a promise — to give some thought to my suggestions that you may have difficulty believing you deserve the good things that happen in your life. And then ---"

"All right, Dr. ---"

"Please. Let me finish, Miss Jacobs. [Pause.] And I will not mention this subject again unless you tell me, after you have given it some thought, that there may be some validity to my premise."

"OK, Dr. Levy. Fair enough. I promise. And you <u>are</u> right. When I make a promise, I don't break it unless there's a darn good reason for it — and believe me, that doesn't happen often. [Pause.] And I can <u>definitely</u> tell you that this is something left from my childhood, when so many people made promises to me they never kept. I swore when I grew up, I would never do anything like that to anyone if I could help it."

[Pause.]

"Was Harry one of those people who made a promise to you as a child that he never kept?"

"Harry? No. Not ever, that I can think of. Not once that I can remember. Perhaps that's another reason he made me feel so at ease. I knew I could trust him."

"Who was it then? Members of your family?"

"Yes, of course. [Pause.] But now that I look back, I suppose they meant well. I suppose, perhaps in their hearts they wanted to do things to make me happy, but the time and money just wasn't there. I guess they were so involved in their own problems that any promise made to me would have to take a back seat to the important issues of survival. [Pause.] You know, you're right. Let me think about that issue some more, and I'll let you know if I think it is something we should discuss in our sessions."

"We have an agreement then, Miss Jacobs?"

"Yes, Dr. Levy. We have an agreement."

[Silence of longer than average length.]

"Dr. Levy, I'm afraid we got off to a bad start today, but if it's all right with you, I'd like to talk about something that's been

380

on my mind a lot ever since these things started happening with Harry."

"Of course, it's all right, Miss Jacobs. [Pause.] And what is it that has been on your mind so much?"

"Well — Reincarnation."

"Hmm. Ah yes. [Pause.] I suspected we would arrive at a point where this subject would be discussed, and I believe that possibility was mentioned previously in one of our sessions."

"Yes, Dr. Levy. I believe it was."

[Silence.]

"What is it about Reincarnation that you would like to discuss, Miss Jacobs."

"It's about Harry, of course, and whether we were possibly together in some prior lifetime. [Pause.] All the songs, at least most of them, have messages about how we'll be united again in the Future. But, I've wondered about whether we were ever together before, in the Past.

"There's that song, 'In the Gloaming', the one that came into my head when I visited Harry's grave. When I read the words, I think I told you how appropriate they were: a man helping his lover of years before come to terms with his death. But there is that one line - and it has always troubled me. It goes: 'What had been could never be'."

[Pause.]

"I've thought of that line over and over. Did Harry simply mean that the closeness we felt when we were together couldn't continue because of his life with his wife and baby? That would be like the words of the other song telling the young girl to go away.

"Or did it mean something more profound? [Pause.] Did Harry want me to know that we had been together in some other lifetime but could not be in this one?"

"What do <u>you</u> think, Miss Jacobs?"

"I don't know, Dr. Levy. But I've thought about it a <u>lot</u>, I can assure you, and I've read a lot about the subject, too. [Pause.] Then there are the circumstances of Harry's birth. Whenever I think of Reincarnation, I think of how Harry was born and to me it seems to be compelling evidence in support of the theory."

"Now you have me quite confused, Miss Jacobs."

"It's just that when I think of the line in that song, and when I think of Harry's birth, I can't dismiss Reincarnation so easily - the way I once did. I used to think of it simply as nonsense. Now I'm not so sure."

"As you may well imagine, I am quite curious to know the circumstances of Harry's birth, and <u>particularly</u> why you think these circumstances lend support to the possible existence of Reincarnation.

"But before you begin, Miss Jacobs, suppose you give me <u>your</u> definition of Reincarnation, so that we may be certain we are discussing the same concept."

"Yes. I understand. [Pause.] You realize, don't you Dr. Levy, that what you're asking me to do is define something that the greatest philosophical and spiritual minds haven't been able to agree upon throughout history. In all the literature I've been reading, no two definitions seem to be the same."

"That's true, Miss Jacobs, I have put you on the spot, so to speak, but I think it is important that I know what <u>your</u> definition is, when you tell me your thoughts about Reincarnation."

"All right. I understand. [Sigh] Here goes. [Pause.] To me, Reincarnation means that a person's soul - yes, I know - what's the soul, and that's even tougher - anyway, the soul, or essence of the uniqueness of a particular entity - how's that - the soul of a person who has died on the earthly plane, returns to live again in the body of another individual. Now that process can happen in several ways, but I believe Reincarnation refers to a soul returning to fulfill the life experience of a newborn individual. [Pause.] How's that?"

"That lets me know how you view the subject. Thank you, Miss Jacobs. [Pause.] Now what has been troubling you about Reincarnation, please."

"No. It's not that anything is troubling me, exactly - more like puzzling me. I think about the concept, and I wonder if it can be true - especially when I think of all those song lyrics about being together again."

"Perhaps Harry meant in Heaven, or some similar type of after-life."

"That could be true. I can't rule that out. But it's the circumstances of how Harry was born that makes me wonder about Reincarnation. Whenever I think of his birth, aside from how funny the entire situation was, I find myself thinking that Harry's character already existed somewhere else before arriving on this plane, and that his birth was just one more typical manifestation of his personality. And if <u>he</u> existed somewhere else before birth, then I could have also, and we <u>could</u> have been together before our recent lifetimes."

[Pause.]

"You certainly have me curious about Harry's birth, so tell me about it Miss Jacobs, please."

383

"Personally, I think it's hilarious, although I don't think Harry's mother did at the time. It must have been a source of terrible embarrassment for her, especially in those days. [Pause.] Still though, Christy told me that Harry's mother worshipped him, as if he were a gift from God. Even Harry's father thought he was something special, and whenever a new toy or gadget or some other plaything came out for kids, Harry was always among the first to have one. Sometimes I wonder if their attitude didn't carry over into his special cockiness on the playing field."

"The birth, Miss Jacobs, please."

"Oh yes. Sorry, Dr. Levy. [Pause.] Harry's parents lived on a farm in this tiny town in Missouri. They had four children, all of whom were born before 1900. Their daughter had married and moved to California; two sons had started a carpenter business in town; and the other son lived with his wife on his parents' farm, as they were getting on in years and needed help."

"What do you mean they were 'getting on in years', Miss Jacobs."

"Well, in 1918, Harry's father was in his mid to late sixties, and Harry's mother was approaching her sixtieth birthday. Neither looked their age, however, as I've seen photos. And when Harry died, his brothers were his Pallbearers, even though they were each somewhere around ninety years old."

"Obviously good genetic material."

"Yes, Dr. Levy, I agree. [Pause.] Anyway, Harry's mother had long since passed the Menopause, and I'm sure the possibility of having more children never entered her mind or her husband's; although it soon became very obvious that they were still enjoying sexual relations.

"Anyway, Harry's mother's abdomen began to swell, and several of the neighbor women told her she was probably having those tumors that women get after their periods are finished. As her abdomen kept growing, she went to the nearest doctor, the one who had delivered her children at least twenty years before, and he agreed that she most likely had a fibroid tumor. [Pause.] Seriously, Dr. Levy, you know because you're a Medical Doctor, surely that man must not have given Mrs. Gault any kind of decent examination."

"I would suspect he did not, Miss Jacobs. Continue, please."

"The month before Harry was born, his brother's wife, the one who lived on the farm, gave birth to a baby boy. That was not the Gaults' first grandchild, either. Meanwhile, Mrs. Gault kept getting heavier and heavier. The family became concerned about her condition, and one of the sons who lived in town talked about how a Dr. Hastings, who had practised in St. Louis, had retired and moved to their area. He wanted to have this Doctor look at his mother, but Mrs. Gault declined because she trusted her family physician. After all, he had assisted with the delivery of her four children.

"Then one day, a month after her grandson was born, Mrs. Gault experienced excruciating pain. She was crying and screaming how she couldn't take it anymore, and so her husband rode into town on his horse to look for this Dr. Hastings."

[Pause, and obvious attempt to restrain laughter.]

"Anyway, he eventually managed to locate the doctor, and apparently Mr. Gault had to do a job of convincing him to come out to the farm to look at his wife, as Dr. Hastings insisted he had retired from the practise of medicine. But I suppose Mr. Gault must have made a convincing case of how his wife was truly suffering from this tumor, and Dr. Hastings took his medical bag along, in the event emergency surgery was needed."

[Pause.]

"The whole thing seems like a silent film or TV episode to me. I can visualize Harry's father riding his horse back to the farm like fury, and Dr. Hastings following in his automobile."

[Snickering.]

"It gets funnier – at least I think so. [Pause.] Dr. Hastings goes to the bedroom where by this time poor Mrs. Gault was screaming her head off in pain. [Pause.] Harry used to get such a kick out of telling this story. I can remember him telling it with such enthusiasm. He was such a good story teller, and this is such a good story.

"Anyway, Dr. Hastings tells Mrs. Gault he's going to have to feel her abdomen, which he does. Then he tells her, apologetically, that he's going to have to examine her private parts. Well, of course both she and her husband couldn't figure out why that was necessary and were somewhat annoyed or – what's a better word – well, they weren't too keen on that idea; but she was in so much pain that they consented.

"Anyway, it didn't take much for Dr. Hastings to figure out what was happening and they did the boiling water routine. I never did understand that – was it primitive sterilization? Anyway, he told the Gaults they were about to become parents again. Mr. Gault went into shock, and Mrs. Gault just wanted to have the pain go away.

"Shortly thereafter, Dr. Hastings presented Mrs. Gault with a very healthy baby boy. His complexion was dark, and he had a head full of jet black hair. Apparently Mr. Gault's first response, upon seeing his newborn son, were words to the effect that he looked like a God-damn Indian[1], but since Mrs. Gault was half Cherokee, she didn't mind — she thought he was beautiful. She wept as she held her newborn son and <u>her</u> first words were to the effect that God had blessed her in her old age.

"The strange thing was that she was so grateful, she insisted on naming the baby after Dr. Hastings - which I think is funny, because what did <u>he</u> have to do with it! And here's what even funnier. The Gaults had little education, and could not spell very well. They asked the doctor his name. It was Harold Hastings. They knew they didn't know how to spell Hastings, so they asked him for that. But they thought they knew how to spell Harold - it was like — [Words interrupted by laughter.] -- I'm sorry, Dr. Levy, but -- [More laughter.] - it was like 'Hark the Herald Angels sing'. You know: [More laughter.] 'Glory to the Newborn King'.

"And who knows, maybe that's what she actually thought. This beautiful infant was a 'newborn king'. So, the actual spelling of Harry's name, on all his official documents, *et cetera*, is H - <u>E</u> - R - <u>A</u> - L - D. Herald

---

[1] Again apologies must be offered to Native American readers for the words of the text. However, in view of the fact that Mr. Gault married a woman of Native American descent and was proud of his son's development, his words clearly do not reflect genuine animosity or disdain.

Hastings Gault." [Laughter continues until eventually under control.]

"Miss Jacobs, it's a delight to see you laughing in my office instead of weeping. [Pause.] But seriously, how does that humorous story of Harry's birth make you believe that there may be some validity to the theory of Reincarnation?"

"OK. I'll try to be serious. [Pause.] WAIT! I just remembered. [Pause.] During the time I knew Harry, our family lived in Brooklyn on <u>Hastings</u> Street. [Pause, then voice tone softer.] That's strange, isn't it. Of course, it could just be another of those coincidences. [Pause.] Still....

"Yes. I know. Reincarnation. [Pause.] But don't you see, Dr. Levy? Don't you see? [Tone almost pleading.] I've told you many times about how Harry liked to play magic tricks. And what better magic trick than the one he played on his own parents. He did a <u>real</u> appearing act out of nowhere, didn't he - deceiving his own mother into thinking he was a tumor - I mean, what a joke! And his name? 'Herald'? As if he were a 'Herald' of great things to come - the 'newborn king'?

"That was the Harry <u>I</u> knew. The one who loved to play magic tricks. Blithe spirit. [Pause, then voice resumes in more serious tone.] You see, Dr. Levy, Harry's mother also thought of him as special because he was the <u>only</u> one of her children who displayed any sign of her Cherokee heritage. The four older children looked like typical mid-west American pioneer stock, fair skinned and fair-haired, whereas Harry's complexion was ruddy, with thick jet black hair. [Voice tone wistful.] But then, he had those sparkling blue-eyes. [Pause.] The other Gault sons were broad-built and stocky, but Harry had the body of an Indian warrior - tall, muscular, wiry. At first his father was annoyed with his appearance, but as Harry grew and demonstrated unique abilities in marksmanship, horseback riding, extraordinary eyesight and agility, even Mr. Gault began to boast about his youngest son - the one who looked so much like an Indian.

"Harry told me his mother used to say she knew the American saying that 'life begins at 40' and that she wanted more than anything to live to see the time when Harry would begin his new life. She died shortly after his 40th birthday, when she was herself almost 100 years old! Mr. Gault was over 100 when he passed away - actually Harry was the youngest in the family to die. [Pause.] In a way, I'm glad she didn't get to see how sad his life turned out. He was still playing ball when she died and perhaps she felt he still had a chance for a new and better life."

[Pause.]

"Anyway, all of this taken together makes me think that Harry's physical appearance and character were already formed and existed somewhere else — PLEASE don't ask me WHERE, Dr. Levy. Remember, I'm only <u>reading</u> these books - I'm not the one who's writing them."

[Pause.]

"But the way Harry made his entry - like a magic entrance onto the stage of life - boy that sounds corny doesn't it? But in some ways it's true. That's why I wonder if indeed, this was <u>always</u> his way - to make magic - and that's what he did <u>this</u> time around on earth."

[Pause.]

"And look what he's doing now to me. Isn't he playing magic tricks with me? Isn't he being a 'Herald' of new experiences for me – experiences with the World of Psychic Phenomena - a World I had not had contact with except through him?

"And so I wonder. Did he come into this earth as a pre-formed package? [Pause.] I <u>know</u> you're thinking, well couldn't Harry have developed the characteristics of love for magic simply <u>because</u> every one around him talked about the miracle of his birth? I suppose that's possible. I thought about that, too."

"Yes. Of course that <u>IS</u> what I was thinking, Miss Jacobs."

"I'm sorry, Dr. Levy. I didn't mean to do that. It just came naturally. [Pause.] Anyway, what I want to say is that the verdict is still out. I haven't decided <u>what</u> I believe about Reincarnation. But the more I think about it, the more examples I seem to find. [Pause.] Of course, those could be mere coincidences as well. I'm aware of that. [Pause.] Let's just say then, that my mind is open."

[Pause.]

"What are your thoughts on the subject, Dr. Levy?"

"You mean you don't know?" [Pause.] Forgive me, Miss Jacobs. That was an uncalled for remark and I sincerely apologize. You deserve an honest answer. [Pause.] As you know, this subject is not an easy one; and as you also know, much has been written about it through the centuries. I would have to say that my opinion is similar to yours, Miss Jacobs, although perhaps not as strong – as I sense you are leaning towards belief. For myself, the verdict is <u>also</u> still out. And to be honest, before <u>you</u> became my patient and raised these questions, I hadn't given the matter much thought. But believe me, I shall now."

[Silence.]

"Of course, it is important to me, Dr. Levy, because it would mean that if Harry and I were together in some other existence before we met here on this earth, then we could possibly be united there again - or even on earth again. [Pause.] Perhaps I'm romanticizing - I can't be sure of anything anymore. And that's again, one more reason why I decided to come to you on a regular basis."

[Silence.]

"Miss Jacobs, in all honesty, sometimes I think you come to me more for a sounding board to test your belief system than for any services I can perform as a Psychoanalyst. But we can discuss that at some future session, as this one is about over, indeed more than over, as is our typical pattern."

"Thank you, Dr. Levy. I know I need to do a lot of thinking about a lot of things."

"Yes. We both do, Miss Jacobs. We both do."

[Pause.]

"Good night, Dr. Levy."

"Good night, Miss Jacobs."

End of Tape 24.

Notes Accompanying Tape 24.

What is there to comment upon? Both Miss Jacobs and I are uncertain about the validity of the theory of Reincarnation, yet we each have indicated that our minds remain open to the possibility - hers more than mine. It is obvious that she wants desperately to believe - in order to support her cherished hope that she and this man Harry will be reunited - together again on either this earthly plane in the future, or together in that special place from which all souls originate.

I must note that she still seems insecure about the role childhood poverty plays in her adult existence. She continues to deny that she has any doubts concerning her self-worth, yet her actions often belie her words. At least she agreed to give the matter her attention, and I trust she will honor her promise.

***

Tape 25

<u>May 22, 1981</u>

4:30 pm

"Miss Jacobs."

"Good afternoon, Dr. Levy."

[Silence of unusual length, as indicated by the next words of Dr. Levy.]

"Miss Jacobs - I have many patients who sit for long periods of time without speaking, and with them I am accustomed to such behavior and do not interfere with their need for silence.

"But for you, Miss Jacobs, it is atypical to have a silence of this length. It will soon be almost one quarter of an hour without any sound from you. I must say this arouses some concern in me, and I feel I must ask if everything is all right."

[Pause.]

"I'm sorry, Dr. Levy. I guess I kinda just spaced out. [Pause.] I was thinking about Harry, as I'm sure you can well believe."

"And what thoughts did you have about Harry this time? They must have been extremely profound, because you were immersed in them for such a period of time. [Pause.] Now I feel I must ask, if I had not spoken, would you have said <u>anything</u> during this session?"

[Pause.]

"I don't know, Dr. Levy. I don't know if I would have spoken. I don't know."

[Pause.]

"What were you thinking about Harry, Miss Jacobs, please."

"I was thinking of several things. One sort of led to another.

"First I was thinking of a vision-type experience I had involving Harry when I was in the Hot Tub at my home in the Berkshires."

"Miss Jacobs! You never told me! When did this happen?"

"Oh, last weekend sometime."

"And you never said anything to me about it?"

"There was no need to. It was strange, but also lovely in a way. I was not frightened at all, and there was really nothing to discuss."

"Perhaps I might think otherwise. [Pause.] Tell me about it, Miss Jacobs, please."

"Well, I suppose so. [Pause.] I was in the Hot Tub, which is in the rear garden. You can see the stars so clearly, and I find it so peaceful and beautiful. [Pause.] Perhaps in a way, almost like Harry found it at his cabin by the Lake – except, instead of a Lake, I have a Hot Tub."

[Pause.]

"Anyway, I was in the Tub, looking at the stars, when I had another of those experiences. I was aware I was in the Tub, yet at the same time I saw myself in the Cemetery, kneeling by Harry's marker. But then, while the me that was kneeling by the grave remained there, I saw my Spirit, or Soul, or whatever you want to call it, get up, leave my body, and walk into a mist where Harry was waiting. What was strange was that we were about the same age – these Souls that met.

"And he said to me, and I'll never forget his words – Harry said – well he didn't really say it, rather he specifically asked it as a very direct question: 'Don't you feel sorry for her?' referring to the me who was kneeling at his marker. I turned to look at this other me, and asked Harry why I should be feeling

394

sorry for this woman kneeling at his grave, because I honestly didn't understand what he meant.

"And again, he said so <u>clearly</u> — so straight-forward and direct - 'Because she thinks she is alive and I am dead.' He paused for awhile; then continued: 'She doesn't know that we are together now, have <u>always</u> been together, and <u>will</u> always be together. We have <u>never</u> been apart. We are together throughout eternity and can <u>never</u> be separated.'

"Hearing those words, I felt such a sense of peace and calm and turned from looking at the self that was me kneeling on the grass by his marker and placed my head on his shoulder and moved close to him. He took my hand and held me tight. [Pause.] Then it was over. The entire scene was gone, and I was once again conscious of myself in the Hot Tub looking at the stars.

"And I wondered: 'What is Reality?' Was reality my sitting in the Hot Tub? Was reality my kneeling by Harry's marker? Was reality the communication between our souls - our forever young, but mature Spirits?'"

[Silence.]

"I think I can understand how you felt, Miss Jacobs. The nature of Reality has always been a troublesome concept. [Pause.] But why did you not tell me about this experience Miss Jacobs, please."

"Because it was so simple. It was there and it was over. I understood the message and it wasn't frightening. It was — in a way — comforting. And because of our previous sessions, I decided to take your advice and accept it for what it was."

[Silence.]

"And then there was more - after I got out of the tub."

"<u>More</u>?"

"Yes. [Pause.] I got out of the tub, and as I reached for my towel, I had the <u>very strong</u> sense of Harry's presence beside me. It was so real, the way it was - like when he first came to me. I knew he was there, I could see him in the way I've described to you before.

"I started to dry myself, and he held me close. The sensation of being in his arms was so vivid that - can you believe this, Dr. Levy? It was so vivid that I <u>actually</u> said out loud, "Don't. You'll get wet!" And he smiled and I laughed at how silly it was for me to have said that. [Pause.] And then he was gone. And I stood there, mechanically drying myself with the towel, weeping, tears streaming down my face, as I thought about everything that had just happened."

[Extended silence, with faint sounds of sobbing in the background.]

"Miss Jacobs — I think you mentioned you had <u>other</u> thoughts about Harry, is that correct?"

"Yes. That's correct. [Pause.] I was thinking about how when I talked to different people who knew him, almost everyone told me how much the poor man - and that's what they said in reference to him - that 'poor man' - how much he suffered. They talked about his suffering in the War, the loss of his beloved wife, and the loss of his daughter, both physically and emotionally - and how he couldn't take it anymore and had to go off and live by himself.

"But none of that was the Harry <u>I</u> knew, Dr. Levy. <u>NONE</u> of that was <u>my</u> Harry.

"<u>My</u> Harry was someone who felt <u>joy</u> in living - it showed in the way he walked, with that jaunty defiant bounce to his long strides. It showed in his impish, irresistible grin, and his wide broad smile. Did they not see that in him?

"And did it not occur to them - Dr. Levy, I've come to believe that people prefer to live in herds, and that they can not comprehend that others have a need for solitude. It doesn't mean they are depressed or angry or in pain. Perhaps it simply means they no longer want to put up with the shit - ooops, I'm sorry, Dr. Levy - I mean, why can't people understand that being alone is not necessarily a bad thing?

[Silence.]

"So then I thought, that perhaps when I knew Harry, he was joyous because he was doing the thing he loved most in the World - playing ball. I never saw him living with Betty's pain. I never saw him when he had to send his little girl away."

"Ah, but Miss Jacobs, you saw him when he had to send <u>you</u> away. How did he look then? I think <u>you</u> even said that his walk no longer had that special bounce as he walked away."

[Pause.]

"And, Miss Jacobs, there is something else. Did it ever occur to you that in addition to playing baseball, another reason Harry may have found such joy in life when you saw him was because he was WITH <u>YOU</u>?"

"<u>WHAT</u>!"

"Just what I said, Miss Jacobs. Did the thought ever occur to you that one of the reasons Harry may have been so happy the times you saw him was the fact itself that he was with you?"

[Pause.]

"No. I never even <u>considered</u> that possibility!"

"And <u>why not</u>, Miss Jacobs, please. <u>Why not?</u>"

"I don't know. It just never dawned on me."

"But does it dawn on you now — now that Harry has come with so many messages of love for you."

"I don't know. I need to think about it. [Pause.] And please, please Dr. Levy, don't ask if I haven't thought of it because I feel unworthy. That's not it at all. It's just that as a kid, how could I have <u>even</u> considered a man like Harry could feel that way about me. After all, he had a wife and baby he loved very much. [Pause.] And I loved them too, because they were his."

"I'm not saying that Harry did not love his wife and little girl, Miss Jacobs. I'm saying that you could have brought happiness into his life as well. After all, you did give him unselfish devotion and unconditional love. You took pride in anything and everything he did - why wouldn't that make a man happy. [Pause.] So, my dear Miss Jacobs, I truly suspect that not only was it playing baseball that made Harry happy when you were with him, but the very fact of being in your company, as well."

[Silence; sounds of weeping; then voice filled with emotion and choked with sobs.]

"I find myself asking over and over: WHY? Sometimes, when I am alone, thinking about Harry, I even ask aloud: WHY? Then I wonder to whom my question is directed? Is it to God? Is it to some Force of Destiny? 'La Forza del Destino?' A Directing Agency? An Intelligent Incomprehensible, or an Incomprehensible Intelligence?

"WHY, if there was so much love between us, WHY weren't we allowed to be together?

"I asked that question of a Psychic once, and she actually scolded me, and said that 'Atheist Energy' – and those were her <u>exact</u> words – 'Atheist Energy' had gained control of my mind, otherwise I would <u>never</u> question The Supreme Being, whose ways are beyond understanding."

[Silence.]

"Dr. Levy – [Pause.] – have you ever wondered WHAT IF a certain event hadn't happened, or if a certain event HAD happened – how your life might have turned out differently?"

[Pause.]

"Yes. I have had such thoughts, Miss Jacobs. I believe most human beings have those thoughts at one time or another."

"Well, I've been thinking about that a LOT lately."

[Pause.]

"In what way, Miss Jacobs, please."

[Pause.]

"I've been thinking WHAT IF I hadn't been a fan of the St. Louis Cardinals, even though I was living in Brooklyn. What a bizarre thing in and of itself. [Pause.] And WHAT IF I hadn't gone to a school within walking distance of the Polo Grounds? [Pause.] And WHAT IF the Gate-keepers hadn't required me to sit by the Visitors' Clubhouse?"

"By this line of thinking, I assume you are referring to the events that led to your meeting with Harry."

"Yes. [Pause.] And WHAT IF I hadn't agreed to meet him outside the Clubhouse that first afternoon. That was a bold thing for a thirteen year-old girl to do.

"And WHAT IF I hadn't gone with Harry to his hotel that night? Would we have continued to see each other and still have been good friends?"

[Pause.]

"But worst of all, worst of all, I keep asking myself: WHAT IF I had gone back to the Polo Grounds the next time the Cardinals were in New York?"

[Pause.]

"And the song that played on Harry's radio the first time I turned it on – where the man asks the girl to go away – it keeps haunting me. He sings that her lips are sweet and their lips must never meet, yet Harry kissed me before I could get into the cab and leave. And he sings about how much it hurts each minute she delays leaving and how hard she is to resist when she is near him. [Pause.] And of course there's the ending – that she MUST leave or else he'll beg her to stay."

[Pause, then voice filled with anguish.]

"WHY did I have to accept being placed in the cab like that? WHY didn't I go back and see him the next time he was in New York?"

[Pause.]

"Oh, Dr. Levy – it's then that my mind wanders and I have all kinds of beautiful fantasies about what could have been. [Pause.] At the very least, Harry and I could have been friends, and he would not have had to be alone during the last years of his life."

"But, Miss Jacobs, just a while ago you were berating people for not understanding that some individuals prefer solitude."

"But Dr. Levy, I'm talking about when Harry was so sick and in physical distress. I can't bear the thought of a man of Harry's character being confined to a Nursing Home. I can't bear it."

[Sounds of sobbing.]

"And so, this afternoon, I found myself in another - what I call my - WHAT IF moods."

[Silence.]

"I've read that there are theories in Physics where some mathematicians or whatever, <u>actually</u> believe there are parallel, or alternate, Universes. Can you believe that! <u>Not</u> Science <u>Fiction</u>, but <u>real</u> Science.

"And so I think - WHAT IF there are other Universes where Harry and I are together? Of course, based on those other choices available in my life, Harry and I might never have met at all. [Pause.] But once we <u>had</u>, I keep thinking over and over WHAT IF, and then I envision all these other possibilities, all having happier endings than ours."

[Pause.]

"But Miss Jacobs, following everything you have told me that has happened to you, <u>especially</u> the <u>messages</u> from Harry — and accepting those messages as real - hasn't he been letting you know that, sad as it may be, the two of you were not meant to be together - at least not in this lifetime. [Pause.] It was not *beschert* [1] — do you understand me, Miss Jacobs?"

[Pause.]

"Yes. I do."

"And, I think you said that you envision all the happy endings that could have existed. Have you also thought of the alternative possibilities that would <u>not</u> have worked well? What if you <u>had</u> gone back to see Harry again, and what if he succumbed to temptation and seduced you - what then? What if you had become pregnant at age 15? What if you had not had been pregnant - would you have been his

[1] Yiddish - the closest equivalent in English would be "pre-destined," or meant to be.

401

teenage Mistress during his visits to New York? Would you have been satisfied with that? And what would have been the consequences if his wife, who you tell me he loved so much, had learned of his affair with you? What then?"

[Pause.]

"I regret if I seem cruel or harsh in what I am saying, but I wonder if you ever thought of endings other than the happy ones?"

[Silence.]

"And what about your career? Look at the positive changes you have brought to your life through your own perseverance and determination. Would you have risen from your level of poverty to the prominence and style of living you have now if your life with Harry had continued? From everything you have told me, you would have dedicated your entire existence to him, and perhaps those Forces or Entities to which you alluded preferred that you have a life of your own, with relative ease and comfort and recognition for your own achievements - not Harry's."

[Pause.]

"Yes. [Audible sigh.] I have thought of the consequences of possibilities other than those of happiness. Probably the same ones you thought of."

[Pause.]

"I have also wondered, Miss Jacobs - [Pause.] - what would you have done if, when you conducted your research to learn what happened to Harry, you discovered he was still alive?"

[Pause.]

"Believe me, Dr. Levy, I've often wondered about that myself - asked myself that question many times."

[Silence.]

"And?"

"I don't know. I am sure I would have, at least I <u>think</u> I would have, tried to contact him - write to him, visit him - [Pause.] - I just don't know."

"Or would you have reacted as his daughter has, and refused to have anything to do with him because of what you perceived as his rejection of you?"

[Silence.]

"Miss Jacobs, I am not in a position to debate Physics or Metaphysics with you. It is possible, I suppose, that there <u>may be</u> alternate Universes, based upon the <u>infinite</u> number of choices each of us is faced with every second of our lives. [Pause.] But tell me. In your opinion, does that theory conflict with your belief that there are NO coincidences in life?"

[Pause.]

"I don't think so. Couldn't it be that in <u>each</u> of these Universes, there are no coincidences?"

[Pause.]

"I don't know, Dr. Levy. Certainly <u>I</u> don't know, as I was merely an average student in Science. So really - how do <u>I</u> know what I'm talking about? I'm just theorizing, based on stuff I've read."

[Pause.]

"Anyway, I guess that's what I was preoccupied with when I was sitting in your office today."

[Pause.]

"I remember there was something I wanted to discuss with you when I came in for today's Session, but when I sat down, before I could put it together to tell you, the memory of the

Hot Tub incident, the memory of all those people telling me how miserable Harry's life had been — and then these WHAT IF thoughts started coming into my mind and it was downhill after that. I guess I got caught up in it and spaced out. [Pause.] And NO, I <u>don't</u> know if I would have snapped out of it before time for the Session to close. I really <u>had</u> lost all sense of time."

"Speaking of time, Miss Jacobs, it IS time for our Session to close. I regret that it seems to leave things somewhat up in the air, so to speak - but at least, you are in good company with all the Philosophers, Scientists, and Metaphysicians who have contemplated this broad general area for centuries. I imagine you must have read a considerable amount of material on these subjects during your personal research."

"Yes, I have, Dr. Levy. And I suppose that is one reason I think about it so much. [Pause.] I apologize if I wasted your time."

"Miss Jacobs. I won't dignify that comment with a response — and you probably know what it would be already. Shame on you, if you need such reassuring."

"Why Dr. Levy. I <u>do</u> believe you're on to me!"

"Not completely, Miss Jacobs, but perhaps some day. [Pause.] Are you spending this coming weekend in your home in the Berkshires? [Some type of affirmative indication.] Yes? Then I hope it is as peaceful and comforting as apparently this last one was, and that you are able to accept any events as well as you did then."

"Thank you, Dr. Levy, and good-bye."

"Good-bye, Miss Jacobs. "

End of Tape 25.

Notes Accompanying Tape 25.

The Emotion of Today's Session was - to use an American idiom - so thick you could cut it with a knife! Only at closing, when she made a half-teasing remark, did Miss Jacobs give any indication of her otherwise lively personality.

I have seen this woman frightened, terrorized (whether real or exaggerated), constantly weeping - but this is the first I have seen her so despondent — almost symptomatic of clinical depression.

I previously believed she had exaggerated when she said she would sit on her bed for hours without moving. Now I believe it to be entirely possible. I do not know, nor does she, if she would have spoken at all if my probing had not snapped her out of her silence. Could she have been in a Trance? I have read where this occurs in persons with verified psychic abilities. But she gave no verbal indication that such was her state today - nor do I think it was.

What depth of subject material! The imponderable.

But did she realize - could she possibly have been aware of the poignancy of her question, when she asked if I had ever wondered what might have happened in my life had certain events —

No. I prefer to think she was merely asking as part of her general musing - as a hypothetical — and not with any specific awareness of my own life experiences. But who is to say how much she can see inside the

405

souls of others? I do not think that even <u>she</u>
knows the extent of her capacity to

Gott!

The Unanswered Question: WHAT IF?

***

Tape 26

"Hello?"

"Dr. Levy?"

"Yes, this is Dr. Levy speaking. [Voice weary and indistinct.] Who is calling please?"

"Dr. Levy, this is Sophie Jacobs, and I —"

"Miss Jacobs, are you aware of what time it is?"

"Yes, Dr. Levy. It's almost 4 o'clock in the morning."

"That is correct, and as it will soon be dawn, perhaps you would like to call when my office is open and make an appointment with my secretary. I promise —"

"Dr. Levy, believe me, I would not be calling now if it wasn't urgent. I need to see you NOW. It can't wait until your office opens. I need to see you NOW!" [Voice desperate, frantic.]

"Miss Jacobs, do you realize what you are asking me to do? Do you really want me to get out of bed, get dressed and go to my office? Is that really what you are asking?"

"YES, that's exactly what I am asking."

"Miss Jacobs, is this not something we can discuss over the telephone? Why is it necessary that I see you at my office?"

"I can't discuss it over the 'phone. It's too involved, and also —"

[Silence.]

"Miss Jacobs? Miss Jacobs? Are you there?"

---

[1] As the Reader may surmise from the time noted, this tape begins with an early morning call to Dr. Levy at his home. (cf. Tape 1, fn. 1.)

"—and also, I'm afraid to talk about it in my apartment. I'm afraid it might happen again. I've got to get out of here! I've got to talk to you, NOW!"

"Miss Jacobs, I can tell you are upset, but I think I know you well enough to believe you will not try to harm yourself, is that correct?"

"Yes. That is correct. And I will not walk in front of a truck either. But I tell you what I <u>WILL</u> do. If you do not agree to see me in your office now, I will go to the hospital where you are on staff — Seymour told me — and I will ask to be admitted <u>immediately</u> and they will call and ask you to come down anyway."

"Miss Jacobs, I have never heard you —"

"I realize what I just said sounds like extortion, but I don't give a damn! You're a psychiatrist — act like one for God's sake! I can't take another episode like this — I just can't. I need to talk to you NOW. It <u>can't</u> wait."

[Pause.]

"All right, Miss Jacobs. Take a taxi and by the time I am dressed and at my office, you should be arriving."

"Thank you. Thank you, Dr. Levy. I am sorry, but I <u>have</u> to do this. I will see you in about a half-hour then."

"Yes, Miss Jacobs. Good-bye."

4:34 am

"Come in, please, Miss Jacobs. Come in."

"Thank you, Dr. Levy. Thank you. I'm so sorry I had to do this to you, but I really do not know how much more of this I can take. And I KNOW I've said that before, many times, I'm sure, but —"

[Hysterical weeping, followed by lengthy silence.]

"Miss Jacobs, I have never seen you like this. You're trembling. What on earth has happened? [Voice tone indicating grave concern.] You are in a state of Hysteria. Perhaps you DO need to be hospitalized — immediately."

[Continued weeping, with no response.]

"Shall I call the hospital, Miss Jacobs?"

[Silence.]

"Do whatever you think is best Dr. Levy. I just know that what happened to me tonight is more than I can bear alone."

"Please, Miss Jacobs, if you can, try to tell me what happened, please. [Pause.] I KNOW you are a woman with great strength of character. You have managed to recover from other incidents which were troubling. Please. Do your best to exercise control and pull yourself together; at least to the point where you can tell me what has made you so desperate. I swear I have NEVER seen you this upset before. [Pause.] Can you do that, Miss Jacobs. Can you pull yourself together, and tell me what on earth happened to put you in this state."

"Believe me, Dr. Levy — what happened to me tonight is NOT of this earth." [Voice filled with emotion.] That is, if it really happened. I can't be sure, with all these things going on, what is real anymore."

"Here, Miss Jacobs. Sit in this armchair, please."

[Sounds of movement of people and furniture.]

"Try to relax. Breathe deeply. [Voice fading away, gradually becoming slower and softer.] Gently. Breathe deeper. Slower. Yes, Miss

Jacobs. You <u>are</u> becoming more relaxed. Softly. Gently. [Pause.] That's better, is it not?"

[Prolonged silence.]

"Continue breathing slowly, Miss Jacobs. Softer. Gently. Slower. You <u>are</u> more relaxed. Your body is less tense. [Pause.] Breathe deeply. Slowly."

[Prolonged silence.]

"Are you able to tell me about your experience, Miss Jacobs?"

[Pause.]

"Yes. [Pause.] I don't know. [Pause.] I think so. [Voice more relaxed, less frantic — then suddenly agitated.] But it was <u>horrible</u>. So <u>horrible</u>." [Sounds of sobbing, followed by more silence.]

"Miss Jacobs, tell me what it is you want to do now. You are calmer, yet you are still having difficulty talking about your experience. If you want me to admit you for hospitalization, perhaps that might be best. At least there you will be under observation and will be given medication to help you sleep and remain calm. Then, I can visit when you are in better physical and mental condition and you can tell me about this incident that has disturbed you so greatly."

[Silence.]

"I'm going to call the hospital now." [Sounds of telephone being dialed.]

"No! Wait! I don't want to be alone in a hospital room. Maybe it could happen again there, too. Please. I'll try. I promise. I'll try again."

"Miss Jacobs. I am not doing this as a threat to get you to talk to me. I am <u>seriously</u> concerned about your condition, and whatever it is that reduced you to this state. You HAVE to talk about it, Miss Jacobs, otherwise, in your present condition, it will become a problem for which you <u>will</u> require hospitalization. [Pause.] I assure you I <u>know</u> what I am talking about."

"All right. I'll try again."

[Silence.]

[Deep breath before resuming. Voice tone quieter, but still agitated.] "I had gone to bed, nothing of any significance had occurred, and then I woke up in the middle of the night to go to the bathroom.

"It happened when I got in bed after coming back from the bathroom."

"<u>What</u> happened, Miss Jacobs, please."

"It was another one of those situations where the walls of my room disappeared. I'm not even sure if I was in my bed or not. But I was an observer. I was part of a scene unfolding before my eyes that was like nothing I have ever experienced before, or could even imagine."

[Silence.]

"It was Winter. It was so cold – so very cold. Snow was heaped high all around, only the snow wasn't completely white — and it wasn't the gray slush that we see here in the City. The snow was piled high, only there was red, deep red, like blood, running down it, and orange, like rust, seeping through it. Directly in front of me was this huge pile of snow, and lying on its side in this snow was a mangled rusting vehicle, a military vehicle, but it was hard to tell what kind, because its metal was twisted and burnt with orange rust oozing from it as if it were bleeding a slow death.

"And the sky. The thing I remember most about the sky was the color orange. <u>Everything</u>

411

was colored orange, except the white of the snow and the red blood running down.

"The entire sky was orange, with gray or black smoke streaking through from time to time. I couldn't tell if it was day or night. It was almost a kind of smog — or haze caused by battlefire. But there was no sound. Everything was muted because of the snow. Snow was everywhere. It was piled so high. It was so deep.

"The air was so cold and it was orange also. Even the air was orange. I know that sounds crazy, but that was how it felt to me. The air was very cold, and orange.

"And the smell. I remember the smell. Smoke, burning metal — burning everything. The air was filled with the smell of orange and gray-black smoke. It was horrible. So horrible."

[Silence.]

"Do you remember seeing any people?"

"I think I remember either hearing or seeing men, soldiers in uniform. They were whispering in German. And there may have been bodies — I'm not really sure."

[Pause.]

"And there was a sign. It was wooden, and had fallen into the snow, almost buried, and the letters were hard to make out, because the sign was frozen also, and had orange icicles hanging from it."

"Could you read the sign, Miss Jacobs. [Voice tone fervent, almost anxious.] Do you know what it said?"

"It was such a strange sign. Almost like something from the 'Wizard of Oz.' It was a country sign, made of wood, but the wood was shattered in places and, like I said, the sign was leaning into a pile of snow. [Pause.] It was a three-way sign. That's it. I remember now. That was one of the things that was so strange about it. It had planks of wood pointing in three directions — at least they would have, if the sign had been erect."

"And could you make out what those signs said, Miss Jacobs? [Fervent, insistent pleading, then pausing.] But first, perhaps I should ask, do you know in what language the signs were written?"

"Yes. They were in French. Definitely in French. One was a city I think I have heard of — Boulogne, I think. And the other two, I never heard of them. One had a three-part name, I know that — something like: V - I - L - L - E - R - S. — I'm trying to see it now, but I can't make it out. But the sign was splintered and bent over into the snow, with orange icicles dangling from it."

[Pause.]

"Everything was so horrible. I don't know which frightened me most: the oppressive orange everywhere, the orange sky — the orange air; or that huge mound of snow with the twisted metal wreckage of the unrecognizable military vehicle. And the smell. That horrible horrible smell of smoke and fire. [Pause.] But it was all so orange. And so cold. So very cold."

"Miss Jacobs, you are shivering. Here, let me get you a covering."

"So cold. So cold."

[Sounds of movement in background, then prolonged silence.]

"Was that the end of your vision, Miss Jacobs, or was there more?"

"My God! Isn't that enough? What more did I have to see? It was so awful, so horrible. I don't even know what it was that I was seeing. I know it had to be something from World War

413

II, it <u>had</u> to be. [Pause.] And probably it was something that Harry had been involved in."

"How did it end, this vision?"

"It just seemed to fade away. It gradually shrank in size, kept getting smaller and smaller until my bedroom walls began to take shape again and I was in my bed."

[Pause.]

"It was <u>so</u> horrible, and I don't know what it was and I don't <u>want</u> to know what it was, it was so unbearable and so miserable.

[Silence.]

"When I close my eyes I can still see it. That orange color everywhere, the orange sky, the orange rust, the snow, the dead vehicle, the fallen sign — ALL of it. [Pause.] And so cold — so <u>very</u> cold."

[Silence.]

"Miss Jacobs, are you familiar at all with the French language?"

"Yes, I am. I speak it fairly well, if I keep in practise. I can read and understand better than I speak, however."

"You told me that the sign you saw, the three-way sign, was in French, is that correct?"

"Yes, that is correct."

"And you thought one of the directions was to a city whose name you thought you might have recognized — Boulogne, perhaps — is that correct?"

"Yes. That's correct."

"Miss Jacobs, if I ask you to concentrate, can you visualize that sign again, please."

"Please Dr. Levy, do I have to? Please don't make me bring it back in detail, please."

"Miss Jacobs, I think I may have an explanation of what you saw tonight — an explanation of your vision. Bear with me, please. I think this may help you."

[Silence.]

"Now, can you see that sign? Visualize it for me, please."

[Pause.]

"Yes. I can see it. It has three wooden planks, split in some places, fallen over into the snow, orange icicles. Yes. I can see it."

"And the city that starts with the letter B. Look at that part of the sign carefully, if you can."

"Yes, but it is damaged."

"Could the city possibly be Bastogne, and NOT Boulogne. Bastogne: B - A - S - T - O - G - N - E."

"Yes, that's it! That _is_ it. [Pause.] But I never heard of a city in France called Bastogne. I assumed it was Boulogne, and I didn't want to see anymore than I had to."

[Pause.]

"But there _is_ something else I saw. I can still see it, but I didn't want to say anything about it because it seemed so insane. But if I'm telling you so much already, I might as well say this also."

"Yes. Please. [Voice excited, animated.] Tell me everything you can see and remember, Miss Jacobs, no matter how strange it may seem to you."

[Pause.]

"On that sign. I could see the name of the city I thought was Boulogne, and I could see the one that had three or four parts to it, the one that started with a V. Maybe it was Ville something, you know, as in French for city. [Pause.] But this other one was so strange."

[Pause.]

415

"You know how Orthodox Jews are not allowed to write out God's name, but write G-hyphen-D instead?"

"Yes. I am familiar with that practise, Miss Jacobs."

"I know this is going to sound crazy, but part of the broken three-way sign had G-hyphen-D printed on it. When I saw that, I knew I had to be insane. [Pause.] Was it a sign pointing to God — to Heaven? But how could it have been when this place was nothing but pure Hell."

[Silence.]

[Tone professorial, but barely disguising excitement.] "Miss Jacobs, the city on that sign was Bastogne, and I believe that the G-hyphen-D might have been part of an indication of the direction of the Grand Duchy of Luxembourg. [Pause.] What you were viewing was a cross-section, perhaps diorama might be a better descriptive term, of a scene from one of the worst battles of the Second World War."

[Silence.]

"Miss Jacobs, have you ever heard of the Battle of the Bulge?"

"Yes."

"What do you know about it."

"Nothing, really. I just know it was, like you just said, one of the worst battles of the War."

"Do you know where it was fought?"

"In France, right?"

"No, Miss Jacobs."

"Germany?"

"No, Miss Jacobs. [Pause.] The Battle of the Bulge was fought in Belgium, where one of the primary languages spoken is French. The fighting was centered around Bastogne and its surrounding Villages."

[Pause.]

"Do you know <u>when</u> the Battle of the Bulge was fought, Miss Jacobs, in what months, in what year?"

"No. I'm sorry, I don't. I was only a little kid when the War was on, and I remember most of the important stuff from the News then, because we barely touched upon it in College. I really don't know much of anything about the Battle of the Bulge, except that it was one of the big ones. It had to have taken place after D-Day, but I don't even remember when <u>that</u> was, to tell the truth."

"Miss Jacobs, D-Day, or the invasion of Europe by the Allies, took place on June 6, 1944. The Battle of the Bulge was the last large offensive by the Germans to regain control of Europe, and it was fought in Belgium in late December 1944 and early January 1945. It was one of the worst battles of the War, and it seems, my dear Miss Jacobs, that you were privy to one of its ordinary moments."

[Prolonged silence.]

"Did I tell you Harry fought in the Battle of the Bulge? I remember when I was a kid and read everything about him in the papers. Of course, with all the Veterans returning and everything, reporters were always asking the ballplayers if they had seen any "action," as they called it. Most ballplayers hadn't. They were used mostly like USO performers, put on teams to perform· for the troops, for morale and so forth, you understand, right?"

"Yes, I believe so."

"But not Harry. He and a few other ballplayers volunteered for active duty, to be regular G.I.s. He went through what every

417

other G.I. suffered, and the Battle of the Bulge was part of it.

"Did I tell you what Harry did during the War — what his assignment was?"

"No. I don't believe so, Miss Jacobs."

"He volunteered for special duty. He was a Jeep Driver in a Special Reconnaissance Unit. The Army asked for volunteers because the work involved was one of the most dangerous assignments and called for special skills. The men chosen for these duties had to have excellent vision, be excellent marksmen, and skilled drivers. Harry knew he could qualify easily because his vision was unusually keen - - in fact, during a routine physical, a team physician told Harry he had the eyesight of an eagle - he was a skilled marksman because of his years of hunting and also an experienced driver. Another thing that appealed to Harry about this assignment was that he would be alone most of the time - scouting. [Pause.] Who knows? Maybe he was an Indian Scout in another lifetime.

"Anyway, the work of the Reconnaissance Jeep Drivers was so secret that it remained classified until fairly recently. I learned from one of the men I talked to in the Government Military Archives that they were even nicknamed "The Stealth Squad" in Division Headquarters, because they were almost like spies. The work they did was very dangerous, but the regular GIs in their own Division never knew they existed, or if they did, what job they had, other than to have it easy riding around in jeeps while the rest of the poor guys had to dog it out on foot. And the Recon drivers could never speak out on their own behalf and explain what their job actually was.

"But what they did was go, alone in jeeps at night, behind enemy lines, and assuming they survived or were not captured, sent radio messages back to Division Headquarters, giving critical information about enemy position, strength, numbers, equipment, — you know, whatever essential information they —"

"Excuse me, Miss Jacobs, in the Battle of the Bulge, Harry would have been in his jeep, behind enemy lines, assuming that was possible, in order to provide essential data to his Division Headquarters, if I understood what you have just told me about his duties during the War."

"Yes. I would think so."

"Then I believe, Miss Jacobs, that what you experienced tonight was part of that Battle, as seen through Harry's eyes when he was on reconnaissance patrol."

"Oh dear God. [Pause.] Oh my God."

"Surely you must have suspected that this is what happened, Miss Jacobs?"

[Silence.]

"Dr. Levy, did I understand you correctly? Are you telling me that I had a vision? You seem to be reacting as if you accept what I've told you as some sort of actual experience that happened to me outside the normal limits of Time and Space — is that right?"

"As if I actually believe what you told me, is that what you mean?"

"Yes. As if you actually believe me, Dr. Levy."

[Pause.]

"I DO believe you, and the events as you saw them this night."

[Pause.]

"Tell me then, how would you explain it, Miss Jacobs?"

419

"I can't. That's why I called <u>you</u> so frantically this morning. I thought I had really lost my mind. I didn't understand anything about what I was experiencing and it was so horrible and so terrifying. [Pause.] And then that part of the sign that seemed to indicate the direction to what I thought must have meant God. [Pause.] Dr. Levy, I knew I needed your help to tell me what I had seen."

"And I just did."

[Silence.]

"You don't think it was some form of hallucination."

"Not the kind that I have been familiar with, both from my studies and my experience in treating other patients."

"You don't think it was my imagination."

"I realize you believe you have a very vivid imagination, Miss Jacobs, but I have <u>never</u> known of imagination in such specific detail, including the names of places with which you were completely unfamiliar. Imagination usually involves expanding upon that with which we are already familiar, even if only through reading or fantasy. But I questioned you and you knew absolutely <u>nothing</u> about the Battle of the Bulge, not even the time of year it occurred. And you saw the surroundings in such detail. I believe I have material at home that can provide you the names of the little villages which were also involved. So, to reiterate — NO, Miss Jacobs. I am firmly convinced it was <u>not</u> your imagination. [Pause.] Besides, would you have been so terrified of your own imagination?"

"Well, people have been known to scare themselves sick over things they imagine. I've even seen that myself with people I know."

"All right. I accept your correction of my statement. But in your situation, I do NOT believe this was an example of your imagination."

[Silence.]

"Miss Jacobs, I realize you have been through a terrifying experience, and I fully appreciate now why you insisted on seeing me this morning. But I feel I must ask you — why do you <u>not</u> want to think of this experience as a paranormal vision?"

"But such things can't happen. I mean, I've never heard of such things before."

"And <u>why</u> can't such things happen, Miss Jacobs. You yourself have told me of your metaphysical research. Surely you have come across people who have had what is known as 'visions'."

"Yes, but — but why would that be happening to <u>me</u>?"

"Oh is that it? Is this an example of an area in which you feel so unworthy that you can not be one of those chosen to be blessed?"

"I don't understand a word you're saying."

"Ah, but I think you DO, Miss Jacobs. I think you DO. [Pause.] From your childhood of poverty and deprivation, I can understand that there would be many areas in which you would feel unworthy. You have yourself told me this in so many ways — your days in your special High School, for example. But you have overcome these areas, perhaps not entirely, but enough so that you have a position with a prestigious firm in a profession in which very few women are accepted. You have proven your worthiness and now live a life of comfort, style, and affluence as much as any person born into such an existence. But here is an area that is totally new, or at least to which

421

you have not been exposed for a considerable time. So I ask you again, Miss Jacobs, do you feel that these experiences are only for a chosen few, and that you are not worthy?"

[Prolonged silence.]

"I really don't know how to answer that question, Dr. Levy. I know, really, I <u>am</u> aware that there are areas, because of my background, in which I feel uncomfortable, but I manage to cope, or at least get by. But this — this is so different. I don't know <u>what</u> to say."

[Pause.]

"All right. Let me ask you this then, do you think that paranormal, or metaphysical, or mystical — whatever you wish to call them, experiences are only for a chosen few?"

"I don't know. I don't think I've given much thought to that idea."

"Miss Jacobs, for some time now, I have been aware that you would rather consider yourself insane than be someone possessed of unusual talent capable of experiencing events outside the realm of so-called normal existence. For example, tonight you were almost ready to have yourself admitted to a hospital with a diagnosis of mental disorder. You would have told the admitting staff that you were suffering from delusions and hallucinations, neither of which are true."

"But how can you be so sure, Dr. Levy?"

"You will just have to trust my professional judgment, just as I would have to trust yours if I consulted you with an accounting problem."

[Pause.]

"But on these matters, Miss Jacobs, I do not have the answers. I blame myself for not providing you sooner with the names of colleagues who have had more experience and understanding of these phenomena than I."

[Pause.]

"Are you angry with me for getting you out of bed, and don't want me to be your patient anymore?"

"My dear Miss Jacobs, that is an unfair remark which is both an insult to me and unworthy of you. I don't believe you are <u>that</u> insecure that you would need to ask such a question, but if you need reassurance, let me state <u>emphatically</u> that I am <u>not</u> angry with you and I am <u>not</u> rejecting you as a patient."

"I'm sorry, Dr. Levy. I'm really sorry. It's just that I don't understand what is happening to me."

"I may not understand it either, but you asked for my professional opinion, and I have given it. I believe you have had a mystical experience which is interconnected somehow with the life of the deceased, Harry, and that you do not suffer from any form of mental disorder. Quite the contrary. If anything, you have <u>overcompensated</u> for what you term your vivid imagination by an <u>extreme</u> use of logic which is <u>itself</u> illogical — if you can possibly understand what I mean."

"Yes, I think I do, Dr. Levy."

[Silence.]

"My dear Miss Jacobs, I think we are both tired and could use some sleep. Do you feel all right now, or is that experience still haunting you?"

"No. What you have said has been very helpful. And you have given me much to think about. Could I really be having mystical experiences? And if so, have I been attempting to dismiss them, not because they are unusual or symptomatic of mental illness, but because I feel unworthy of receiving them?"

"Precisely the issue. You <u>do</u> have a keen analytical mind, Miss Jacobs."

[Pause.]

"But still, Dr. Levy, these incidents <u>do</u> frighten me. They frighten me because they are terrifying in and of themselves, like tonight — I mean, this morning's episode. So — is it really a blessing, as you put it, to be the recipient of such experiences?"

"It may not appear that way to you now, Miss Jacobs, but perhaps with the proper instruction and guidance, you might see these experiences as gifts, and truly learn to appreciate them."

"That will take time, Dr. Levy, LOTS of time."

"Yes, I have no doubt that it will. And believe me, I do not mean it as a rejection of you, but I wish you would give serious consideration to consulting a therapist who has familiarity with paranormal phenomena. There are not many, as I'm sure you can understand, and please forgive me for procrastinating — but I will do some research and provide you with names in the near future.

"In the meantime, however, please call if you wish to be seen before your next regularly scheduled appointment."

"My regularly scheduled appointment is for this afternoon."

"Oh."

"I think I'll go back to my apartment. It's daylight now, but perhaps I can still get some sleep. I'll cancel this afternoon's appoint- ment and see you at the regular time on Friday — assuming I can hold out 'til then."

[Sounds of movement.]

"Dr. Levy, I can't thank you enough for seeing me this morning. I really am very grateful."

"Actually, Miss Jacobs, I, too, am grateful; grateful for the opportunity to hear about these visions and related experiences. [Pause.] I also think we have covered much material this morning, do you agree?"

"Yes, I do. And thank you again, Dr. Levy, for seeing me like this."

[Pause.]

"I can truly appreciate how terrifying this was for you, Miss Jacobs. But think of yourself as a Time Traveler. You have experienced something that only those who were actually there can understand. You have been given an extraordinary opportunity to relive a moment in history, no matter how brief. In a way, I envy you, despite how terrifying it must have been."

[Pause.]

"I never would have thought of it that way Dr. Levy, but I rather like the concept of myself as Time Traveler."

"Good. And now it is time to say, I presume, 'Good Morning'."

"Yes. Good morning, Dr. Levy. Thank you so much again for everything. I promise to think about the issues and about seeking the services of a specialist, but I really believe I am getting all the help I need from you."

"Thank you, Miss Jacobs. Good-bye."

"Good-bye, Dr. Levy."

End of Tape 26.

Notes Accompanying Tape 26.

After reviewing the tape of the telephone call and of the session itself, I think they are self-explanatory and need little, if any, comment. I have brought into the open Miss Jacobs' preference for a dx of mental illness, with the added insight, which occurred to me only at the time of this Session, that she might be reluctant to accept these experiences for what they are because she considers herself unworthy of receiving them. Perhaps now, with this further insight, she will have a new perception of what is happening and be less frightened and less critical of herself.

It is interesting — when confronted with the actual possibility of admission to a mental health facility, Miss Jacobs responded quickly and related the incident. This, to me, is further indication that at the subconscious level she is aware she is not delusional.

However, her frequent concerns about hallucinations raises another interesting question. Could all patients who have been diagnosed as hallucinatory actually be seeing things which are inaccessible to those of us who are bound to a fixed system of Time and Space?

It was fascinating to see how easily she forgot her fears and became lively and animated when talking about Harry. Her sense of pride in his accomplishments was quite evident. And rightfully so, it appears, if he went through that Hell — particularly since he volunteered for this dangerous special assignment when he could have performed much easier duties in his chosen occupation.

But why would Harry want her to experience the Hell he suffered? Perhaps it is part of his search for the Peace he never found in Life.

What a Magnificent Experience! Of course she was terrified. But what a privilege to be, no matter how briefly, an observer of a dramatic moment in History.

How pathetic poor Miss Jacobs sounded — almost like a child — when she asked if I wanted to refer her to someone else as punishment for getting me out of bed to come to the Office. There were actually tears in her eyes. It is obviously a reflection of her tragic childhood, where apparently she was shifted from relative to relative. (This I learned from Seymour, in one of <u>his</u> sessions!) Perhaps switching doctors would be a painful repetition of this unfortunate aspect of her childhood. But I must also acknowledge my own selfishness in wanting to retain her as my patient, which is why, I am sure, I have neglected to investigate other possibilities for her. But I DO believe the help she needs in dealing with these experiences lies with a different specialist. I must force myself to do my part in obtaining that help for her.

***

Tape 27

May 29, 1981

4:30 pm

"Miss Jacobs."

"Good afternoon, Dr. Levy."

"Please sit down, Miss Jacobs. And I must say that it is good to see you looking so refreshed after what happened just a few days ago."

"I have you to thank for that, Dr. Levy. Really. I _mean_ that."

"Thank you, Miss Jacobs. [Pause.] But I want to point out something I find very interesting, especially in light of our earlier discussion."

"Yes?"

"You seem to have NO trouble at all in subscribing to the metaphysical belief that, as you put it, 'there are NO coincidences'; in fact, you seem to believe it with your entire heart and soul."

"Yes. I _do_, in fact."

"Then, tell me, Miss Jacobs please. Why is it you have so much difficulty accepting the belief that these events which you find so disturbing in your life are also _not_ coincidences, but part of the larger picture as well."

[Pause.]

"Incidentally, I did some research, and the information I obtained further substantiates the accuracy of your vision. Remember how you described some of the letters on the sign appearing to be a V followed by an I and some other letters? The other part of the sign you saw would have included Villers-La-Bonne-Eau, a village where heavy fighting occurred near Bastogne during the Battle of the Bulge. So your vision was completely accurate, Miss Jacobs."

[Silence.]

"I don't know. [Tone very serious and subdued.] I honestly don't know. [Pause.] Perhaps it's because the theory you proposed during our last session is correct. I haven't had much time to think of it since then, but I promise, I will. And I <u>mean</u> that."

"Yes, Miss Jacobs, please. I want you to give these questions your careful consideration. [Pause.] Or do you wish to explore them now?"

"No. [Pause.] Actually, I thought I would continue talking about what Harry went through in the War, since I already opened the wound by talking about the vision."

"What are you referring to as a 'wound', Miss Jacobs?"

"Harry's War experiences in general — they were so terrible."

"By the way, Miss Jacobs, I've been wanting to ask you — was Harry wounded during the War?"

"Not physically — only emotionally. You know what I'm trying to say."

"Yes. I understand, Miss Jacobs."

[Pause.]

"How did you find out about his experiences, Miss Jacobs? From what you have related in our sessions, I received the distinct impression that Harry, himself, hardly, if ever, talked about the War."

"Yes. That's true. The only time he talked about the War was if some reporter asked about it, and he provided only minimal information. Part of the reason, as I found out later, was that his duties were classified. But the other part, I'm sure, was because what he had been through was so horrible. [Pause.] And whenever he did talk about his War experiences, it was always to tell a humorous incident. I thought they were funny then, as a kid, but now as I look back on them, I realize that even those incidents took place in the heat of combat, despite their humorous element."

"Can you provide an example, Miss Jacobs, please."

"He joked about keeping his pitching arm limber and his aim accurate while getting food for himself and some of his fellow jeep drivers. He would sneak up on chickens and pigeons, or anything else that would make a meal, and aim a rock at its head and knock it over. All this had to be done very quietly of course, so as not to alert the Germans of his presence. So you see, there is humor in the story he told about how he would get their food, but the real truth was that this was one of the only ways he and the men could get something to eat to survive on, because of course, there were no GI food rations being delivered behind enemy lines! Do you see what I mean, Dr. Levy?"

"Yes. I do. The humor masks the reality of the terror of their situation. They must have lived every day on the edge."

"YES!" [Spoken very emphatically.] That's exactly what Harry's Brother-in-law said. Harry lived every day 'on the edge'."

"So, was it from Harry's Brother-in-law that you learned the true extent of Harry's War experiences?"

"Yes. Mainly from him and also from George and from the Government Military Archives, which has the recently declassified information."

"Tell me, Miss Jacobs, how did you meet Harry's Brother-in-law, and how did you get him to tell you about Harry's War experiences, which were obviously very private and personal to Harry."

"I met him during that emotion-packed week I spent in Missouri. Harry's friends, George and Lil, arranged it, and I met Harry's Brother-in-law on my last day there — the Sunday I left."

"Yes. Continue please, Miss Jacobs."

"And the incredible thing was that after he told me about how he had known and worshipped Harry since they were children, and how he wanted to be a ballplayer just like Harry, and all that sort of family stuff — he almost immediately began to launch into how much Harry had suffered because of the War. It was amazing to me, because it was the same with Harry's close friends, George and Lil. It seemed almost as if they couldn't wait to unload upon me how much Harry had suffered during the War."

"Perhaps Harry wanted you to know about it."

[Pause.]

"What's going on here, Dr. Levy? Now YOU are the one who is sounding metaphysical."

[Tone very somber.] "Perhaps it was hearing about your vision, Miss Jacobs. It was very compelling for me, as a listener, as well."

[Extended silence.]

"You may resume whenever you are ready, Miss Jacobs, please."

"Yes, Dr. Levy."

[Pause.]

"What did Harry's Brother-in-law tell you about Harry's War experiences."

"Christy — that was the family nickname for Harry's Brother-in-law — he was younger than Harry and always said he wanted to be a pitcher just like Harry, and since his name was Christopher, Harry and Betty teased and called him 'Christy,' after the great pitcher, Christy Mathewson. [Pause.] The irony in that is Christy Mathewson died as a result of illness sustained from being gassed as a soldier in the First World War."

"Who is Betty, Miss Jacobs?"

"I know I've said her name before, Dr. Levy. She was Harry's wife — Christy's sister. They were sweethearts since they were little kids, and Christy always used to follow them around, because he idolized Harry so much."

"Yes, I remember now. Continue, Miss Jacobs, please."

"Anyway, when the War in Europe ended, Harry's Division served in the occupation of Germany, and then were to be sent back home and given a 30-day furlough to visit their families, before being shipped out to fight in the Pacific. Can you believe that? These men fight at Omaha Beach, the hedge-rows in Normandie, the Battle of the Bulge, meet the Russians at the Elbe, liberate a Concentration Camp — and then they're supposed to go and fight in Japan! What did the Government think these men were? Supermen?"

"In effect they were, Miss Jacobs. In effect they were. Our World would not be as we know it today if it were not for the bravery of these ordinary men, who brought forth their best under extraordinary circumstances. The Government may have expected much because these men had already demonstrated how much they were capable of achieving."

[Pause.]

"Did you say Harry's Division took part in the liberation of a Concentration Camp?"

"Yes. In fact, Harry, on one of his typical reconnaissance missions, was the first to come upon it. [Pause.] According to Christy, it was something Harry could never forget, but also could never speak of. And not just because his duties were classified, but because it was so painful, not only to him, but to the entire Division. But for him it was worse than for anyone. Because he got there first."

"Did Harry's Brother-in-law happen to mention which one, which Camp it was, that Harry's Division liberated?"

"He did, but I don't remember, because it wasn't one of the well-known ones, like Dachau, or Buchenwald, or Auschwitz, but it still had the same purpose and the same things occurred within its walls. Harry could testify to that, according to Christy. [Pause.] I think I wrote it down somewhere. I'll have to check."

"I can certainly understand why these men do not want to discuss an event so painful in their lives, but in a way, I wish they would, in order to counter the effect of these so-called Revisionists who want to say the Holocaust never occurred. [Pause.] But forgive me, Miss Jacobs. I did not mean to deliver a Lecture. Continue, please."

"Dr. Levy, I imagine this must be difficult for you to hear about. I've read that you escaped just in time before the War began. You must have lost family members — but I hope not."

[Silence.]

"Miss Jacobs, I am sorry to have interrupted your narrative of Harry's War experiences. Continue, please."

Tape 27

[Pause.]

"Where was I? Oh, yes. Harry's Division returned to the States after the War ended. Eventually he was discharged and went home to Betty and to the baby girl he had never seen. And like most of the other returning GIs, his job was waiting for him, and also like the others, he was expected to return and perform his work as if nothing had happened.

"In Harry's case, what that meant was he got discharged in late December 1945 and had to report earlier than the other ballplayers for training, because he had been away from the game for so long. So in less than six weeks from Discharge, he was off to Florida for training before the Baseball Season began. Work as usual, no counseling, no period of adjustment, and it was like that for all those men. They did what was expected of them, and kept what they had been through to themselves, just as Harry did. In learning about Harry, I've come to understand how much we owe these men — but now I guess I'm the one who is starting to lecture."

[Silence.]

"Sometime, a few years later, Christy thought it was, he and Harry went duck-hunting. I've surmised, both from Christy and from Harry's friend George, that duck-hunting is just an excuse for men to sit in a boat, freeze, tell tall-tales and/or jokes, but mainly to drink themselves blotto. Not that Christy or George actually said that, but it certainly is what I picked up, based on what they told me.

"Anyway, on this one particular day of duck-hunting, no ducks ever showed up and Harry just kept on drinking. Eventually, he loosened up enough to talk to Christy about his War experiences, and it was something Christy said he will never forget.

"Christy had been in the War too, but because he was younger than Harry, did not enter it until almost the end, and then served on a carrier in the Pacific. He saw almost no action, but he could still relate to what Harry told him that day.

"The worst part, according to what Harry said, was just the every-day struggle to stay alive. He was alone most of the time, constantly in danger, without proper food, always facing the possibility of detection, capture, torture, sniper fire, land mines — all those things. One time he got out of his jeep to look through his binoculars at what seemed to be an enemy encampment, and his jeep rolled a little and was blown to bits by a mine. He scrambled out of there as fast as he could, and eventually was rescued by one of his Platoon buddies.

"Another thing that was painful for him was to see the plight of the civilians, especially the children. If he or his buddies ever <u>did</u> get anything to eat, they shared it with whatever civilians were around.

"Actually, there's a rather weird, almost amusing story about how Harry captured an entire unit of German soldiers."

"He did <u>what</u>, Miss Jacobs?"

"Just what I said. [Pause.] The War was almost over, and Harry, alone in his jeep as usual, drove into this German village — oh yes, by then they were well into Germany, almost to Berlin. The Burgomeister came out and told Harry in English that there was a unit of German soldiers waiting for him in the house at the end of the block. Well, according to Christy, Harry figured his life would soon be ending, but he still drove his jeep to where the building was located.

"When he reached the house, out stepped this German Captain, in full dress uniform, and told Harry, in perfect English, that he was surrendering himself and his entire unit to Harry.

"Anyway, out comes this unit of German soldiers, single file, and first they place their weapons and paraphernalia in the back of Harry's jeep, then they place their hands behind their heads in typical surrender position, like you see in all those old World War II movies. The Captain told Harry that he and his men had reached this decision because they knew the Russians were in the vicinity, and that they would surrender themselves to the first Americans they saw, rather than be around when the Russians arrived. And considering what the Germans did to the Russian population, it was a wise move on the Captain's part.

"It must have been a comical sight. According to the way Christy described it, it sounded like the procession from Prokofiev's 'Peter and the Wolf'. First came the German Captain, then his troops, all with their hands behind their heads and in full dress uniform; then came Harry, with his machine gun leveled at them, and all these German weapons and other paraphernalia loaded into his jeep."

[Pause.]

"What Harry did next shows, at least to me, at any rate, how the War clouded his thinking — had warped his sense of judgment. For some reason, he took all these weapons and other pieces of equipment that he had taken from the Germans, including their Regimental Flag, packed them in a crate and shipped them home to his wife. I can't imagine this was within Military Regulations, but I think it shows how distorted Harry's thought processes had become by that time.

"But Betty, Harry's wife, apparently didn't think of it that way, and was proud of him. So shortly after he returned from the War, in the few weeks he had at home before he had to report back to baseball practise, she called the paper in their tiny town and they printed an article about their local hero along with a photo of Harry and all the assorted weapons and paraphernalia displayed on his kitchen table.

"Christy showed me the article. Harry looks so serious, surrounded by all this stuff – I can imagine the memories it brought to his mind – but he said nothing about how he obtained these implements of War. He just told the reporter they were War souvenirs. All his activities were still classified, and also Harry was someone who was modest and would not have wanted to provide the details anyway, I'm sure. All Harry wanted to talk about was how precious his little girl was to him, and how grateful he was to have been able to survive the War and to see her. Apparently his daughter was crawling around while the reporter was taking the photos. 'Isn't she pretty and sweet', Harry said. [Voice filled with emotion.] 'Isn't she pretty and sweet'."

[Silence.]

"Was the capture of this Unit before or after he found the Internment Camp? Do you know, Miss Jacobs?"

"According to Christy, it was before. So you can imagine how much worse Harry's emotions must have been when he came upon the Camp. And besides, if it had been after, he probably would have killed them all."

"What do you mean by that, Miss Jacobs, please."

"Next to the Camp, the single worst thing Harry saw, he told Christy, was what made him resolve to kill any NAZI soldier in sight, no questions asked."

"What was that, Miss Jacobs. It must have been horrible, as the man you describe as Harry was ordinarily a quiet, calm person, is that not correct?"

"Yes, but I can understand why he would feel that way, although I'm not sure he ever acted upon those feelings."

[Pause; then voice resumed filled with emotion.]

"Harry was doing his usual routine, driving his jeep alone behind enemy lines, with several other jeep and small military vehicles not too far behind him. He had almost reached the Concentration Camp, only of course he didn't know that then, when he saw, in a clearing in the woods, a single S.S. trooper with a rifle aimed at an unarmed women holding a little girl. Harry stopped the jeep, got out, and moved stealthily to get a better look at the situation, and watched the Trooper shoot with the woman's back toward him.

"This woman and the little girl she was holding so tight to her chest, Harry said, never had a chance to escape, or to do anything except be slaughtered. Harry told Christy that in his mind he pictured Betty and his own baby girl, who he had never seen, and how much he had wanted, and always wished, he could have killed that trooper – and Harry could have done it too, because he was an excellent marksman – but he was behind enemy lines and to do so would have alerted the Germans not only to <u>his</u> presence, but to his men who were not far behind. Harry was by then a Sergeant and had to be sure he followed orders and didn't do any wild renegade act on his own. [Pause.] But he did do the next best thing, however. He took his camera and photographed this unbelievable atrocity."

[Pause.]

"Christy said it was this merciless execution that made Harry swore he would kill any German soldier he saw on sight, no questions asked."

[Pause.]

"Somehow, I think Harry must have had this incident in his mind as he stood by his kitchen table, looking so serious, surrounded by all those German weapons, and his baby girl crawling around. 'Isn't she pretty and sweet?' He said it more than once, according to the article."

[Lengthy silence.]

"Did Christy tell you how it was that Harry came upon the Camp. If I understood you correctly, it was shortly after he saw the S.S. trooper execute this poor woman and her child in cold blood."

"Yes. It was. And he could not tell it without crying, and I'm not sure if I can, either."

[Pause. Sigh, then deep audible breath.]

"The War was only days from ending, but of course Harry did not know that. I imagine only the top Military figures on both sides really knew. [Pause.] The way Christy told it — I can visualize it so readily, and can understand so <u>clearly</u> how and why Harry reacted the way he did. It's not that Christy was such a dynamic narrator, it's just that the facts themselves are so — so — compelling.

"I guess the Germans, knowing the War would be ending soon and that the Russians were close by, were trying to speed up their exit and eradicate any sign of what was and had been going on within this Camp. But they had no way of knowing that Harry and the other drivers were already there, and also, apparently some Russians, as well.

"Harry was the first to arrive. Some of the prisoners were in the process of escaping and the Germans were firing at them. The first thing Harry observed was the barbed wire. It looked like a typical prison, with guard towers and all. Then he saw this man, looking like a skeleton, barely able to move, yet trying to go as fast as his feeble legs would allow. And you know by now, as do we all, the familiar striped uniform the victims wore. Well poor Harry, his mind incapable of grasping what he was about to find, wondered, he told Christy, what was this poor guy doing in pajamas. Isn't that funny? Harry was thinking this Concentration Camp victim was wearing pajamas!"

[Sounds of sobbing. Then lengthy silence. When voice resumes, choked with emotion.]

"The man flagged Harry down. He was well-educated and spoke English, and warned Harry about what was ahead. But no amount of warning could prepare Harry for what he found.

"Harry told the man to wait on the side of the road, that other Americans in military vehicles would be arriving shortly, and that the man could ride with one of them. Harry had his Orders and had to move on.

"Christy said that when Harry started to describe what he found in the Camp, Harry broke down and wept for a long time."

[Pause.]

"Did Harry tell Christy what it was that he and later, the other men saw?"

"Yes."

"Can you tell me, Miss Jacobs, please. If you can. If you feel that you can."

"I'll try."

[Pause.]

"When Harry was on the perimeter of the Camp, prisoners were still escaping and German soldiers were still firing upon them. Harry could also hear the sound of massive machine gun fire from within the Compound. When the Germans saw Harry in his jeep, rather than kill him, for some reason they started escaping themselves, but not before setting a particular building on fire.

"Harry got out of his jeep, and what he saw was incomprehensible to him. By then, the other drivers from his Platoon had arrived. Their reaction was the same as Harry's. There were the things we now think of as typical of those Camps, but for which, at the time, Harry and his men were totally unprepared."

"What things, Miss Jacobs. Tell me, please, even if you think they are familiar to me."

"There were the Ovens, there were buildings filled with dead bodies, buildings filled with people barely alive. The building that the Germans started to burn as Harry drove up, had bodies piled upon bodies. Harry and his men pulled some of the bodies from the burning building, hoping to save lives, but soon found that they were risking their own lives for nothing. The people were already dead. They had been killed by the machine gun fire Harry

441

had heard as he approached the Camp. Harry told Christy that he and his men counted one hundred and one dead bodies in that building alone.

"They did see some survivors, and as was the man Harry had pathetically assumed was dressed in pajamas, they were all emaciated, and in similar clothing, if they had clothing at all. And the weather was still cold, even though it was late April or early May. Christy wasn't sure and Harry could no longer remember. He had never told anyone about this experience before, not even Betty.

"Harry took a few of his reconnaissance men and used an armored scout car - Christy showed me a picture of one, it looks almost like a cross between a jeep and a small tank — anyway, Harry and his men drove off to see if they could find where the German soldiers had gone and on their way, met up with their Russian counterpart - a Soviet reconnaissance vehicle. Fortunately, the commander spoke English and told Harry that Russian troops were not too far from the area, and that he had just come upon something horrible that Harry should see, and gave directions. At that time, it seems that the Americans were to have control of the area, until Orders came from higher up - so after relaying this information to Harry, the Russians drove off.

"According to Christy, all this in one day was almost more than Harry could bear. They drove past the field where the poor woman and child had been executed and Harry radioed for someone from his Division to come and retrieve their bodies. Then as they drove through that field following the directions given to them by the Russian Officer, they came upon the ruins of a barn that was still smoldering, filled with bodies of Camp victims, who it was later determined, had been burned alive. The S.S. had shot the victims in the knees so that they could not walk or run, then had heaped hay on top of them, then set the hay on fire. Once again Harry had to radio grim news to Division Headquarters.

"When the Division arrived at the Camp, they rescued any survivors they could find and captured the nearby Village. Harry said it was incredible that these Infantrymen, who had seen everything, from Omaha Beach through the hedgerows in Normandie, the slaughter at St. Lo, through the Battle of the Bulge — were hardened to almost anything, but not to this, and most broke down and wept at what they saw, which was beyond their comprehension. What bothered them most, Harry said, was how this could be done to women and little children — how anybody could have been this barbaric to innocent children.

"The GIs counted over one-thousand victims who had been burned alive in that field barn. Then, by Order of General Eisenhower, every civilian in that Village was assigned a specific victim or victims, and a mass burial ceremony took place. After the War, the German population of the Village was to care for the graves of their assigned victims for the remainder of the Villagers' lives.

"Harry had been an amateur photographer before the War. He used this skill to take photos all during his overseas duty, including that horrible execution he witnessed, the Camp, and the burial ceremony. While serving in the Army of Occupation in the City outside the Camp, Harry developed the photos. He gave them to Division Headquarters and kept copies for himself. He took photos of the Statue of

Liberty as his Division sailed into New York Harbor on the Queen Mary after the War ended. Then Christy said, as far as he knew, Harry never took another photo in his life, except of Betty and their little girl when he returned home."

"Did you have an opportunity to see those photos, Miss Jacobs?"

"Yes, I did. Harry really was a skilled photographer, and the photos are graphic and sickening. I can sense what his emotions were as he took them, and it does not surprise me that he would never want to take another photo again, except for the Statue of Liberty. Just to hold a camera in his hands would have brought too many painful associations, I imagine."

[Pause.]

"But what troubled Harry most, according to Christy, and what he had to live with every day of his life, was the horrible choice he was forced to make. By not killing the SS trooper, he allowed the execution of an innocent woman and child. [Tone almost pleading.] But how could he be sure there weren't other Germans he couldn't see? His shot might have brought death not only to himself but to his men as well, for whose lives he was responsible. That choice haunted him forever. [Pause.] But at least he took the photo as proof of NAZI brutality."

[Silence, then voice filled with emotion.]

"Christy told me that he had known Harry since he was little, and not once had he ever seen Harry cry, not even when they were kids -- until that day, when Harry sobbed uncontrollably. Christy said he cried like a baby, too. [Pause.] He didn't know how to comfort Harry, so even as they were crying, they just kept drinking until they were almost ready to pass out. Christy never did say how they managed to get home, but he kept repeating how Harry had suffered through so much in the War."

[Pause.]

"Do you remember at all the name of this Camp, Miss Jacobs? Has it returned to your memory?"

[Pause.]

"No. I'm sorry, Dr. Levy, I just can't remember. I don't know if it's because I'm blocking it out because it all was so horrible, or because the name is difficult to remember - I just don't know. But I am sure it was not one of those familiar ones the whole World knows. [Pause.] I'm fairly certain I have it written down somewhere though, and I promise to try to find it for you."

"Thank you, Miss Jacobs."

[Pause.]

"In the tape they made of the family Reunion — did I tell you about that, Dr. Levy?"

"I'm not sure, Miss Jacobs. Tell me again, though, even if you have."

"Well, some of Betty's relatives came to Missouri from one of the Dakota states, I forget which, to visit Christy and his family, and of course they wanted to see Harry. By that time, Harry had long since been ensconced in his cabin in the Ozarks, so they all just took a gamble that he would be there and drove the distance.

"What was interesting was that someone decided to tape the family gathering. I don't know if they did it because they knew Harry did not have much longer to live — Christy didn't tell me, and I didn't feel like asking

— or whether it was just to preserve family history.

"It was fascinating, because, naturally, Harry was NOT there when they arrived. He had chosen that particular day to make the long drive to the nearest town for groceries. So of course, he made this dramatic entry upon his return. He still was the same Harry I know and love. Still the Spellbinder."

[Pause.]

"And of course they took pictures. Christy showed them to me. These were the last photos ever taken of Harry. He would have been about 60 then. His face looks weathered and worn, but his blue eyes were still sharp and clear, with that sparkle of mischief. His body was lean and wiry, unchanged at least in outer appearance. And Christy told me that Harry still had the agility and grace of an athlete. Of course, he hunted and fished and walked so much in the woods... [voice trails off before resuming]. He was wearing some kind of baseball cap, but you could see that he still had a full head of hair underneath, only it was salt and pepper instead of jet black. And he was wearing denim carpenter overalls and a plaid workshirt with purple socks showing out from tan loafers."

[Pause.]

"Two things about the tape were very painful for me, though."

"What were they, Miss Jacobs, please."

"Well, one of the very first things out of his mouth was that he chose this beautiful secluded area in which to live because he needed to get away from the War — decades later, and he still was searching for peace from the War. Now I understand, of course, and I'm still learning. I suppose you could say the experience of the other night has been just one more thing to show me how deep an effect the War had on Harry.

"But worst of all for me about this tape, which Christy kindly made a copy of for me, was to hear Harry's cough. He was coughing continually. Even interrupting his story-telling. His body was wracked by that terrible cough. And a little over a year later, he was dead. In the meantime though, he was in and out of hospitals and even in a Nursing Home. I think part of what killed him must have been having to leave his cabin. George and Lil had quite a struggle to get him to leave, and didn't succeed until he was too weak to put up a fight."

[Silence.]

"What are you thinking, Miss Jacobs, please."

"I guess I am thinking what a sad end for such a good man. It just doesn't seem fair somehow. If only I had known. I would have done anything to help Harry, anything."

"Miss Jacobs, I'm sure that is a loving and romantic ideal, but what really could you have done for this man. Really."

"I'm not sure. But I know that he was a good person to me and a positive influence. It seems only fair that I should have had a chance to help him when he needed it."

"But Miss Jacobs, as you know, we all make choices, and Harry's choice was to be alone."

"But perhaps he would have wanted me to be with him, if I had been aware —"

"But remember the words of the song that came to you as you sat by his gravesite? Perhaps he did not want pity or comfort — just solitude, as you yourself once suggested,

<u>especially</u> after all that he had been through in the War."

[Pause.]

"You may be right, Dr. Levy, but I still wish I could have been at his side in those last painful months. Perhaps I could have helped him remain in his cabin. It's so sad — no TRAGIC, to think of a man like Harry Gault in a Nursing Home, for God's sake."

[Silence.]

"Miss Jacobs, I see we have considerably exceeded our allotted time. [Pause.] We have had two <u>very</u> emotional sessions this week, both involving the Second World War."

"Yes. You're right."

[Pause.]

"Good-bye, Dr. Levy, and thank you again, for everything."

"Yes. Good-bye, Miss Jacobs."

End of Tape 27.

Notes Accompanying Tape 27.

Once again, the tape of our Session is self-explanatory and needs little comment. It was primarily anecdotal, with no reference, that I can recall, to psychic or psychiatric material.

The loyalty and devotion displayed by Miss Jacobs toward Harry is indeed touching. What a compassionate woman she can be and fiercely protective. I don't know anything about his wife, but Harry did certainly suffer a loss when he put young Sophie into the taxicab. Yet what else could he have done?

I continue to be impressed by her natural warmth and compassion for people, not just this man Harry. She is also politically aware and concerned — perhaps because of the Socialist background she has made reference to.

What did she mean she "read" about my "escape" from Europe. Has she been — but why should I be surprised? She is a natural researcher and compulsive about obtaining facts. Of course she would want to know about the Therapist to whom she would pay money for services.

And that scene Harry photographed - it is horrible to think that this could be - **NO** - it can not be. I must not allow myself to become overwhelmed by emotions Miss Jacobs is experiencing and believe things that CANNOT POSSIBLY BE!

I wonder if Miss Jacobs will be able to obtain the name of the Camp. As compulsive as she is, if she has retained the information, I have no doubt she will produce it.

But how could I possibly respond to questions about loss of family members in the Camps. Then I would have been crying as well — something absolutely *verboten*[1] for Therapists!

***

---

[1] German = forbidden.

Tape 28

2:30 pm

"Miss Jacobs?"

"Yes, Dr. Levy?"

"Miss Jacobs - forgive me, it's just that I was, I mean, for a —."

"I know, you were going to say you almost didn't recognize me. No - it was that you weren't sure it was me, because you've never seen me dressed like this and also, it's not my regular appointment."

"Forgive me, Miss Jacobs, but that is true. For a moment, I was taken off guard, so to speak, because I -"

"I know. You're used to seeing me dressed in a business suit, or a dress with a blazer, or, at the least, a pants-suit worn by pro-fessional women, and high-heels. You're used to seeing my face made-up, and my hair tied back neatly - except of course, for the time I came to your office in the early morning."

"Miss Jacobs, try to - -"

"And today when I come for this unscheduled appointment, I have no make-up, my hair is in its natural wild and woolly state, and I'm wearing a tee-shirt and dungarees, with socks and sneakers on my feet."

"Miss Jacobs, it is quite obvious that you are very upset over something. Please tell me what it is, if you are able."

[Silence.]

"Miss Jacobs?" [Tone of concern.]

[Pause.]

"I had another of those bizarre experiences last night."

"And you did not call me?" [Tone astonished.]

"Please, Dr. Levy, I've disturbed you enough times already by getting you out of bed upon demand. So, I decided this time to see if I could handle it myself. [Pause.] Obviously, I did not succeed too well, as you can tell from my appearance."

"What happened, Miss Jacobs, please." [Tone indicating considerable concern, although with attempt to conceal.]

"After the experience occurred — -"

"When was that, please?"

"In the middle of the night, I would guess about 2 am or so. I was so distraught — I guess that is about the best word for how I felt - I just got out of bed and got dressed into the first things I could find. I <u>knew</u> I could not stay in that house another minute."

"Ah. I was going to ask, but it is clear now that you were in your country home."

"Yes. [Pause.] Anyway, I got into my car and drove back to the City and went to my apartment. I believe it was close to 5 am when I arrived, since I was driving as if I was on the Autobahn. Fortunately, no Troopers were around. In the condition I was in, they probably would have taken me straight to the nearest mental hospital."

"Miss Jacobs, you <u>keep</u> making statements like that, as if you <u>wish</u> someone <u>would</u> put you in one."

"Dr. Levy, you know why that is - we've talked about it so many times. When these things happen that are <u>SO bizarre</u>, I sometimes feel that is the <u>only</u> place where I'll be safe."

"Safe? [Pause.] "Safe from <u>what</u>, Miss Jacobs, please."

452

"YOU know. And what's more, you <u>know</u> that <u>I</u> know that you know!"

"Miss Jacobs, I'm not sure I understand. What you said just now makes no sense to me."

[Silence.]

"Dr. Levy — when these events are THIS bizarre, they are so overwhelming, that I am willing to do <u>anything</u> to make them stop, including treatment for being mentally ill, if that's what it will take."

"But, Miss Jacobs, surely you know what effect a diagnosis of mental illness might have upon your career."

"I'm not so sure it would be that devastating, Dr. Levy. I've been a dedicated worker for so many years, that it just might be attributed to overwork on my part. [Pause.] Besides, Harry might not be so tempted to visit me in a mental hospital!" [Words spoken with intense sarcasm.]

"How can you be sure, Miss Jacobs? You and Seymour were convinced he wouldn't be around in your new house, and look at the number of experiences you've had with him there in just a few weeks!

"I still want to know why you did not call me, Miss Jacobs."

"Because I was ashamed. I really feel that I've been selfish, <u>particularly</u> that last time when I threatened to go to the hospital if you didn't agree to see me immediately, remember?"

[Pause.]

"Also, because of our talks, I thought I could handle the experience by myself - that all I would have to do was remember our discussions and the conclusions we reached and I would be able to get it under control and take it in my stride. [Pause.] I did it with the Hot Tub incident, remember? [Pause.] Only this time, it didn't work.

"So — I sat around my apartment for awhile, decided I was in too much of a state to go to work, called in sick, then 'phoned Sarah, to see if I could possibly see her, and she said I could come over right away. [Pause.] I suppose I must have sounded pretty upset."

"Sarah? I'm not sure I heard you mention her before. Why did you not go to Midge, upon whom you regularly rely in situations like this."

"I was <u>trying</u> to be a good girl, Dr. Levy. I wanted to see if I could tough it out until my regular appointment. Anyway, Midge and her husband took a three-day weekend to Atlantic City, so they won't be back until tonight.

"And Sarah is a good friend, also. I'm pretty sure I mentioned her before. Sarah's a hypnotherapist."

"I am <u>absolutely</u> positive that you never mentioned having a friend who is a hypno-therapist, Miss Jacobs."

[Pause.]

"Wait! [Voice excited.] It was when I told you about the cardinal music box. Sarah's the one who left the cardinal statuette by my apartment door and it later turned out to be a music box. Remember?

"Perhaps I never mentioned what she does because, although that is her profession, she has refused to treat me in any way, shape, or form. She claims it would be unprofessional and unethical. [Pause.] But she still has been a very good friend and a good listener, who has provided some rather unique insights of her own. [Pause.] In fact, because of the nature of this particular experience, I think that even if Midge had been available, I would have gone to see Sarah anyway."

"And why is that, Miss Jacobs, please."

"Because Sarah is more cerebral and serious in the way she approaches paranormal phenomena. Midge accepts it straight away – no questions asked. She believes ANYTHING is possible; whereas Sarah is more deliberative about the process, before she will reach a conclusion."

[Pause.]

"When you telephoned Sarah this morning, it was to see her as a friend then, not as a client."

"That's right; because as I said, she refuses to see me professionally. I visited her in her apartment, not her office."

"I understand. Continue Miss Jacobs, please."

"Anyway, Sarah listened as I told her what happened and we sat and talked for a long time. I think you would be interested in her theories, as they are <u>really</u> unique."

"Perhaps I would. [Pause.] But what did you do after you left your friend Sarah?"

"I called for an appointment from her apartment, and, as usual, you had another convenient coincidental cancellation. Then I came here."

"Do you mean you have been with Sarah since early this morning and did not leave until you came for this 2:30 appointment?"

"That's true. Sarah doesn't schedule clients on Mondays, so she was able to spend the time with me."

"Miss Jacobs, it seems to me that not only were you seeking advice and friendship from this woman Sarah, but that you also did not want to be alone."

[Silence.]

"You're probably right, Dr. Levy. After what happened this morning, I guess I did not want to be alone. [Pause.] I certainly was in no shape to go into the office, that's for sure."

[Pause.]

"Miss Jacobs, I feel like scolding you for not contacting me sooner. Please do not think of the effect upon me of your early morning calls. I may sound, euh, perhaps, euh, grouchy, as it is said. [Pause.] However, the choice to have the telephone by my bedside is my own, and I have made that choice just so that my patients could contact me in situations where they are incapable of resolving their problems alone. [Pause.] I would never have wanted you to make that drive to the City during the early morning hours, particularly if you made it in an agitated mental state at the speeds you have intimated."

"Well, what could I have done then, Dr. Levy, as I felt I could not stay in that bedroom another minute."

"That's an interesting statement, Miss Jacobs. I thought it was the house, itself, that you could not stay in. Now is it only the bedroom?"

"Well, primarily the bedroom. But how was I to be sure about the rest of the house?"

"Permit me to suggest the possibility that you and I could have talked on the telephone while you were in another room, and that perhaps you would have been able to feel more comfortable and then return to the City later, under less harried circumstances."

[Pause.]

"This is somewhat awkward for me to say, Dr. Levy, as I truly respect and admire you, but you <u>can</u> be rather intimidating when you are awakened in the middle-of-the-night."

"That may be so, Miss Jacobs, but we have always been able to work something out, haven't we?"

"Yes, Dr. Levy. I can't deny that."

[Silence.]

"Now, Miss Jacobs — [Pause.] - whenever you feel ready, please tell me what it was that had you in such a state that you felt you had to leave the house immediately. [Pause.] Was it similar to the experiences which we have been referring to as 'visions'?"

"No. Not at all. Perhaps I could have handled another of those in a more reasonable manner, now that I understand them better. But this was like nothing I've <u>ever</u> gone through before."

[Silence.]

"Whenever you are ready, Miss Jacobs, please."

[Pause, then deep breath.]

"By now, I'm sure, you're probably aware that I have this habit of reading in bed before turning out the lamp and going to sleep. I have the same habit in my country home.

"When this started, I was sitting in bed, reading, when I began to feel a strange sensation in my right arm. It started at the shoulder, where the top of my arm joins, and progressed slowly from there down the rest of my arm."

"What did this sensation feel like? Are you able to describe it, please."

"I don't know if I can. It was so strange. I never felt anything like it before in my life. My arm began to feel numb, then dead, then when the feeling returned, it wasn't like it was my arm at all."

"Do you think you were dreaming, Miss Jacobs?"

"NO. I can assure you, Dr. Levy, I was wide-awake. In that respect it was exactly the same as those other episodes. I was wide awake when it happened."

"Yes. Go on, Miss Jacobs, please."

"Anyway, this change in the feeling of my arm continued to work its way down into my right hand. My hand gradually went numb, then when the feeling returned, it did not feel like my own hand, either."

"In what way did your arm and hand feel different?"

"They were stronger, more muscular, like the strong right arm and hand of a physically-fit man. It was such a strange sensation. The book had fallen from my hands onto the bed, and I was staring at my arm as these changes happened. At first I just thought that my arm was falling asleep, you know, like when you lay on it in a bad position, except that I was sitting upright with both hands on the book I was reading.

"Then when I realized what was happening, I kept staring at my arm. It never changed in appearance. It remained the same size to my eyes, but it felt so different. Then, after my hand changed, the really strange stuff started happening.

"I was still sitting up in bed, staring at my arm and hand, which felt like that of a muscular athletic man – who, of course had to be Harry – right(?) – when I heard, not audibly, but in my mind, the sound of this voice."

"**What** voice, Miss Jacobs, please. Did you recognize it as Harry's voice?"

"No. It definitely was **not** Harry's voice. [Pause.] It was not a voice inside my head exactly, but it was not a voice that could be heard aloud. It was as if this voice were speaking to me from somewhere to the left, a few feet from where I was sitting up in bed."

[Heavy sigh.]

"Was it a man's voice or a woman's? Was it the voice of someone else you knew, or **had** known?"

"It was a man's voice, but not one that I could identify. It was almost — and I know this sounds crazy —

[Voice inflection raised, as if asking a question.] like I was hearing a message from God?"

[Silence.]

"Go on Miss Jacobs, please."

"The voice told me, I heard it in my mind, although it emanated from outside me, it told me very specifically: 'Let it happen.' And it told me not to be afraid; to just 'let it happen.' So I did.

"My right arm, which looked but did not feel like my right arm, moved up to my face. The fingers of my right hand touched my forehead. At this time it became more difficult to see my fingers, and something about the way the voice spoke reassured me to just sit back and 'let it happen,' whatever **it** was.

"I'm not sure just when 'it' happened, but I no longer thought of the fingers and hand as being my own, but as Harry's. It was as if he was touching me with his strong fingers — strong, but **gentle** fingers." [Voice tone soft, weepy.]

[Silence.]

"Go on Miss Jacobs, please."

"His fingers touched and felt and stroked the right side of my face, starting first with my forehead, then going oh so slowly and gently down to my cheek. It didn't feel as if it were a lover's touch, it felt more like, and I know this sounds weird, but more like his fingers wanted to explore the <u>feeling</u> of touch, what it felt like to touch and stroke something -- to know what the sensation of touch was. And at that point, when I somehow understood this, I felt a sense of compassion and empathy - almost pity — and it became easier for me to 'let it happen.'

"His fingers continued to move slowly down my face, the tips touching my cheek oh so gently. Then when his fingers reached my lips, their touch became more of a caress, and with this same emotion of compassion, I— without thinking, I kissed the fingertips with my lips."

[Momentary silence, then agitated speech.]

"That's when the spell was broken. Immediately my hand and arm and fingers were once more my own and I was repulsed at the thought of having stroked and caressed my own face and kissed my own fingertips. <u>What was I thinking of</u>? Had I gone stark raving mad? I was completely back to myself again, and all I could think of was hearing voices coming from thin air, and having the crazy idea that my own right arm belonged to a dead man."

[Silence.]

"Miss Jacobs, I can not help but ask, if you felt compassion for Harry wanting to experience the feeling of touching your face-"

[Interrupting, but voice tone calmer.]

"I know. It's almost — [Pause.] -- 'Touch her soft lips and part' — isn't it?"

460

[Pause.]

[First phrase spoken slowly, as if with deliberate contemplation.] "That's - very - interesting, Miss Jacobs -- and I think an appropriate analogy. In a way, it seems to be a *leitmotif*[1] that runs throughout your relationship with Harry, doesn't it? [Pause.] But what I wanted to ask was, if you felt such compassion, what made it turn into terror - indeed, such terror that you felt you had to leave your house under the most unfavorable conditions. And also, such distress that you were unable to report to work this morning."

[Pause.]

"I think I was unable to go to work because I had no sleep and was a nervous wreck not just because of the experience, but also because of the long, frantic drive."

"But again, Miss Jacobs, like the experience of the Cardinal serenading you on your balcony, why should you be terrified of what was meant to be a loving gesture?"

"You sound as if you believe all this."

"Come now, Miss Jacobs. Don't you?"

"Don't I what!"

"Don't you really, after all that you and I have discussed, after all the experiences that you have related - don't you really believe it was Harry trying to know what it would be like to experience the feel of human touch again?"

[Tone very agitated.] "Dr. Levy, it was not YOUR face upon which he was experimenting. What am I? Harry's plaything in the Afterlife? What does he want from me? [Pause.] I tried to explain how I felt when I fled after the bird serenaded me. He wants me in that house as his

---

[1] German; used commonly as a musical term; denoting a specific theme associated with a particular person or situation in a continuing saga.

bride. I told you it felt like being carried over the threshold.

"He means to turn <u>my</u> house - especially my <u>bedroom</u>, into OUR house. You should see my bedroom. It is like a Honeymoon Suite. There are photos of Harry all over, in <u>addition</u> to my favorite one of him, plus the painting I bought at the Institute, and the framed photo of the real Cardinal as it sat perched in that tree I told you about.

"Then there's the Cardinal Alarm Clock - I never <u>did</u> tell you about the experience with that; and the Cardinal Music Box - you know about that one -."

"Excuse me, Miss Jacobs, but I must ask - how did these items get into your bedroom? Am I correct in assuming that it was <u>you</u> who took them from your apartment in the City and placed them in your bedroom suite yourself?"

[Pause.]

"Yes. I brought them to the Berkshire house. [Pause.] But at this point, what does it matter? I still feel that if I stay in that bedroom another - -"

"Are you afraid Harry might eventually become an Incubus, and you would not be able to resist?"

[Silence.]

"I don't know whether to think you're a dirty old man, Dr. Levy - or worse, if there's some truth to what you say."

[Pause.]

"My dear Miss Jacobs, it is simply that I am having difficulty understanding why, when you tell me how much you love Harry, how you plan to wear your ring as a vow of eternal love which will not be broken for any living man during your lifetime, and how you are frightened at the possibility that these

462

other-worldly contacts between the two of you might cease -- it is difficult for me to comprehend why you run in terror when the very thing you want the most, a loving relationship with this man, even though he is now deceased, is being offered to you."

[Silence.]

"I don't know, Dr. Levy. Except perhaps that, I am ambivalent – that when it <u>is</u> offered, the nature of <u>what</u> our relationship is, that of a dead man with a live woman, frightens the Hell out of me!"

"Do you feel unworthy even of the love of someone who is deceased?"

"Oh, here we go again with that unworthy stuff. No. I don't think that is it either. WHY is it so difficult for you to understand that it could just be as scary as Hell?"

[Silence.]

"Miss Jacobs, if I remember correctly, during your experience in the Hot Tub, didn't Harry's Spirit feel pity for <u>you</u>, because you mistakenly believed you were alive and he was dead, when in essence there is no difference in the essential state of existence between the two of you."

"Now <u>you're</u> beginning to frighten me, Dr. Levy. [Pause.] But you're right. That <u>is</u> what Harry told me during that experience."

[Silence.]

"What does your friend Sarah think? I assume you discussed this latest experience at length with her, is that correct?"

"Yes. I did."

"And how did she react?"

"She's one of my friends who thinks Harry should be exorcised, for my own good. She <u>believes</u> that all this is happening – at least that is what she tells me - but she thinks he is gaining too much control over my life, and that this experience is just one more example. She sincerely believes he should be exorcised, and has told me that many times."

"Was that the idea you referred to earlier that I might be interested in hearing?"

"Well that - but primarily something else. [Pause.] You remember what you and I refer to as my 'visions', right?"

"How could I forget, Miss Jacobs."

"Well — [Pause.] — it is Sarah's belief that as I am experiencing what is happening to Harry in his past, he is also experiencing the fact that I am there with him, taking part in his life at that very moment.

"I realize that may sound convoluted, but were you able to follow what I just said, Dr. Levy?"

"Yes, Miss Jacobs, I was. Hmm. [Pause.] Very interesting. [Pause.] Very interesting indeed."

[Silence.]

"WELL? What do you think of her theory?"

"It is unusual. Let me think about it for awhile. But first, to be sure I understand - what she is saying is, for example, when you experienced a moment in history from the Battle of the Bulge through Harry's eyes, Harry himself, while living this part of his life, was aware somehow that you were actually there with him, watching it through his eyes."

[Tone very excited.] "Exactly."

[Pause.]

"And what do you think of Sarah's theory, Miss Jacobs?"

"I really don't know what to think, but it certainly is fascinating."

"How did Sarah develop this idea - do you know?"

"It has to do with her belief system concerning Time and Space. She believes that all Time is One, and that - well to oversimplify it - that instead of looking at Time as if it were a line, if it were turned and viewed as a point, everything would be seen as happening simultaneously. There would be no Past, Present, or Future, only the - -"

"The Eternal NOW."

"Are you reading my mind, Dr. Levy?"

"No. But I have come upon this theory many times. I hate to inform you that it is not original with Sarah. [Pause.] However, her way of utilizing it to interpret your experiencing the battle scene is - to say the least - fascinating."

"She also applied it to my experience of being in Harry's bedroom - you know, the very first incident I told you about."

"Hmmm. [Pause.] Fascinating."

[Pause.]

"Miss Jacobs, I see our time is almost up. How are you feeling now?"

"Better, thank you."

"I am still concerned, however. [Pause.] Will there ever be a time when you will feel comfortable in your country home? [Pause.] I remember how excited you were when you bought it and when you left for your first week there. What can you do about this fear? [Pause.] Have you contemplated getting a room mate? [Pause.] Have you thought of removing all those items associated with Harry?"

[Pause.]

"I remember when once before we spoke about the possibility of Harry being an Incubus, you felt he meant you no harm. Indeed, none of these experiences you have related seem to indicate any harm is intended toward your person."

[Pause.]

"Miss Jacobs, you will need to make a decision about your house. [Pause.] Knowing how you react whenever I raise this question, I am somewhat reluctant to ask. However, could it be possible that you really DO feel unworthy of owning a house - particularly one which seems - and you, yourself, I believe, have used the word - 'sinfully' palatial; and are using these events as reasons not to stay in it?"

[Silence.]

"I think I'll take the convenient excuse of noting that my session time is over, and not answer any of those questions - especially the last one. But I will promise to think about them, and discuss them at a future session."

"Fair enough, Miss Jacobs. [Pause.] What will you do tonight?"

"I plan to return to my apartment, and then go back to work as usual tomorrow."

"And your house?"

"As I told you, I will have to think about that situation. I'll see after we discuss it in future sessions."

"Agreed. [Pause.] You're sure you'll be all right, Miss Jacobs."

"Yes. I'm fine now, thanks. Goodbye, Dr. Levy."

"Goodbye, Miss Jacobs."

End of Tape 28.

Notes Accompanying Tape 28.

This experience is truly extraordinary. I remember at one point in our Sessions, Miss Jacobs asked if I believed in these experiences. It would seem that I must. Certainly for purposes of her treatment, I should conduct myself with the assumption that they are, in actuality, as described, both in form and content. But time and time again, I have reviewed the various possibilities and find myself compelled to accept them as related.

The poor woman.

She is in torment because of her ambivalence. She yearns for this man desperately, but is terrified by his actual advances. And I cannot say that under the circumstances this is an inappropriate response. Indeed, my colleagues would say that she is clinging to reality by a thread, in a frantic attempt to salvage her sanity. But they have not talked with this woman, nor noted the depth of her analytical mind, as I have.

Assuming these events are "true" (but then, WHAT IS TRUTH!) - is what her friend Sarah suggests - "exorcism" - the only appropriate remedy for the *angst*[2] Miss Jacobs is suffering? And how exactly would this "exorcism" be accomplished in this Day and Age?

How utterly bizarre to be referring to exorcism of an Incubus - something I'm sure has not been heard of nor discussed since the Middle Ages, I would suspect!

But, in the alternative, if she were to "let it happen," as was suggested by some unknown

---

[2] German; difficult to translate. Perhaps rendered as heightened anxiety, accompanied by emotional discomfort.

voice, what would total surrender mean? What would it involve? What would be the result if she "let it happen" – whatever "IT" is, as she wisely questioned.

This situation is far beyond my capabilities to treat – if there is indeed anything here that is treatable.

Still, I MUST CONTINUALLY ASK MYSELF - <u>WHY</u> have I been so delinquent in seeking proper assistance for Miss Jacobs? I have not even tried to discuss her situation with Singer.

What is **MY** problem here, I must ask again.

* * *

Tape 29

4:30 pm

"Hi, Dr. Levy."

"Miss Jacobs. How good it is to see you again. You look splendid."

"Why, thank you, Dr. Levy."

"But it is true. This trip must have done wonders for you. You have a lovely tan, you are somewhat slimmer — I think, but perhaps I should not ask, your hair is even somewhat lighter in color."

"Yes, but that's natural. I've always been natural. You know that, Dr. Levy. This happens every Summer, when I am outside a lot without anything covering my head."

"Whatever it is, the combination is very flattering. [Pause.] You also seem more relaxed, perhaps even a bit more self-assured. Or is that wishful-thinking on my part?"

"No. I believe I do feel the way you describe."

"Am I to surmise then, that in the several weeks you have been gone, you were free of contact with Harry, and that is why you are more relaxed?"

"No. At least not entirely. [Pause.] Harry was very much with me — except for Paris and Wales. [Pause.] Now that's interesting. [Pause.] I'll have to give that some thought. [Pause.] Hmmm. [Pause.] I wonder what that means."

[Silence.]

[Spoken simultaneously.] — "Miss Jacobs." — "Dr. Levy."

[Laughter, sounding forced.]

[Silence.]

"Dr. Levy, were you surprised when I canceled my sessions so abruptly?"

"Not really, Miss Jacobs. [Pause.] I knew you were under <u>considerable</u> stress before you left. What <u>did</u> surprise me however, was how <u>suddenly</u> you went to Europe. Trips such as the one you took usually require <u>months</u> of planning. And I know that YOU, in particular, plan things with <u>great</u> care. Had you planned this trip but not informed me?"

"No. Of course not! [Pause.] It's just another of those contradictions in my character. [Pause.] My basic character is the way I was when I knew Harry: spontaneous, carefree, creative, imaginative, *et cetera*. But, in repressing all of that and becoming super-logical over what is now the major portion of my life, no one knows of the basic elements of my true nature. I appear to be <u>extremely</u> neat, efficient, industrious, and well-organized. But those characteristics are <u>deliberate</u> tactics I use to compensate for the fact that I'm really a lazy disorganized slob."

"You certainly deceived <u>me</u>, Miss Jacobs. I could have sworn your character consists of those traits which border on obsessive-compulsive, as I have stated several times."

"The only reason I went off on that tangent was to explain that I really am <u>not</u> as compulsive as you think, and that I frequently act <u>impulsively</u>. However, I usually cover my tracks with some reason that sounds well-considered."

[Pause.]

"What I'm trying to say, is that I often act on impulse. I always keep my Passport in order — just in case. Actually, that turns out to be an asset for my work, since I am one of the few, being single, and also fairly conversant in French, who can take off to Europe on a moment's Notice.

"This time, there just 'happened' to be an opportunity to develop a client contact in Paris, and I volunteered. I told the Managing Partner that if I was successful, I would stay overseas for awhile to reward myself, and he had no problem with that.

"I guess because of what we now refer to as my quote - psychic abilities - unquote, I can see opportunities where others can not. Of course, at work, this is just referred to as "woman's intuition." They are somewhat in awe of what they consider my almost uncanny ability to discover client possibilities, and develop ideal strategies for the firm.

"As a result, off to Paris. I canceled all my regular standing appointments, including yours, and went on what was in some ways a vacation, but also turned into another Pilgrimage. [Pause.] Oh. In case you're interested, I resolved the client situation very smoothly and quickly and had most of the time to myself. I even took in Wales as a side-trip."

"Yes, I know. I received your card. Thank you for thinking of me."

[Pause.]

"Actually, Dr. Levy. I wrote you a long and emotional letter. I just never mailed it. I was in Nice at the time, and I poured my heart out. I debated about sending it, and I even wrote in the last paragraph that I was having difficulty deciding. I also wrote that if I didn't mail it, I would bring it to my first session when I returned. And I did. [Pause.

Sounds of paper rustling.] Here. Please read this when you have time."

[Pause.]

"Thank you, Miss Jacobs. I'm flattered that you would write a long letter to me. Of course, I shall read it, but can you give me some indication of what it contains, please."

"WHAT! And spoil the suspense! Never!"

[Feigned disappointment.] "Miss Jacobs."

"All right. I suppose we <u>do</u> have to become serious at some time or another."

[Pause.]

"I saw the client opportunity as a convenient way to escape a situation that was becoming unbearable. I felt I was spiraling out of control. It seemed like another avenue of escape. I would be away from you, from Seymour, from Midge, from Sarah — and hopefully — although I <u>know</u> you are aware of how ambivalent I am — away from Harry, as well.

"Of course, I should have known better. No sooner did I get off the plane in Paris, when I felt another one of those compulsions, and I <u>had</u> to go to Normandie. And just as it worked out that the only time I could get free to go to Missouri was on the anniversary of Harry's death, there I was in Normandie exactly 37 years after Harry landed at Omaha Beach."

"From what you are saying, I gather that there were paranormal experiences shortly after you arrived in Europe."

"The moment I got off the plane, Dr. Levy. The moment I got off the plane."

[Pause.]

"And the same things happened all over again with the radios, too. [Pause.] When I arrived in Paris, I canceled my hotel reservations, rented a car and headed straight for

Normandie. As I entered the area, the radio started playing 'Our Love is Here to Stay' — in English — can you believe it? And when I left the area, the radio played Walton's music from 'Henry the Fifth,' only this time it wasn't 'Touch Her Soft Lips and Part,' — if it had been I probably would have crashed the car — it was the ancient ballad about the English King waging a victorious battle in Normandie and defeating the foe — again sung in English. And how ironic — after I spent well over a week there viewing the Museums and the battlegrounds of the Second World War, in which the English King waged another victorious battle in Normandie. And of course, the film was produced as part of the morale effort for British civilians during the War."

[Pause.]

"And I saw Harry, too. He tried to make me feel better about things. [Pause.] Perhaps my being there and seeing and feeling, experiencing what he went through with all that I took in and learned — perhaps that gave him the strength to be there for me when I needed him."

"I'm not sure I understand what you mean, Miss Jacobs."

"It will probably become clear when you read the letter, Dr. Levy. But I can tell you that I went to all the Museums I could in the time I had allotted, and I learned things about what our GIs suffered that I never realized before — and that only the soldiers themselves would know because we civilians were never told. It was so horrible.

"Also, on two separate occasions, on the exact day 37 years after Harry would have been in that very spot, I saw two different jeeps, exactly restored to appear as they would have

473

at the time Harry was driving them. Each time I saw one of those jeeps, Harry appeared, and comforted me. I understood how he felt, and I knew he understood how I felt, being there, seeing those jeeps, knowing with my heart and in my soul, what it was that he went through."

[Pause.]

"Another time he was with me as I stood on a hill, overlooking a little village that had been part of a ferocious battle. Everything was so peaceful. Children were running and playing. Life was so normal. Thirty-seven years before it would have been ruin and rubble. Eighty percent of Harry's Division had been lost. I prayed aloud that Harry and all those brave men who had fought there, living or dead, could see through my eyes the peace they had brought. But I was crying so much, I don't know how they could have seen anything. [Pause.] Harry didn't appear to me, and he didn't say anything, but I could sense his presence."

[Pause.]

"I don't know if I told you this, Dr. Levy, but I learned that Harry never even touched a cigarette before the War. He didn't smoke until the Battle of the Bulge. Maybe he started so he could feel a little heat, I don't know. But that was another thing I learned from Harry's friend George. So, in a way, the War was ultimately responsible for Harry's death."

[Pause.]

"Remember how, when I came to you so frantic the morning I had that vision about the War, and you asked questions that revealed my total ignorance as to dates and times and places. Well, I can assure you Dr. Levy, that has changed. After visiting those Museums and

474

monuments and especially the D-Day Memorial and Cemetery, I will never forget those dates and places again. Never."

[Silence.]

"Miss Jacobs, I can't help but notice a distinct difference in your entire demeanor. It is not just your physical appearance, nor is it that air of confidence I ascribed to you earlier. It is as if you have gained more maturity, even more tranquillity. For the first time since I have known you, you spoke of subjects which were deeply emotional involving Harry, yet you did not weep. Not that I am implying that it was wrong for you to shed tears, but it is more — it is as if you have reached a deeper understanding of the tragedies of this man's life and have come to terms with them."

"Or perhaps <u>he</u> has come to terms with them through me. As I told you, it was Harry who was comforting <u>me</u>, as I wept at what I saw over there."

[Pause.]

"Thank you for the compliments though, but I'm not sure you would have given them to me if you had seen all the weeping I was doing in Normandie."

"But weeping for what you saw and felt <u>there</u> would be appropriate, and amply justified, in my opinion, Miss Jacobs."

"But I also cried in Paris, over a simple thing, really. I was eating lunch in a café. I know people must have thought I was — OK — I won't say it. And the French are so emotional, perhaps it is not unusual for them to see a woman alone, crying for no apparent reason. [Pause.] What set me off was just that three young women came in, they seemed to be working girls, secretaries perhaps, I'm only guessing

475

in stereotypes. One was blonde and blue-eyed —
very Aryan-looking; another was brunette —
Semitic or Mediterranean in appearance; and
the third was African. They were all speaking
French, and obviously good friends enjoying
each other's company. And I thought, this
would never have taken place in NAZI-occupied
France. The simple fact of these three young
women sitting together in a restaurant in
Paris, enjoying the pleasure of each other's
company, was a direct result of the sacrifices
of our GIs — guys like Harry, and George, and
all the others, who fought in Europe."

[Sounds of weeping.] "There, you see. I'm
not that much improved after all. Sorry to
disappoint you, Dr. Levy."

"Far from it, Miss Jacobs. Those are
beautiful and true sentiments you expressed.
[Pause.] But alas, you will not put them to
paper to share with others."

"Oh, but I have, Dr. Levy. I wrote a letter
to you!"

"That doesn't count, Miss Jacobs. That
doesn't count, and you know it!"

[Silence.]

"Did anything else happen that you wish to
share with me today, Miss Jacobs?"

"Well, I can tell you what prompted me to
write the letter that I never sent."

"And what was that, Miss Jacobs, please."

"After the successful conclusion of my
business meetings in Paris, I went to Nice to
relax. And I really did! [Pause.] And since
you're such a dirty old man, Dr. Levy, and
you're also bound by medical ethics not to
reveal my secrets — I'll confess to you that I
actually went TOPLESS on the Riviera. Isn't
that a kick! I just wanted to see what it
would be like. What a blast! [Pause.] And I

swear I'll have your license if Seymour teases me about this, because you're the ONLY person I've told this to!

"But that's not what prompted me to write. What I wanted was to let you know that Harry had been with me, but that our last contact in France was fun and loving. [Pause.] I had brought along this tape of Peggy Lee songs that I know Harry liked, and besides his favorite standards, there was one I'd never heard before, and when I listened to it, I had to laugh, right there on the Boulevard des Anglais in Nice. It was about a gal trying to escape her lover, and he tells her that it doesn't matter where she goes — and get this — 'even to the South of France' — because he'll keep returning to her, like a boomerang! [Pause.] I swear, Dr. Levy, I had never heard that song until then, in Nice. I had always skipped over it to listen to what I thought were Harry's favorites. Well, now I know about this one. And I got such a kick out of it, I felt I had to share it with you."

"Thank you, Miss Jacobs. I appreciate that. And you can be sure I will read your letter at the very first opportunity. [Pause.] Was there anything else?"

"Just to tell you that after a few days in Nice, I thought about how I always wanted to see a certain area of Wales — absolutely nothing to do with Harry, believe me — so I picked up and went. And, since you said you received my card, you know that I was fortunate enough to stay in the very cottage in which Noel Coward wrote his ghost-love story, 'Blithe Spirit.'"

"Miss Jacobs, permit me to correct you about something."

"Yes, Dr. Levy?"

"You said earlier, I believe, that Harry was not with you at all in Wales. I would dispute that, since you yourself wrote on your postcard, and I can remember you even telling me, about how this one particular sportswriter admired Harry and referred to him often as a 'blithe spirit'. So I think that means Harry was there with you in Wales, wouldn't you?"

[Pause.]

"I think you win that one, Dr. Levy. Perhaps you're the one who should write the book!"

"I'm surprised you even brought that subject up again, Miss Jacobs, since you protest it is so distasteful to you."

[Pause.]

"Well, since you explained how he was with me in Wales, can you explain how he was with me in Paris, Dr. Levy?"

"I'm not sure, except that perhaps he was out and about sight-seeing, while you were busy conducting business."

"Not bad, Dr. Levy. Not bad."

[Pause.]

"This has been, for me at least, a very rewarding session, Miss Jacobs. It is good to see you so relaxed, and so much more accepting of your experiences with Harry, and with the World in general. This trip has been a blessing to you, and I am glad you had the opportunity to take it. Perhaps even the break from therapy has been good for you, as well. Things were becoming extremely intense and you were seeing me almost on a daily basis. But now, I think I can even begin the weaning process, as I call it."

"I'm not sure whether I should feel complimented, insulted, fearful, or sad about that. Really. [Pause.] But I know I _am_ glad to see you and pleased to resume our sessions

478

again. [Pause.] I can also tell you I've been to my house in the Berkshires with no problems, and that I plan to go there again to spend the weekend. In fact, I'm driving up as soon as I leave here."

"Marvelous, Miss Jacobs. I am indeed <u>very</u> proud of you. [Pause.] And with that I see our time is almost up, and this will be a good place to end today's session."

"Thank you, Dr. Levy."

"Thank <u>you</u>, Miss Jacobs. Thank you for the letter, and welcome back."

End of Tape 29.

Notes Accompanying Tape 29.

I am writing these Notes after having listened to the tape of Miss Jacob's Session and also having read the letter she handed me.[1] This letter is indeed *very* emotional, although I find her introductory paragraph about paying my Fees somewhat humorous. And she says she is not obsessive-compulsive! She is trying to fool *herself* as well as me and the rest of the World with her denial. She has done such an excellent job of repressing her creative spontaneous character traits, they have become barely recognizable.

However, perhaps that was Harry's assignment as Liliom — to return to her those characteristics she had buried — (that is an interesting analogy - or perhaps, slip!) for so long. It took the shock of his "psychic assaults" — as she once referred to them, to bring her out of the intellectual materialistic trench she had dug for herself. (I see I have done it again — who is choosing these words for me!)

Once again she related Harry's speech in Biblical terminology. "Lo, I am with you always." How strange — especially because, again, I believe this is from the New Testament. However, even though Miss Jacobs is Jewish, perhaps Harry, being Christian, would speak those words. These Biblical phrases could support the "Liliom" theory as well — that Harry has been sent on a mission from a Divine Entity.

The change in this woman's appearance is indeed remarkable. And there *has* been a distinct improvement in her demeanor, as well.

---

[1] The original handwritten letter and postcard sent from Ms. Jacobs to Dr. Levy were attached to his Notes with a paper clip.

Love and Remembrance

I was <u>not</u> using flattery to stimulate her self-confidence. She seems to have gained that on her own. It is difficult to say what has caused this noticeable difference — there could be several possibilities: e.g., being away from familiar surroundings, being in a different environment, being away from the stress of the therapeutic sessions, — perhaps it is even possible that the discussions in our therapeutic sessions finally made an impact upon her, once she was removed from her daily environment, or just through the passage of time.

It is obvious that the events of the Second World War have made an enormous impression upon Miss Jacobs. It is difficult to know why, except that she sees it through the eyes of her loved one, and relates to it through her increasing knowledge of the pain and suffering <u>he</u> endured. For whatever reason, I cannot help but feel this serves a purpose. As many people as possible should be made to understand the horror of that War, and the Great Good that resulted from the actions of those brave soldiers. Miss Jacobs was <u>absolutely correct</u> in her assessment of the experience involving the three young women. NEVER could anything like that have happened, not just in France, but ANYWHERE IN THE WORLD had the NAZIS not been stopped. Indeed, <u>she and I</u>, <u>ourselves</u>, would <u>never even have had this discussion</u>, because, as Jews, we would have been among the first to be victimized in this country.

It was interesting to hear her evaluate her work performance. I have <u>never</u> for one moment believed her exaggerated fears that her professional abilities were endangered because of her contacts from Harry. This woman, despite the seriousness of her concerns, has

481

never really lost control of her behavior. Nor do I see that as a possibility at ANY time. Indeed. Here is where she has let her overactive imagination gallop away with terrifying possibilities of consequences that could never occur. And I believe, in truth, that she knew they could never occur, but used this possibility as a tactic to gain my attention. Perhaps as a child she had to be overly dramatic for anyone to even acknowledge her existence!

Indeed. Despite her repression of many of her creative abilities, she has remained imaginative and manipulative, particularly when it suits her purpose. It was fascinating to hear her reveal, in today's session, how she uses her psychic abilities to ferret out potential client activity. It is obvious then, that she knows how to make use of them when it furthers her own interests. And why not? But the problem arose when she saw that it was not easy to control what Harry was confronting her with.

But now she seems less terrified of these experiences, and more accepting. Hopefully, she will find a way to incorporate them into her persona and utilize them as she has done with the minor psychic tools she uses in her profession. Perhaps then, these "assaults" from Harry will become fewer, and she will accept them for what they are, and cherish their memory. That is the goal which we should work for in the continuation of our therapeutic sessions. I do not envision this as a lengthy process, considering the improvement she has evidenced today, unless, God forbid, there should be some unfortunate relapse. It will be interesting to see how she will react to what I referred to as the "weaning" process. She seemed uneasy when I presented that possibility to her. But then, with patients, this is a normal reaction to the beginning of the end of the therapeutic process.

I can not help but wonder why she mentioned being "topless" on the Riviera. Sometimes I still think this woman is a Seductress, as I have often suspected and expressed, I believe, in my Notes. But perhaps she believes she is harmlessly teasing an old man. With her, it is not easy to discern.

This process of separation will not be that simple for me, as well. I have never before treated, nor do I expect again in this late stage of my profession, to find a patient as fascinating and provocative as Miss Jacobs.

***

Hotel West-End
Nice, France
July 1, 1981

Dear Dr. Levy,

I know I probably shouldn't be writing to you like this, but so much has happened that I didn't want to wait until I got back to the U.S., and perhaps forget some of the important things I want to tell you. Please don't think I am trying to escape paying your fees by detailing my experiences via the mail. Please feel free to charge me for whatever time you spend reading this letter. Also, the things I remember to include in this letter will generate many future therapy sessions, I am sure (!), so in the long run I don't think you will lose money from my writing to you.

At our last session, I felt so overwhelmed by all the "paranormal" phenomena to which I was being subjected, that I felt I just had to get away. So, I canceled all my appointments and took this trip to Europe. As it turns out, Harry is here with me, too, and aside from the rather humorous incident that just occurred and prompted me to write this letter, everything else that has happened from <u>the very first day I arrived in France</u>, has been very emotional.

When I arrived at the airport I fully intended to go directly to Paris, but instead, I had this very strong feeling - I <u>had</u> to rent a car and drive to Normandie.

Before I even got there, as I drove into Normandie (there was a sign posted with that information), I turned on the radio, and strangely, the song which has had so much meaning for Harry and me - "Our Love is Here to Stay" - was playing! And, amazingly, it was being sung in English, just as it would have been in the 1940s. It was then I began to realize that this trip would not be what I had envisioned.

As I drove deeper into Normandie, I saw signs with directions to the American Military Cemetery. I could not ignore them. And so, within hours of arriving in France, I had driven to the Memorial to our brave GIs who lost their lives on D-Day and in the battle to liberate Normandie. By the time I arrived there were very few people around, and I was virtually alone. Except for the crosses. Row upon row of them.

I walked to the railing, and looked out at the sea where the greatest Armada in history had unloaded its soldiers. And of course, how could I be there without thinking of Harry, and how it must have been for him to land at Omaha Beach.

It began to get late. I felt Jet Lag catching up with me, and had not found a place to stay (I had canceled my hotel reservations in Paris). I left the Cemetery and looked for somewhere to spend the night. Eventually I stopped at a Hotel 6 Juin — so many businesses in Normandie bear that name in honor of D-Day.

I left the hotel early the next morning, exactly 37 years to the day Harry landed. It was cold and very foggy. It never occurred to me that it could be this cold and foggy in Normandie in June; but of course, it makes sense now that I remember what it is like in San Francisco in the summer. (Somehow I think cold and fog were the last things on the minds of those young soldiers.)

I drove to Omaha Beach, parked as close as I could, and walked the rest of the way. (I learned later that the very place I left the car was the debarkation point for jeeps such as Harry drove, and other motorized vehicles.) Large twisted wrecks of landing vessels remain, themselves serving as grave markers.

I walked and thought of how Harry told George about having to drive his jeep along this very beach, up the hill, being shot at while driving over bodies of dead and wounded GIs. My mind was so immersed in thought that I almost walked into it. There on the beach was a jeep just like the one Harry had driven 37 years ago to the day.

I walked up to the jeep and looked at it in awe. I was sure it was the real thing. It had the same markings as the jeeps in Harry's photos and had scribbled across it "All This and Heaven Too!" (A somewhat ironic statement, in view of what has been happening to me!)

I was inspecting it closely when a couple about my age walked up. I asked them, in fairly decent French, if this was a true jeep from World War II. They looked at me with blank stares. After several attempts at miscommunication, it turned out that the couple was from England and spoke only English! The husband explained that he had been a child during the War and lived on the coast where the GIs shipped out for the invasion. He had seen many jeeps pass by and fell in love with them. When he was a teenager, he located this old one, left from the War in France, and was able to get it very cheaply. He restored it fully and tried to get it to look exactly as it would have when a GI was driving it during the War.

By that time I was in tears, and when they asked why, I told them that someone I loved dearly had driven a jeep like this on Omaha Beach exactly 37 years before. They were very compassionate, and the husband let me do something the wife told me he almost never let anyone do - that is, get inside the jeep on the driver's side.

As I sat there, my hands on the steering wheel and tears streaming down my face, I "saw" Harry. He was sitting on the hood of the jeep, leaning toward me. Young Harry, as he would have looked as a GI in uniform. He smiled that little crooked grin of his and told me, "Don't cry, Sandy. Don't cry. You'll have fun, you'll see." Then he was gone.

The husband asked if I would like to go for a ride. Of course I told him yes. So off we went, driving along the very route that Harry would have taken exactly 37 years ago to the day. And Harry was right. Not being shot at, not having to drive over bodies of dead and dying soldiers, it was as if we were driving along a beautiful beach in a dune buggy. And we did have fun.

When we got back to where we started, I showed the couple a photo of Harry in uniform I had brought along. They remarked at how "smashing" Harry was (I guess that is something like "handsome"). We exchanged addresses, and they drove off. I found myself crying as I waved goodbye.

The rest of the time in Normandie I spent in Museums. I learned that almost every village, town or city, no matter what the size or population, has its own monument and/or museum to commemorate the experiences of occupation by the Nazis and liberation by the GIs. It was in these museums that I saw for the first time what the French population and our soldiers had suffered. The war in Europe was far more horrible than American civilians ever imagined.

There were photos taken by French civilians that had never been shown to us in the States. I guess our government did it for reasons both of morale and security. It would not be encouraging for anyone to know how horribly the war was going for our guys.

In one of these museums, I managed to learn the route Harry's division had taken in Normandie. I followed it, and tried to be in each location on the very day Harry would have been there.

One place that had NO museum was St. Lo. No one there would even speak of the War to me. It was not until I went to the Museum in a city nearby that I learned why. St. Lo had been completely destroyed during the War by both the Germans and the Americans. The GIs had made it through horrible, slow, almost hand-to-hand combat in the dangerous hedge-rows that separate farmlands in Normandie, then Harry's Division was trapped and held motionless in St. Lo. Neither side had the advantage, and a lengthy siege developed. Then the fog lifted and our bombers got through. They bombed everything in sight and we lost as many GIs to our own bombers as to the Nazis. Maybe more. In the end the cost to gain St. Lo was staggering. Not one building was standing and Harry's Division had lost over 80% of its men. I can understand why there is no museum in St. Lo. There was no victory to commemorate. St. Lo seems to be one of the best kept secrets of the War. How many Americans have heard of it!

I proceeded on the path of Harry's division after St. Lo. They received much needed replacements and continued the battle of Normandie. In one spot, I stood at the top of a hill and looked down at the peaceful village below. It was late afternoon and children were playing ball. I thought of how this village was today, 37 years later, and how it was rubble and ruin when Harry and the other GIs were here. I felt Harry's presence strongly, and I prayed aloud that he and <u>all who had fought here</u>, survivors and <u>especially</u> those fallen – could see through my eyes, could see the peace and joy of life as it was in this village on this day. The horror and sacrifice these men endured had made this possible. But how could they see through my eyes, which were so filled with tears?

The next day, in a different village, I came upon <u>another</u> jeep. At first my eyes couldn't believe what I was seeing, and I thought maybe it was the English couple again. But no. It was yet another authentic World War II jeep. I was in such shock that I parked haphazardly on the narrow village street. I walked to the jeep, parked so casually along the curb, so different from how Harry, might have parked his, if there had even been a curb remaining 37 years before to the day when he had been there.

I looked inside the jeep at the gauges and once again I "saw" Harry beside me, in his GI uniform, except it was dirty and torn. His young face seemed so war-weary. He looked at me intently and said, so slowly and seriously: "Lo, I am with you always." And then he was gone.

I never got inside that jeep. No one came to claim it. I just walked back to the car and wept. My poor dear Harry. He kept so much inside, so much. That was all I could think about.

By the time I left Normandie, going to Paris seemed almost anti-climactic. (I bet Paris has never been described in those terms before!) As I left Normandie, there was a sign proclaiming departure, just as the other had proclaimed entry. Then another "strange" thing happened on the radio, comparable to when I entered Normandie. As the sign came into view, the radio played Sir William Walton's choral setting of the medieval "Agincourt Song;" the words which are, in part:

> Our King went forth to Normandy
> With grace and might of chivalry
> There God for him wrought marvelously….

Again it was in English on this French station. Yes, the English "King" and the Americans had gone forth to Normandie, and had won their battle. But at what cost to life and soul! ("Strange" also, I thought, that this was Walton's music from the film "Henry the Fifth," filmed during the War to bolster civilian morale; the same film with the lyrical "Touch her soft lips and part.") It was difficult not to cry with all the memories evoked.

My stay in Paris almost made me forget what I experienced in Normandie, but I <u>know</u> I have to return someday. I need to learn more about what <u>really</u> happened there.

When I got to Nice, I felt I could really relax. And I did. Nice is fun. Then today, listening to a tape of Harry's favorite songs on my cassette player, I decided to hear one which I usually skip over. It turned out to be about a gal trying to get away from her lover; however, he tells her it doesn't matter where she goes, "even to the South of France", because he'll keep returning to her, like a boomerang!

When I heard those lyrics, I had to laugh out loud, right there on the Promenade. This was Harry the way I remembered him, always teasing. And I felt warm and good again, and decided to write this letter to you. Now that I'm done, I'm not even sure I'll mail it, but at least it's out of my system. If I don't mail it, and if I don't destroy it, I'll bring it to my next session, so at least you'll be able to know what my so-called "vacation" was like in France.

Sincerely,
Sophie Jacobs

GWYNEDD, WALES
[Undated.][2]

After an emotional time in France, I needed a vacation from my vacation! I always wanted to visit this area of Wales, and amazingly, there just "happened" to be a vacancy in the <u>very cottage</u> where Noel Coward wrote "Blithe Spirit." What irony: "Blithe Spirit" is a <u>ghost/love</u> story, AND the term that sports reporter used to refer to Harry. It's very beautiful here, and I'm told I really "lucked out," as this cottage is usually booked <u>years</u> in advance, and this was a last minute cancellation! Be seeing you. — SJ

---

[2] Large postcard, with lovely scenic representation of Snowdonia Province, Wales; and tiny handwriting in order to fit entire message and address on the reverse.

Tape 30

<u>**July 15, 1981**</u>

4:30 pm

"Hi, Dr. Levy."

"Good afternoon, Miss Jacobs."

"Dr. Levy, I couldn't wait to see you today! I'm <u>so</u> excited!"

"That's fairly obvious, Miss Jacobs, and whatever it is you want to tell me about, it is quite obvious that it is something that makes you happy. Not only can I tell from your demeanor, but also from the fact that although you could not wait to see me, you did not feel the need to call during the night or make arrangements for an earlier visit."

"Why Dr. Levy. [Teasing tone.] I do believe you're becoming psychic!"

"No, Miss Jacobs. That is YOUR department – not mine, I can assure you. [Pause.] Please. Sit down and tell me what it is that has you so excited."

"I saw a Psychic this weekend!"

"Did you go with your friend Midge? I think you may have mentioned that possibility previously."

"No, Dr. Levy. I went on my own. [Pause.] And that's another example of how there are no coincidences."

"Explain please, Miss Jacobs."

"Well, the weather was gorgeous this weekend, and as I had never been to the Village before, I decided to take a leisurely drive and investigate. Seymour has always been telling me how charming it is. And guess what!"

[Pause.]

"No, WHAT, Miss Jacobs." [Hint of irritation in tone.]

"THERE WAS A PSYCHIC FAIRE GOING ON! [Pause.] Well - isn't that incredible! Isn't that simply amazing!"

[Pause.]

"My dear Miss Jacobs, considering the events that have happened in your life, the fact that the neighboring Village had a Psychic Faire seems rather trivial."

"Where is your sense of magic, Dr. Levy? At least I thought it was wonderful that there was a Psychic Faire the very first weekend I decide to visit the Village."

"I can understand why that must have been a pleasant surprise for you, Miss Jacobs. Tell me the parts you think I should hear about, please."

"You mean be relevant and stick to the point, right? I know I have a tendency to ramble and I'll try to rein myself in.

"The Faire had taken up what I guess is usually the Village Square. The Village itself is quite old, and probably dates from the time when any of its inhabitants who had experiences similar to mine were burned at the stake, or whatever. So, to me at least, there was a certain irony that a Psychic Faire was being held in the Public Square."

"I can appreciate that sense of irony myself, Miss Jacobs."

"Anyway, I walked around and what I saw was mostly New Age stuff, which you know already I have no interest in and don't particularly like. But there was an area set aside for Psychic readings, in a tree-lined part of the Square, to provide shade for the people sitting and also, I would imagine, to provide less light in order to add to the mystique of the experience. [Sarcastic tone.]

"What struck me as being peculiar right away was that, along with the typical person I had envisioned would be a Psychic - you know the stereotype - well, in case you don't: thirtyish White woman with long straight hair, lots of beads, a long dress which copies one originally Third World in origin or American Indian, and flowers somewhere - usually in the hair.

"But what was so odd - [Pause.] - it really was SO odd that I am wondering now if it was real, or if perhaps I imagined the entire experience, or - if it DID happen, if it happened only to me!"

"What do you mean, Miss Jacobs, please. You have me quite confused."

"Along with these women, but sitting off to himself somewhat, was a middle-aged man. He was Caucasian, and he looked rather scholarly. At first I assumed he was a Professor of some sort, from one of the many private schools or Universities that are in the area. He looked rather bookish. His hair was gray, and he was wearing bifocals. He was even wearing a suit and tie, even though the weather was far too hot for such an outfit.

"I had such a strange feeling, seeing this man with these women. My logical mind told me that he was a Professor sitting down to get some shade. But then when I saw he was sitting behind a card table, just as the female Psychic Readers were, I felt drawn to approach him. I went to his table and asked if he did Readings, and when he replied that he did, I asked him to do mine."

"What was your opinion of his ability, Miss Jacobs? Do you think he had insight into your situation? And if he did, could it just have been through keen powers of observation coupled with intuition, rather than any special psychic ability?"

"You have several questions there for me to answer, Dr. Levy. I will try to do so - but really, I want to describe the entire experience. It was — that is, if I am able to describe it, it was so unusual.

"First, he not only KNEW me, he WAS me!"

"What on earth do you mean by that, Miss Jacobs."

"He looked at me with blue eyes that seemed to pierce my soul, even with the bifocals he was wearing. He took my hands and -. [Pause.] I know you don't watch television Dr. Levy, but I think I spoke to you about a Science Fiction program in which there is a character with whom I identify. His name is Spock. Spock is from another Planet, and he is supremely logical, but he also has extraordinary powers of perception - one of which is to be able to read the thoughts of others by melding with their minds. [Pause.] That is what it felt like when the Reader and I touched hands. It was as if our minds were melded into one mind — as if our minds were joined together in one great link, and we shared each other's thoughts. [Pause.] I haven't had such an experience since the time I was with Harry."

[Pause.]

"It is one thing to be able to know what another individual is thinking. It is quite another to know that simultaneously, that person also knows what you are thinking. [Pause.] And that is what happened in this situation - with this man."

[Pause.]

"I think he was as surprised as I when it happened. He was probably used to just being able to read the other person's mind, but not to have someone read his back. Then he proceeded to speak freely with me. He knew there was no need for pretense, because he was aware I would know if what he was saying was accurate."

"And was it, Miss Jacobs?"

"One thousand per cent, Dr. Levy. Believe me, this man was no phony."

"But Miss Jacobs, could it be that he was — if he could read your thoughts — simply relaying back to you what you expected to hear?"

[Pause.]

"That thought crossed my mind also, but then what this man did went beyond merely reading my thoughts. He told me things that had <u>never</u> been in my mind before. [Pause.] Unless, of course, the thoughts were there and I had been afraid or unwilling to acknowledge them."

[Silence.]

"Tell me about this experience, Miss Jacobs, please."

"It was incredible, Dr. Levy. As he held my hands, he told me he could see a man walking up to stand next to me. He told me that the man was holding up the letter 'H' and I told him it stood for Harry. Then he said the man was holding his chest, to indicate the cause of his death."

"I fail to see anything remarkable in that Miss Jacobs, as heart disease is the primary killer of adult males."

"Yes, but Harry died from Emphysema, and I told the man that the indication was correct. [Pause.] If that were all he had said, then I

497

might agree with you Dr. Levy, but there was so much more."

[Pause.]

"Then he told me that the man standing beside me was showing him a large crate - filled with guns and other implements of War. Of course, this was what Harry sent to his wife after he captured that Unit of German soldiers.

"He told me the names of the Aunt and Uncle with whom I was living at the time I knew Harry. Then he said that Harry was holding up the letter 'S', and it had something to do with the color of my hair and how Harry used to refer to me. Of course that stood for Harry's nickname for me - 'Sandy'. And the man just kept on and on with this type of information, which he said Harry was supplying to him in order to validate, in my mind, that Harry was actually present.

"The man also said, and believe me Dr. Levy, I did NOT want to hear this -- that there were MANY people from the Spirit World hanging around me besides Harry, and that I was actually someone who should be a professional Medium. [Pause.] You can see right there an example of something definitely NOT already in my mind for him to read!"

[Pause.]

"Then he said he saw me surrounded by numbers and logic, and asked if I was a Math teacher. I had to snicker, because of the Male Chauvinism revealed by his statement, and told him I was a CPA. He had no particular reaction except to acknowledge that his sense that I was involved with numbers was correct."

[Pause.]

"The man asked if I had any questions to ask Harry. And of course the first and most important thing I needed to know was why Harry came back to me as a Spirit after there had been no contact between us for so many years.

"The man indicated <u>immediately</u> that there <u>HAD</u> been contact between us, such as a horse, a young neighbor of Harry's, and even a small city in which I lived at one time. Can you imagine his knowing these things? Isn't that wild! The man said Harry was responsible for these events -- causing them to happen in order to make sure I would remember him as my life progressed.

"But here's what was <u>really</u> EXTRAORDINARY, Dr. Levy. In explaining that contacts HAD existed between Harry and me between the time I last saw him and the time he appeared to me after his death, this guy said something like, 'and there was a friend who would frequently remind you of a very dramatic psychic incident that occurred between you and the man who is now a Spirit. This frequent reminder also served to keep his memory alive in your mind.'"

[Pause, then voice tone very excited.]

"Dr. Levy - isn't that <u>absolutely</u> <u>incredible!</u> Can you believe that! Of course, <u>now</u> I know why Seymour would continually bring up the incident with Ed - it was Harry's way of making sure I remembered him and the psychic energy we shared."

[Pause.]

"NOW I UNDERSTAND! It's as if a light bulb just went on in my head! NO WONDER Seymour didn't want to talk about it anymore. He didn't <u>have</u> to! Once Harry was back in my life full force, even as a Spirit or whatever, there was no <u>need</u> for Seymour to throw this incident in my face because I was not about to forget Harry with all that was happening now!"

[Silence; then voice tone subdued and serious upon resumption.]

"But the reason Harry returned, according to what he told the Psychic, was that there was unfinished business between us -- things that remained unresolved after Harry's death. [Pause.] It really sounded like the script of 'Liliom', and gave me a rather eerie feeling."

[Silence.]

"What unresolved business, Miss Jacobs, please."

"Well, there was the way we parted – the way Harry just put me into that cab without any explanation. [Pause.] And there was another thing. [Pause.] The man said that Harry was standing next to me with a small bouquet of country flowers – daisies, he thought – and that Harry kept saying, 'I'm sorry. I'm so sorry'."

"Did the Psychic indicate what it was that Harry was sorry about?"

"Of course I had to ask that very question. He explained that Harry was sorry for the way we parted, but that he didn't know what else to do. [Pause.] Then he said that Harry tried to explain how he felt back then using the words of a song that played on a radio. [Pause.] I guess he meant 'Go Away, Little Girl'. The man indicated that Harry had given a friend the suggestion to make a present of a radio, so he could send that message to me."

[Pause.]

"The man also indicated that there were other things Harry wished he had done differently in his life, but he knew of no other way at the time – and I took that to mean how Harry regretted having to send his little girl to his sister."

[Pause.]

"Ultimately then, what Harry came back for was the unresolved business between us: to tell me how sorry he was for the way he sent me away; to let me know how much he loved me, and to get me to stop denying how much I loved him, as well."

[Pause.]

"Oh yes. And this I found really peculiar. [Pause.] Apparently another reason Harry came back was to let me know that I had <u>enormous</u> Psychic abilities which I had repressed, and that I must now bring back into prominence.

"The man stated that I should be using these abilities to help people, as I had helped Harry to find peace at last on the Other Side. [Pause.] At that point, I asked if Harry really was at peace now, and the man replied that Harry indicated he was - because of what I had done through love to help him."

[Pause.]

"Then the man suggested again that I become a Medium, and even asked if I had considered writing a book about my psychic experiences."

"I suppose if I wanted to inject humor at this moment, Miss Jacobs, I could say something to the effect that 'Great Minds think alike'."

[Sarcastic tone.] "Very cute, Dr. Levy, very cute. [Pause; then emphatic.] I told him the same thing I told you and everyone else: <u>NO WAY</u> will I <u>EVER</u> write any book on <u>this</u> subject!"

[Pause.]

"He indicated that Harry and I had been lovers in a previous life and would definitely be together again, although he could not ascertain who would play which gender roles! I thought that was funny. But then he said that the next time we would be as husband and wife and would never be apart again. [Pause.] He said we were true 'Soulmates'. That was the exact expression he used."

[Pause.]

"Then the man asked if I remembered the experience at the Cemetery where Harry and I were so close as we watched the valley below, and if I remembered the vision from the Hot Tub. [Pause.] Dr. Levy, I was stunned —. You are the <u>only</u> person I <u>ever</u> told about those experiences. [Pause.] He said the reason he asked those questions was that Harry wanted me to remember the feelings we shared at those times - emotions which revealed how we were Soulmates who <u>had</u> been and <u>would</u> be together forever."

[Pause.]

"But when he asked about the ring — [Voice considerably lower in pitch and choked with emotion.] — and he said it in the strangest way - he said that Harry referred to it as 'our ring of vows' —"

[Silence.]

"WHO asked about the ring, Miss Jacobs, please. Was it Harry, or the Psychic?"

[Pause; then sigh.]

"The Psychic told me that Harry was asking if I remembered how we had made our sacred vows together, with special music, indicating that nothing, not even Death, would part us now. [Pause.] And I started to cry."

[Silence, interrupted by sounds of crying.]

"I can't help but be curious, Miss Jacobs. Did the Psychic offer Harry's opinion of your having therapy sessions?"

"No. [Pause.] Sorry to disappoint you, Dr. Levy, but that subject never came up."

[Pause.]

"But it made me feel good to know Harry had at last found peace, even if it <u>was</u> after his death, and to know that <u>I</u> had been the one to help him - who knows, perhaps even as a result of these therapy sessions."

"Thank you, Miss Jacobs. That is very kind of you to say."

[Pause.]

"Did anything else of significance occur during your Psychic Reading? For instance, did this man forecast what the future held for you?"

[Pause.]

"Not that I can recall. [Pause.] I'm sorry, Dr. Levy, but I guess reliving the impact of that reading has unnerved me. I can't remember what else - [Pause.] - except he did seem to place <u>unusual</u> emphasis on my psychic abilities and how I should be using them to help others, both the living <u>and</u> the dead. [Pause.] I thought that was strange and <u>very</u> creepy."

[Pause.]

"And what else was strange was that after I paid the man and left, I walked around the rest of the Faire, and then went back to the tables, because I thought of some other things I wanted to ask, but the man was gone. And when I asked the women Psychics about him, they each looked at me as if I was <u>really</u> crazy because they swore no such man had been there giving readings.

"Then I wondered if I might have sat in the tree-lined area, dozed off and dreamed the whole thing - but I checked my wallet, and the money I had put in the glass jar he had on the table - that money wasn't there, and I hadn't bought anything while I was at the Faire, and my purse had been in my control the entire time."

"Unless, of course, as you stated, you had sat down, drifted off, dreamt the entire episode, and someone had taken the money while you were sleeping."

"There's two reasons why that theory won't work, Dr. Levy. [Voice tone street tough!] One is that NOBODY takes anything out of a purse of someone from Brooklyn without a fierce struggle -- I don't care how sound asleep they might be. [Pause; then normal voice tone resumed.] But also, even assume someone managed to do that - why wouldn't they have taken the entire purse? Why leave me with more than $35.00 still in my wallet?"

[Silence.]

"It seems you had a <u>most</u> intriguing afternoon, Miss Jacobs. [Pause.] Did anything eventful happen after - -that is, after the Faire and before you returned to the City for your work?"

"Nothing. Nothing at all. [Pause.] At first it felt strange to me - the entire experience. But then the strangeness wore off and I felt uplifted and excited by everything that happened. I don't know if that man was real or not, but he looked and seemed real enough to me, although I can't explain why no one else around saw him but me. And the more I thought about it, I felt such joy and happiness — I guess it carried over into my Session with you today."

"I am pleased to see you in such good — I almost said 'Spirits' —. But I am pleased with how you have reacted to this occurrence, which, in previous situations, might have caused you considerable distress."

"You're right about that, Dr. Levy. I can't explain it, but I feel so much better about everything."

"I see our time is almost up, Miss Jacobs. Is there anything else you wish to tell me?"

"No. Except to thank you again for all the help you have given me. I don't think I could have reached this ability to accept what happened had it not been for the discussions we've had."

[Pause.]

"That is very kind of you, Miss Jacobs. Thank you. And you see - we are well on our way toward the weaning process."

[Pause.]

"Good evening, Miss Jacobs."

"Yes. Good evening, Dr. Levy. [Pause.] Ooooh. Dr. Levy - I almost forgot. You know how I <u>always</u> keep my promises. Well, I found where I had written the name of the Camp that Harry came upon. I had copied it from the back of one of those horrible photos Christy showed me that Harry had taken. It was called Neuengamme. I hope I pronounced it correctly. [Pause.] Here. I wrote it on this paper for you. [Pause.] I'm sorry it took so long for me to get it to you, but I didn't find it until I was unpacking after my trip. I knew you were interested as to which Camp it was."

"Yes. Thank you, Miss Jacobs. Good night."

"Goodnight, Dr. Levy."

[Extended Silence; then voice filled with anguished emotion.]

"Neuengamme. *Mein Gott! Mein Gott!*"

End of Tape 30.

Tape 30 (Notes)

Notes Accompanying Tape 30.[1]

I sit and I cannot concentrate. I try to listen to the tape of Miss Jacobs and her visit to the Psychic, but I find my mind is on one thing and one thing only - the piece of paper I hold in my hand on which she wrote the name of the wretched Camp that this poor man Harry came upon, unaware of the horror
Neuengamme.

WHAT TERRIBLE IRONY OF FATE has brought this dreadful example of synchronicity home to me. WHY OF ALL THE CAMPS that this man - about whose suffering in the War she has spoken so often - WHY OF ALL THE CAMPS IN THE WORLD - I do not

---

[1] The Notes accompanying Tape 30 end abruptly in mid-sentence, presumably for the reasons revealed in the final personal Notes written by Dr. Levy; which are reproduced separately following the entry for Tape 30.

PERSONAL NOTES AND LETTERS OF DR. LEVY

[These explanatory remarks to the personal Notes of Dr. Levy precede as text rather than Footnotes, because I want to ensure that the reader does not miss the full impact of this material, which was presumably written during the night and morning immediately following what was the last visit of Ms. Jacobs to Dr. Levy (although unknown as such to either at the time).

The Notes transcribed below were written entirely in German (with the exception of a few incidental phrases and religious references), and were barely legible, both because of scribbled handwriting and the presence of many stains and rips. I took these pages to a former colleague of Dr. Levy for translation. This aged Professor, himself a survivor of one of the infamous Camps of the Holocaust, who respected and admired Dr. Levy and his work, felt compelled, after a preliminary review of the material, to perform his translation with the utmost care and dedication, as he wanted to preserve the emotional tone, content, and significance of the Notes to the fullest extent possible.

The Professor explained that the style of German utilized was highly impassioned and dramatic, such as would be found in older romantic German poetic works; nevertheless he attempted to translate Dr. Levy's words into contemporary English while doing his best to retain the emotionally charged impact of the original. This pursuit of accuracy also applies to sentences which appear fragmented. These were retained in their original format, as were the structure and formation (or lack

507

thereof) of punctuation, paragraphs, and large spaces between written material. Words in bold print are those whose letters the Doctor had traced repeatedly.

The Professor believes that many of the blurs on the pages could be from fallen tears; and the circular smears from a glass containing some variety of alcohol. The torn paper upon which the text appears probably resulted from an attempt by Dr. Levy to destroy that which he had written. Because of the condition of these pages, there were words which the Professor could only infer, and some which he could not decipher at all. Such words, phrases, etc., are indicated by suitable markings and/or spaces where warranted. The text is often rambling, repetitive, and incoherent; no doubt resulting from the "Schnapps" frequently referenced, as well as the powerful emotions experienced by Dr. Levy. One must also consider the possibility of delusional thought processes resulting from alcoholic, rather than incorporeal spirits.

The writing of these personal thoughts begins several lines below where Dr. Levy discontinued the Notes he had begun while attempting to listen to the tape of Ms. Jacobs' last session.]

[Final fragment of the entry following the
Tape of July 15, 1981:

" WHY OF ALL THE CAMPS IN THE WORLD - I do
not "]

Neuengamme.

Neuengamme.

My Dearest, Beloved, Gerda. Is this a sign?
Did G-D,[1] the Almighty One, send this Jacobs
woman to me, as Harry was sent to her, so that
I, too, might experience love and remembrance

---

[1] It is interesting that in these final personal Notes, Dr. Levy chose
to follow the traditional practice and belief of Orthodox Jewry, that
the name of the Deity must not be written in its entirety. Colleagues
of Dr. Levy had thought of him as a man who held the typical
intellectual view of religion, bordering on Atheism, or at the least
Agnosticism.

But My Dearest, My Beloved Gerda, I have NEVER forgotten. How could I? You were the Love of my Life, the Great Love of My Life.

And our Darling Hannah, our Darling Hannah.

NO

As long as I live I can NEVER forget you you and the Darling Child of our Love.

Can you ever ever forgive me? Because I have not spoken of you does not mean I do not remember. But HOW could I speak of you without the Tears, which now flow so freely, bursting like a shattered dam.

Have I forgotten? Have I become so ----- (?) and self-absorbed (absorbed with self) that I now place more attention on the Material than the Spiritual World? I concentrated so much on treating Sophie[2] for a possible disorder of the rational mind, that I failed to see the profound Spiritual Message she brought with her.

---

[2] For some unknown reason, Dr. Levy refers to Ms. Jacobs by her given name, "Sophie," throughout the pages of these Final Notes.

Surely, G-D, The Almighty One, sent Sophie to me.

The Psychic she saw, if he existed, was correct.

SHE HAS THE POWER

It is because of HER that I saw You tonight,

You and our Darling Hannah.

Because of Sophie.

The Medium said her POWERS were to be used to help the LIVING AND THE DEAD! Is that what she did?

help me, help You, my Dearest

To bring G-D's gift

One precious moment more

Of being together

After this night, Nothing is the same.

Now I understand

I was never able to give Sophie another Therapist.

It was meant, from G-D, that she should stay with me until I was ready to receive this -- this Blessing

it was beschert

WHY did I doubt?

WHY?

All the signs

I outlined them myself. Sophie was NOT neurotic. She was NOT psychotic. I suspected, but refused to believe the ONLY TRUE MESSAGE. SHE HAS THE GIFT. SHE HAS THE POWER.

She had it as a child. Her only problem was repression

THE GIFT -- failure to accept SHE HAS THE POWER.

And Harry came to her, as Messenger, as Liliom, to tell her - to remind her not only of her Love for him, and his for her, but of THE POWER she buried since the time of their parting.

And SHE came -- NO, WAS SENT, to me, By He Who is Almighty, to have me remember -- remember my Love for YOU

Dearest Gerda, and my love for our little Hannah.

THE LOVE THAT NEVER DIES.

THE LOVE that lives as long as it is remembered.

BUT WHO WILL UNDERSTAND?

   WHO CAN UNDERSTAND ALL THAT HAPPENED HERE TONIGHT.

   WHO?

Only Sophie

but how can I go to her and tell her what happened.
G-D help me ----------   Pride, False Pride, ------   . WHO can I tell? Not even Singer. False Pride.   NO ONE.

WHAT IF?

Sophie asked over and over and I began to wonder.

WHAT IF?

WHAT IF I had **INSISTED** you and little Hannah come with me? WHY did I permit myself to believe when you said no harm could come to you?

WHY was I so blind to what was happening?

The Sin of False Pride.

Or, was it, as I told Sophie, not meant to be

Was it part of the plan of G-D or of those other Forces of which Sophie spoke - "*La Forza del Destino,*"

"The Incomprehensible Intelligence"...?

WHAT IF you and our child had come with me to America as I begged, then it would be YOU AND I who would have been married, not Esther, and Nunya[3] would not have been born nor would Shoshannah. Was their existence on this Earth predestined? Were they meant to be here for reasons of deeds they must accomplish on this Earth?

WHY DID IT HAPPEN TONIGHT?

WHY THIS NIGHT AND NOT ANY OTHER?

There was nothing special about THIS session with Sophie. She did not speak of visions or other unusual events involving Harry that have now become usual for her. We spoke only of her visit to the Psychic.

WHAT DISTINGUISHES THIS NIGHT FROM ALL OTHER NIGHTS?[4]

---

[3] My father, Dr. Nehemiah Levy, was called "Nunya" (an affectionate diminutive) by his parents, Doctors Eliahu and Esther Levy.
[4] This sentence was written in Hebrew. It is part of the traditional Jewish Ceremony of Passover.

<u>NOW I AM GUILTY OF THE VERY THING OF WHICH I ACCUSED(?) SOPHIE SO OFTEN</u>.

<u>WHY</u> do I analyze what happened instead of … .. grateful - - falling on my knees and (?) to the ALMIGHTY ONE that I have been blessed with such a vision.

To see MY MOST BELOVED

MY DEAREST DEAREST GERDA.

MY DEAREST LOVE.

<u>IT WAS EXACTLY AS SOPHIE SAID!</u>

I WAS SITTING IN THIS SAME CHAIR -- TRYING TO LISTEN TO THE TAPE BUT I COULD HEAR NOTHING.

ALL I KNEW WAS THE PAPER IN MY HAND WITH THAT ACCURSED NAME

Neuengamme

OH MY DEAREST GERDA, do you forgive that I married Esther and we had a child of our own? I wanted so much to marry and it was ALWAYS YOU who refused. Wait for this MADMAN HITLER to be out of the way and it will be safe for Jew and Gentile to be man and wife.

But what of our baby?

You were so pleased with her golden hair and blue eyes.

A German Aryan baby. She will be safe, you said.

waiting

I waited and waited and it was only after it was confirmed 1946, that which I had feared the most both you and our Beloved Hannah G-D, I can NOT write the words . .. . .

Esther is good. But she NEVER was you, MY DEAREST GERDA, she never was You.[5]

---

[5] It is I, at this time, who is grateful to the Universe that my Grandmother, Dr. Esther Oppenheim Levy, was not alive at the time these writings were uncovered.

I did not talk to Esther until worst fears confirmed.

We did not marry soon.

Nunya was born in 1948.

<u>I did not rush</u> - -

I swear this upon my life.

    <u>I DID NOT RUSH</u>.

    DO YOU KNOW ALL THIS?   ARE THOSE WHO HAVE GONE ON –

DO SPIRITS

ARE SOULS, AWARE OF WHAT IS HAPPENING HERE?

    HOW CAN I EVER EVER AS LONG AS I LIVE EVER FORGET WHAT HAPPENED THIS NIGHT?

    "Verklärte Nacht" [6]

    Sophie asked if there was a day that would live forever in my memory

---

[6] "Transfigured Night." Cf. Tapes 22,23 and Notes for prior reference.

sitting in the chair, trying to listen

all was paper crumpled in my fist   ---

        neuengamme

the wall lined with books on shelves from
floor to

ceiling began to fade away and

Sophie told me she will always remember the
way Harry looked as the taxi drove away   --
how he walked to his hotel

I have <u>always</u> kept in memory you and the
Railway Station as the train pulled away. You
waved your hand and so did little Hannah,
with her bright red fur coat and bonnet,
looking for all The World to see, *Le Petit
Chaperon Rouge.*[7]

WHY? GERDA - WHY?

---

[7] French equivalent of the English "Little Red Riding Hood."

"Do not worry," you told me. You even laughed.

"I am not a Jew. I am not even married to a Jew! I am only the Mistress of a Jew! They won't be interested.

My Father is Gauleiter[8] of our Region.

Also, I am needed here. You understand what I mean."

So I let myself believe you would be safe.

I would send for you as soon as I got established.

There would be no War. It was early 1939. Hitler had gotten what he wanted.

WHY did I not see?

WHY, G-D, did I allow myself not to see what the Whole World could see? Was I so filled with Self? WHY could I not see the Truth, when all but I could see it?

Then when I tried - I DID TRY

YOU **KNOW** I TRIED

YOU **MUST** KNOW THAT I TRIED

---

[8] Gauleiter = A Position of Vast Power in the NAZI Party system; the District Leader of a specific region of Germany within the Third Reich.

to get you out of Germany

it was too late.

Fate sealed -- you, helping Jews escape as you helped me. YOU with such courage   -   and I such a <u>COWARD</u>.

<u>And I loved you so</u>.

THE WALLS WERE GONE AND YOU WERE THERE.
NO ----------   YOU WERE <u>HERE</u> !
STANDING ON THE RAILROAD PLATFORM AS THE
TRAIN MOVED.
I SAW YOUR GOLDEN HAIR
YOU holding the hand of our little
Hannah,
with her red fur bonnet and coat.[9]

YOU WERE **<u>HERE</u>**.
THE WALL WAS GONE AND YOU WERE **<u>HERE</u>**.
WAVING AND SMILING
          DISAPPEARING
smaller and smaller
     lost in the distance

and then there was VOID

VAST EMPTINESS extending to Eternity

---

[9] And my father, the late Dr. Nehemiah Levy -- I can be grateful as well, that he did not live to learn that he had an older Gentile sister, and was not his father's only child.

and the walls returned and the shelves lined with books

from floor to ceiling

<u>I am numb</u>.

I want to scream but I can do nothing.

I CAN do something I can go to the kitchen[10]

more Schnapps.

---

[10] The Office used by Drs. Eliahu and Nehemiah Levy, and now by myself, is a converted apartment, spacious, with many rooms, and fully equipped with kitchen, bathrooms, etc.

I MUST see my son. I MUST see the one child who remains with me and his own darling Shoshannah. And I will hold sweet Shoshannah in my arms and for a moment, if only a moment, I will remember how it was to hold our Hannah in my arms, so close, so warm, so safe.[11]

After this night, perhaps my own son will not want me in his house, and G-D also knows that our relationship has never been --------- ---------- (?)

TOO MUCH SCHNAPPS

---

[11] I have a memory of an occurrence I had previously thought was a dream. In this memory, I am a little girl, and my Grandfather is holding me in his arms, rocking me back and forth. There is a strong smell of something on his breath, most likely alcohol. I can hear the voices of my father and mother arguing, with my mother saying she did not want a drunken old man waking her little girl, and my father saying he had never seen Dr. Levy behave in this manner and that something must be terribly wrong. My father had no concern for my safety and the matter was resolved that my father would remain in my bedroom while my Grandfather was with me. I can remember feeling almost smothered being held so close, until my Grandfather, weeping beyond control, handed me to my father and staggered out of my room. When I awoke later in the morning and asked my parents about this strange experience, both asserted vehemently that I had been dreaming. They told me Grandfather Levy would never behave so strangely, and as I felt that was true, had no reason to doubt their statement. Until reading these Notes, I had stored the memory in my subconscious merely as a dream.

I wanted to be in the office, in the room where I sat in the chair trying to listen - when - when everything

I wanted to see if you would be there.

If instead of the wall filled with books, there would be the Railway Station, with You and Hannah waving but I could not.   I was afraid.

Of what?   I DO NOT KNOW.

So I told the taxi driver to take me home instead.

NOW I KNOW ONCE MORE HOW SOPHIE FELT.

So I sit in our livingroom while Esther sleeps. Unknowing. And I write more thoughts - - - what has happened to me on this night, now unto morning?

Could it be that Shoshannah is the reincarnation of our darling Hannah?   I remember when Sophie

Reincarnation

how Harry was born

BUT HOW COULD IT BE?

COULD SUCH A THING BE?

BUT WHAT IS TRUTH ?

The slip of paper in my hand with Sophie's writing

THAT is TRUTH

neuengamme

neuengamme

Personal Notes

My dearest Gerda

Do you think I did not search for you?   I
went from government office to government
office to government office where I thought
there might be some word, something, anything

I went to Europe searched Refugee Camps for
you for our Hannah.   I would not could not
believe you were gone from me forever.

In one Camp I was fortunate to meet a kind,
gentle, Social Worker from N.Y., an American
Jew - I will never forget his name or anything
about him   -- Leon Lefkowitz -- tiny in
stature but with the soul of a Giant of Great
Strength.

He told me he had read many of my Papers and
was a follower of my theories in his own
private practise - in America anyone can
become a Therapist -- this man was NOT a
medical doctor, not even a Doctor of
Philosophy, which at least Nunya is   -- this
man Lefkowitz has only a Master's Degree[12] -
still he was a man of good will and good
heart[13] He had temporarily suspended his
Practise to help the repatriation of Jews
fortunate to have survived.

---

[12] Even in his apparent anguish, Dr. Levy still distinguished standards
of educational training.
[13] The word "mensch" was used, which has almost no counterpart in the
English language.

He did everything he could.

DID <u>YOU</u> KNOW?

DID YOU KNOW HOW <u>HARD</u> LEFKOWITZ LOOKED to try to find you and our baby?

And Lefkowitz -- I often wonder -- an avowed Marxist. In the Spanish Civil War, part of the Lincoln Brigade. His Communist ties helped him get information that others could not in their search for the missing.

Did McCarthy and his Fascists get this poor decent man?

Because of him I learned

Your work to help Jews escape was discovered and You and Our Darling were taken.

Your Fate was not to be so bad because of your Father.

A Camp for Political Prisoners, where punishment was work for the German War Effort. The War almost at an end. Forced Labor. That was all.

neuengamme

and now to know you and our Hannah were

the camp where Sophie's Harry found the slaughtered and Harry himself a witness to your execution.

HOW IS THIS POSSIBLE!

HOW CAN I BEAR THIS!

It IS as Sophie says.

THERE ARE NO COINCIDENCES!

Lefkowitz learned

He sat with me

how can I -- NO.

I CAN <u>NEVER</u>

He showed me the photograph.
by some G.I. Lefkowitz said
some Sergeant - Lefkowitz did not know who

I never truly believed

I never understood

how could it be?

how could an American, an American soldier

have taken

this photo

it had to be another SS -- proud of their

handiwork

How could an American GI shoot the photo

not the trooper

How could an American soldier allow this beast

slaughter you and our baby

and do nothing but photograph

Now to know it was Sophie's Harry.
how <u>he</u> suffered this moment forever in
<u>his</u> life
as I in mine.
MY G - D!   MY G - D!

Lefkowitz asked, so gentle, so kind -
did I want to know everything or just to know
that you and Hannah were no more - but

neuengamme

In this supposed Work Camp there was no place
for children. Hannah was to be taken away.
You would not let them.

OH MY BRAVE GERDA

BUT AT SUCH A PRICE

SUCH A PRICE.

the S.S. Commander wanted an example for the
workers. Another Officer told him your Father
was Gauleiter, but this made no difference.

He wanted others to see what would happen to those who did not obey.

So he led you to a clearing in the fields near a barn

where other prisoners watched, and

with Hannah still in your arms,

this crazed beast shot you both.

I saw the photo.

Gerda with our Little Hannah held tight to your breast.

    The solitary soldier with the rifle

      The War only days from ending.

    Sophie's Harry hiding   seeing it all.
    The devastating decision.
    The MOMENT FROZEN IN TIME for him, for
me,
    for those we held dear

HARRY, Sophie's Harry who took the photograph that records your EXECUTION as part of History. When Sophie told how he wanted to kill not only that SS beast but all other German soldiers, I would not believe this was THE PHOTO

HOW COULD I BELIEVE?

HOW COULD

How could I accept that the photograph Harry had taken was the photograph I had seen with my own eyes!

But accept I <u>must</u>, and understand why Harry suffered

<u>SYNCHRONICITY</u>
the burden of Harry's choice

where is that photograph?

destroyed perhaps,

along with all other photos of that

wretched Camp

neuengamme

You with Hannah clutched to your bosom, were what Harry and the men of his Unit saw, that made them weep at the cruelty to women and children

Years after the War, when Esther and I were already married, and Nunya was a little boy, I saw Lefkowitz at a conference.   And I asked - - We hear of Aushchwitz   We hear of Dachau

We hear of Buchenwald   Why do we not hear of
Neuengamme?

And he answered

   - he said

We will NEVER hear of Neuengamme

NEVER

   -- even though only the Camps of Buchenwald
and Dachau held more prisoners -- even though
more than twice the number of people met death
at Neuengamme than in Dachau -- even though
infamous medical experiments were performed   -
we will NEVER hear of Neuengamme

Lefkowitz said it was because the Capitalist
Military-Industrial complex would not want the
now respectable German corporations to be
tainted by their history of using Slave Labor
- people who worked until they could work no
more - people who went without food or medical
care - people who, when they could work no

more, were sent to gas chambers - gas chambers that were part of Neuengamme

AND WOMEN WHO WERE MURDERED IN COLD BLOOD BECAUSE THEY WOULD NOT SURRENDER THEIR CHILDREN WHO WERE TOO YOUNG TO WORK FOR THE FAILING NAZI WAR EFFORT
(the burden of Harry's choice)

NO, Lefkowitz told me. We in the West will NEVER learn of Neuengamme. It would not be in the best interest of the developing Capitalist industry in the NEW Germany!

Sophie says THERE ARE NO COINCIDENCES.

Is that why she and I were brought together?
So that Harry's suffering and mine - caused by the same atrocity

so that we Harry and I could confront the horror we tried to shut away

bring it to the open look it straight in the face tell it
BE GONE!

it had done its work and no longer
held power over us.

We know what it did and can move on

I accept and understand the burden of Harry's choice.

accept, understand, and now

ALSO <u>FORGIVE</u>

<u>FORGIVE</u>

<u>RELEASE</u>

  now Harry can sleep in peace until Sophie comes to him
                    Sleep, LILIOM[14]

                      Sleep

                    Dear boy

                  Sleep in peace

                  Dear LILIOM

you have accomplished the assignment of the ALMIGHTY

          And I?

I shall embrace all that G-D has given to replace my loss – dear Esther, our Nunya, and most precious, G-D's great gift to me, my

---

[14] cf. Tape 22, pages 346-347.

bright darling Shoshannah, sweet image of lost Hannah.

WHAT IF!

WHAT IF !

Sophie asked

I had no answer for her and I have no answer for myself

AND

AND

How can I continue this mockery - this Radio Program?

How can **I**

who now knows what it is to receive

a vision from G-D

tell others of the TRUTH they have seen or heard?

WHAT IS TRUTH ???

Before this night and morning, I thought I knew

what Reality is.

NOW, **HOW CAN I TELL ANYONE** about events called by the World "bizarre"?

Surely G-D sent Sophie to me.

G-D sent Sophie to remove me from my self-anointed Pedestal, and bring me to my knees.

I am humble, Oh G-D of my People, Oh G-D of Israel.

> May thy glory, O King of Kings, be exalted
> Thou who shall renew the World
> and resurrect the dead.
> May thy reign, Adonai, be proclaimed by us,
> Sons of Israel.
> Today, tomorrow, and forever.
>
> Let us all say: Amen.[15]

---

[15] Excerpt from Kaddisch -- traditional Hebrew Prayer of Mourning.

I shall no longer work for WMMD.
Let them find The One who can proclaim
TRUTH and discern REALITY for others.

I do not know if I should continue my practise.

But even if I do

I can NOT continue to see Sophie   never
NEVER AGAIN

How can I have her as a patient when

IT IS **I** WHO SHOULD BE SEEKING HER FOR HELP
AND TREATMENT !

NO

I will have Carol[16] telephone and cancel her appointment

I will send a letter to Sophie by personal messenger

a professional letter ending the - our relationship.

---

[16] Carol was Dr. Levy's personal secretary.

There is NO OTHER WAY

My Dearest Gerda.

To see You
to be with You and Our Darling Hannah
this tiniest moment of time is such measure of
comfort.

And as Sophie's Sarah believes, YOU also felt
MY presence there with You Both <u>from the
Future</u>, <u>One</u> <u>with You</u> <u>in the Past</u>.

I do not know if I make sense

Too much SCHNAPPS

But I KNOW WHAT I <u>MUST</u> DO

And I know

    I do not want to stop

        writing

            it is if

I continue to write

        I continue to keep You and Hannah

        alive in the Train Station

I do NOT want to stop

    I want

        moment in time

            continue forever

540

forever

            f

                o

                   r

                      e- - -[17]

---

[17] The writing begins to wander on the page, and it would appear as if the pen may have fallen from Dr. Levy's hand.

July 16, 1981[1]

Sophie Jacobs
129 West 54 Street
New York City, N.Y. 10019

[Delivered by Hand]

Dear Miss Jacobs;
   Thank you for the opportunity to analyze your intriguing case as my patient. The experiences you have related are fascinating and quite compelling, and I feel honored that you chose to share them with me.
   Although I have enjoyed working with you as an individual, and have gained considerable knowledge about the subject of paranormal experiences (with which I was previously unfamiliar) because of our therapeutic relationship, I feel the time has come when that relationship must end.
   It has become apparent to me that there are no additional services which I can offer you. My review of your case has enabled me to conclude that you have no illness which is treatable within my area of specialization. You are not prevented by neurosis from normal functioning, and you are <u>certainly not</u> an individual who suffers from psychosis, despite your concerns that you might be "losing your mind," as you have frequently stated.
   Therefore, although I have felt enriched as a person and as a professional by our therapy sessions, I do not think it ethical for me to continue to see you as a patient when there is nothing for which you need treatment. I would

---

[1] This document is a reproduction of a carbon copy of the original; thus it does not bear the letterhead of the stationery upon which it was typed.

542

urge however, as I have recommended in several of our sessions, that you contact legitimate professionals who investigate the field of Parapsychology and share your experiences with them. This would not only be of benefit to yourself, but to researchers and to other individuals who might face situations similar to your own.

Again, let me convey my appreciation for the experience of working with you. I wish you continued success with your career. You should feel proud of your many accomplishments, and move forward with courage.

Yours sincerely,
[signature]
ELIAHU S. LEVY, M.D.
ESL:cg

Personal Notes (Document)

TO WHOM IT MAY CONCERN:[1]

I, ELIAHU S. LEVY, M.D., being fully aware of the ethical obligation to destroy any and all patient records remaining in my possession upon my termination of the active practise of medicine, have with full knowledge and intent, made the deliberate decision NOT to destroy the records of the Therapeutic Sessions (including, but not limited to all Tapes, Notes, and any and all other material pertaining thereto) relating to the treatment of MISS SOPHIE JACOBS. This deliberate decision was made with the intent that any persons finding said material after my demise, should explore the possibility of publication of said material (in its entirety or in relevant portions thereof) in Scientific, Medical, Psychiatric, Metaphysical and/or Parapsychological Journals, or other related methods of dissemination deemed appropriate under the circumstances and conditions at the time of discovery.

I have reached this decision because of my sincere belief that the contents of said material, in their entirety, have the potential for enormous expansion of the knowledge of the above-named Fields of Study, as well as the potential for great benefit to the general Public.

14 July 1984
[s]Eliahu S. Levy, M.D.
ELIAHU S. LEVY, M.D.

---

[1] The language of this document suggests that it was either prepared by an attorney, or by Dr. Levy after consulting with an attorney.

EPILOGUE

When the transcription and printing of both the tapes and Notes of the sessions between Dr. Levy and Ms. Jacobs were completed, I sent copies to her for approval. In addition, I sent a copy of Dr. Levy's Personal Notes, in the belief that Ms. Jacobs should be made aware of their content, as so many references contained therein were to her. Ms. Jacobs telephoned when she concluded her review and made an appointment to discuss the material. She invited me to her home in the Berkshires so that we could be together in an environment less stressful than New York City.

As all our previous contacts had been by electronic communication (i.e., telephone, computer, facsimile, etc.), this was my first in-person meeting with Ms. Jacobs. She seemed much as I had envisioned her through the tapes and Notes made by Dr. Levy, except, of course, considerably older. She was tall and attractively built; and was wearing a man's purple shirt (open at the collar, with sleeves rolled up), a plaid scarf draped casually across her shoulders, and green-checkered slacks[1]. When I commented on her still bright red hair, she grinned and indicated that this was something "only her hairdresser knew for sure." Then she winked.

After a moment or two of awkward silence, Ms. Jacobs expressed how sad she had felt when she learned of Dr. Levy's death from Lung Cancer. She admitted she was somewhat

---

[1] I observed that Ms. Jacobs was wearing a highly distinctive and unique silver ring on the third finger of her left hand. Although I did not inquire, for fear of raising a sensitive issue [cf. Tape 17], I can only assume it was the very ring so passionately discussed by Ms. Jacobs with Dr. Levy.

unsettled by Dr. Levy's interpretation of their sessions, as revealed in his Notes (which, of course, she had not seen previously). Miss Jacobs also stated that although she felt somewhat hurt that Dr. Levy had chosen the rather impersonal tool of a written document to conclude their therapeutic relationship, she had merely assumed this was the formal means he utilized to terminate his analysis of a patient's case.[2]

Ms. Jacobs indicated she had been deeply moved by the emotional content of Dr. Levy's last Notes, and admitted to weeping profusely upon reading them. She also stated she felt touched by the real reason behind Dr. Levy's decision to terminate his radio program. When she learned of the abrupt cancellation of "Ask Dr. Eli," Ms. Jacobs had assumed, as did most of the general public at the time, that it was the result of a decision by management. She had not been aware of the profound effect her purported psychic abilities had upon Dr. Levy. His demeanor, always professional and detached at their sessions, including the one which turned out to be their final meeting, - even his manner in handling her frantic middle-of-the night telephone calls - gave no hint of the depth of his personal reactions to her experiences.

Ms. Jacobs affirmed that the material contained within the transcriptions was as she remembered, and that they and the Notes[3] should be published, so that both the public and the scientific community could obtain what she considered to be much-needed documentation of

---

[2] Ms. Jacobs had no way of knowing otherwise, as her friend, Seymour Cohen, was still continuing therapy with Dr. Levy at the time this letter was written.

[3] Of course, Ms. Jacobs had no way of attesting to the accuracy of the Notes made by Dr. Levy after each of their sessions.

paranormal phenomena, from a highly-respected impartial source. She added that this should please Dr. Levy, "wherever he is now," as she remembered his insistence that she write a book about her psychic experiences.

Ms. Jacobs then stated the following: "You were wondering whether I still visit Harry's grave each year on the anniversary of his death. Of course, I do. It's become an annual Pilgrimage to me that has great meaning."[4]

While in Missouri, Ms. Jacobs visits George and Lil and Christy and his wife. After reading Dr. Levy's personal Notes, Ms. Jacobs stated she plans to talk with Christy about whether Harry's photos of the Concentration Camp can be donated to the Holocaust Museum or some other Historical Society, so that what happened at Neuengamme is revealed to the Public.

When I inquired[5] about whether she had any additional contact from Harry during the years since she had seen Dr. Levy, Ms. Jacobs smiled and answered, "Of course," and elaborated briefly.[6]

"The contacts were decreasing at the time my therapy concluded. I had assumed that was a consequence of my increased awareness of my confused thought processes, thanks to Dr. Levy, and abandonment of childhood insecurities and feelings of unworthiness. After reading these notes though, I'm not sure what to think.

---

[4] Although I had not verbalized the question, that thought was precisely what I was thinking at the time Ms. Jacobs made her comment.
[5] My inquiry was solely for scientific purposes, of course, and not for reasons of personal curiosity.
[6] The meeting between Ms. Jacobs and myself was taped, with her permission; therefore, the words attributed to her are her actual responses.

"Anyway, the contacts continued to diminish, and were — I don't know how exactly to describe it, except maybe to say they stabilized? No, that's not the exact word – anyway, they became less frequent - more routine and consistent. There no longer were unexpected surprises or dramatic events. I believe that is because, as that Psychic told me - the one I saw just before what turned out to be my last visit to Dr. Levy - Harry is finally at peace. Now it's as if Harry is a loving companion, watching over me like some kind of Guardian Angel, alerting me to anything I need to take care of, or watch out for. I can give you an example of something that happened recently to illustrate what I mean.

"Often, when I sit down to read, wherever I am, if I turn on a light, it will flicker briefly. I know that this means Harry is with me and this is his way of greeting me. It makes me feel warm and comfortable and I usually say, 'Hi, Harry'.

"Well, this one time when I turned on the lamp on my nightstand so I could read in bed, the light flickered and I gave my standard hello. Then I heard his voice loud and clear in my mind, the way I used to hear it when I was a kid, and he said, 'It's NOT me this time. There's a short in the god-damn wiring in the lamp and if you don't turn it off now and unplug it, you'll burn your expletive deleted[7] palace down.' His message came across so strongly that I did exactly as instructed. The next day I called an electrician, and when he turned the lamp switch on, sparks flew every-which-way. The electrician told me it

---

[7] Those were the exact words used by Ms. Jacobs. They were not inserted by me, in an attempt at censorship.

was a good thing I turned the lamp off when I did because there was a short in the wiring that could have started a fire."

[Pause.]

"I'm semi-retired now. As a full partner in my firm, I can pretty much dictate my own schedule. I gave up my apartment in the city and commute to the office only when absolutely necessary. I do most of my work through these new marvelous computer systems and their incredible technology. So I'm home most of the time, and have Harry and my cats for company."

[Thoughtful pause.]

"Yes, Harry still hangs around. It's as if all the initial frenzy and passion has calmed down and we are now just an old country couple, used to each other and taking each other for granted. [She grinned.] Darby and Joan who <u>never</u> were Jack and Jill. We're just the folks who live on the hill." [She laughed at what was obviously a private joke.]

I thanked Ms. Jacobs for her consent and expressed my appreciation on behalf of myself, the scientific community, and the public in general. As I backed my car slowly out of her driveway, I could see Ms. Jacobs as she returned to her house. Her hands were thrust deep inside the pockets of her green-checkered slacks, and there was a bounce or spring to her tan shoes as she took long strides up the pathway.

Shoshannah Levy-Goldstein, NMD.
High Falls, New York

May 18, 1999

About the Author

   D. Jovanovic is a musician and retired psychiatric social worker, with an intense interest in the personalized history of the Second World War, and an active involvement in programs for veterans of that conflict. Metaphysical subjects also intrigue Jovanovic, particularly the investigation of paranormal phenomena.